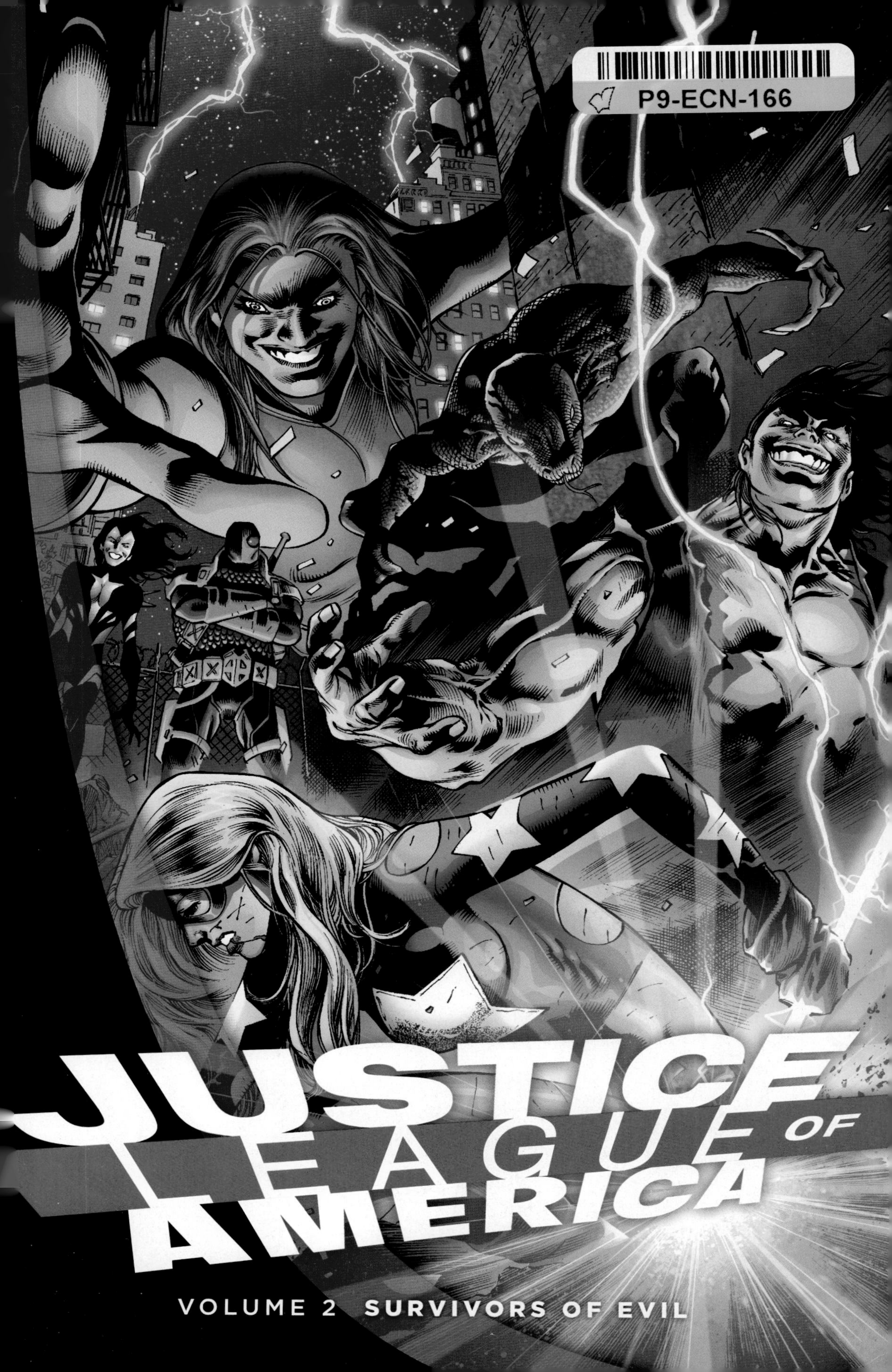
JUSTICE LEAGUE OF AMERICA
VOLUME 2 SURVIVORS OF EVIL

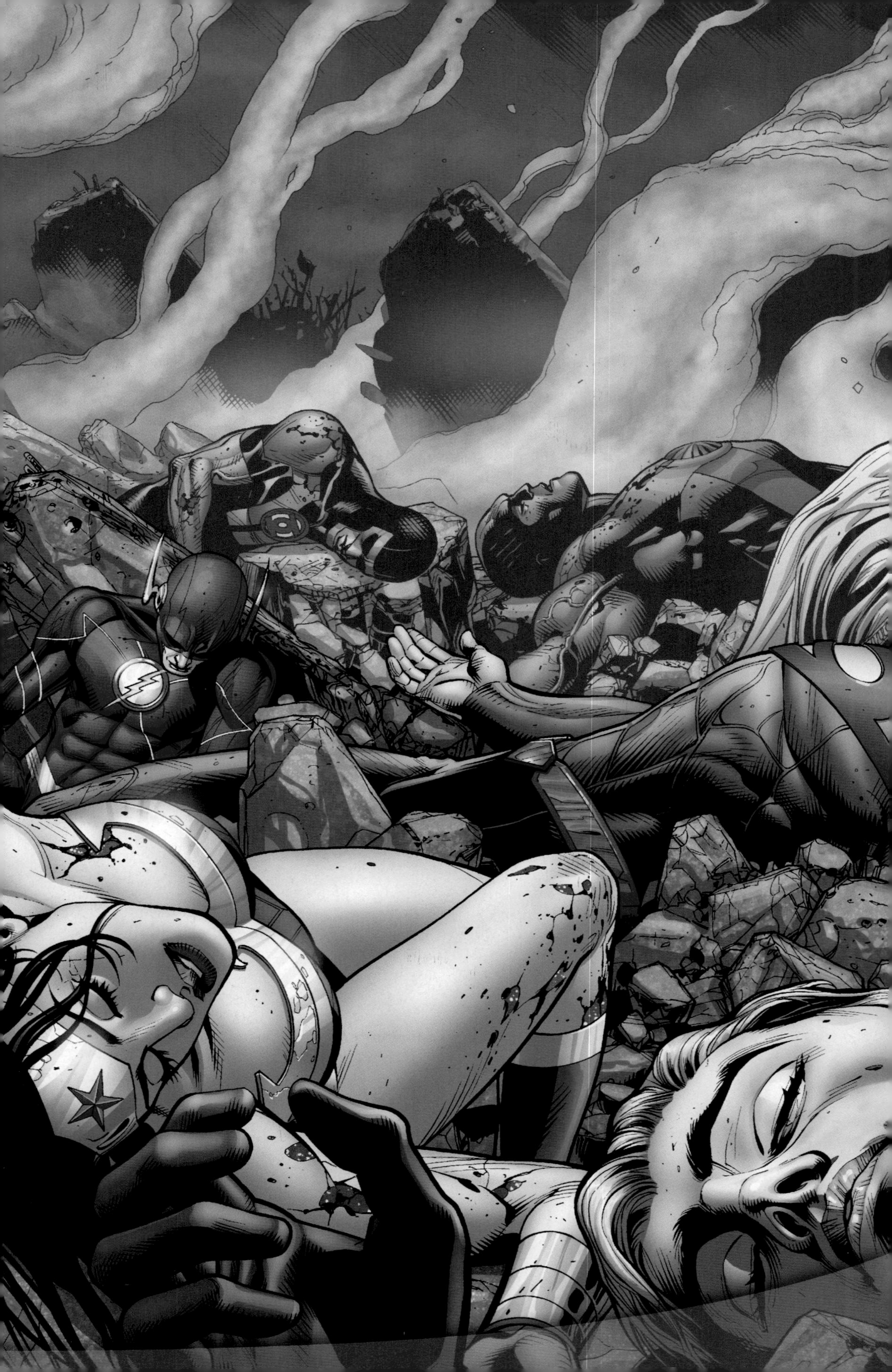

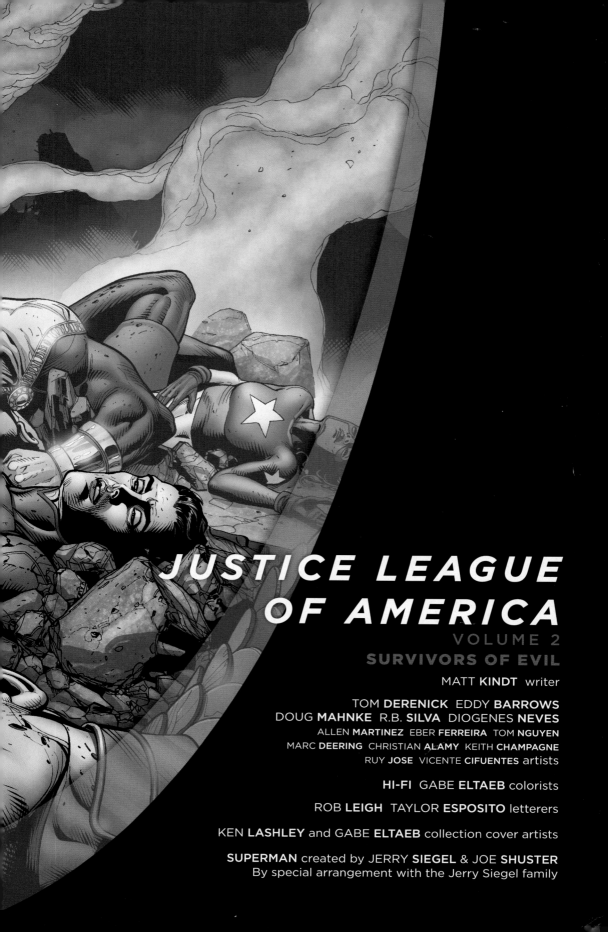

JUSTICE LEAGUE OF AMERICA

VOLUME 2
SURVIVORS OF EVIL

MATT **KINDT** writer

TOM **DERENICK** EDDY **BARROWS**
DOUG **MAHNKE** R.B. **SILVA** DIOGENES **NEVES**
ALLEN **MARTINEZ** EBER **FERREIRA** TOM **NGUYEN**
MARC **DEERING** CHRISTIAN **ALAMY** KEITH **CHAMPAGNE**
RUY **JOSE** VICENTE **CIFUENTES** artists

HI-FI GABE **ELTAEB** colorists

ROB **LEIGH** TAYLOR **ESPOSITO** letterers

KEN **LASHLEY** and GABE **ELTAEB** collection cover artists

SUPERMAN created by JERRY **SIEGEL** & JOE **SHUSTER**
By special arrangement with the Jerry Siegel family

EDDIE BERGANZA Editor – Original Series RICKEY PURDIN Associate Editor – Original Series
ROBIN WILDMAN Editor ROBBIN BROSTERMAN Design Director – Books ROBBIE BIEDERMAN Publication Design

BOB HARRAS Senior VP – Editor-in-Chief, DC Comics

DIANE NELSON President DAN DIDIO and JIM LEE Co-Publishers GEOFF JOHNS Chief Creative Officer
AMIT DESAI Senior VP – Marketing and Franchise Management
AMY GENKINS Senior VP – Business and Legal Affairs NAIRI GARDINER Senior VP – Finance
JEFF BOISON VP – Publishing Planning MARK CHIARELLO VP – Art Direction and Design
JOHN CUNNINGHAM VP – Marketing TERRI CUNNINGHAM VP – Editorial Administration
LARRY GANEM VP – Talent Relations and Services ALISON GILL Senior VP – Manufacturing and Operations
HANK KANALZ Senior VP – Vertigo and Integrated Publishing JAY KOGAN VP – Business and Legal Affairs, Publishing
JACK MAHAN VP – Business Affairs, Talent NICK NAPOLITANO VP – Manufacturing Administration SUE POHJA VP – Book Sales
FRED RUIZ VP – Manufacturing Operations COURTNEY SIMMONS Senior VP – Publicity BOB WAYNE Senior VP – Sales

JUSTICE LEAGUE OF AMERICA VOLUME 2: SURVIVORS OF EVIL

DC Comics, 1700 Broadway, New York, NY 10019
A Warner Bros. Entertainment Company.
Printed by RR Donnelley, Owensville, MO, USA. 2/13/15. First Printing.
ISBN: 978-1-4012-5047-8

Library of Congress Cataloging-in-Publication Data

Kindt, Matt, author.
Justice League of America. Volume 2, Survivors of Evil / Matt Kindt, Doug Mahnke, Christian Alamy.
pages cm
ISBN 978-1-4012-5047-8
1. Graphic novels. I. Mahnke, Doug, illustrator. II. Alamy, Christian, illustrator. III. Title. IV. Title: Survivors of Evil.
PN6728.J87K63 2014
741.5'973—dc23
2014011707

SUSTAINABLE FORESTRY INITIATIVE

Certified Chain of Custody
20% Certified Forest Content,
80% Certified Sourcing
www.sfiprogram.org
SFI-01042
APPLIES TO TEXT STOCK ONLY

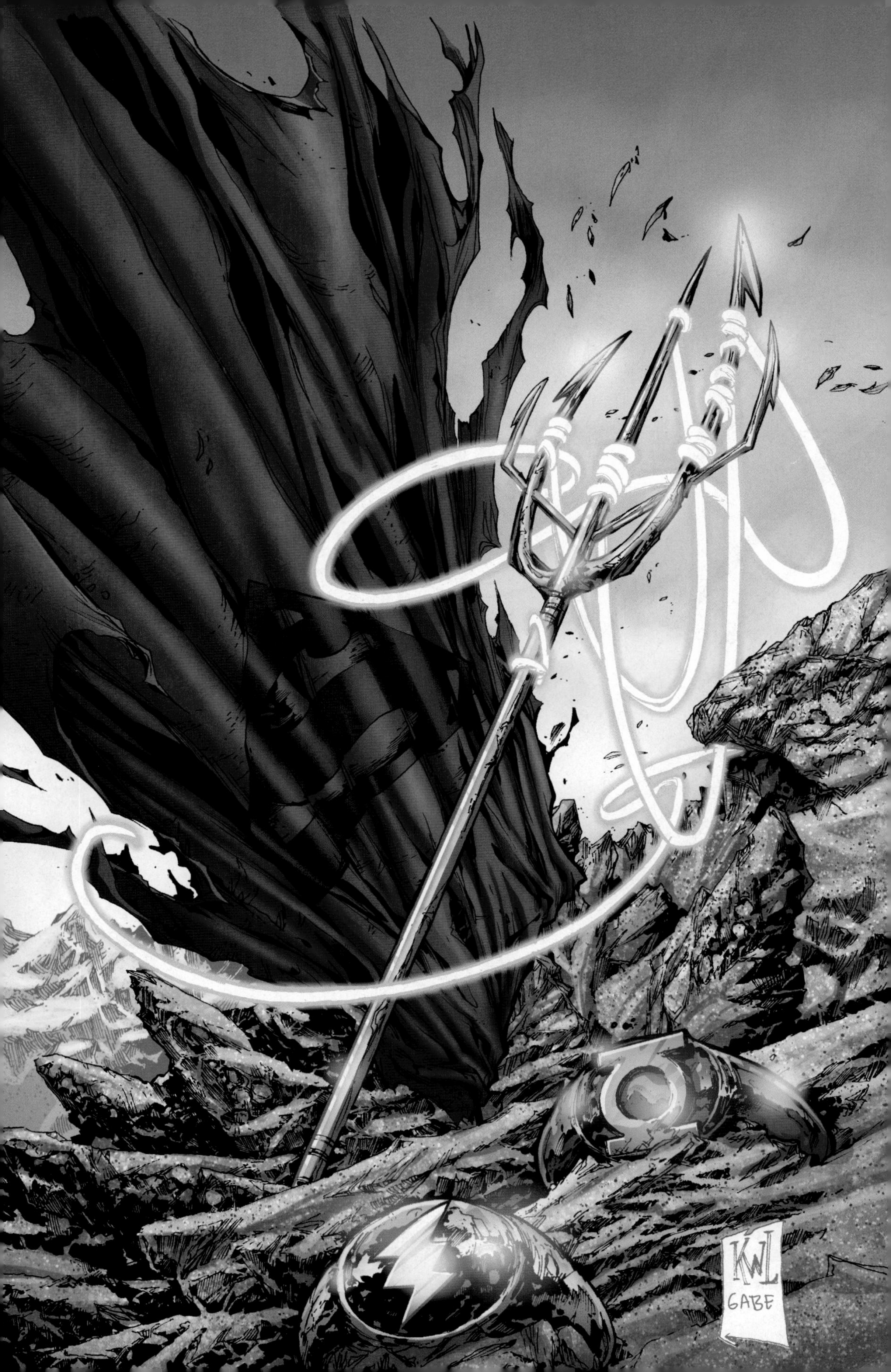
KWL
GABE

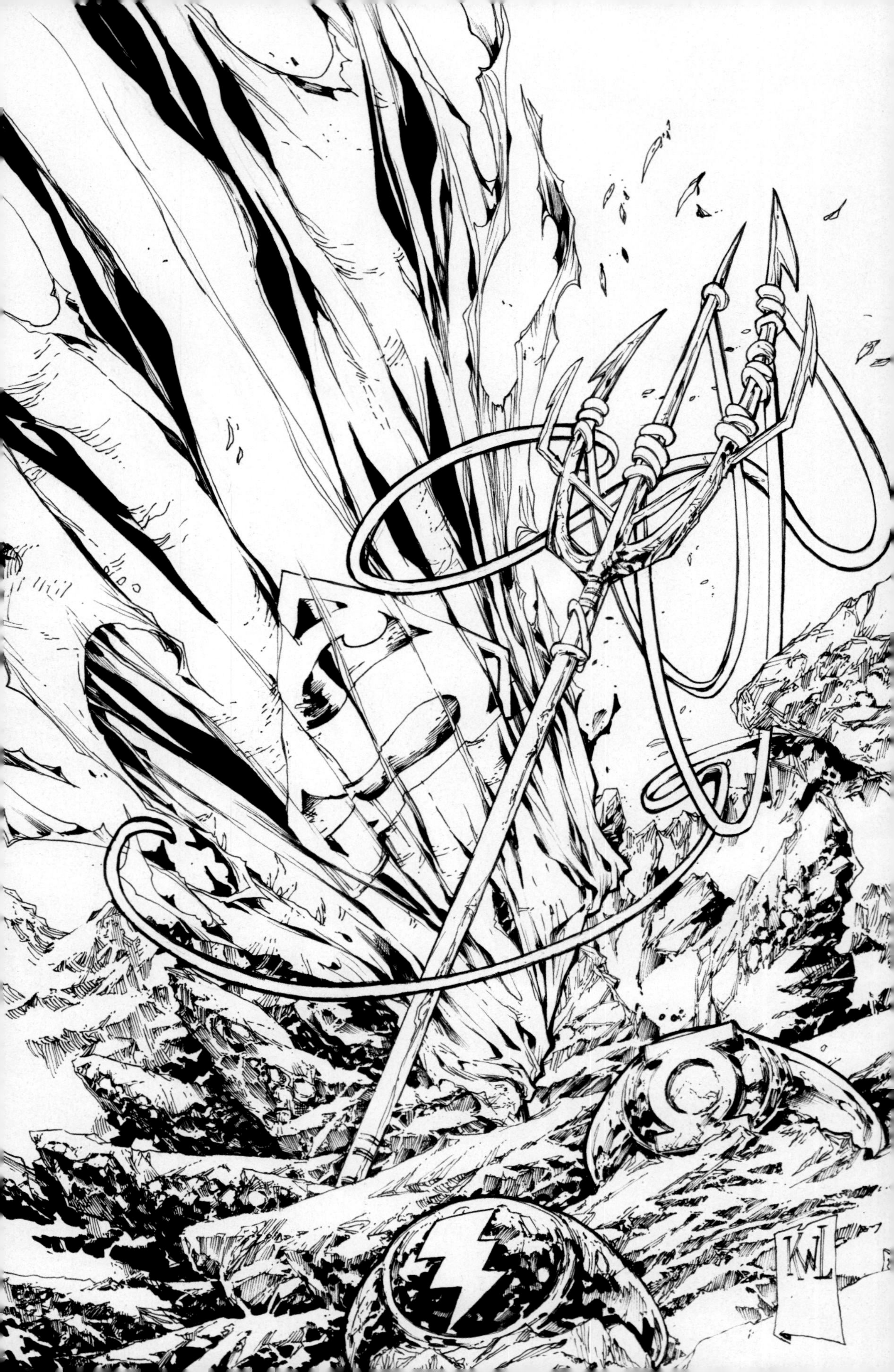

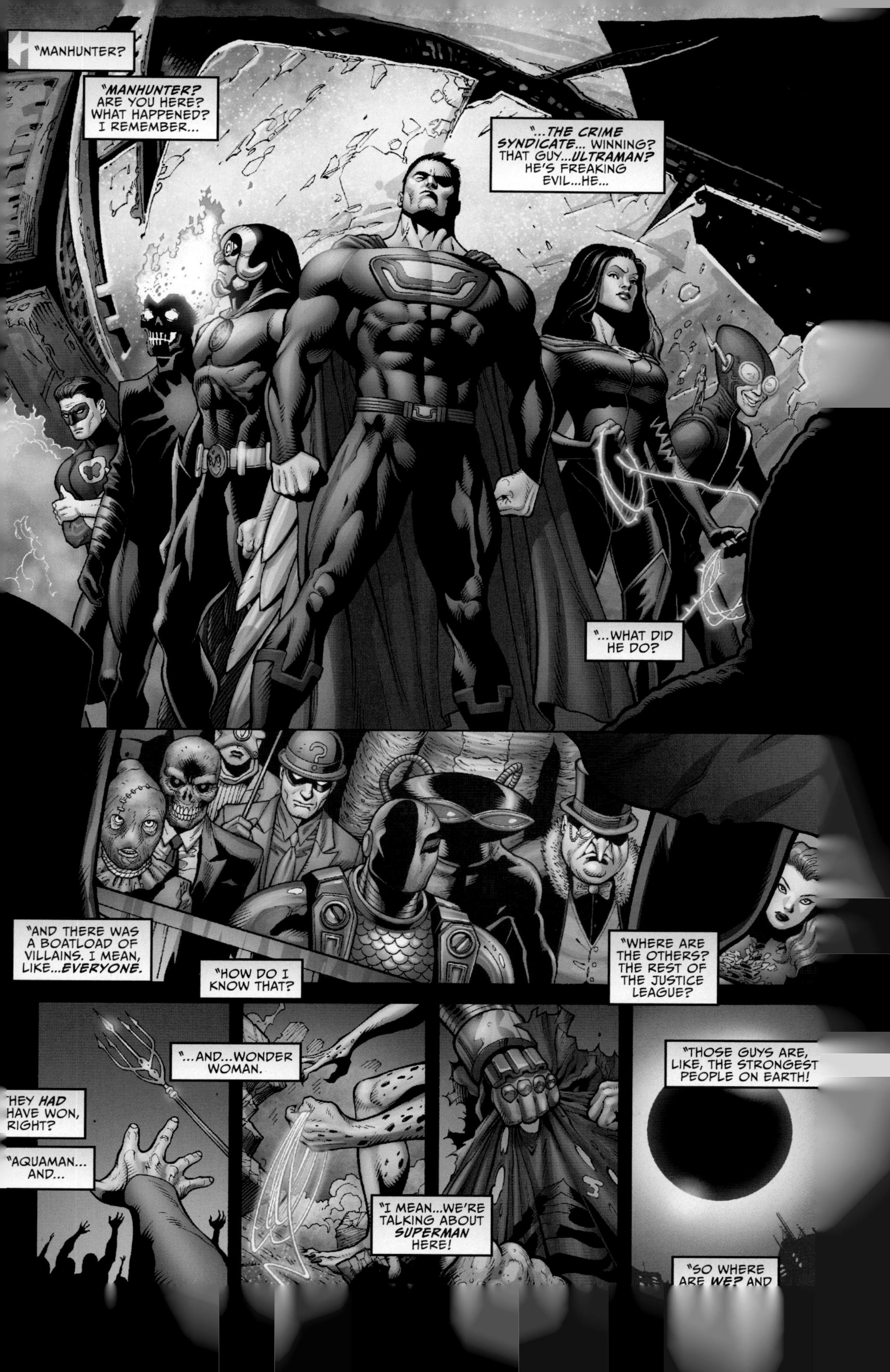
"MANHUNTER?
"MANHUNTER? ARE YOU HERE? WHAT HAPPENED? I REMEMBER...
"...THE CRIME SYNDICATE... WINNING? THAT GUY...ULTRAMAN? HE'S FREAKING EVIL...HE...
"...WHAT DID HE DO?
"AND THERE WAS A BOATLOAD OF VILLAINS. I MEAN, LIKE...EVERYONE.
"HOW DO I KNOW THAT?
"WHERE ARE THE OTHERS? THE REST OF THE JUSTICE LEAGUE?
HEY HAD HAVE WON, RIGHT?
"AQUAMAN... AND...
"...AND...WONDER WOMAN.
"I MEAN...WE'RE TALKING ABOUT SUPERMAN HERE!
"THOSE GUYS ARE, LIKE, THE STRONGEST PEOPLE ON EARTH!
"SO WHERE ARE WE? AND

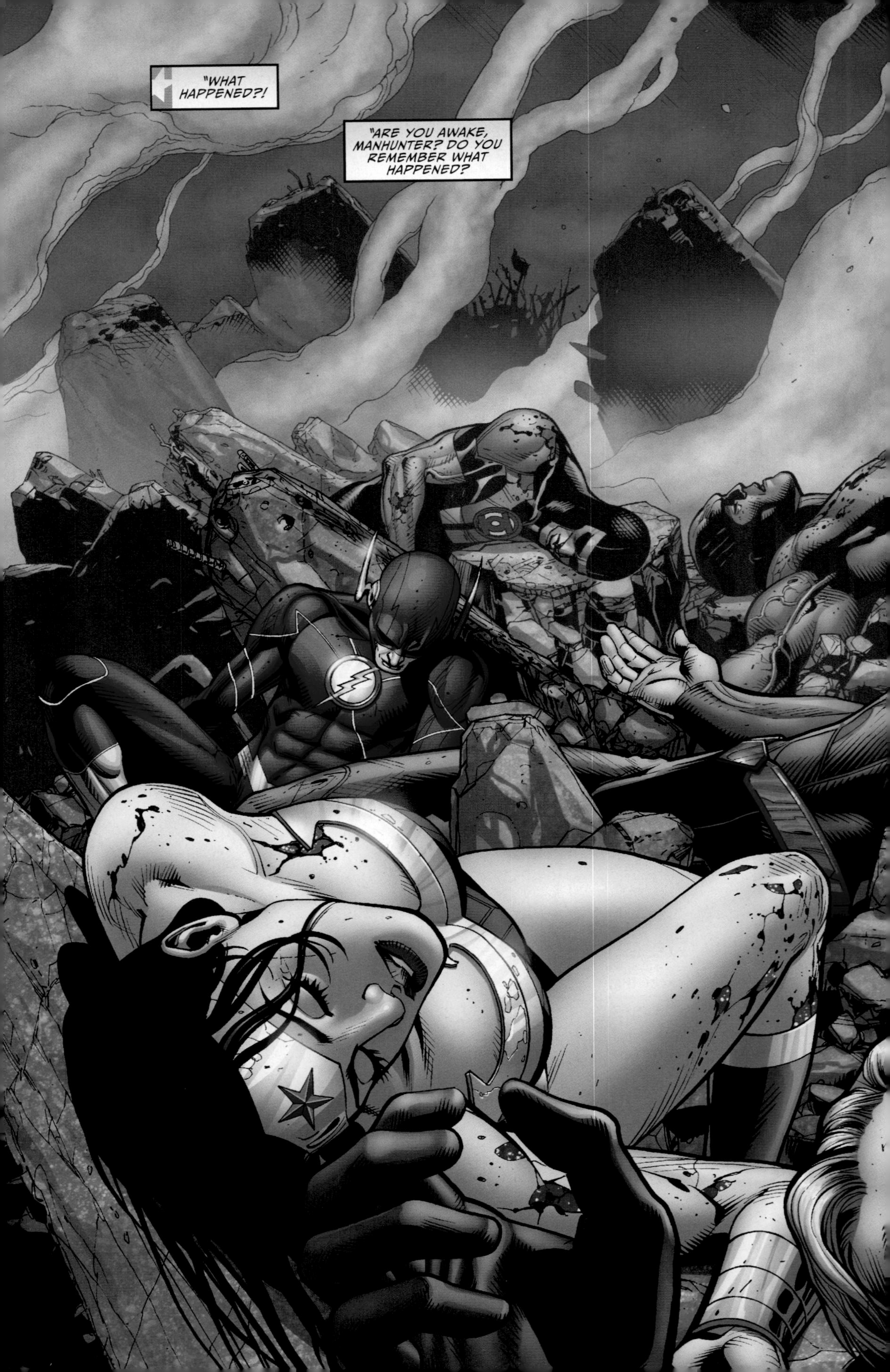
"WHAT HAPPENED?!
"ARE YOU AWAKE, MANHUNTER? DO YOU REMEMBER WHAT HAPPENED?

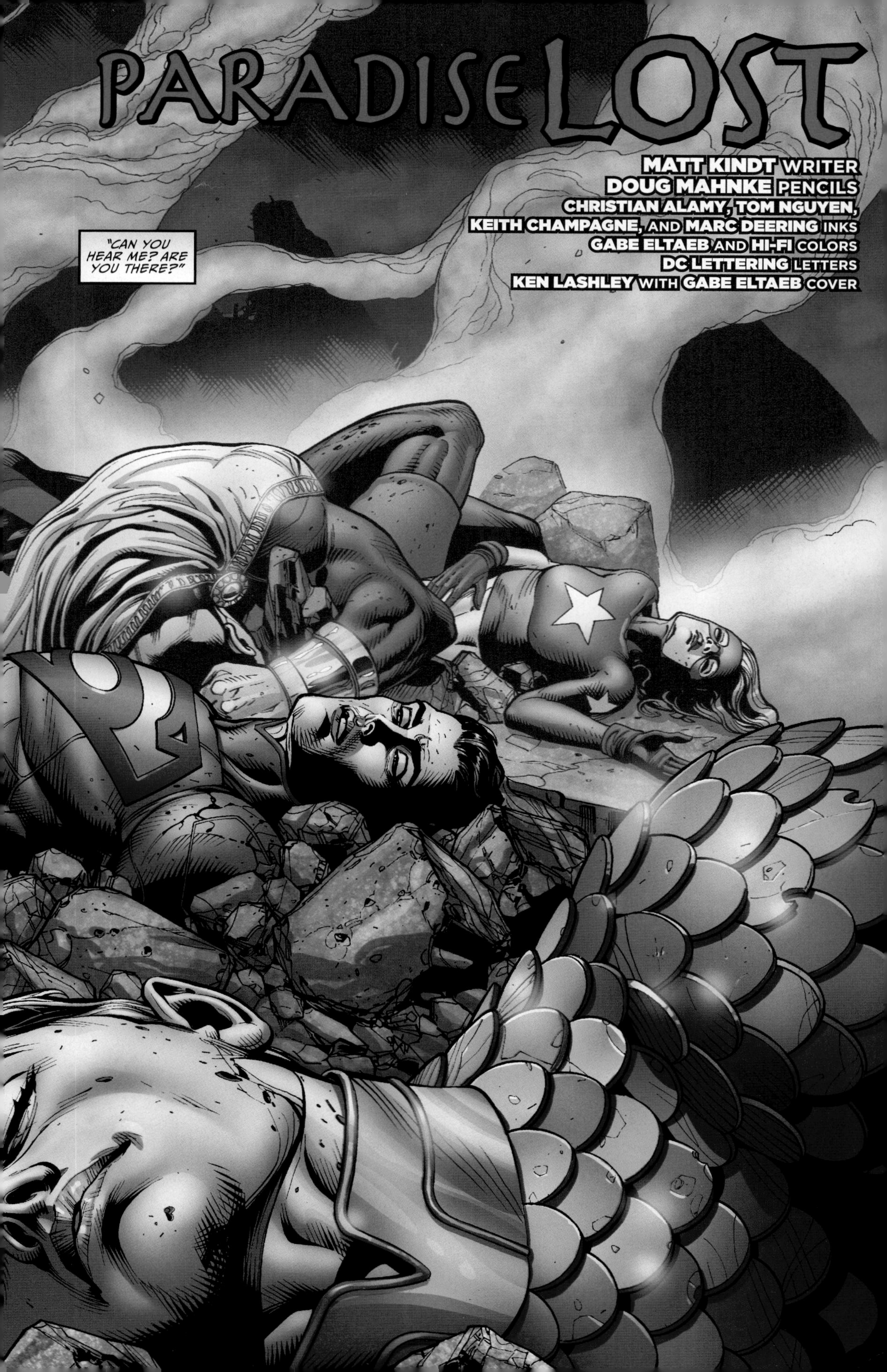
PARADISE LOST
MATT KINDT WRITER
DOUG MAHNKE PENCILS
CHRISTIAN ALAMY, TOM NGUYEN,
KEITH CHAMPAGNE, AND MARC DEERING INKS
GABE ELTAEB AND HI-FI COLORS
DC LETTERING LETTERS
KEN LASHLEY WITH GABE ELTAEB COVER
"CAN YOU HEAR ME? ARE YOU THERE?"

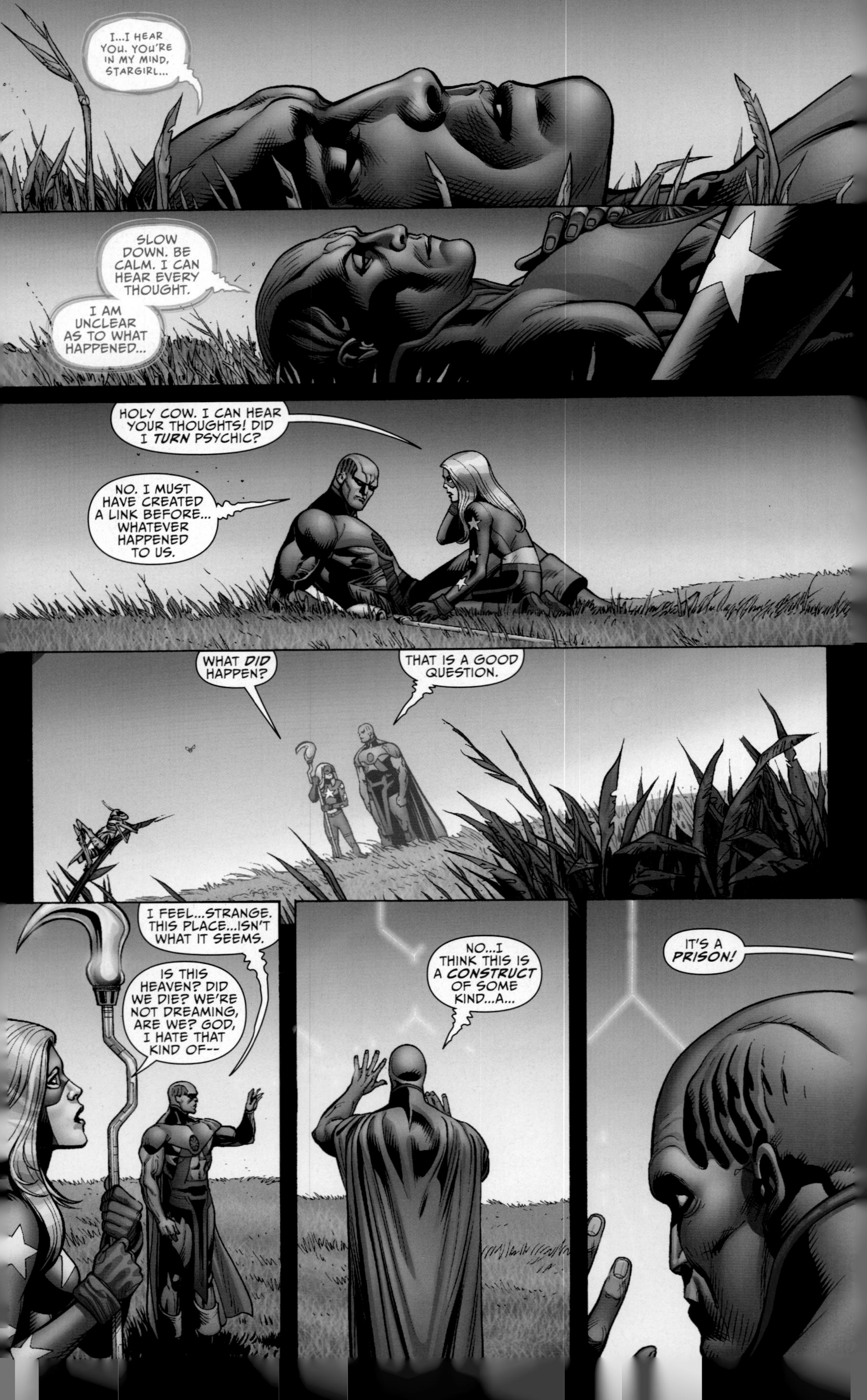
I...I HEAR YOU. YOU'RE IN MY MIND, STARGIRL...
SLOW DOWN. BE CALM. I CAN HEAR EVERY THOUGHT.
I AM UNCLEAR AS TO WHAT HAPPENED...
HOLY COW. I CAN HEAR YOUR THOUGHTS! DID I TURN PSYCHIC?
NO. I MUST HAVE CREATED A LINK BEFORE... WHATEVER HAPPENED TO US.
WHAT DID HAPPEN?
THAT IS A GOOD QUESTION.
I FEEL...STRANGE. THIS PLACE...ISN'T WHAT IT SEEMS.
IS THIS HEAVEN? DID WE DIE? WE'RE NOT DREAMING, ARE WE? GOD, I HATE THAT KIND OF--
NO...I THINK THIS IS A CONSTRUCT OF SOME KIND...A...
IT'S A PRISON!

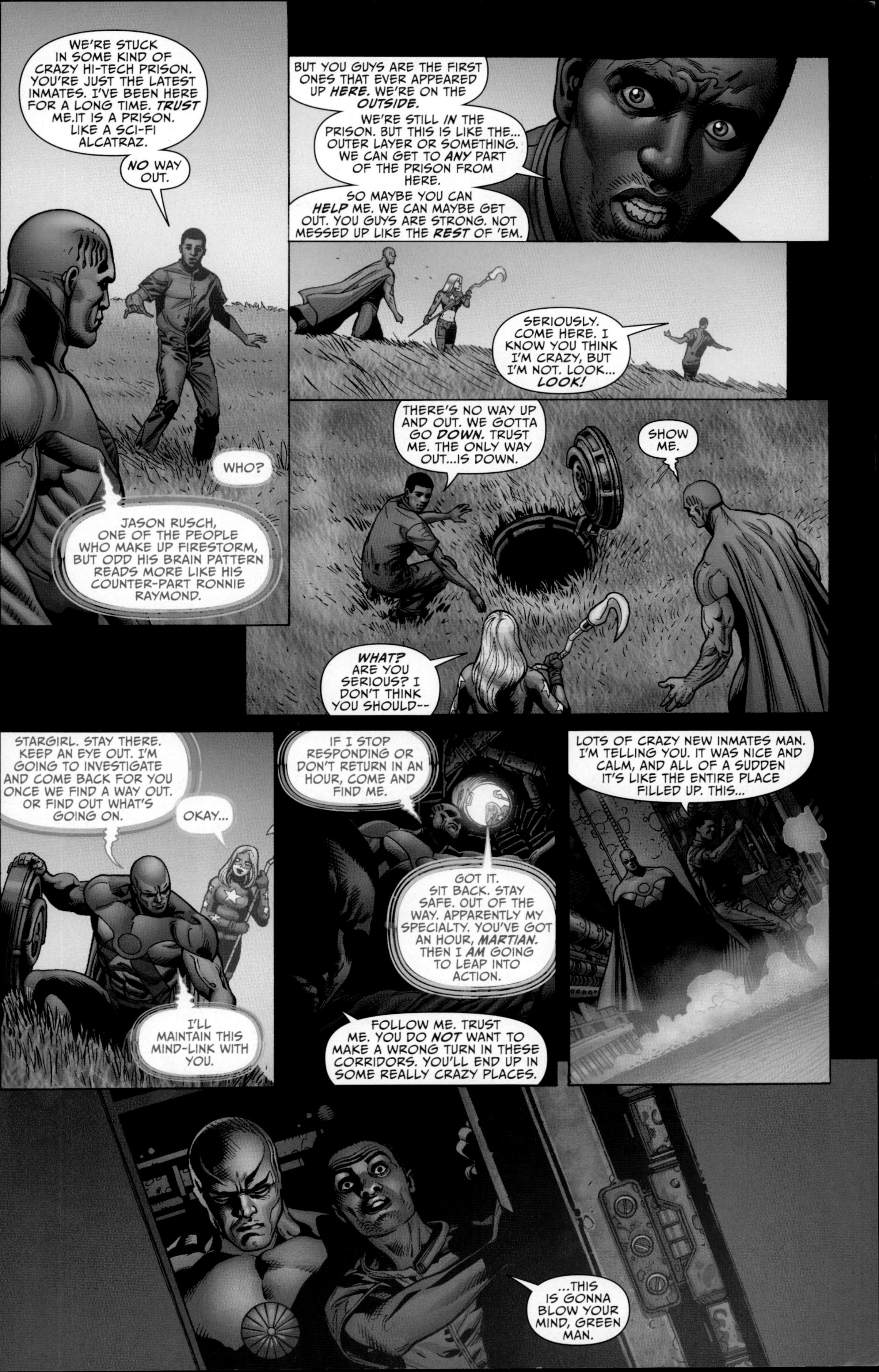
WE'RE STUCK IN SOME KIND OF CRAZY HI-TECH PRISON. YOU'RE JUST THE LATEST INMATES. I'VE BEEN HERE FOR A LONG TIME. TRUST ME.IT IS A PRISON. LIKE A SCI-FI ALCATRAZ.
NO WAY OUT.
WHO?
JASON RUSCH, ONE OF THE PEOPLE WHO MAKE UP FIRESTORM, BUT ODD HIS BRAIN PATTERN READS MORE LIKE HIS COUNTER-PART RONNIE RAYMOND.
BUT YOU GUYS ARE THE FIRST ONES THAT EVER APPEARED UP HERE. WE'RE ON THE OUTSIDE.
WE'RE STILL IN THE PRISON. BUT THIS IS LIKE THE... OUTER LAYER OR SOMETHING. WE CAN GET TO ANY PART OF THE PRISON FROM HERE.
SO MAYBE YOU CAN HELP ME. WE CAN MAYBE GET OUT. YOU GUYS ARE STRONG. NOT MESSED UP LIKE THE REST OF 'EM.
SERIOUSLY. COME HERE. I KNOW YOU THINK I'M CRAZY, BUT I'M NOT. LOOK... LOOK!
THERE'S NO WAY UP AND OUT. WE GOTTA GO DOWN. TRUST ME. THE ONLY WAY OUT...IS DOWN.
SHOW ME.
WHAT? ARE YOU SERIOUS? I DON'T THINK YOU SHOULD--
STARGIRL. STAY THERE. KEEP AN EYE OUT. I'M GOING TO INVESTIGATE AND COME BACK FOR YOU ONCE WE FIND A WAY OUT. OR FIND OUT WHAT'S GOING ON.
OKAY...
I'LL MAINTAIN THIS MIND-LINK WITH YOU.
IF I STOP RESPONDING OR DON'T RETURN IN AN HOUR, COME AND FIND ME.
GOT IT. SIT BACK. STAY SAFE. OUT OF THE WAY. APPARENTLY MY SPECIALTY. YOU'VE GOT AN HOUR, MARTIAN. THEN I AM GOING TO LEAP INTO ACTION.
FOLLOW ME. TRUST ME. YOU DO NOT WANT TO MAKE A WRONG TURN IN THESE CORRIDORS. YOU'LL END UP IN SOME REALLY CRAZY PLACES.
LOTS OF CRAZY NEW INMATES MAN. I'M TELLING YOU. IT WAS NICE AND CALM, AND ALL OF A SUDDEN IT'S LIKE THE ENTIRE PLACE FILLED UP. THIS...
...THIS IS GONNA BLOW YOUR MIND, GREEN MAN.

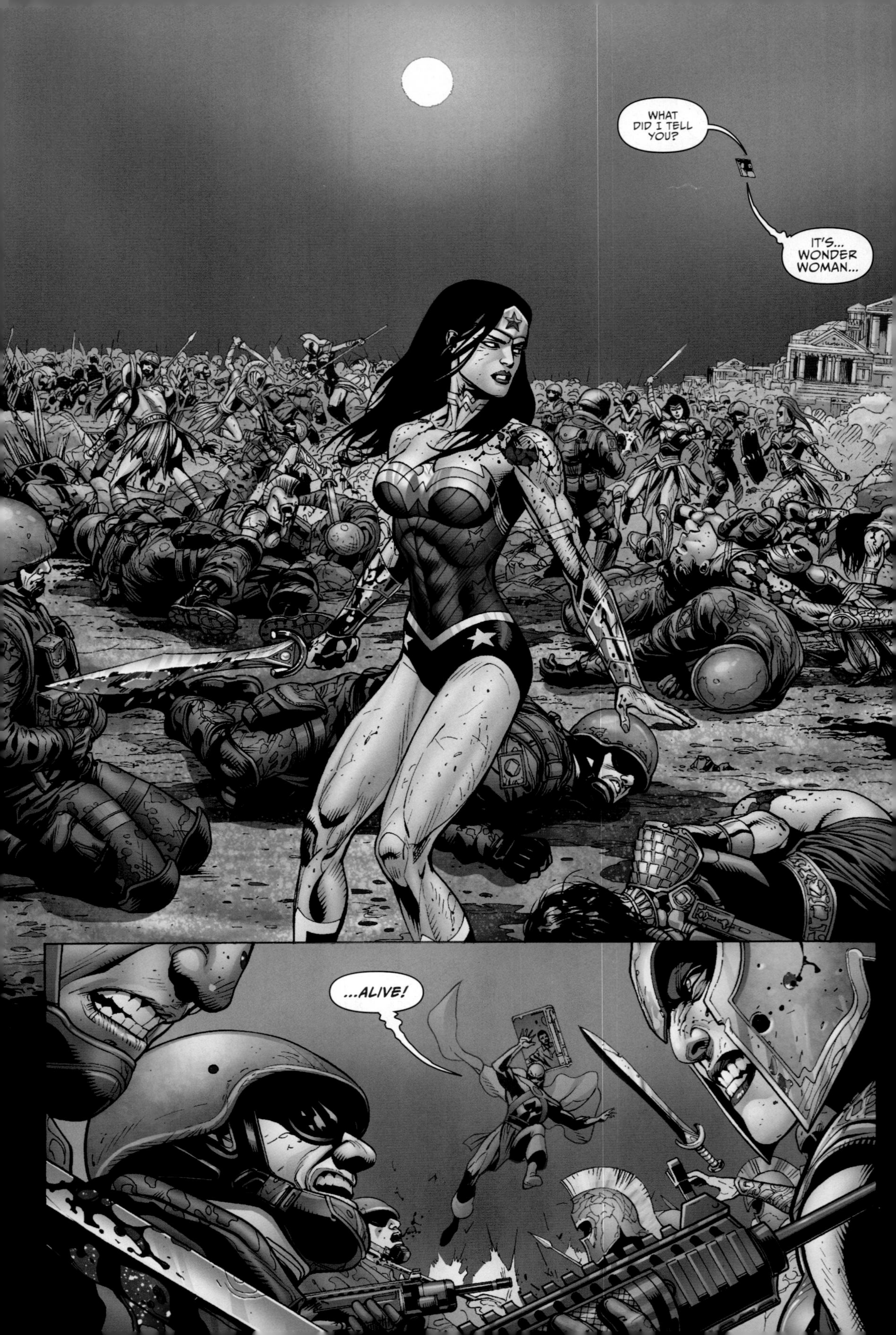
WHAT DID I TELL YOU?
IT'S... WONDER WOMAN...
...ALIVE!

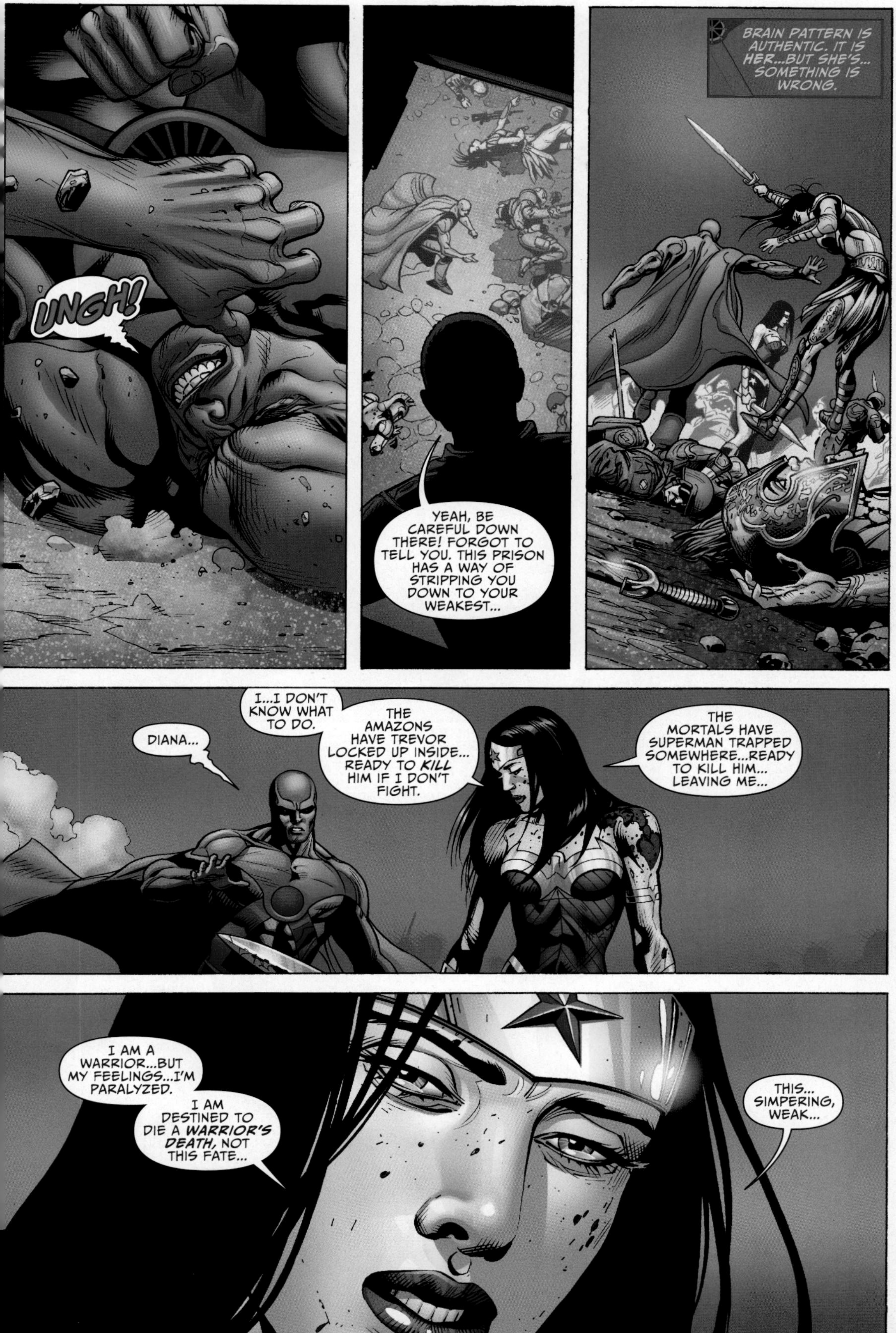
UNGH!
YEAH, BE CAREFUL DOWN THERE! FORGOT TO TELL YOU. THIS PRISON HAS A WAY OF STRIPPING YOU DOWN TO YOUR WEAKEST...
BRAIN PATTERN IS AUTHENTIC. IT IS HER...BUT SHE'S... SOMETHING IS WRONG.
DIANA...
I...I DON'T KNOW WHAT TO DO.
THE AMAZONS HAVE TREVOR LOCKED UP INSIDE... READY TO KILL HIM IF I DON'T FIGHT.
THE MORTALS HAVE SUPERMAN TRAPPED SOMEWHERE...READY TO KILL HIM... LEAVING ME...
I AM A WARRIOR...BUT MY FEELINGS...I'M PARALYZED.
I AM DESTINED TO DIE A WARRIOR'S DEATH, NOT THIS FATE...
THIS... SIMPERING, WEAK...

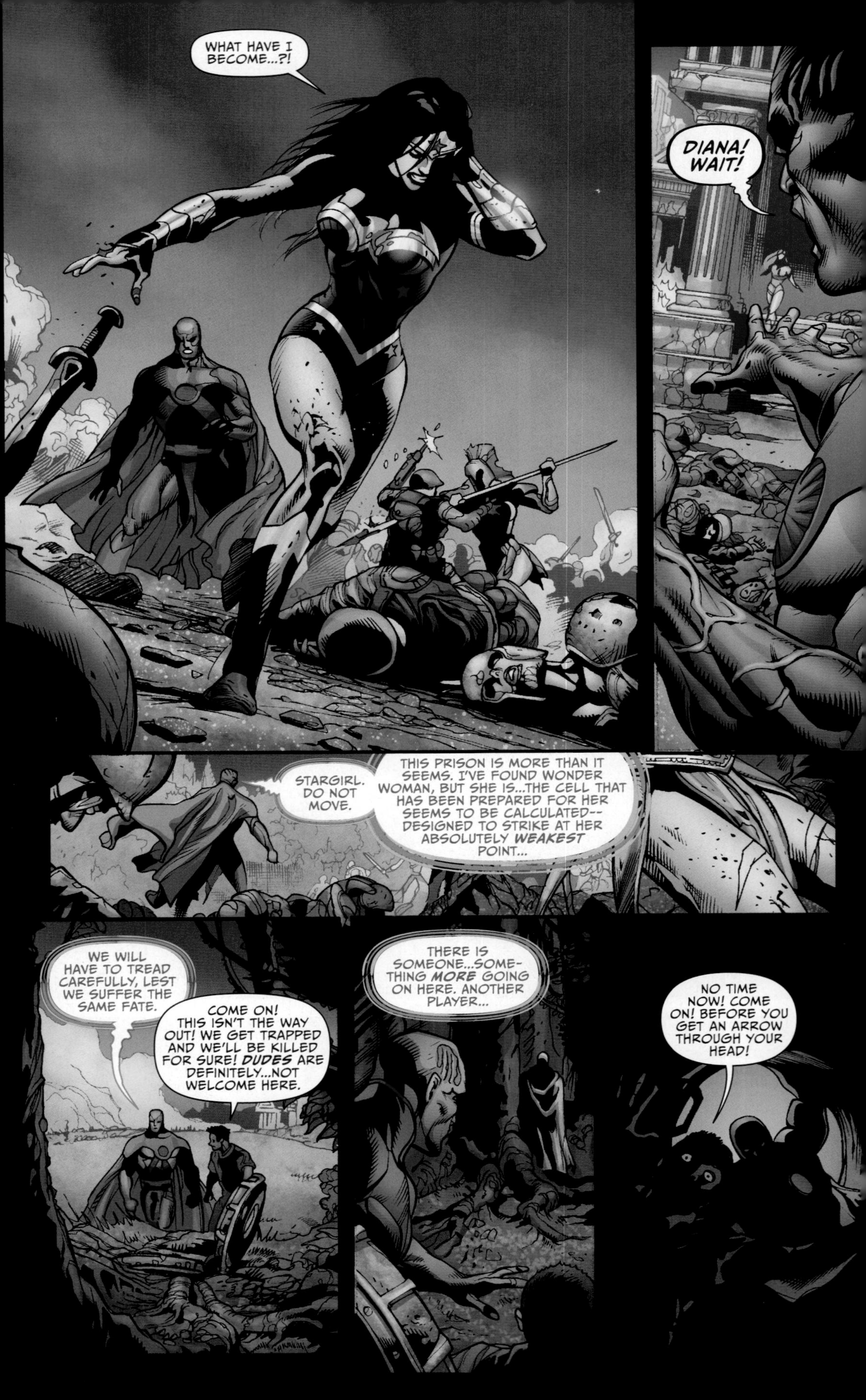
WHAT HAVE I BECOME...?!
DIANA! WAIT!
STARGIRL. DO NOT MOVE.
THIS PRISON IS MORE THAN IT SEEMS. I'VE FOUND WONDER WOMAN, BUT SHE IS...THE CELL THAT HAS BEEN PREPARED FOR HER SEEMS TO BE CALCULATED-- DESIGNED TO STRIKE AT HER ABSOLUTELY WEAKEST POINT...
WE WILL HAVE TO TREAD CAREFULLY, LEST WE SUFFER THE SAME FATE.
COME ON! THIS ISN'T THE WAY OUT! WE GET TRAPPED AND WE'LL BE KILLED FOR SURE! DUDES ARE DEFINITELY...NOT WELCOME HERE.
THERE IS SOMEONE...SOME-THING MORE GOING ON HERE. ANOTHER PLAYER...
NO TIME NOW! COME ON! BEFORE YOU GET AN ARROW THROUGH YOUR HEAD!

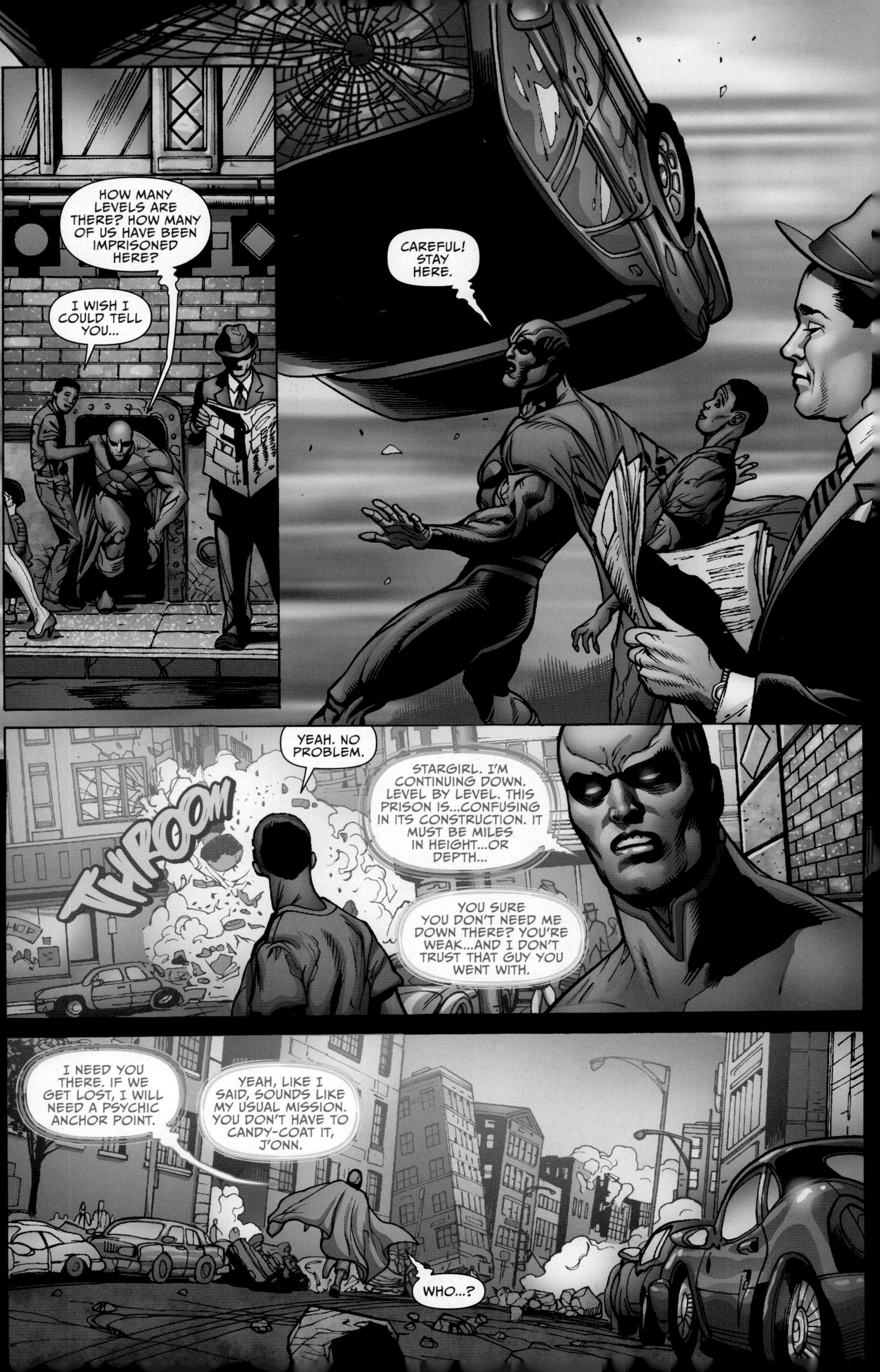
HOW MANY LEVELS ARE THERE? HOW MANY OF US HAVE BEEN IMPRISONED HERE?
I WISH I COULD TELL YOU...
CAREFUL! STAY HERE.
YEAH. NO PROBLEM.
THROOM
STARGIRL. I'M CONTINUING DOWN. LEVEL BY LEVEL. THIS PRISON IS...CONFUSING IN ITS CONSTRUCTION. IT MUST BE MILES IN HEIGHT...OR DEPTH...
YOU SURE YOU DON'T NEED ME DOWN THERE? YOU'RE WEAK...AND I DON'T TRUST THAT GUY YOU WENT WITH.
I NEED YOU THERE. IF WE GET LOST, I WILL NEED A PSYCHIC ANCHOR POINT.
YEAH, LIKE I SAID, SOUNDS LIKE MY USUAL MISSION. YOU DON'T HAVE TO CANDY-COAT IT, J'ONN.
WHO...?

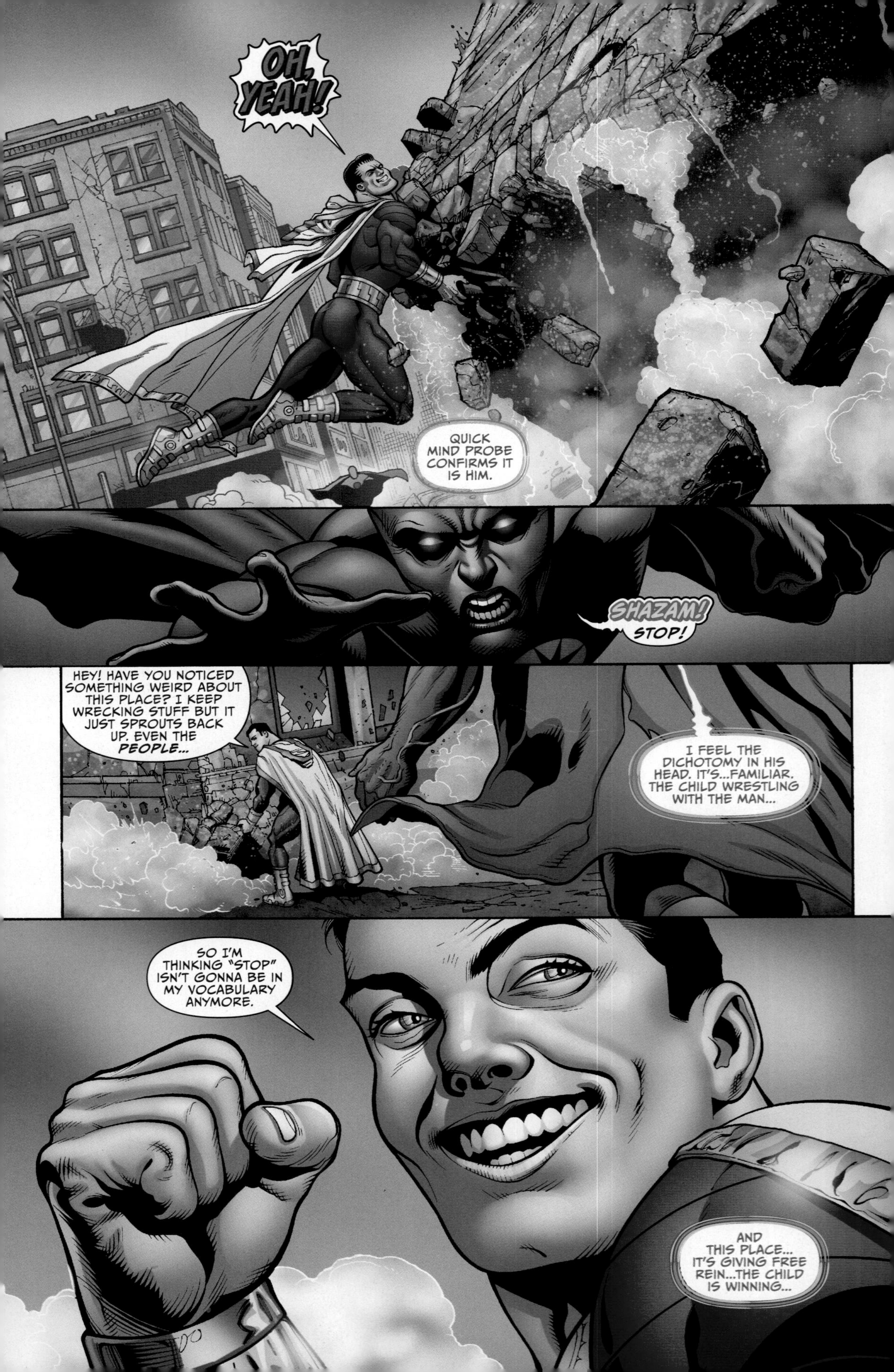
OH, YEAH!
QUICK MIND PROBE CONFIRMS IT IS HIM.
SHAZAM! STOP!
HEY! HAVE YOU NOTICED SOMETHING WEIRD ABOUT THIS PLACE? I KEEP WRECKING STUFF BUT IT JUST SPROUTS BACK UP. EVEN THE PEOPLE...
I FEEL THE DICHOTOMY IN HIS HEAD. IT'S...FAMILIAR. THE CHILD WRESTLING WITH THE MAN...
SO I'M THINKING "STOP" ISN'T GONNA BE IN MY VOCABULARY ANYMORE.
AND THIS PLACE... IT'S GIVING FREE REIN...THE CHILD IS WINNING...

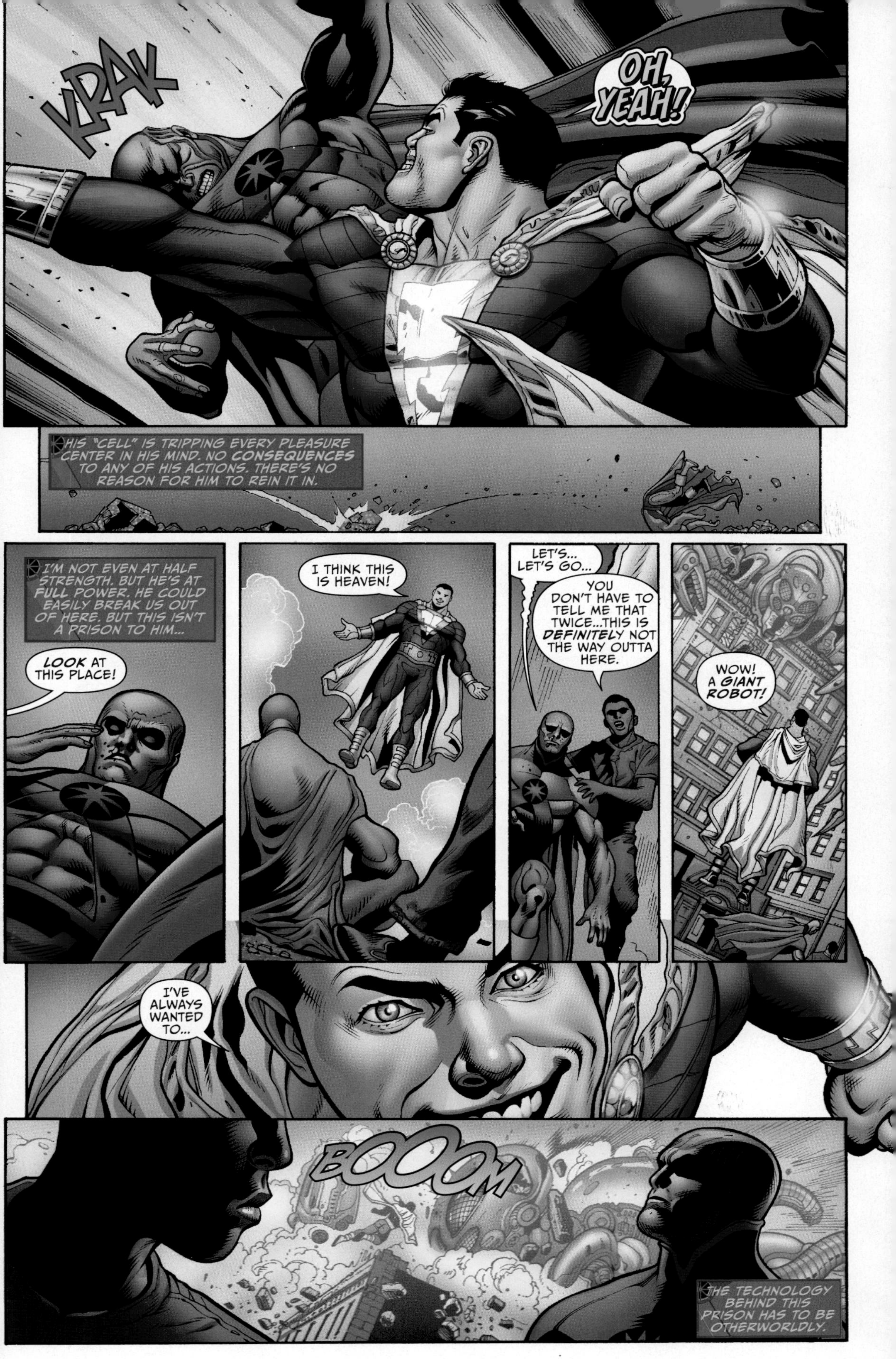
KRAK
OH, YEAH!
HIS "CELL" IS TRIPPING EVERY PLEASURE CENTER IN HIS MIND. NO CONSEQUENCES TO ANY OF HIS ACTIONS. THERE'S NO REASON FOR HIM TO REIN IT IN.
I'M NOT EVEN AT HALF STRENGTH. BUT HE'S AT FULL POWER. HE COULD EASILY BREAK US OUT OF HERE. BUT THIS ISN'T A PRISON TO HIM...
LOOK AT THIS PLACE!
I THINK THIS IS HEAVEN!
LET'S... LET'S GO...
YOU DON'T HAVE TO TELL ME THAT TWICE...THIS IS DEFINITELY NOT THE WAY OUTTA HERE.
WOW! A GIANT ROBOT!
I'VE ALWAYS WANTED TO...
BOOOM
THE TECHNOLOGY BEHIND THIS PRISON HAS TO BE OTHERWORLDLY.

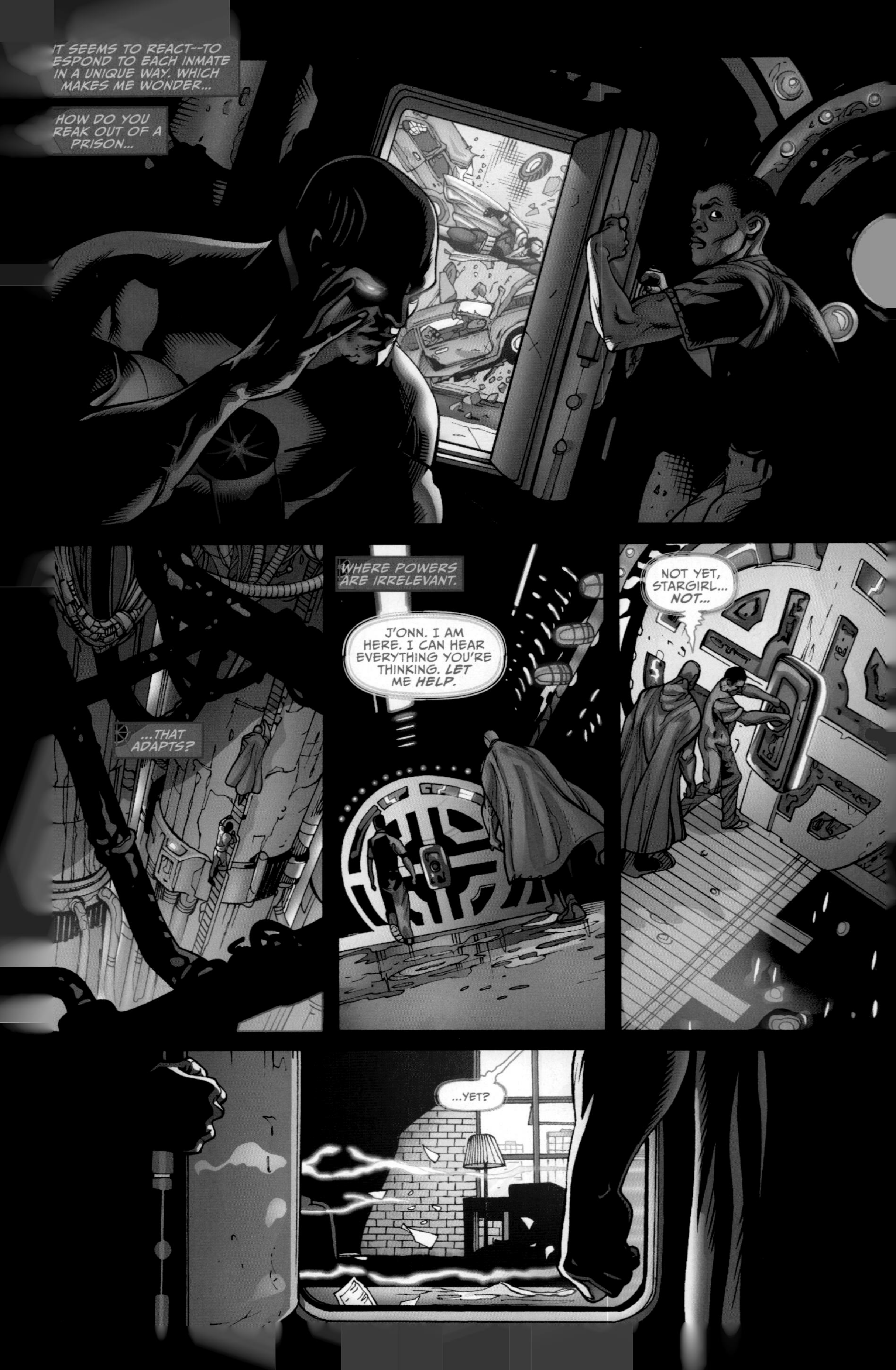
IT SEEMS TO REACT--TO RESPOND TO EACH INMATE IN A UNIQUE WAY. WHICH MAKES ME WONDER...
HOW DO YOU BREAK OUT OF A PRISON...
...THAT ADAPTS?
WHERE POWERS ARE IRRELEVANT.
J'ONN. I AM HERE. I CAN HEAR EVERYTHING YOU'RE THINKING. LET ME HELP.
NOT YET, STARGIRL... NOT...
...YET?

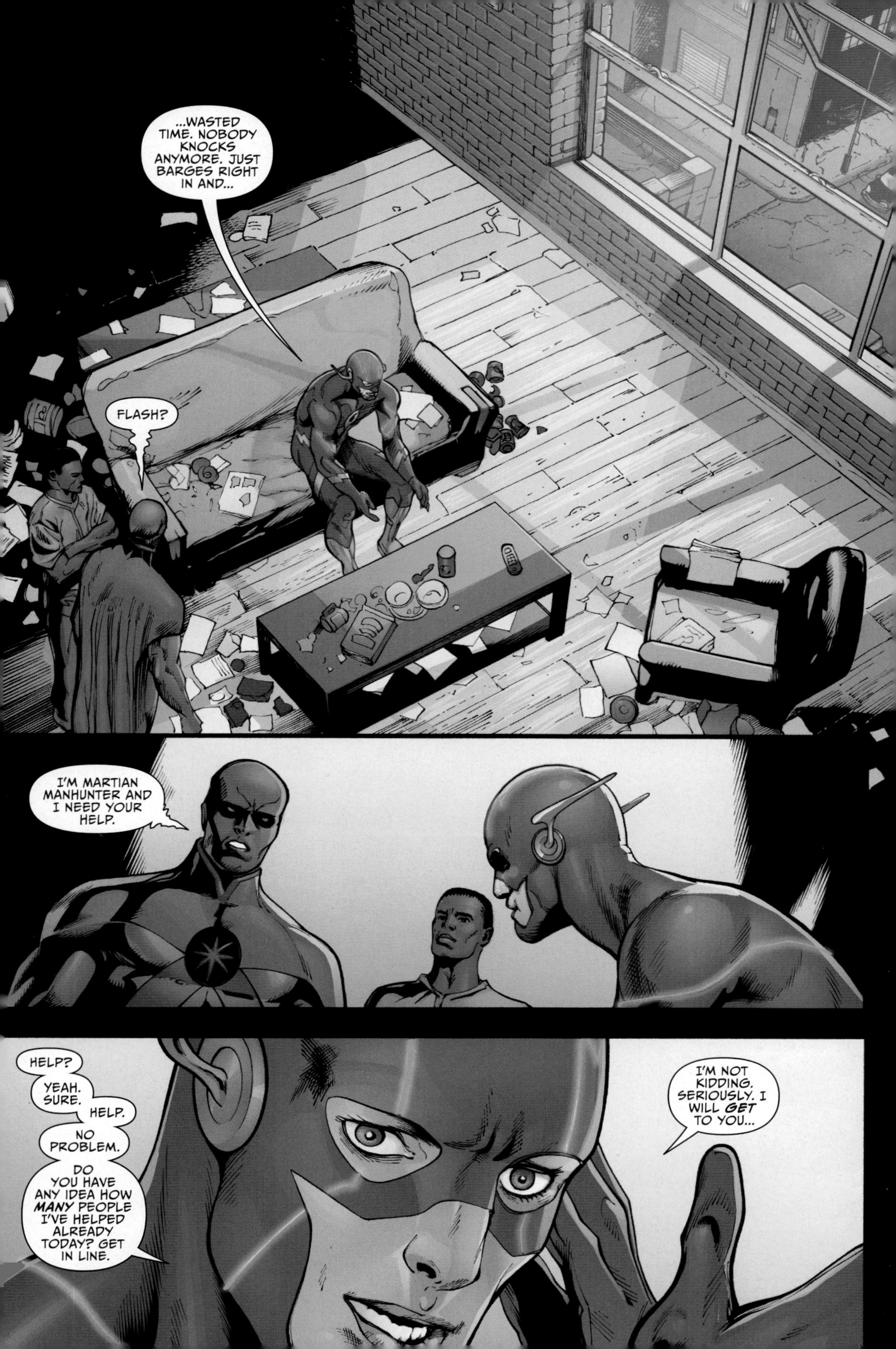
...WASTED TIME. NOBODY KNOCKS ANYMORE. JUST BARGES RIGHT IN AND...
FLASH?
I'M MARTIAN MANHUNTER AND I NEED YOUR HELP.
HELP?
YEAH. SURE.
HELP.
NO PROBLEM.
DO YOU HAVE ANY IDEA HOW *MANY* PEOPLE I'VE HELPED ALREADY TODAY? GET IN LINE.
I'M NOT KIDDING. SERIOUSLY. I WILL *GET* TO YOU...

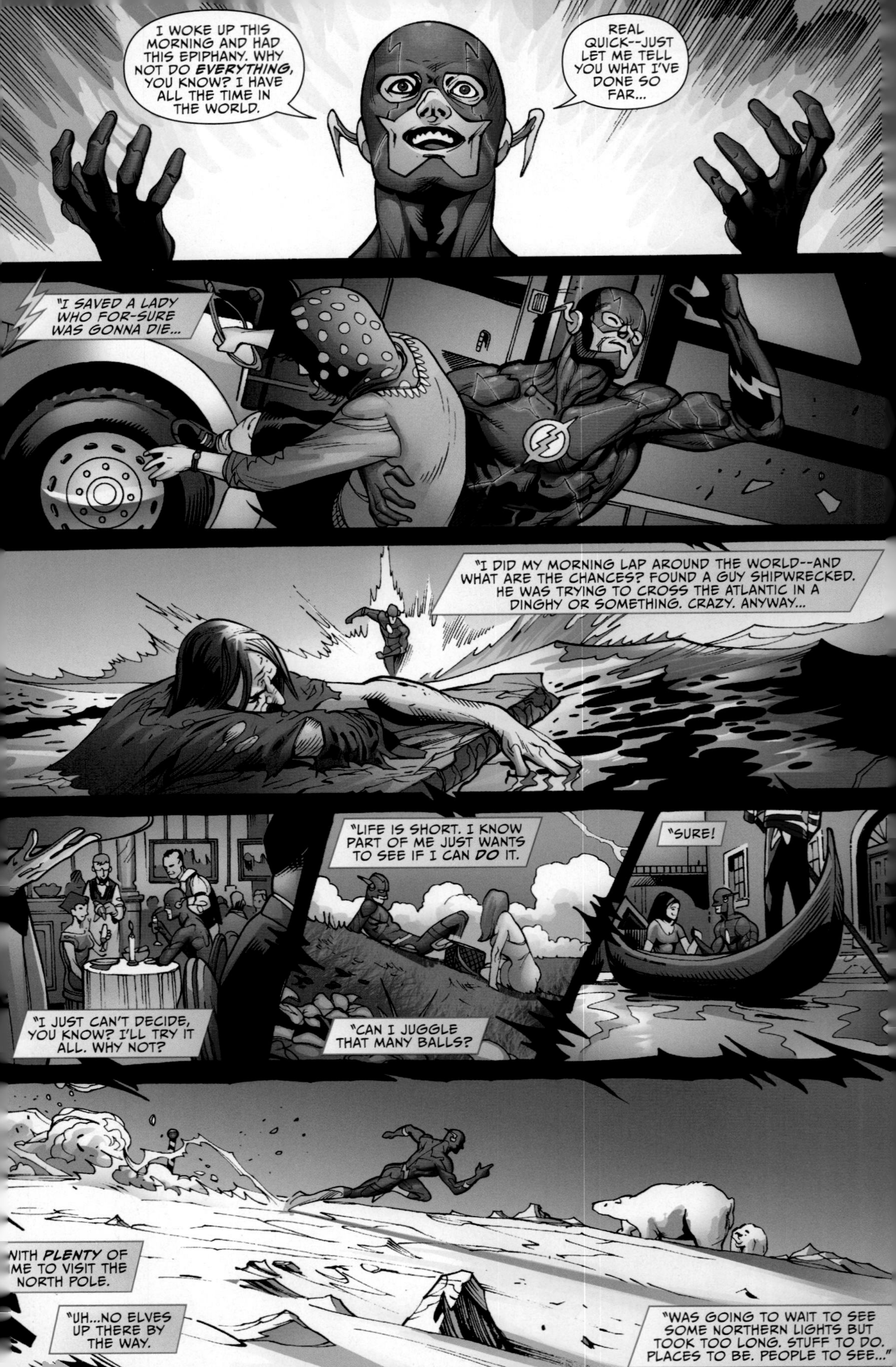

I WOKE UP THIS MORNING AND HAD THIS EPIPHANY. WHY NOT DO *EVERYTHING*, YOU KNOW? I HAVE ALL THE TIME IN THE WORLD.
REAL QUICK--JUST LET ME TELL YOU WHAT I'VE DONE SO FAR...
"I SAVED A LADY WHO FOR-SURE WAS GONNA DIE...
"I DID MY MORNING LAP AROUND THE WORLD--AND WHAT ARE THE CHANCES? FOUND A GUY SHIPWRECKED. HE WAS TRYING TO CROSS THE ATLANTIC IN A DINGHY OR SOMETHING. CRAZY. ANYWAY...
"LIFE IS SHORT. I KNOW PART OF ME JUST WANTS TO SEE IF I CAN *DO* IT.
"SURE!
"I JUST CAN'T DECIDE, YOU KNOW? I'LL TRY IT ALL. WHY NOT?
"CAN I JUGGLE THAT MANY BALLS?
WITH *PLENTY* OF ME TO VISIT THE NORTH POLE.
"UH...NO ELVES UP THERE BY THE WAY.
"WAS GOING TO WAIT TO SEE SOME NORTHERN LIGHTS BUT TOOK TOO LONG. STUFF TO DO. PLACES TO BE. PEOPLE TO SEE..."

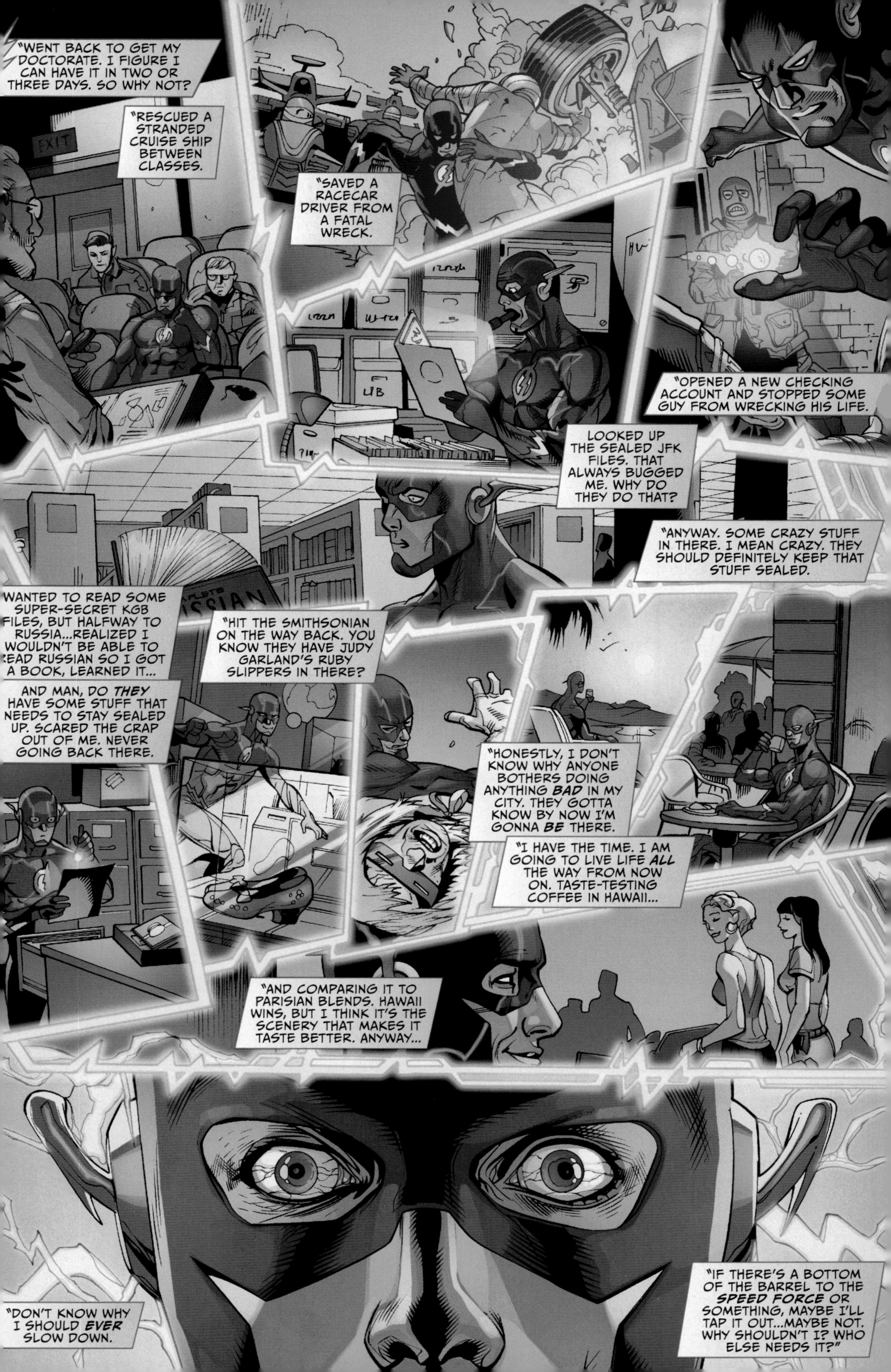
"WENT BACK TO GET MY DOCTORATE. I FIGURE I CAN HAVE IT IN TWO OR THREE DAYS. SO WHY NOT?
"RESCUED A STRANDED CRUISE SHIP BETWEEN CLASSES.
"SAVED A RACECAR DRIVER FROM A FATAL WRECK.
"OPENED A NEW CHECKING ACCOUNT AND STOPPED SOME GUY FROM WRECKING HIS LIFE.
LOOKED UP THE SEALED JFK FILES. THAT ALWAYS BUGGED ME. WHY DO THEY DO THAT?
"ANYWAY. SOME CRAZY STUFF IN THERE. I MEAN CRAZY. THEY SHOULD DEFINITELY KEEP THAT STUFF SEALED.
WANTED TO READ SOME SUPER-SECRET KGB FILES, BUT HALFWAY TO RUSSIA...REALIZED I WOULDN'T BE ABLE TO READ RUSSIAN SO I GOT A BOOK, LEARNED IT...
AND MAN, DO *THEY* HAVE SOME STUFF THAT NEEDS TO STAY SEALED UP. SCARED THE CRAP OUT OF ME. NEVER GOING BACK THERE.
"HIT THE SMITHSONIAN ON THE WAY BACK. YOU KNOW THEY HAVE JUDY GARLAND'S RUBY SLIPPERS IN THERE?
"HONESTLY, I DON'T KNOW WHY ANYONE BOTHERS DOING ANYTHING ***BAD*** IN MY CITY. THEY GOTTA KNOW BY NOW I'M GONNA ***BE*** THERE.
"I HAVE THE TIME. I AM GOING TO LIVE LIFE ***ALL*** THE WAY FROM NOW ON. TASTE-TESTING COFFEE IN HAWAII...
"AND COMPARING IT TO PARISIAN BLENDS. HAWAII WINS, BUT I THINK IT'S THE SCENERY THAT MAKES IT TASTE BETTER. ANYWAY...
"DON'T KNOW WHY I SHOULD ***EVER*** SLOW DOWN.
"IF THERE'S A BOTTOM OF THE BARREL TO THE ***SPEED FORCE*** OR SOMETHING, MAYBE I'LL TAP IT OUT...MAYBE NOT. WHY SHOULDN'T I? WHO ELSE NEEDS IT?"

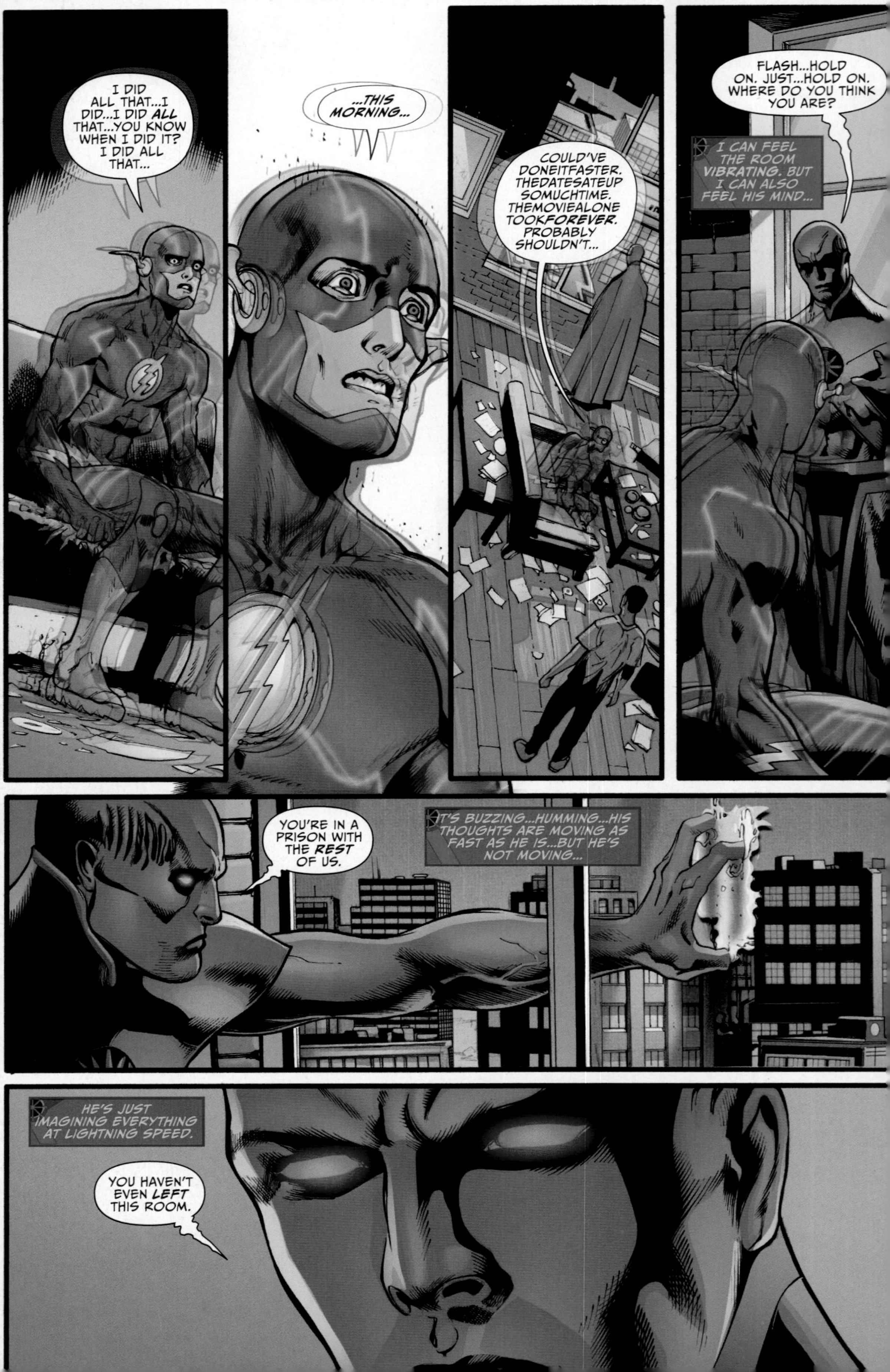
I DID ALL THAT...I DID...I DID ALL THAT...YOU KNOW WHEN I DID IT? I DID ALL THAT...
...THIS MORNING...
COULD'VE DONEITFASTER. THEDATESATEUP SOMUCHTIME. THEMOVIEALONE TOOKFOREVER. PROBABLY SHOULDN'T...
FLASH...HOLD ON. JUST...HOLD ON. WHERE DO YOU THINK YOU ARE?
I CAN FEEL THE ROOM VIBRATING. BUT I CAN ALSO FEEL HIS MIND...
YOU'RE IN A PRISON WITH THE REST OF US.
IT'S BUZZING...HUMMING...HIS THOUGHTS ARE MOVING AS FAST AS HE IS...BUT HE'S NOT MOVING...
HE'S JUST IMAGINING EVERYTHING AT LIGHTNING SPEED.
YOU HAVEN'T EVEN LEFT THIS ROOM.

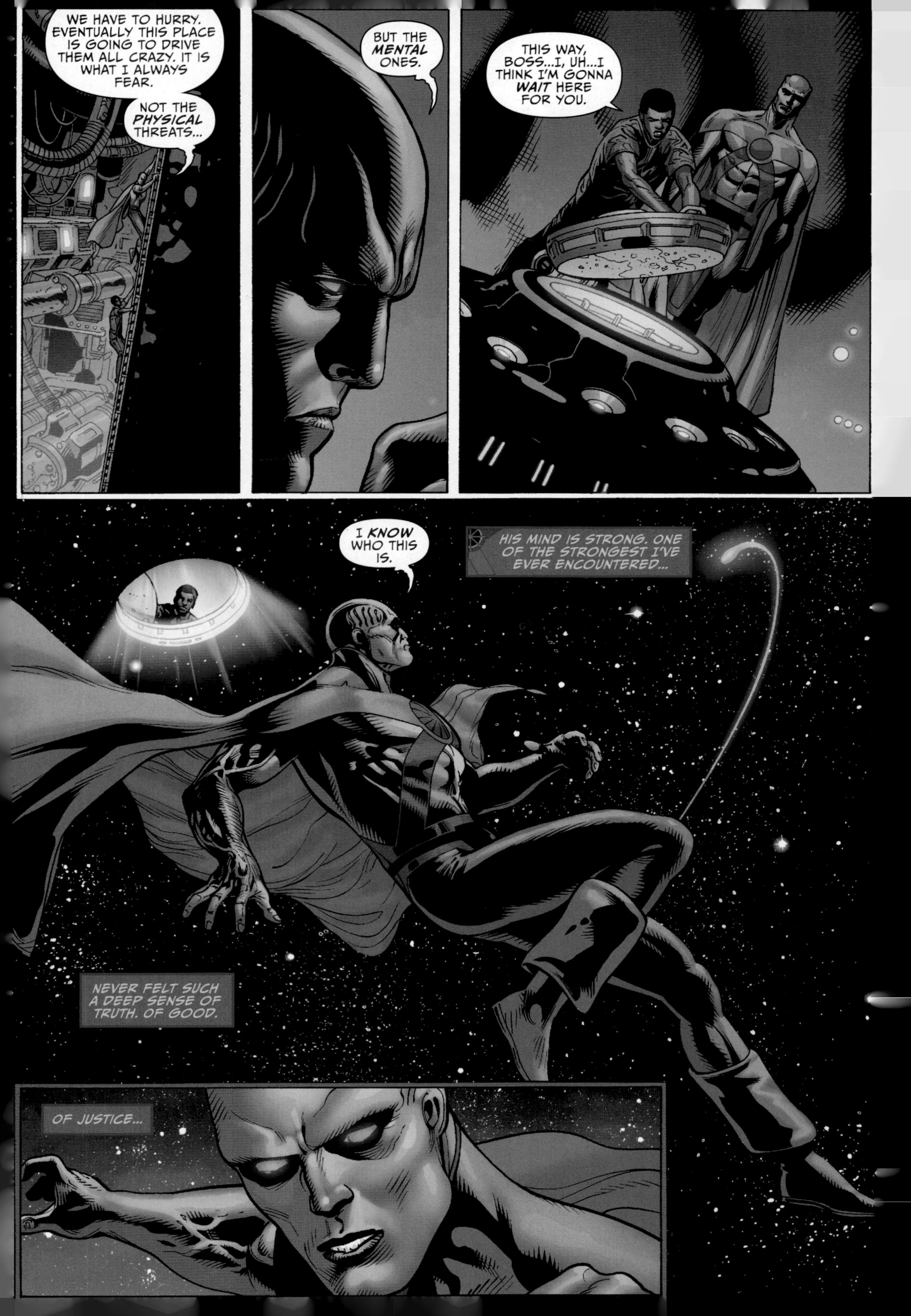
WE HAVE TO HURRY. EVENTUALLY THIS PLACE IS GOING TO DRIVE THEM ALL CRAZY. IT IS WHAT I ALWAYS FEAR.
NOT THE PHYSICAL THREATS...
BUT THE MENTAL ONES.
THIS WAY, BOSS...I, UH...I THINK I'M GONNA WAIT HERE FOR YOU.
I KNOW WHO THIS IS.
HIS MIND IS STRONG. ONE OF THE STRONGEST I'VE EVER ENCOUNTERED...
NEVER FELT SUCH A DEEP SENSE OF TRUTH. OF GOOD.
OF JUSTICE...

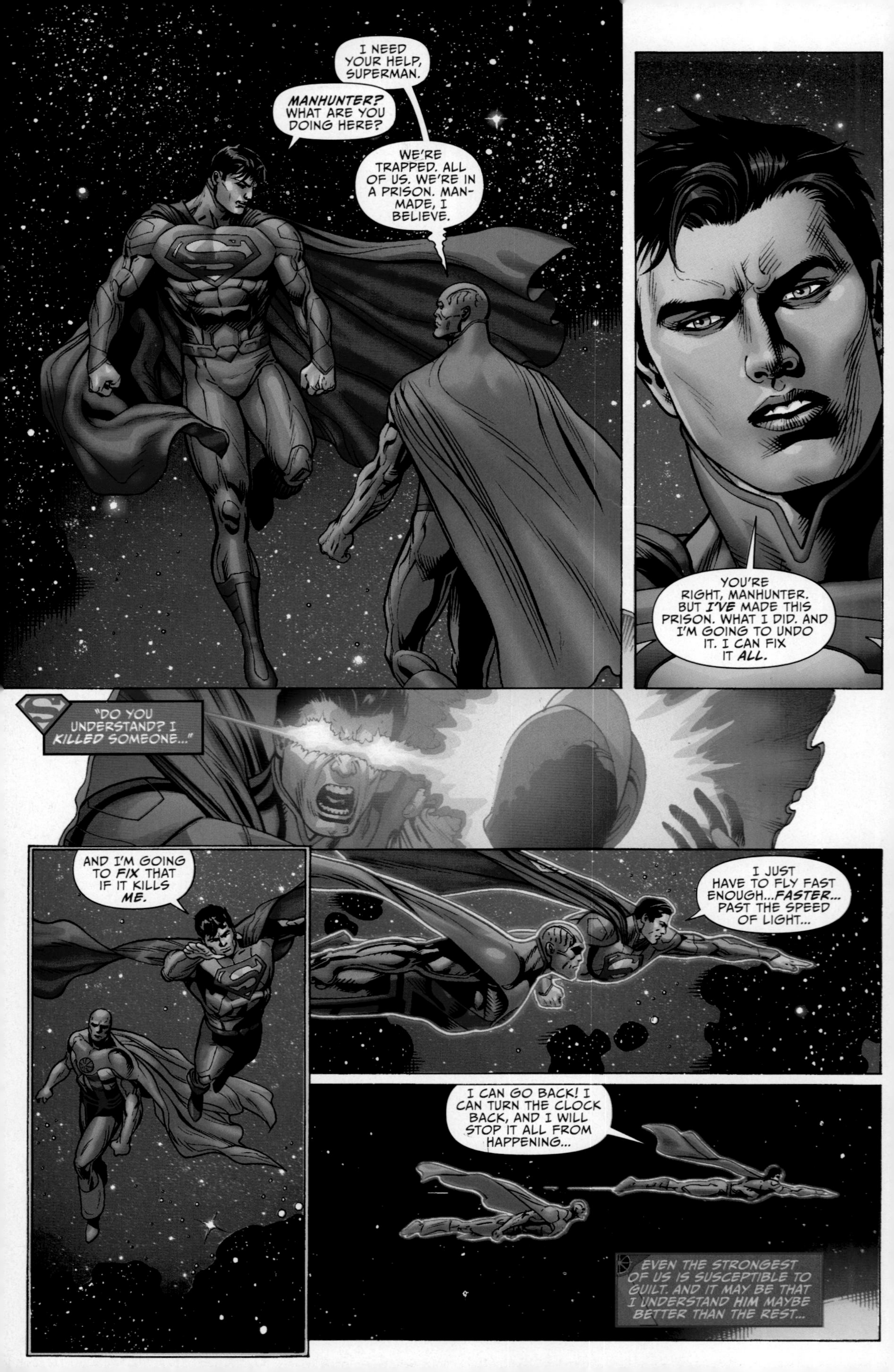
MANHUNTER? WHAT ARE YOU DOING HERE?
I NEED YOUR HELP, SUPERMAN.
WE'RE TRAPPED. ALL OF US. WE'RE IN A PRISON. MAN-MADE, I BELIEVE.
YOU'RE RIGHT, MANHUNTER. BUT I'VE MADE THIS PRISON. WHAT I DID. AND I'M GOING TO UNDO IT. I CAN FIX IT ALL.
"DO YOU UNDERSTAND? I KILLED SOMEONE..."
AND I'M GOING TO FIX THAT IF IT KILLS ME.
I JUST HAVE TO FLY FAST ENOUGH...FASTER... PAST THE SPEED OF LIGHT...
I CAN GO BACK! I CAN TURN THE CLOCK BACK, AND I WILL STOP IT ALL FROM HAPPENING...
EVEN THE STRONGEST OF US IS SUSCEPTIBLE TO GUILT. AND IT MAY BE THAT I UNDERSTAND HIM MAYBE BETTER THAN THE REST...

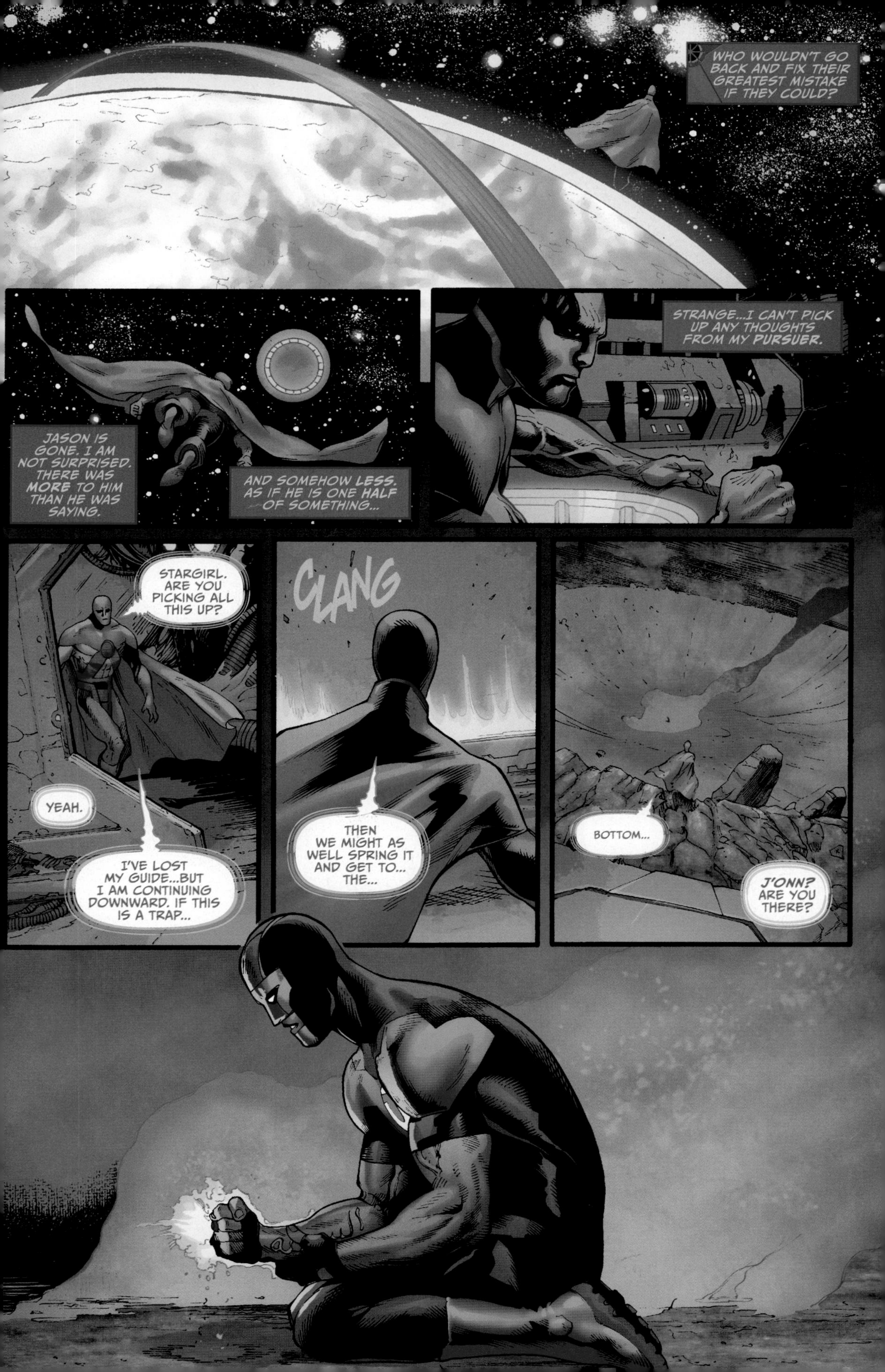
WHO WOULDN'T GO BACK AND FIX THEIR GREATEST MISTAKE IF THEY COULD?
JASON IS GONE. I AM NOT SURPRISED. THERE WAS MORE TO HIM THAN HE WAS SAYING.
AND SOMEHOW LESS. AS IF HE IS ONE HALF OF SOMETHING...
STRANGE...I CAN'T PICK UP ANY THOUGHTS FROM MY PURSUER.
STARGIRL. ARE YOU PICKING ALL THIS UP?
YEAH.
I'VE LOST MY GUIDE...BUT I AM CONTINUING DOWNWARD. IF THIS IS A TRAP...
CLANG
THEN WE MIGHT AS WELL SPRING IT AND GET TO... THE...
BOTTOM...
J'ONN? ARE YOU THERE?

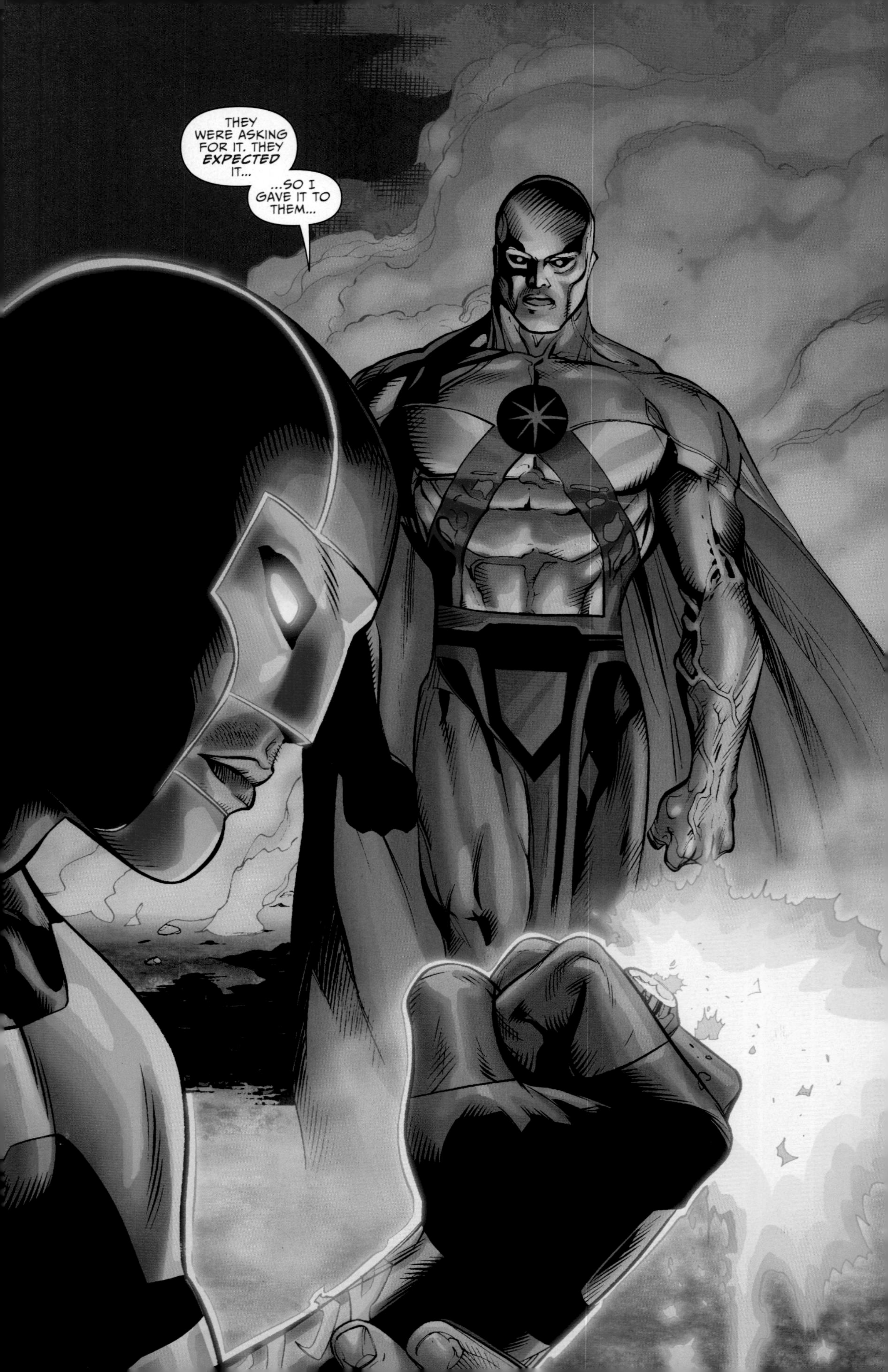
THEY WERE ASKING FOR IT. THEY *EXPECTED* IT...
...SO I GAVE IT TO THEM...

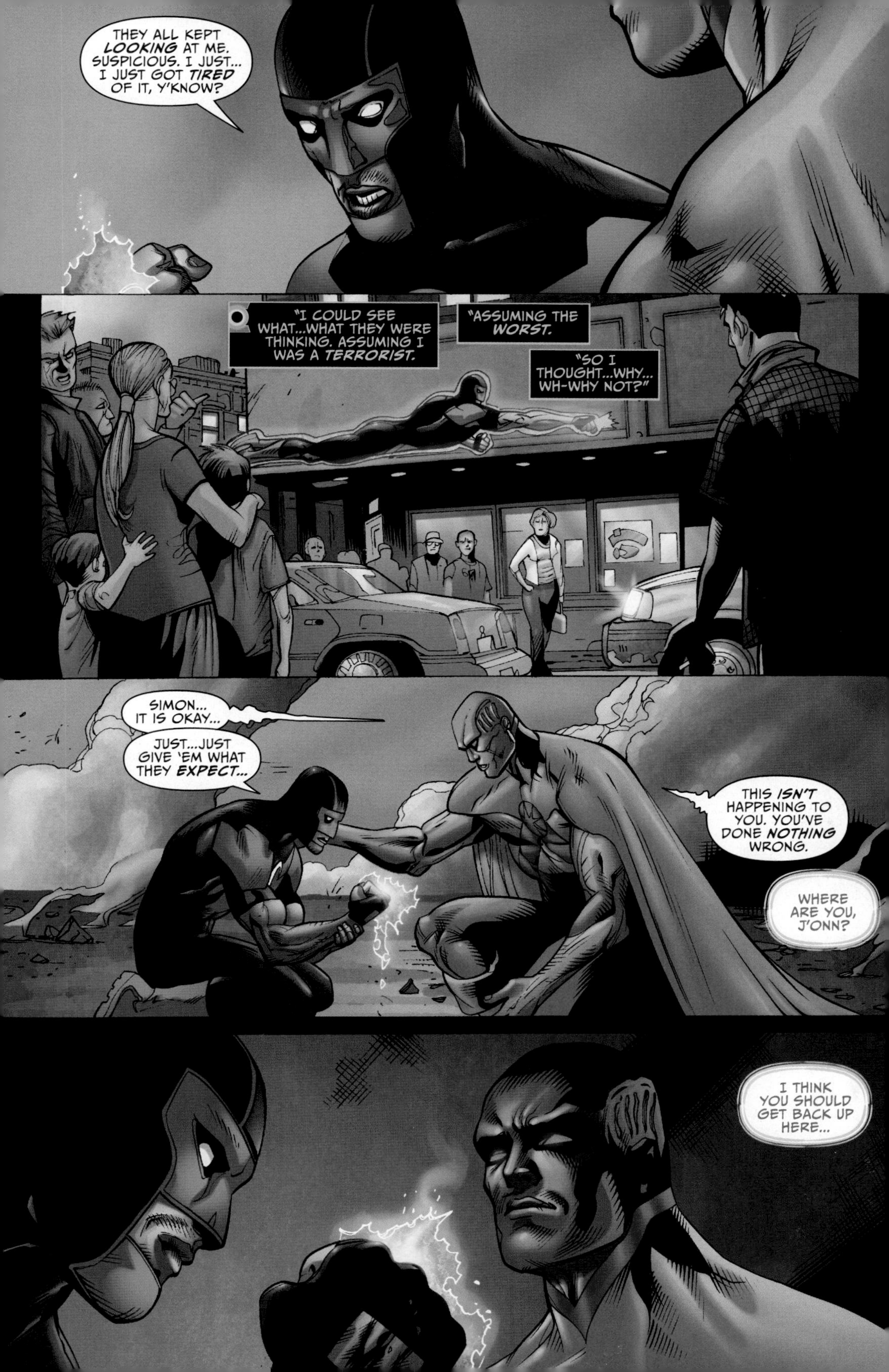
THEY ALL KEPT LOOKING AT ME. SUSPICIOUS. I JUST... I JUST GOT TIRED OF IT, Y'KNOW?
"I COULD SEE WHAT...WHAT THEY WERE THINKING. ASSUMING I WAS A TERRORIST.
"ASSUMING THE WORST.
"SO I THOUGHT...WHY... WH-WHY NOT?"
SIMON... IT IS OKAY...
JUST...JUST GIVE 'EM WHAT THEY EXPECT...
THIS ISN'T HAPPENING TO YOU. YOU'VE DONE NOTHING WRONG.
WHERE ARE YOU, J'ONN?
I THINK YOU SHOULD GET BACK UP HERE...

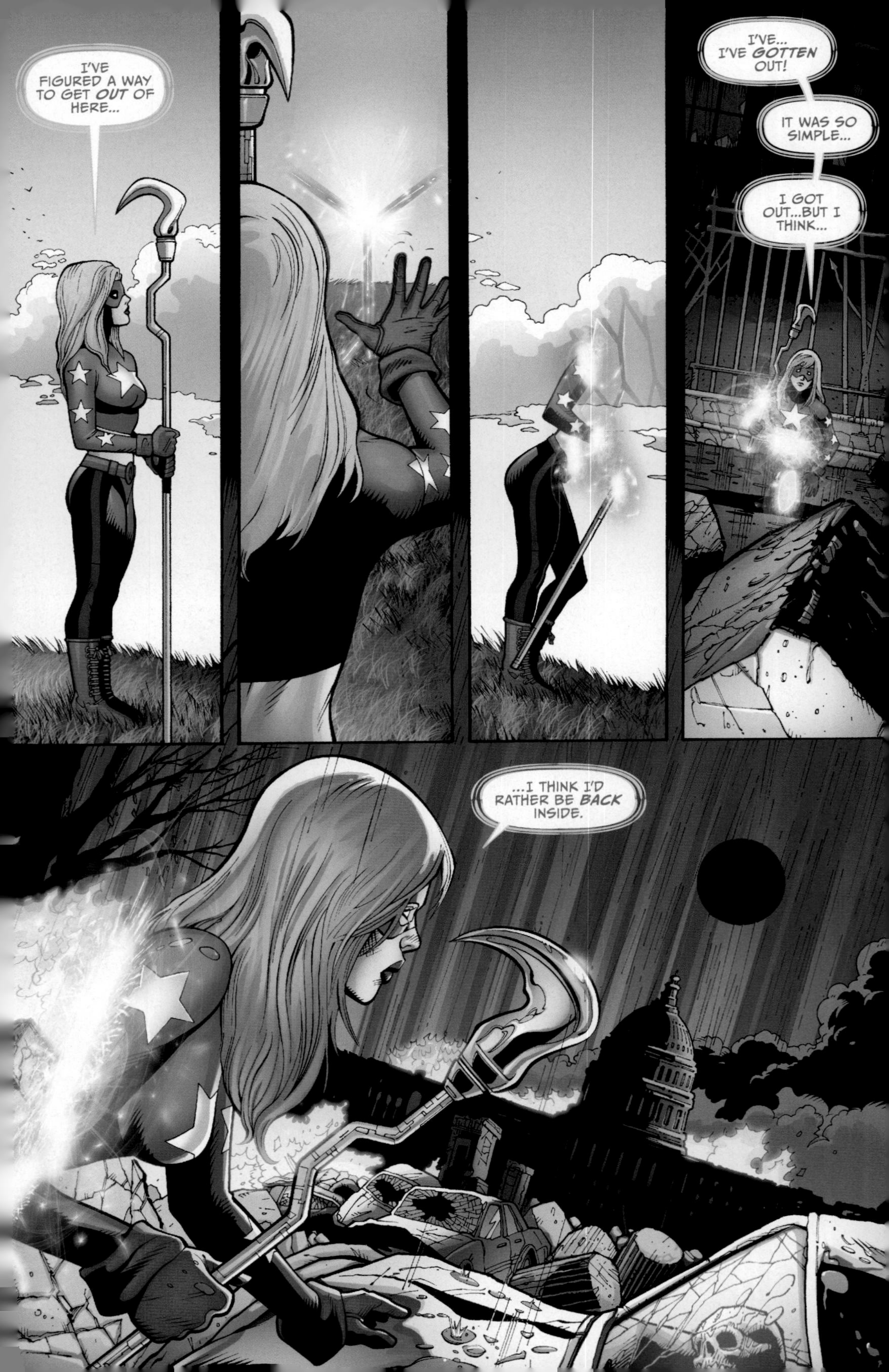
I'VE FIGURED A WAY TO GET *OUT* OF HERE...
I'VE... I'VE *GOTTEN* OUT!
IT WAS SO SIMPLE...
I GOT OUT...BUT I THINK...
...I THINK I'D RATHER BE *BACK* INSIDE.

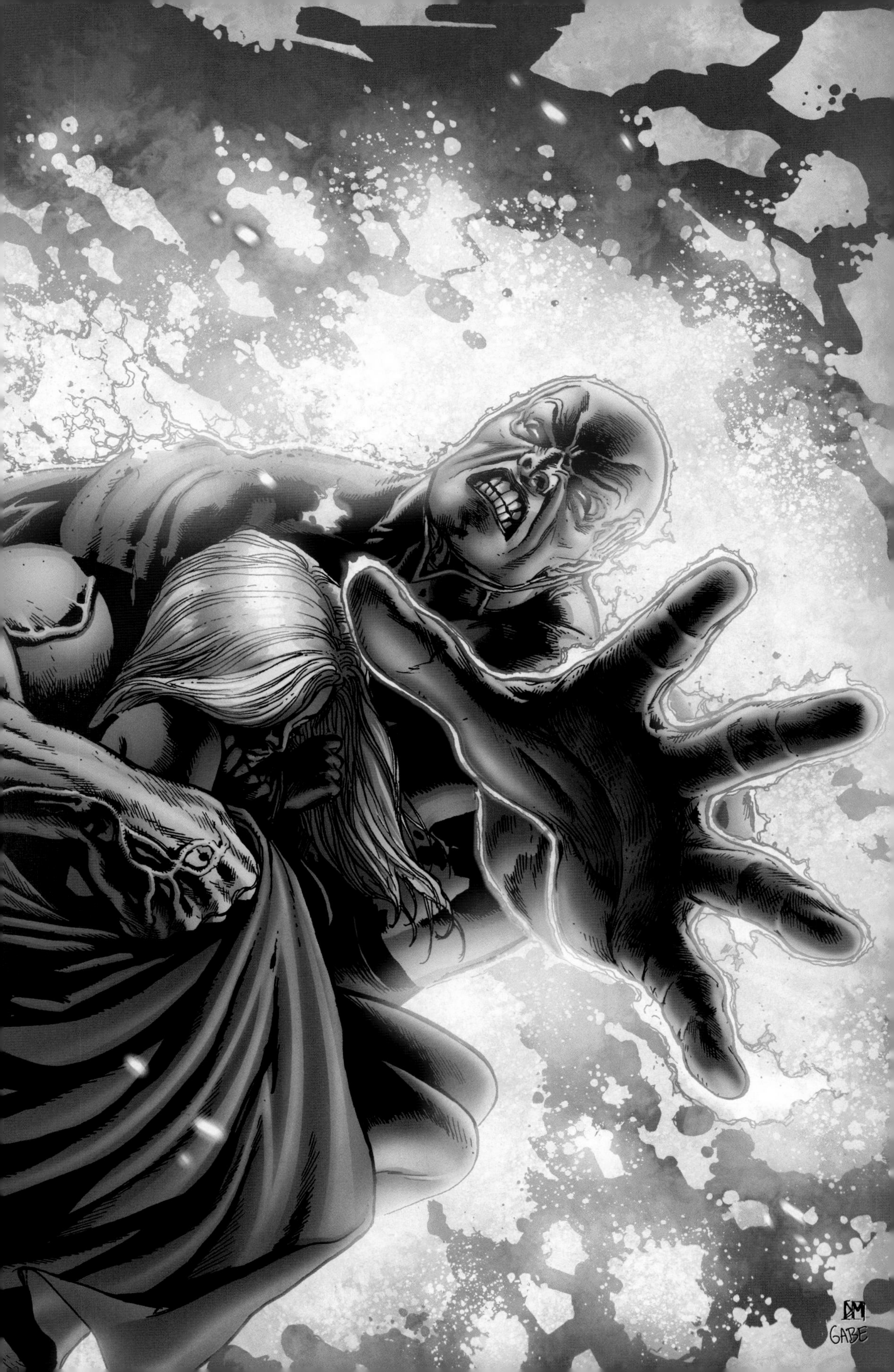
GABE

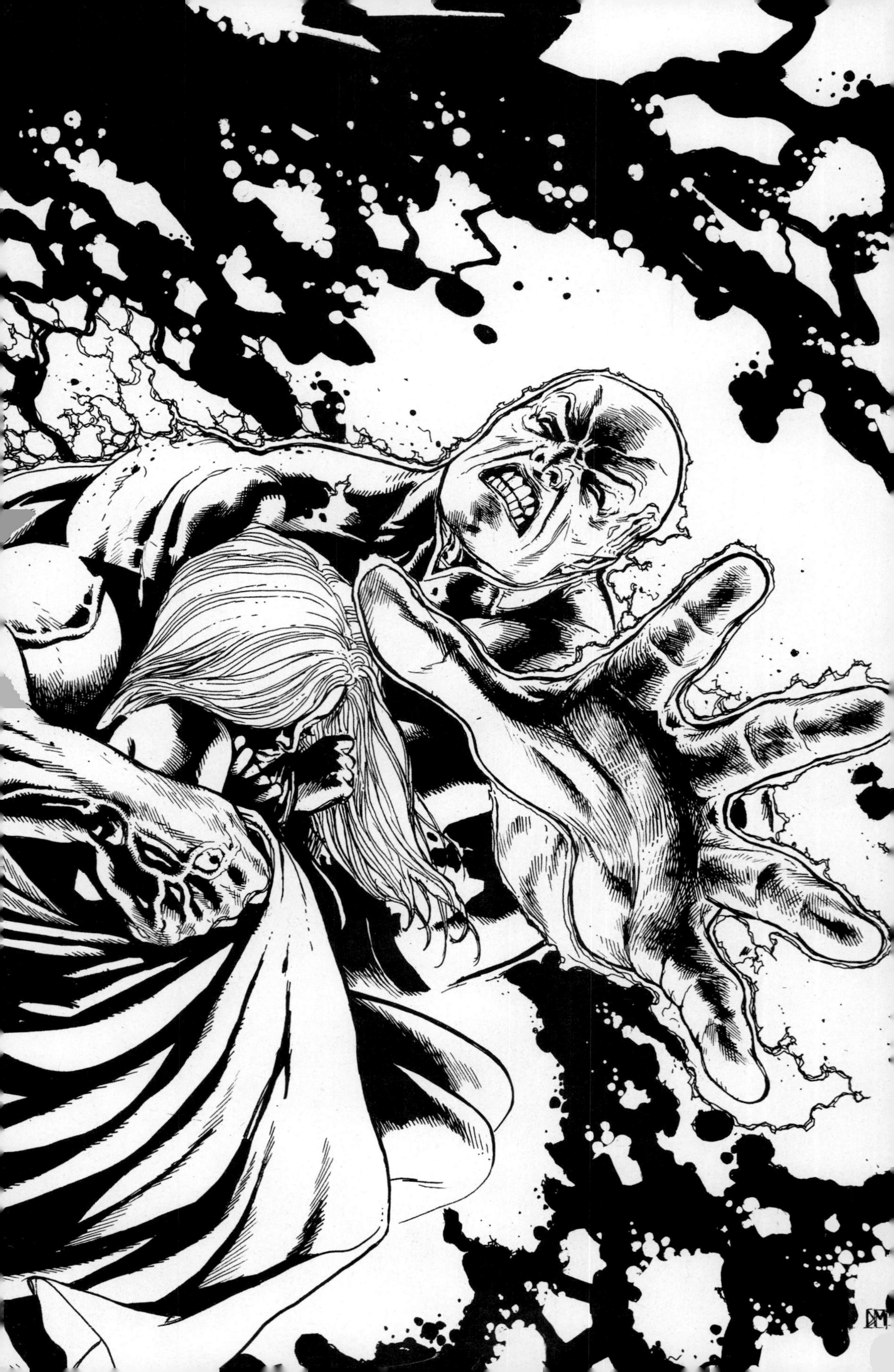

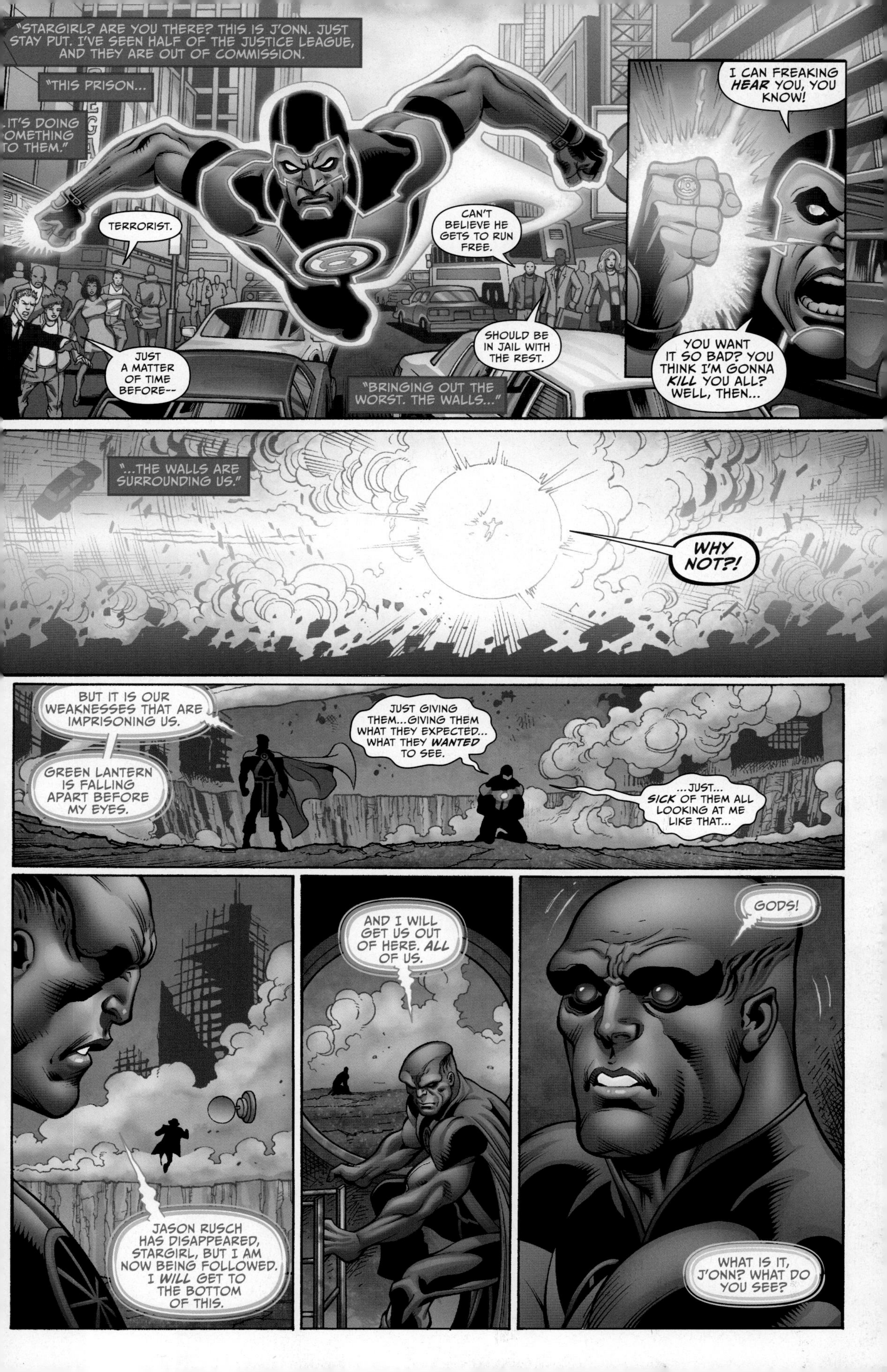
"STARGIRL? ARE YOU THERE? THIS IS J'ONN. JUST STAY PUT. I'VE SEEN HALF OF THE JUSTICE LEAGUE, AND THEY ARE OUT OF COMMISSION.
"THIS PRISON...
...IT'S DOING SOMETHING TO THEM."
TERRORIST.
CAN'T BELIEVE HE GETS TO RUN FREE.
JUST A MATTER OF TIME BEFORE--
SHOULD BE IN JAIL WITH THE REST.
"BRINGING OUT THE WORST. THE WALLS..."
I CAN FREAKING HEAR YOU, YOU KNOW!
YOU WANT IT SO BAD? YOU THINK I'M GONNA KILL YOU ALL? WELL, THEN...
"...THE WALLS ARE SURROUNDING US."
WHY NOT?!
BUT IT IS OUR WEAKNESSES THAT ARE IMPRISONING US.
GREEN LANTERN IS FALLING APART BEFORE MY EYES.
JUST GIVING THEM...GIVING THEM WHAT THEY EXPECTED... WHAT THEY WANTED TO SEE.
...JUST... SICK OF THEM ALL LOOKING AT ME LIKE THAT...
JASON RUSCH HAS DISAPPEARED, STARGIRL, BUT I AM NOW BEING FOLLOWED. I WILL GET TO THE BOTTOM OF THIS.
AND I WILL GET US OUT OF HERE. ALL OF US.
GODS!
WHAT IS IT, J'ONN? WHAT DO YOU SEE?

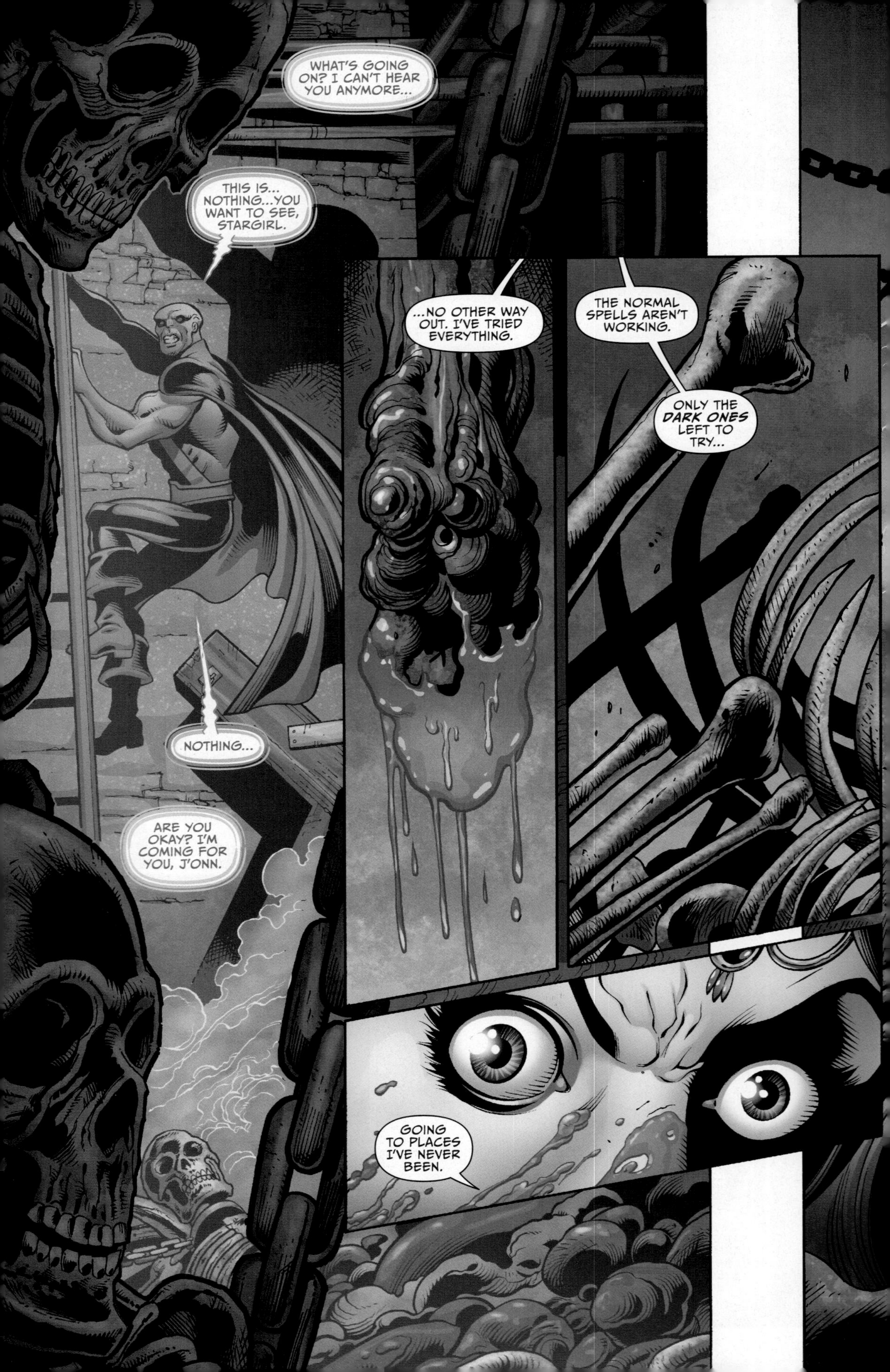
WHAT'S GOING ON? I CAN'T HEAR YOU ANYMORE...
THIS IS... NOTHING...YOU WANT TO SEE, STARGIRL.
NOTHING...
ARE YOU OKAY? I'M COMING FOR YOU, J'ONN.
...NO OTHER WAY OUT. I'VE TRIED EVERYTHING.
THE NORMAL SPELLS AREN'T WORKING.
ONLY THE DARK ONES LEFT TO TRY...
GOING TO PLACES I'VE NEVER BEEN.

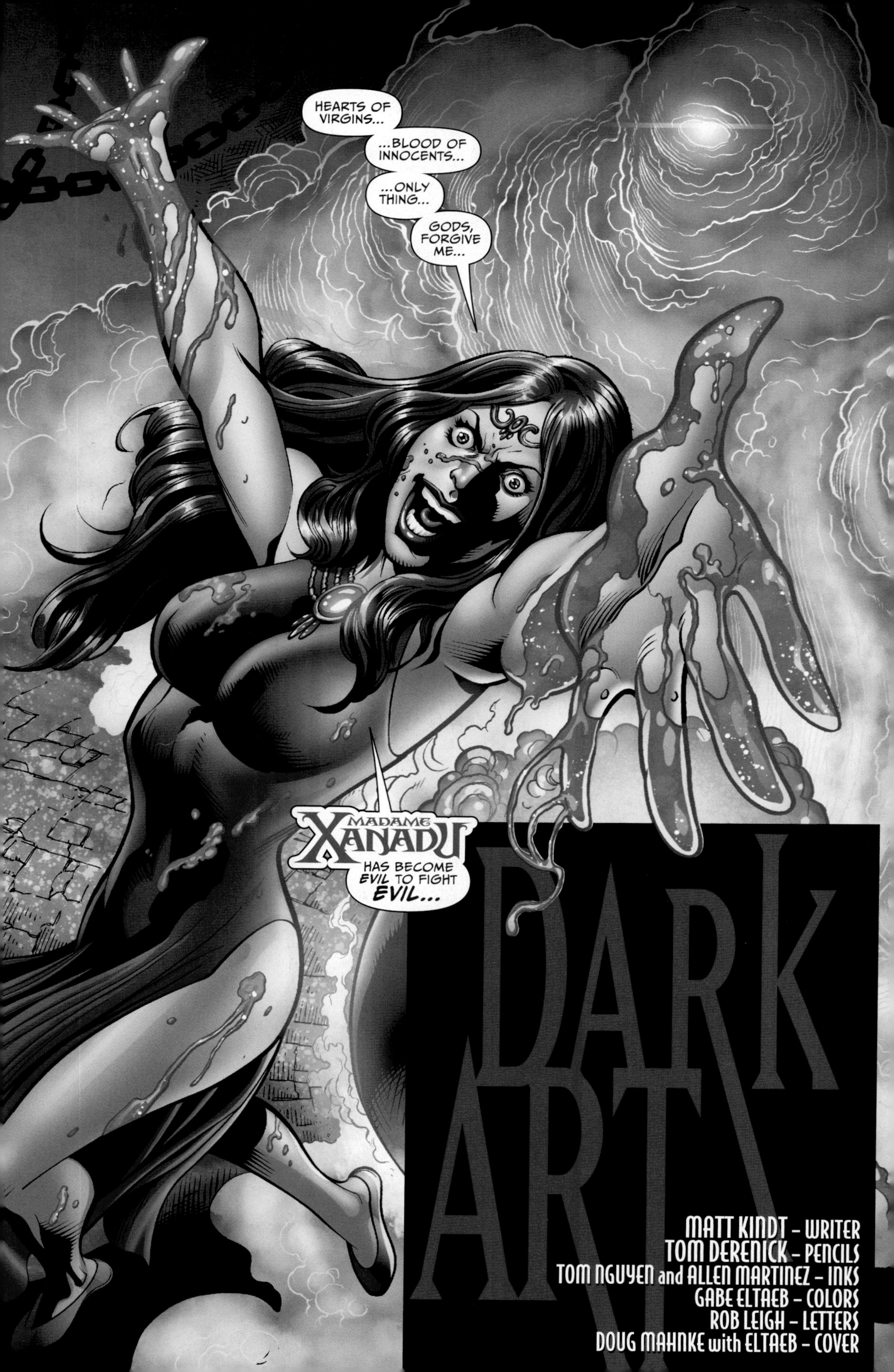
HEARTS OF VIRGINS...
...BLOOD OF INNOCENTS...
...ONLY THING...
GODS, FORGIVE ME...
MADAME XANADU HAS BECOME EVIL TO FIGHT EVIL...
DARK ARTS
MATT KINDT - WRITER
TOM DERENICK - PENCILS
TOM NGUYEN and ALLEN MARTINEZ - INKS
GABE ELTAEB - COLORS
ROB LEIGH - LETTERS
DOUG MAHNKE with ELTAEB - COVER

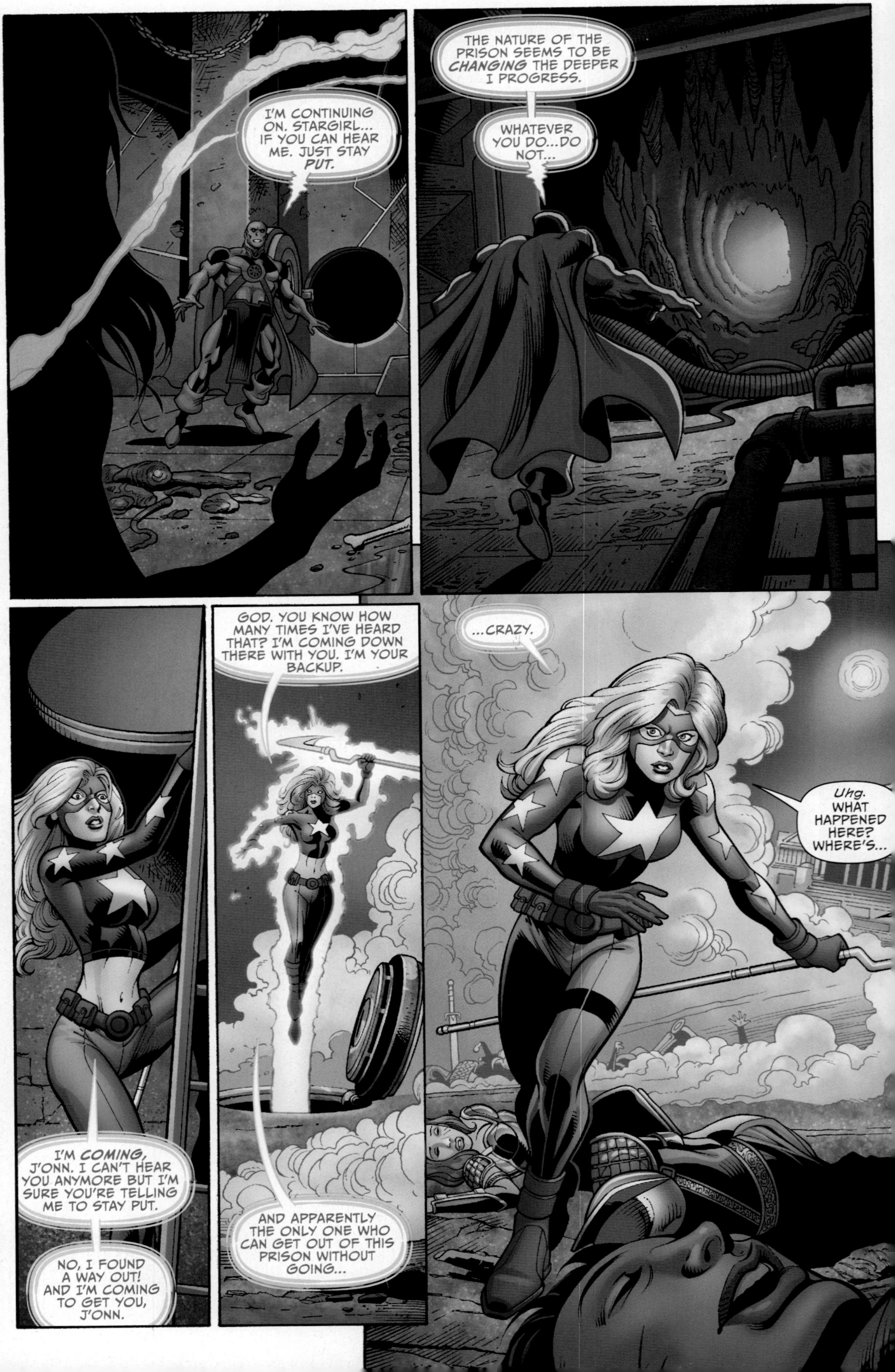
I'M CONTINUING ON. STARGIRL... IF YOU CAN HEAR ME. JUST STAY PUT.
THE NATURE OF THE PRISON SEEMS TO BE CHANGING THE DEEPER I PROGRESS.
WHATEVER YOU DO...DO NOT...
I'M COMING, J'ONN. I CAN'T HEAR YOU ANYMORE BUT I'M SURE YOU'RE TELLING ME TO STAY PUT.
NO, I FOUND A WAY OUT! AND I'M COMING TO GET YOU, J'ONN.
GOD. YOU KNOW HOW MANY TIMES I'VE HEARD THAT? I'M COMING DOWN THERE WITH YOU. I'M YOUR BACKUP.
AND APPARENTLY THE ONLY ONE WHO CAN GET OUT OF THIS PRISON WITHOUT GOING...
...CRAZY.
Uhg. WHAT HAPPENED HERE? WHERE'S...

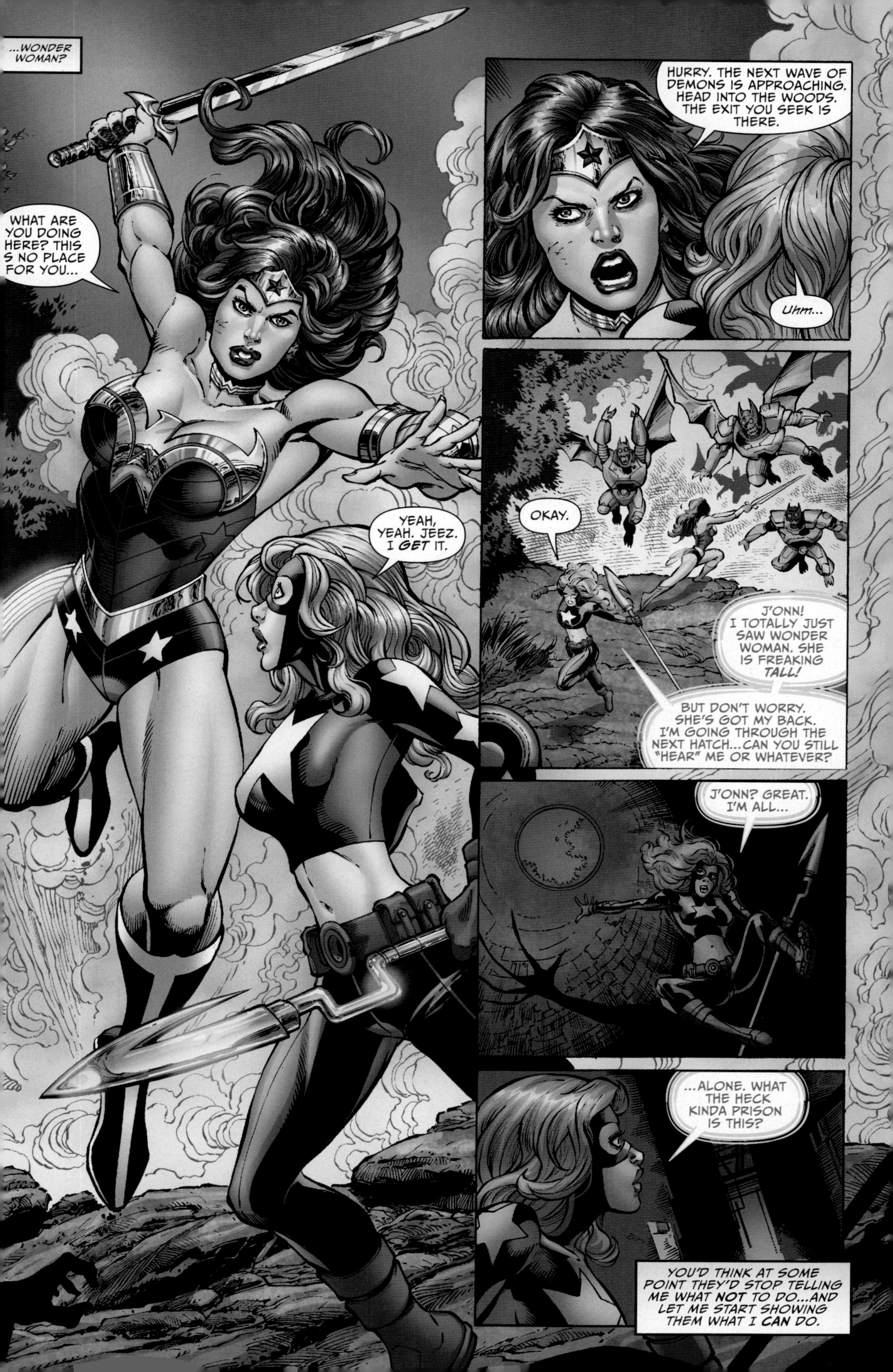
...WONDER WOMAN?
WHAT ARE YOU DOING HERE? THIS S NO PLACE FOR YOU...
YEAH, YEAH. JEEZ. I GET IT.
HURRY. THE NEXT WAVE OF DEMONS IS APPROACHING. HEAD INTO THE WOODS. THE EXIT YOU SEEK IS THERE.
Uhm...
OKAY.
J'ONN! I TOTALLY JUST SAW WONDER WOMAN. SHE IS FREAKING TALL!
BUT DON'T WORRY. SHE'S GOT MY BACK. I'M GOING THROUGH THE NEXT HATCH...CAN YOU STILL "HEAR" ME OR WHATEVER?
J'ONN? GREAT. I'M ALL...
...ALONE. WHAT THE HECK KINDA PRISON IS THIS?
YOU'D THINK AT SOME POINT THEY'D STOP TELLING ME WHAT NOT TO DO...AND LET ME START SHOWING THEM WHAT I CAN DO.

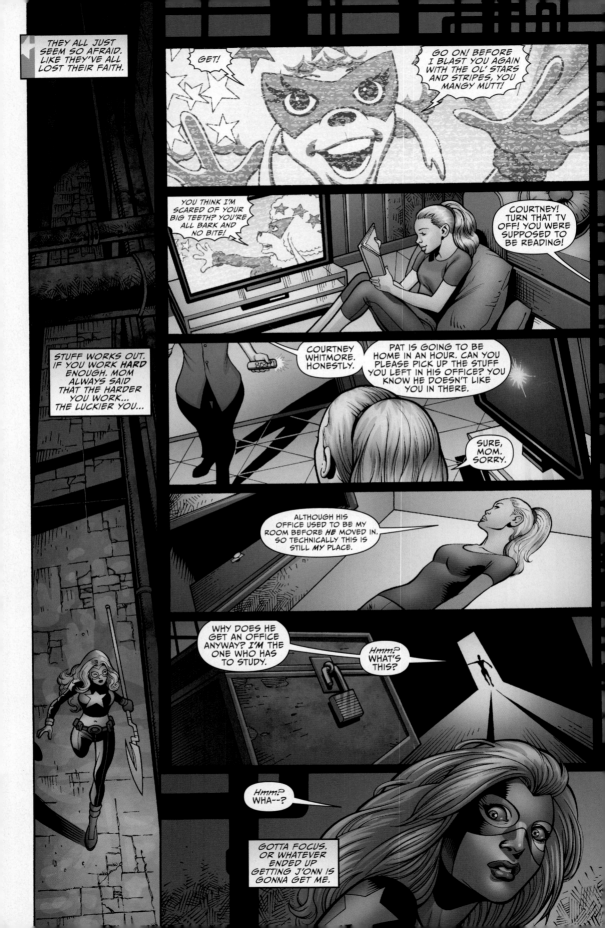

THEY ALL JUST SEEM SO AFRAID. LIKE THEY'VE ALL LOST THEIR FAITH.

GET!

GO ON! BEFORE I BLAST YOU AGAIN WITH THE OL' STARS AND STRIPES, YOU MANGY MUTT!

YOU THINK I'M SCARED OF YOUR BIG TEETH? YOU'RE ALL BARK AND NO BITE!

COURTNEY! TURN THAT TV OFF! YOU WERE SUPPOSED TO BE READING!

STUFF WORKS OUT. IF YOU WORK HARD ENOUGH. MOM ALWAYS SAID THAT THE HARDER YOU WORK... THE LUCKIER YOU...

COURTNEY WHITMORE. HONESTLY.

PAT IS GOING TO BE HOME IN AN HOUR. CAN YOU PLEASE PICK UP THE STUFF YOU LEFT IN HIS OFFICE? YOU KNOW HE DOESN'T LIKE YOU IN THERE.

SURE, MOM. SORRY.

ALTHOUGH HIS OFFICE USED TO BE MY ROOM BEFORE HE MOVED IN. SO TECHNICALLY THIS IS STILL MY PLACE.

WHY DOES HE GET AN OFFICE ANYWAY? I'M THE ONE WHO HAS TO STUDY.

Hmm? WHAT'S THIS?

Hmm? WHA--?

GOTTA FOCUS. OR WHATEVER ENDED UP GETTING J'ONN IS GONNA GET ME.

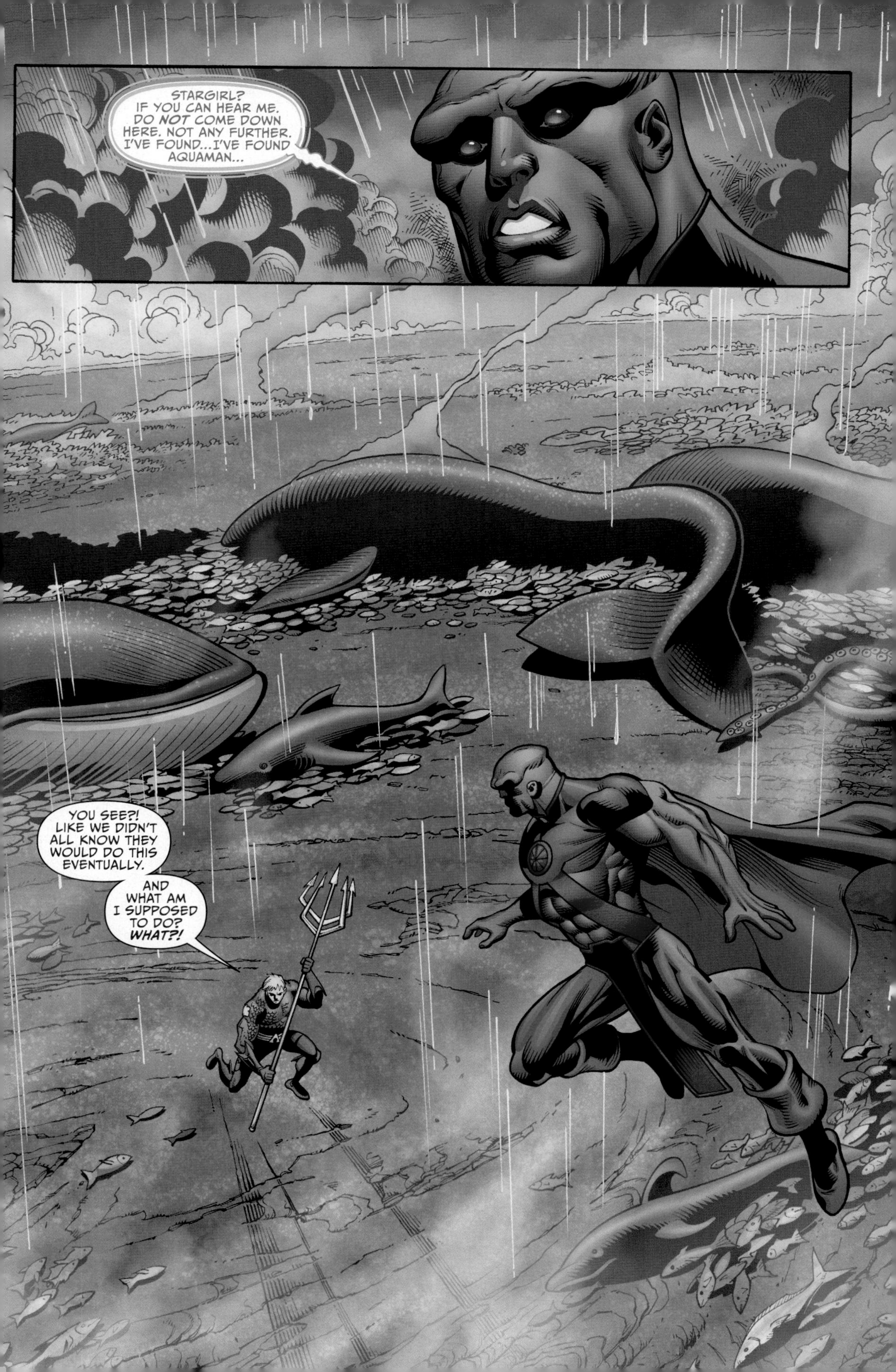
STARGIRL? IF YOU CAN HEAR ME. DO *NOT* COME DOWN HERE. NOT ANY FURTHER. I'VE FOUND...I'VE FOUND AQUAMAN...
YOU SEE?! LIKE WE DIDN'T ALL KNOW THEY WOULD DO THIS EVENTUALLY.
AND WHAT AM I SUPPOSED TO DO? ***WHAT?!***

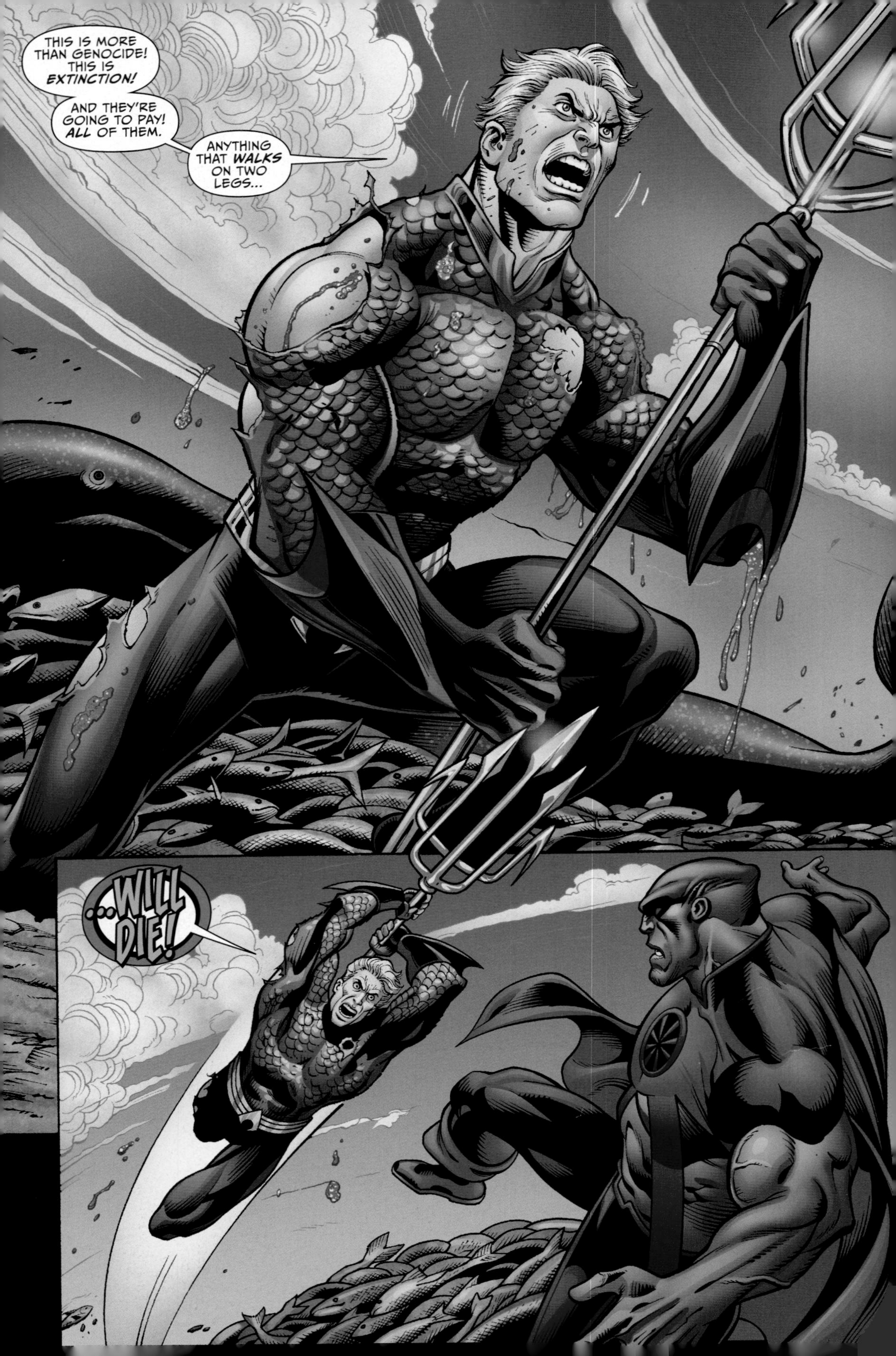
THIS IS MORE THAN GENOCIDE! THIS IS EXTINCTION!
AND THEY'RE GOING TO PAY! ALL OF THEM.
ANYTHING THAT WALKS ON TWO LEGS...
...WILL DIE!

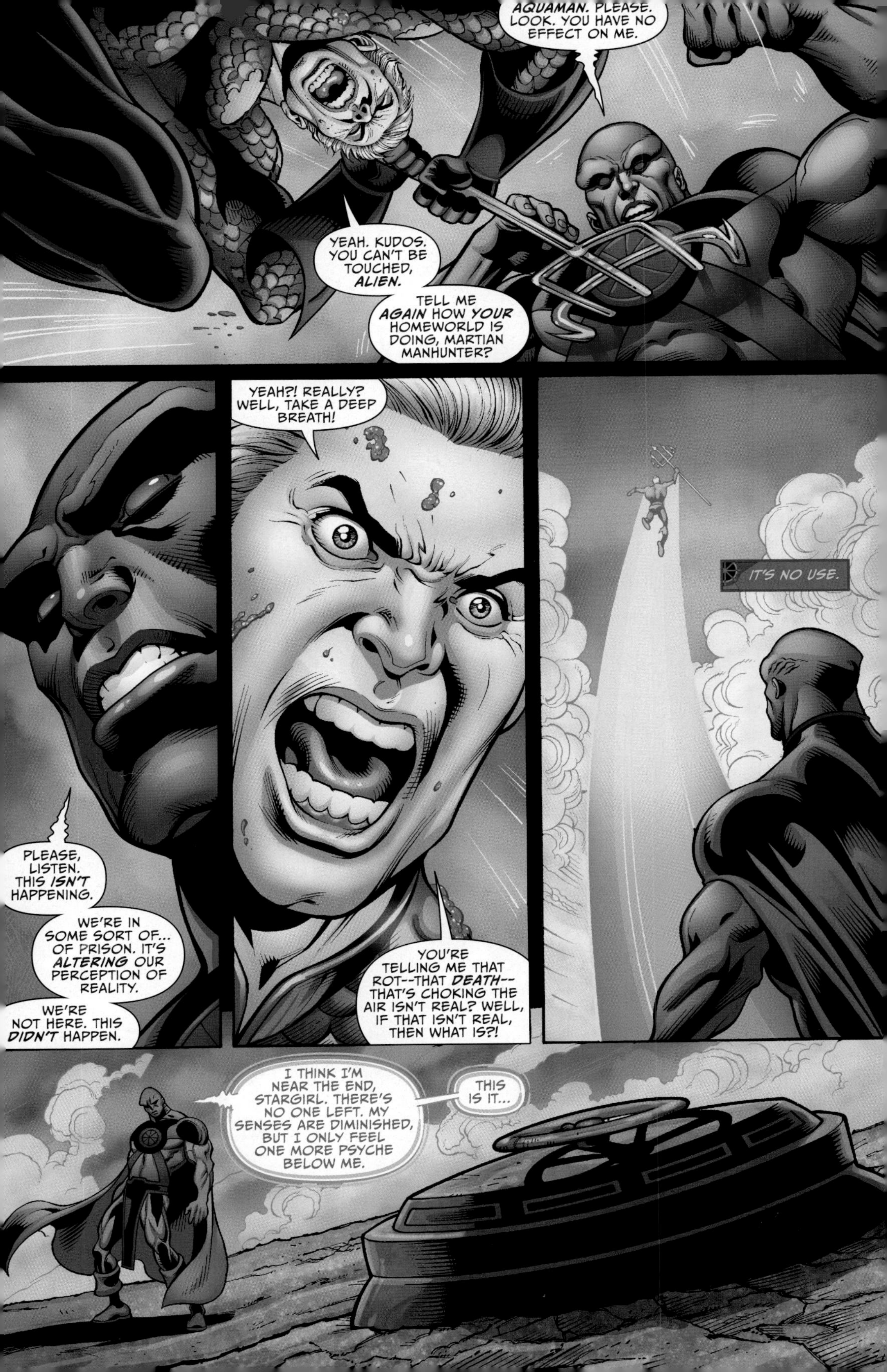

AQUAMAN. PLEASE. LOOK. YOU HAVE NO EFFECT ON ME.
YEAH. KUDOS. YOU CAN'T BE TOUCHED, *ALIEN.*
TELL ME *AGAIN* HOW *YOUR* HOMEWORLD IS DOING, MARTIAN MANHUNTER?
PLEASE, LISTEN. THIS *ISN'T* HAPPENING.
WE'RE IN SOME SORT OF... OF PRISON. IT'S *ALTERING* OUR PERCEPTION OF REALITY.
WE'RE NOT HERE. THIS *DIDN'T* HAPPEN.
YEAH?! REALLY? WELL, TAKE A DEEP BREATH!
YOU'RE TELLING ME THAT ROT--THAT *DEATH*--THAT'S CHOKING THE AIR ISN'T REAL? WELL, IF THAT ISN'T REAL, THEN WHAT IS?!
IT'S NO USE.
I THINK I'M NEAR THE END, STARGIRL. THERE'S NO ONE LEFT. MY SENSES ARE DIMINISHED, BUT I ONLY FEEL ONE MORE PSYCHE BELOW ME.
THIS IS IT...

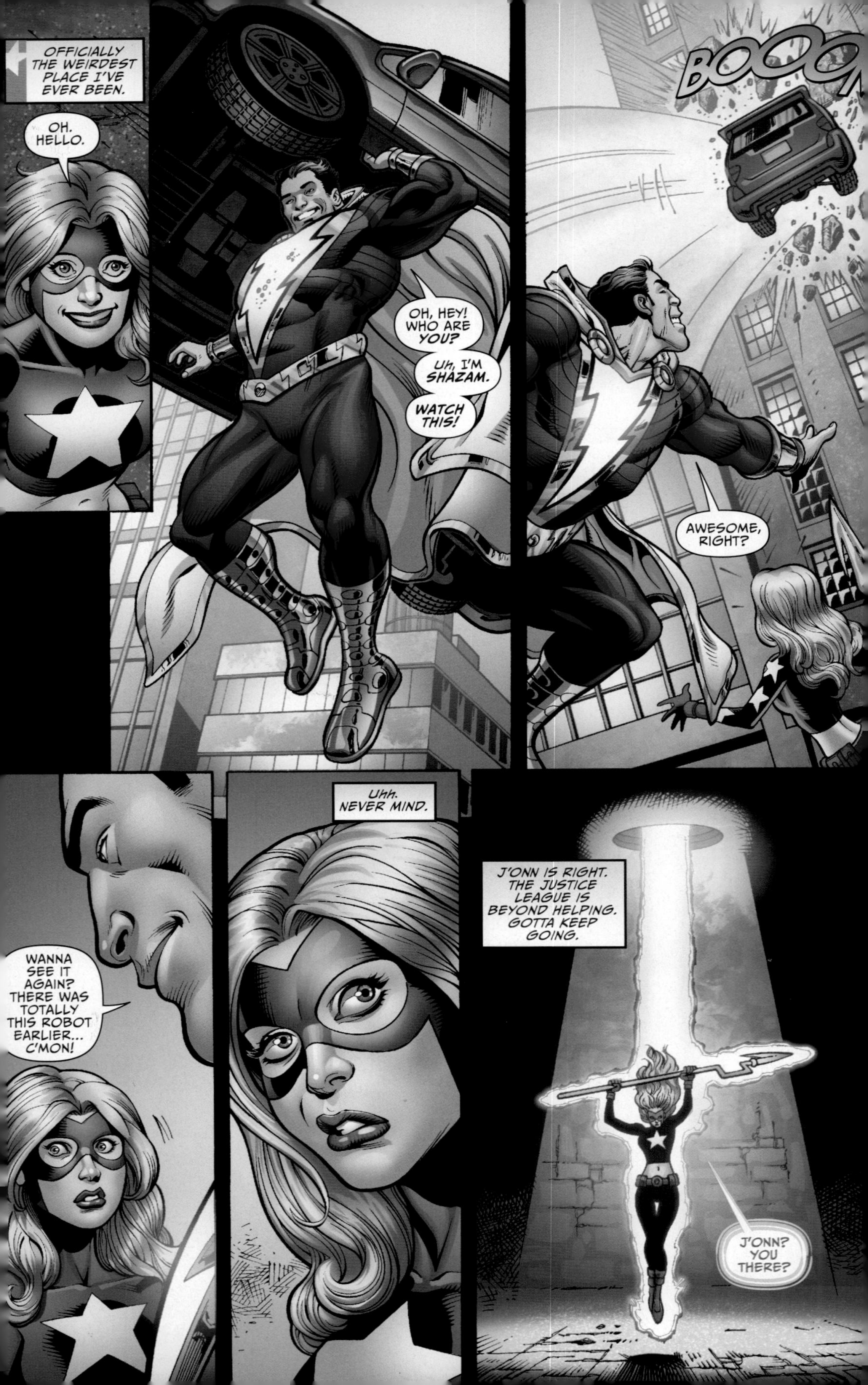
OFFICIALLY THE WEIRDEST PLACE I'VE EVER BEEN.
OH. HELLO.
OH, HEY! WHO ARE YOU?
Uh, I'M SHAZAM.
WATCH THIS!
BOOO
AWESOME, RIGHT?
WANNA SEE IT AGAIN? THERE WAS TOTALLY THIS ROBOT EARLIER... C'MON!
Uhh. NEVER MIND.
J'ONN IS RIGHT. THE JUSTICE LEAGUE IS BEYOND HELPING. GOTTA KEEP GOING.
J'ONN? YOU THERE?

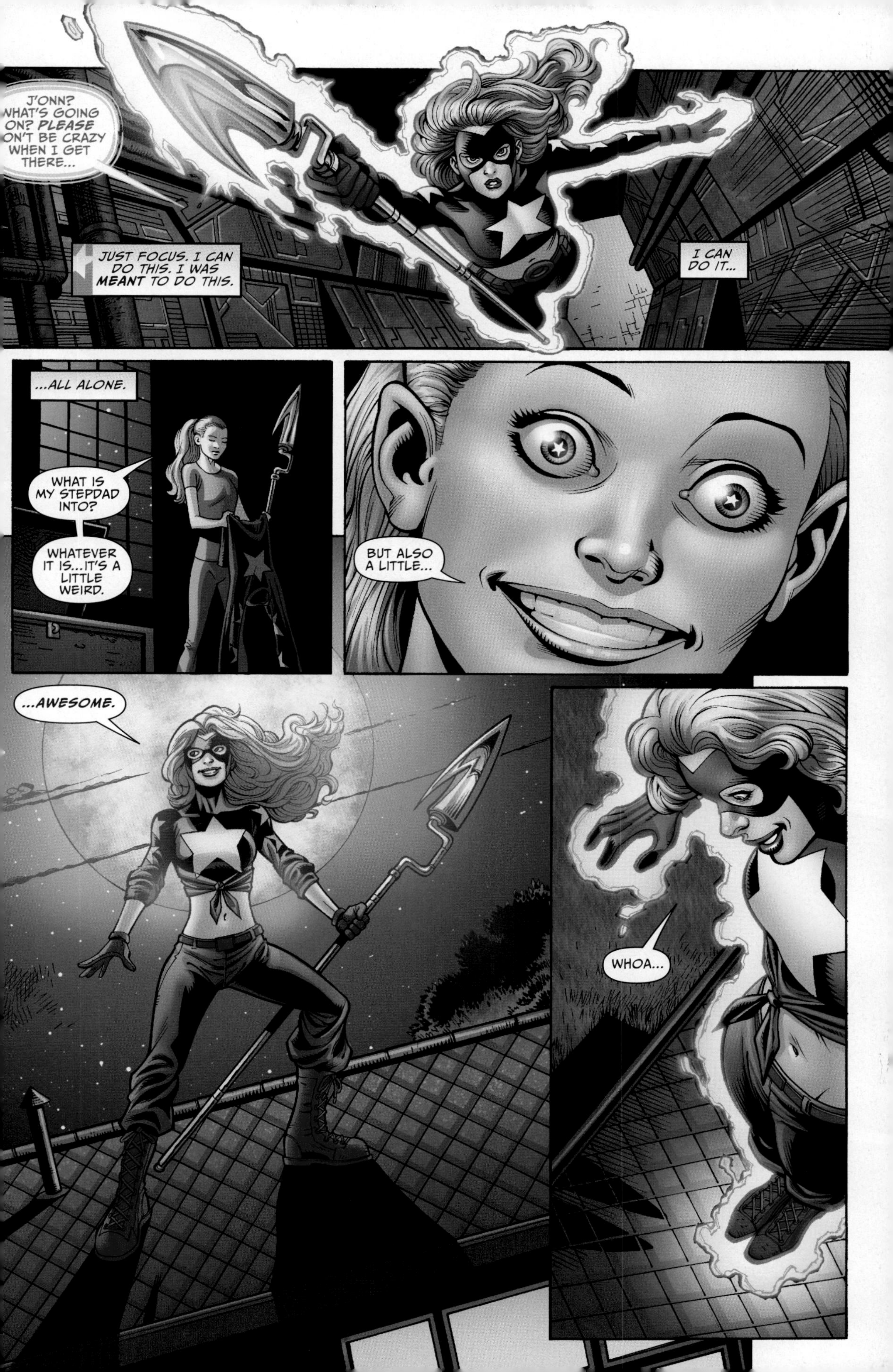
J'ONN? WHAT'S GOING ON? PLEASE DON'T BE CRAZY WHEN I GET THERE...
JUST FOCUS. I CAN DO THIS. I WAS MEANT TO DO THIS.
I CAN DO IT...
...ALL ALONE.
WHAT IS MY STEPDAD INTO?
WHATEVER IT IS...IT'S A LITTLE WEIRD.
BUT ALSO A LITTLE...
...AWESOME.
WHOA...

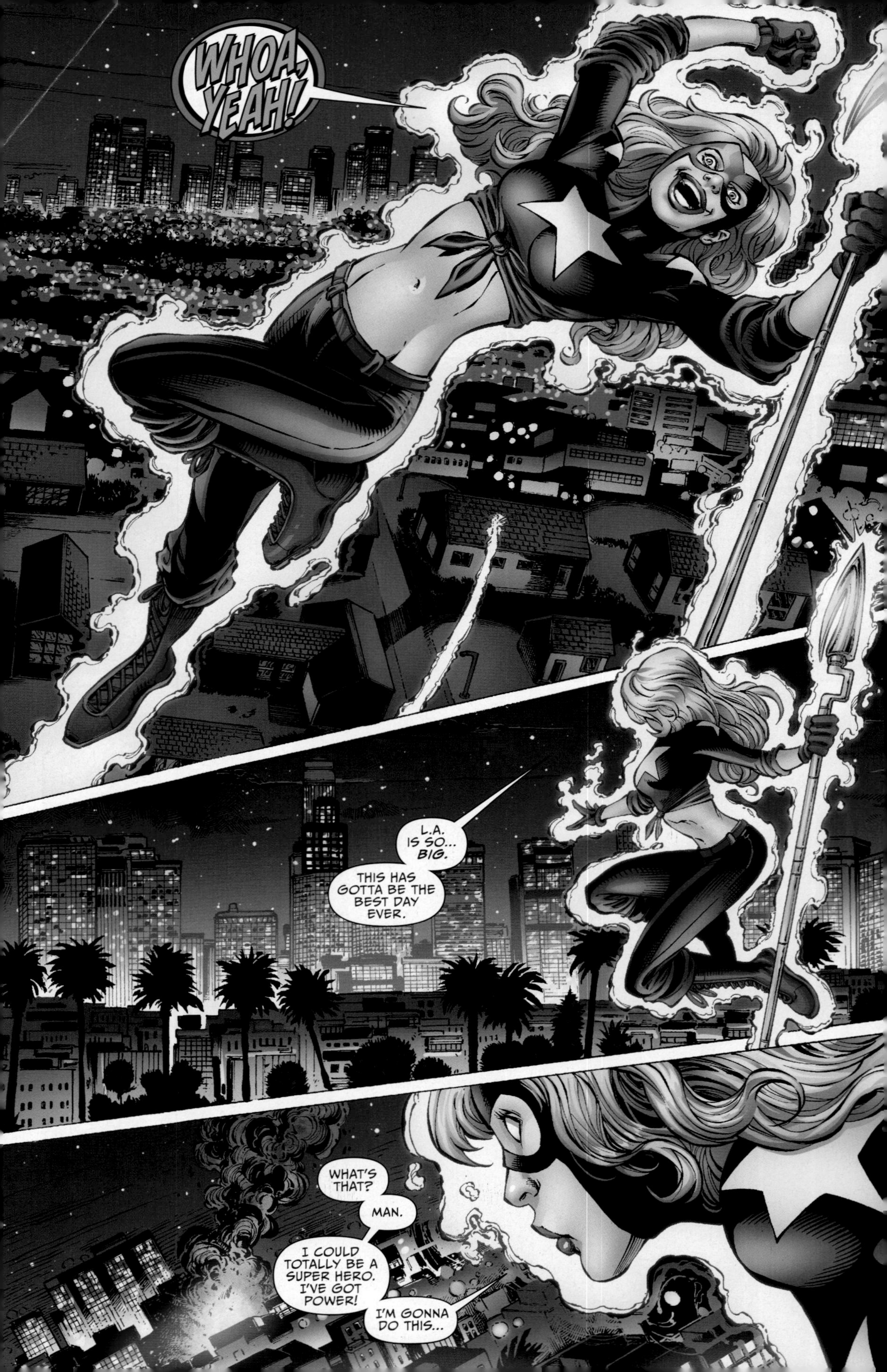
WHOA, YEAH!
L.A. IS SO... BIG.
THIS HAS GOTTA BE THE BEST DAY EVER.
WHAT'S THAT?
MAN.
I COULD TOTALLY BE A SUPER HERO. I'VE GOT POWER!
I'M GONNA DO THIS...

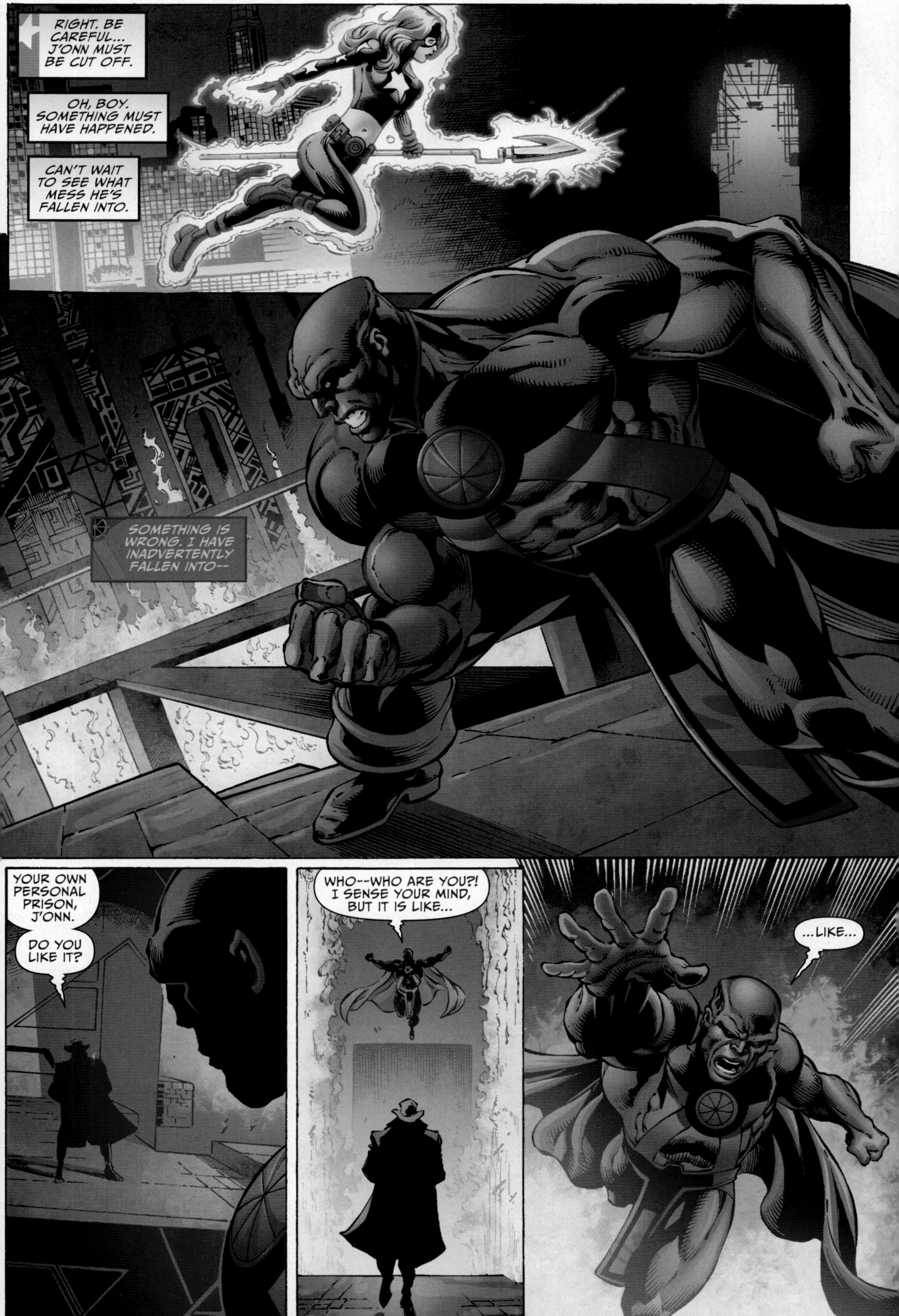
RIGHT. BE CAREFUL... J'ONN MUST BE CUT OFF.
OH, BOY. SOMETHING MUST HAVE HAPPENED.
CAN'T WAIT TO SEE WHAT MESS HE'S FALLEN INTO.
SOMETHING IS WRONG. I HAVE INADVERTENTLY FALLEN INTO--
YOUR OWN PERSONAL PRISON, J'ONN.
DO YOU LIKE IT?
WHO--WHO ARE YOU?! I SENSE YOUR MIND, BUT IT IS LIKE...
...LIKE...

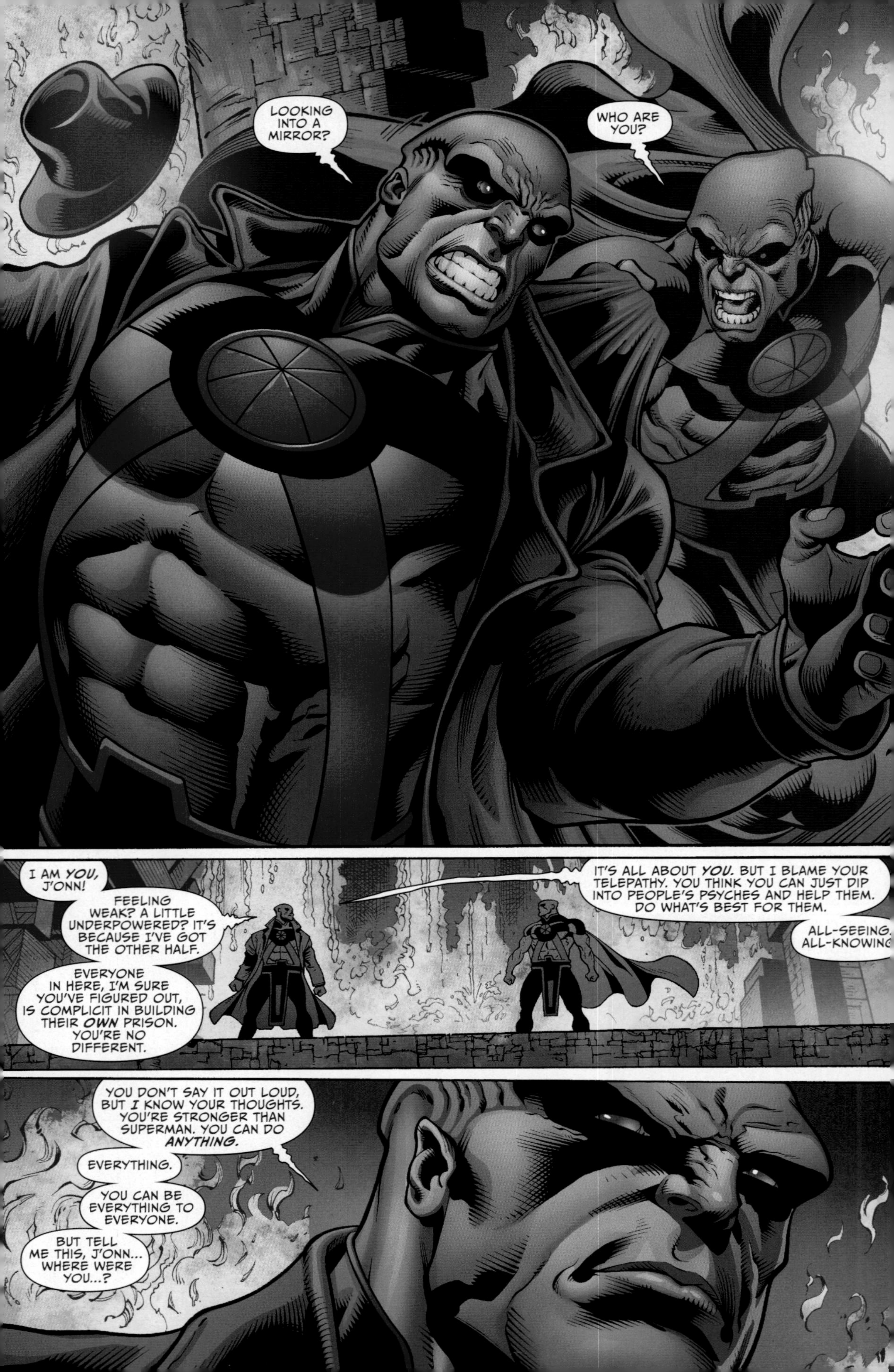
LOOKING INTO A MIRROR?
WHO ARE YOU?
I AM YOU, J'ONN!
FEELING WEAK? A LITTLE UNDERPOWERED? IT'S BECAUSE I'VE GOT THE OTHER HALF.
EVERYONE IN HERE, I'M SURE YOU'VE FIGURED OUT, IS COMPLICIT IN BUILDING THEIR OWN PRISON. YOU'RE NO DIFFERENT.
IT'S ALL ABOUT YOU. BUT I BLAME YOUR TELEPATHY. YOU THINK YOU CAN JUST DIP INTO PEOPLE'S PSYCHES AND HELP THEM. DO WHAT'S BEST FOR THEM.
ALL-SEEING. ALL-KNOWING
YOU DON'T SAY IT OUT LOUD, BUT I KNOW YOUR THOUGHTS. YOU'RE STRONGER THAN SUPERMAN. YOU CAN DO ANYTHING.
EVERYTHING.
YOU CAN BE EVERYTHING TO EVERYONE.
BUT TELL ME THIS, J'ONN... WHERE WERE YOU...?

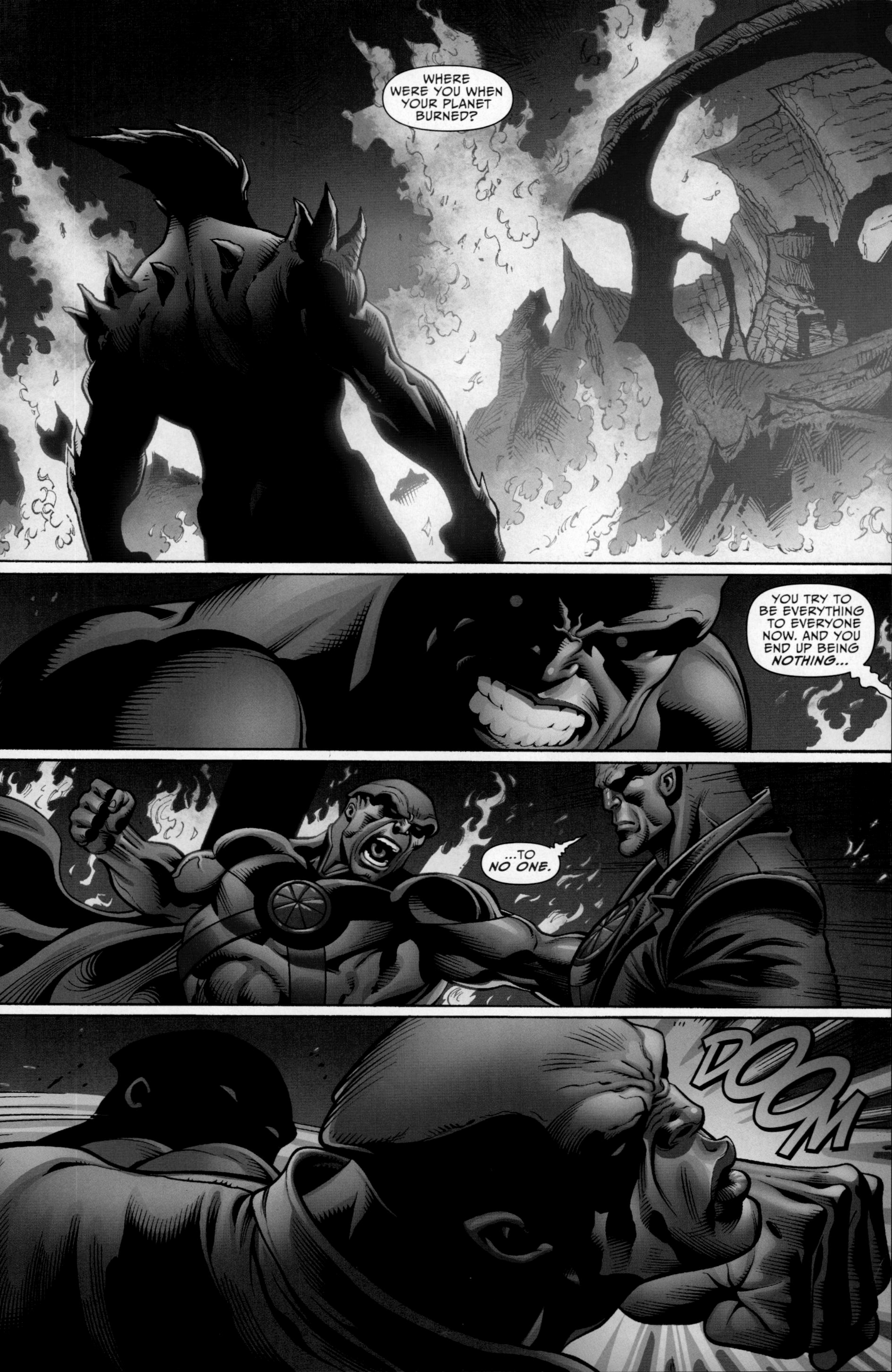
WHERE WERE YOU WHEN YOUR PLANET BURNED?
YOU TRY TO BE EVERYTHING TO EVERYONE NOW. AND YOU END UP BEING *NOTHING...*
...TO *NO ONE.*
DOOM

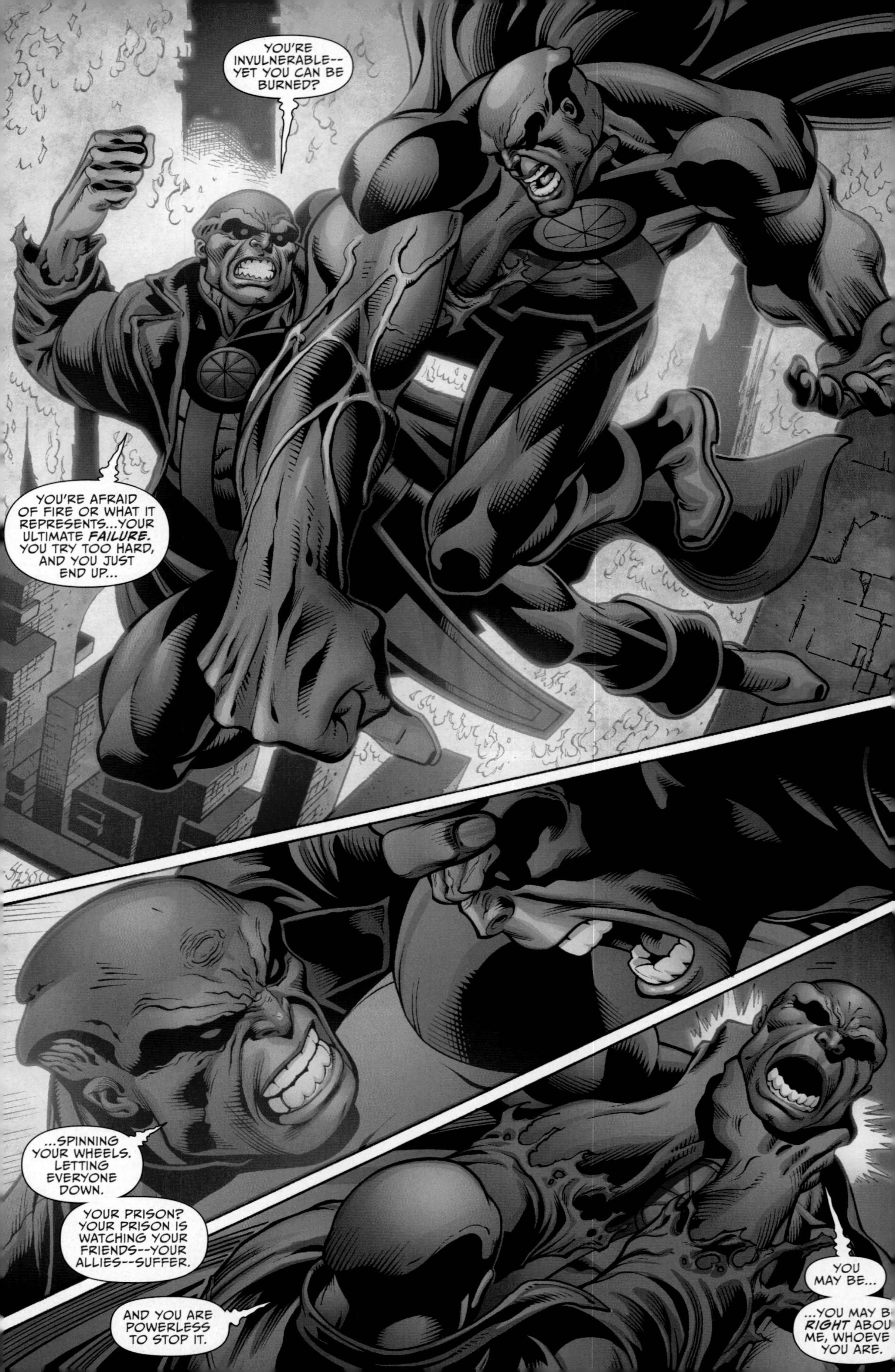
YOU'RE INVULNERABLE-- YET YOU CAN BE BURNED?
YOU'RE AFRAID OF FIRE OR WHAT IT REPRESENTS...YOUR ULTIMATE FAILURE. YOU TRY TOO HARD, AND YOU JUST END UP...
...SPINNING YOUR WHEELS. LETTING EVERYONE DOWN.
YOUR PRISON? YOUR PRISON IS WATCHING YOUR FRIENDS--YOUR ALLIES--SUFFER.
AND YOU ARE POWERLESS TO STOP IT.
YOU MAY BE...
...YOU MAY B RIGHT ABOU ME, WHOEVE YOU ARE.

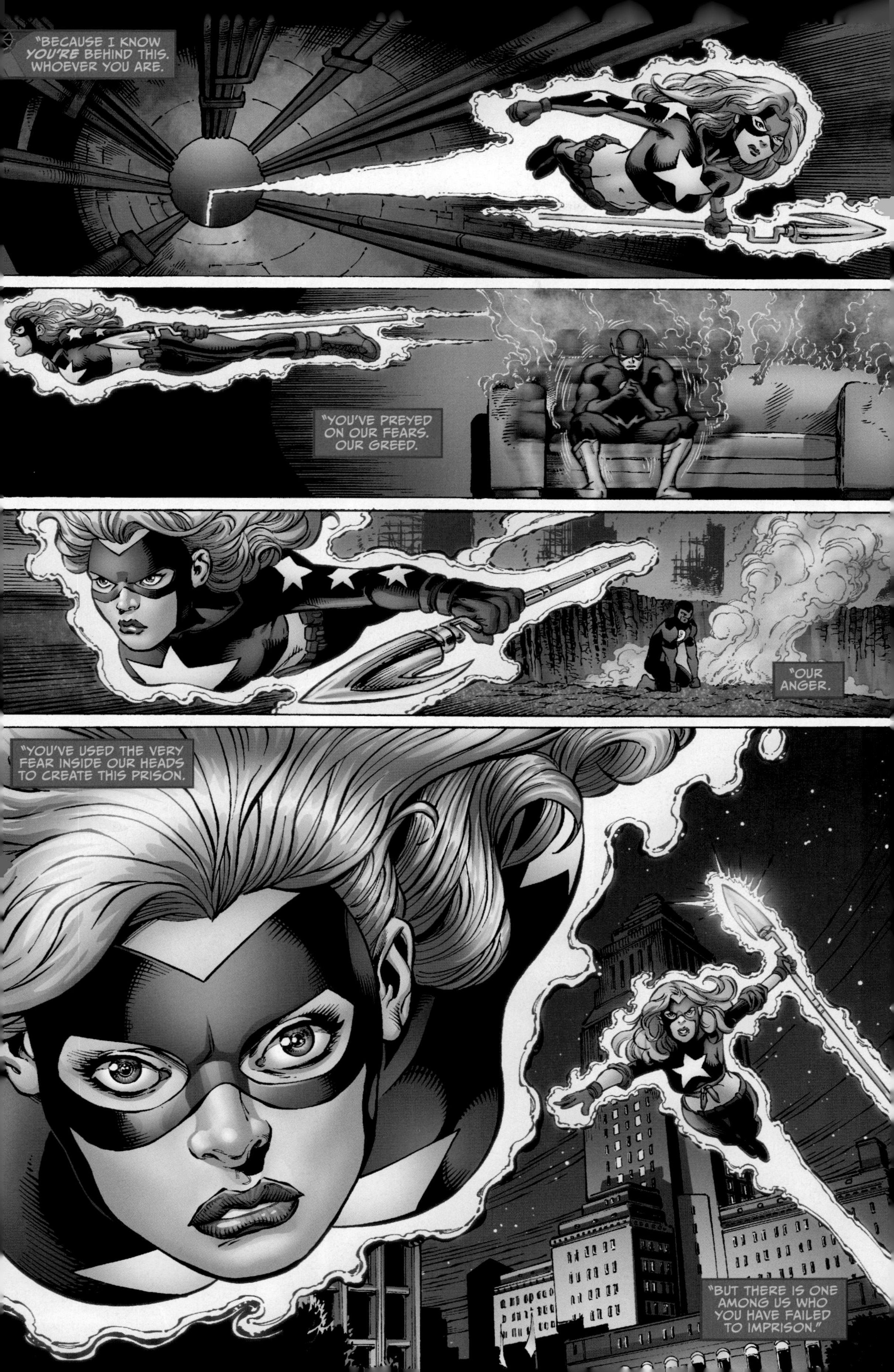
"BECAUSE I KNOW *YOU'RE* BEHIND THIS. WHOEVER YOU ARE.
"YOU'VE PREYED ON OUR FEARS. OUR GREED.
"OUR ANGER.
"YOU'VE USED THE VERY FEAR INSIDE OUR HEADS TO CREATE THIS PRISON.
"BUT THERE IS ONE AMONG US WHO YOU HAVE FAILED TO IMPRISON."

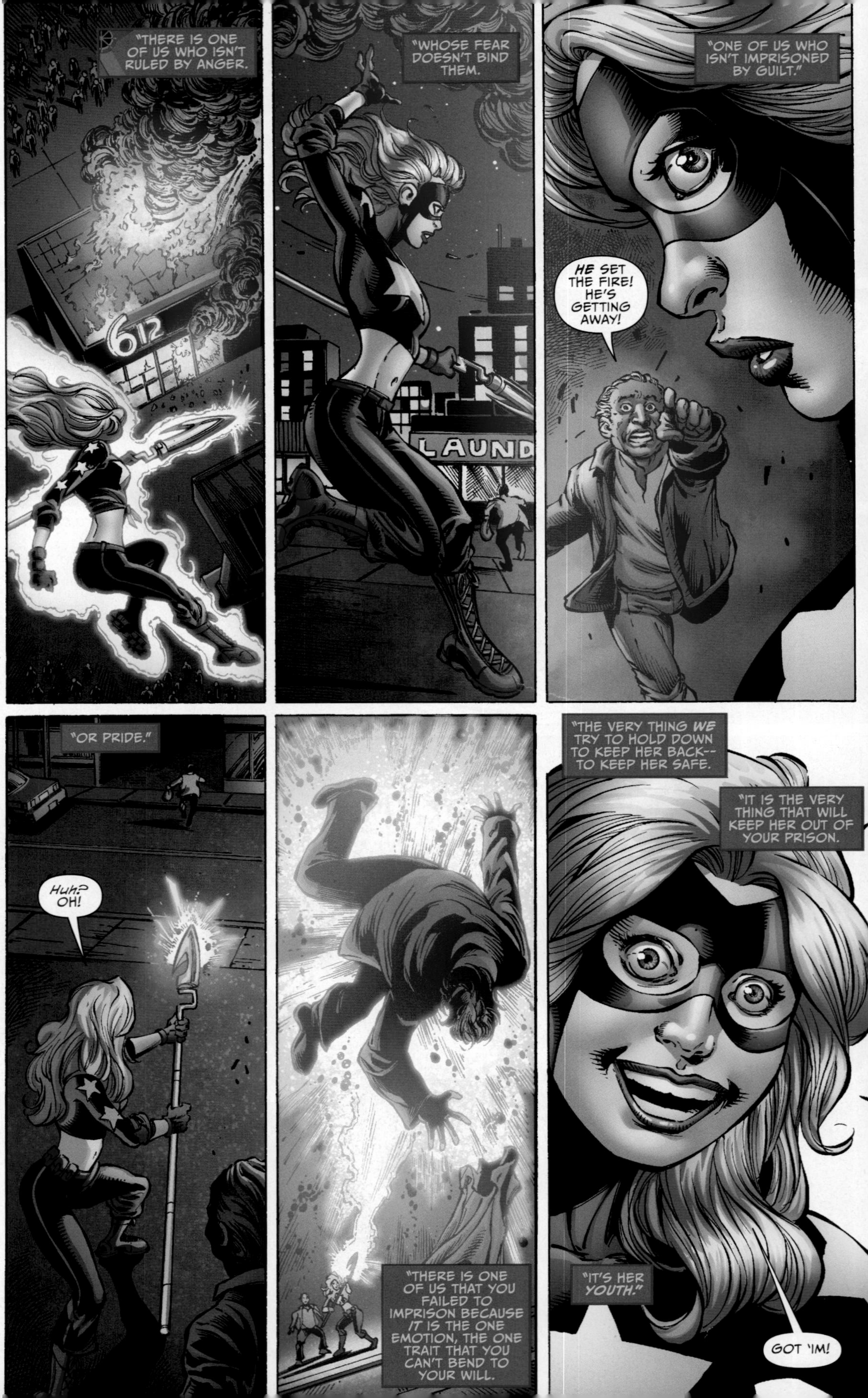
"THERE IS ONE OF US WHO ISN'T RULED BY ANGER.
612
"WHOSE FEAR DOESN'T BIND THEM.
LAUND
"ONE OF US WHO ISN'T IMPRISONED BY GUILT."
HE SET THE FIRE! HE'S GETTING AWAY!
"OR PRIDE."
Huh? OH!
"THERE IS ONE OF US THAT YOU FAILED TO IMPRISON BECAUSE IT IS THE ONE EMOTION, THE ONE TRAIT THAT YOU CAN'T BEND TO YOUR WILL.
"THE VERY THING WE TRY TO HOLD DOWN TO KEEP HER BACK-- TO KEEP HER SAFE.
"IT IS THE VERY THING THAT WILL KEEP HER OUT OF YOUR PRISON.
"IT'S HER YOUTH."
GOT 'IM!

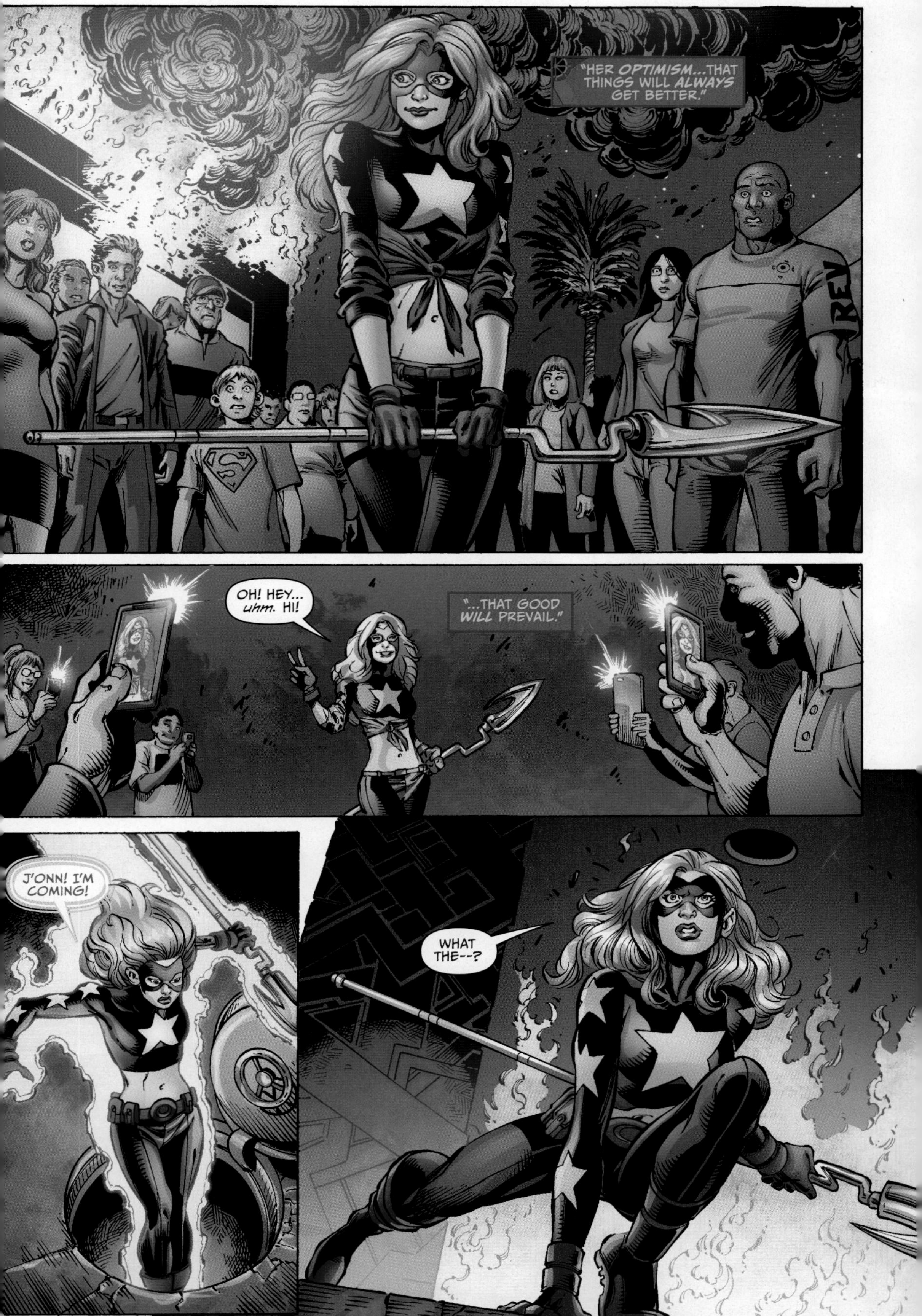
"HER *OPTIMISM*...THAT THINGS WILL *ALWAYS* GET BETTER."
OH! HEY... *uhm.* HI!
"...THAT GOOD *WILL* PREVAIL."
J'ONN! I'M COMING!
WHAT THE--?

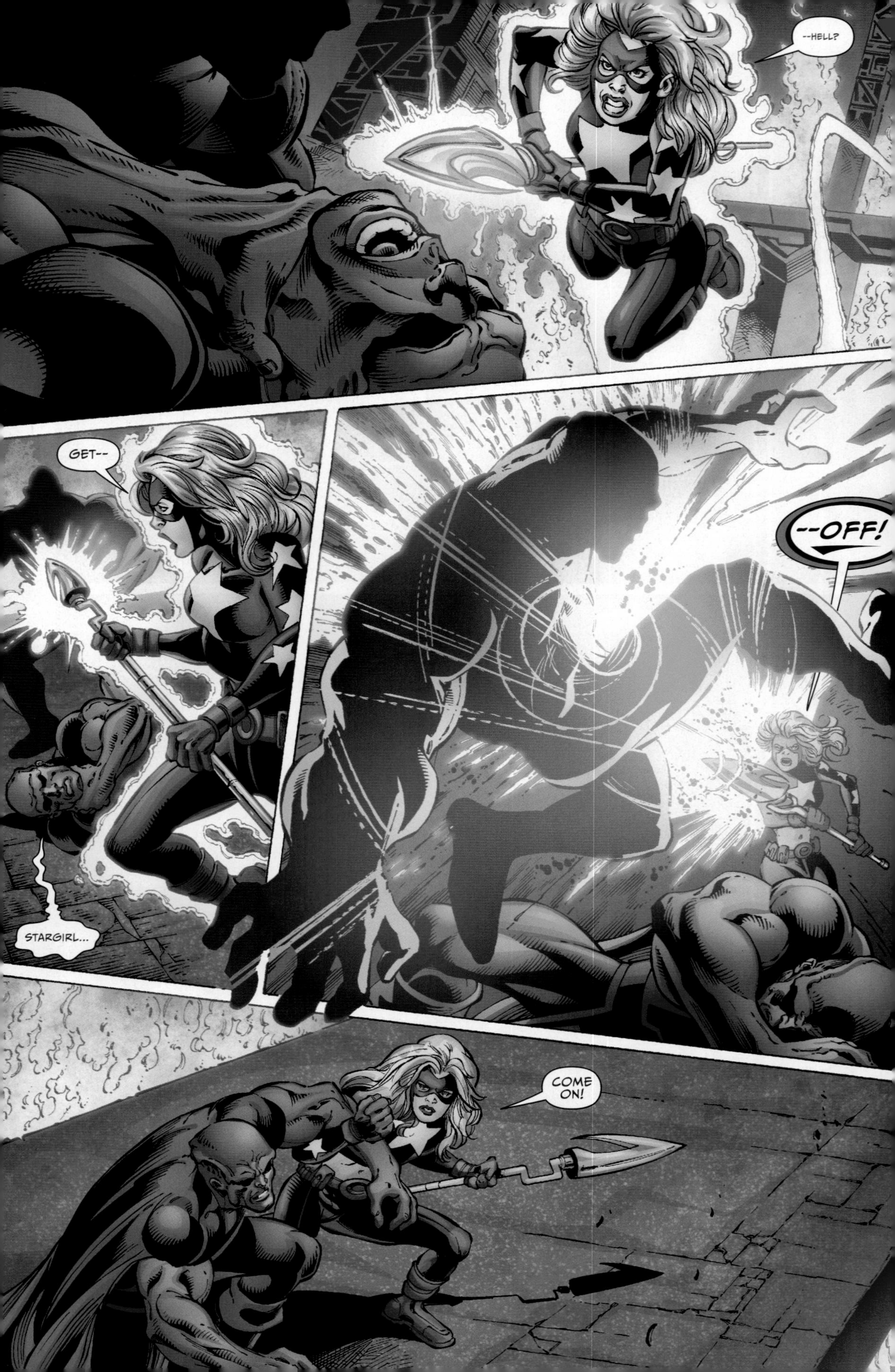
--HELL?
GET--
--OFF!
STARGIRL...
COME ON!

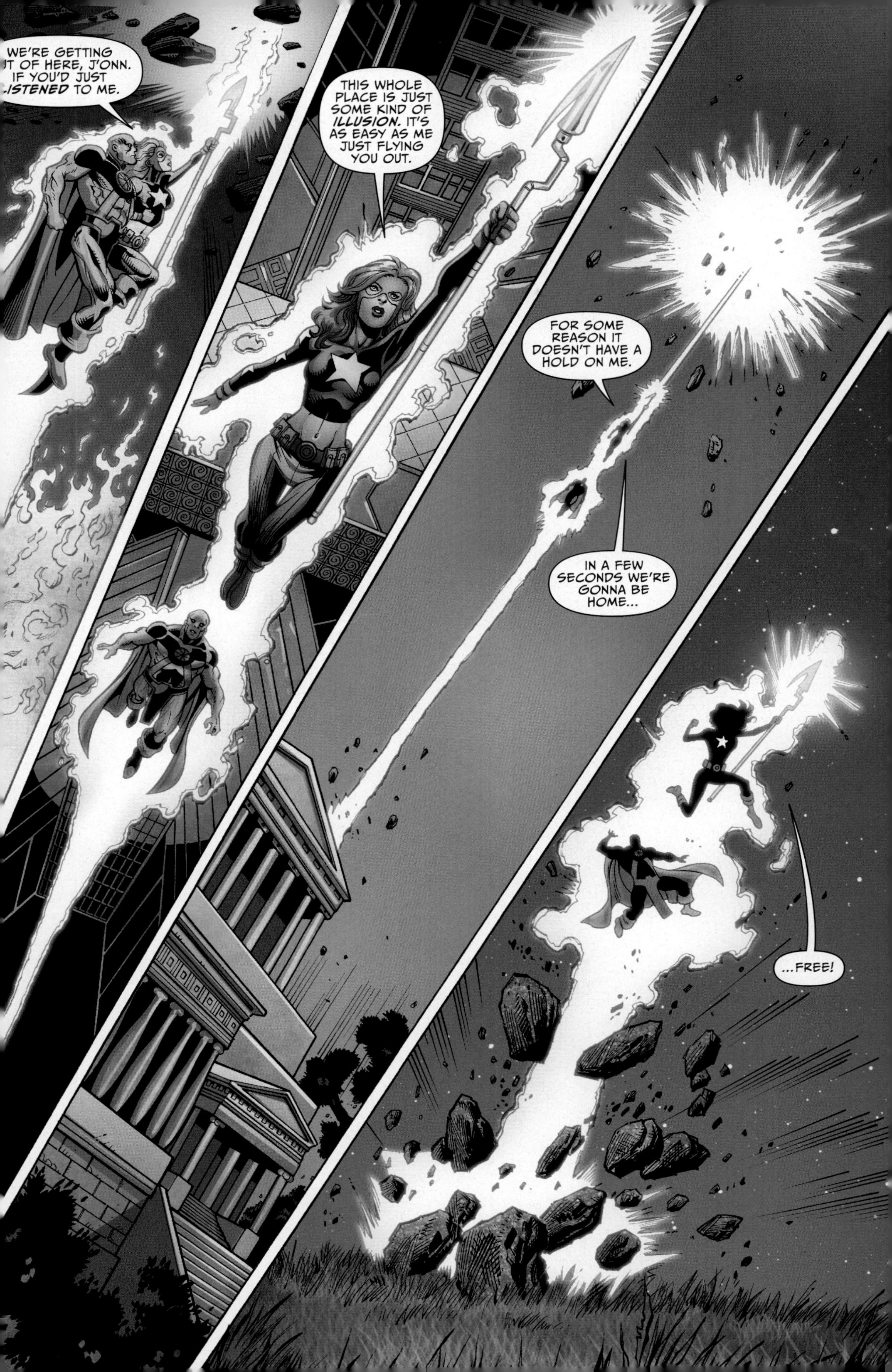
WE'RE GETTING
UT OF HERE, J'ONN.
IF YOU'D JUST
LISTENED TO ME.
THIS WHOLE PLACE IS JUST SOME KIND OF ILLUSION. IT'S AS EASY AS ME JUST FLYING YOU OUT.
FOR SOME REASON IT DOESN'T HAVE A HOLD ON ME.
IN A FEW SECONDS WE'RE GONNA BE HOME...
...FREE!

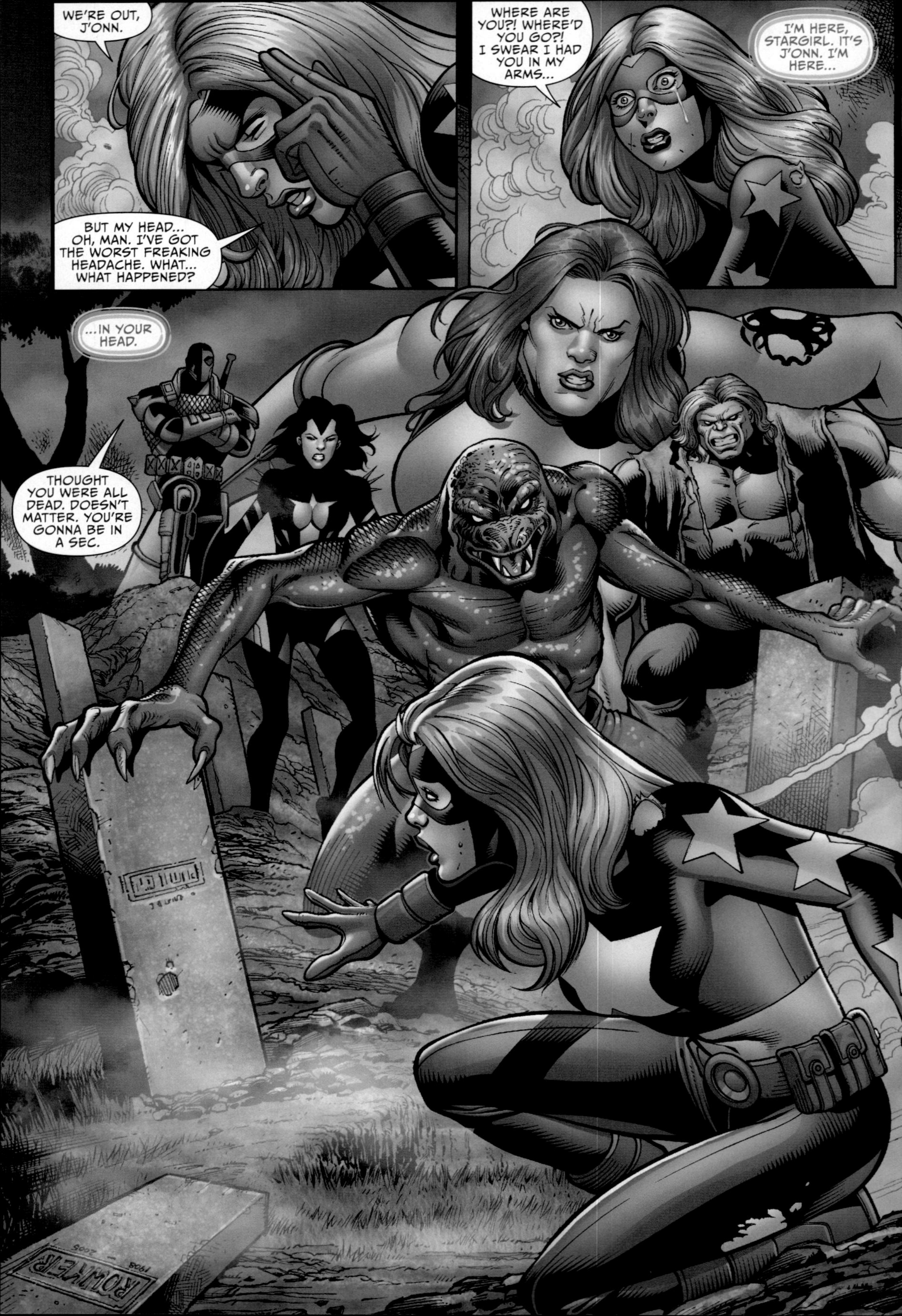
WE'RE OUT, J'ONN.
BUT MY HEAD... OH, MAN. I'VE GOT THE WORST FREAKING HEADACHE. WHAT... WHAT HAPPENED?
WHERE ARE YOU?! WHERE'D YOU GO?! I SWEAR I HAD YOU IN MY ARMS...
I'M HERE, STARGIRL. IT'S J'ONN. I'M HERE...
...IN YOUR HEAD.
THOUGHT YOU WERE ALL DEAD. DOESN'T MATTER. YOU'RE GONNA BE IN A SEC.

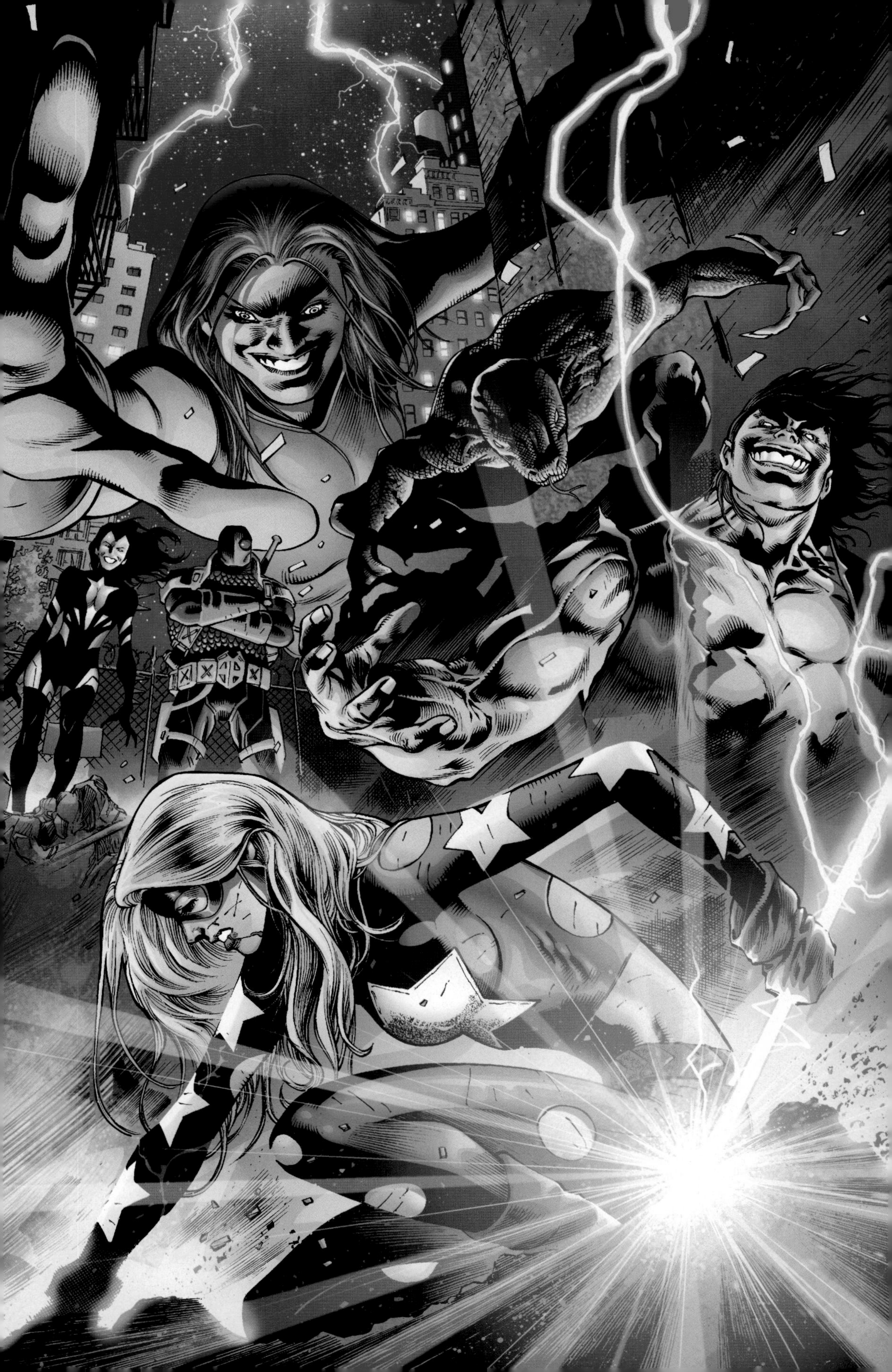

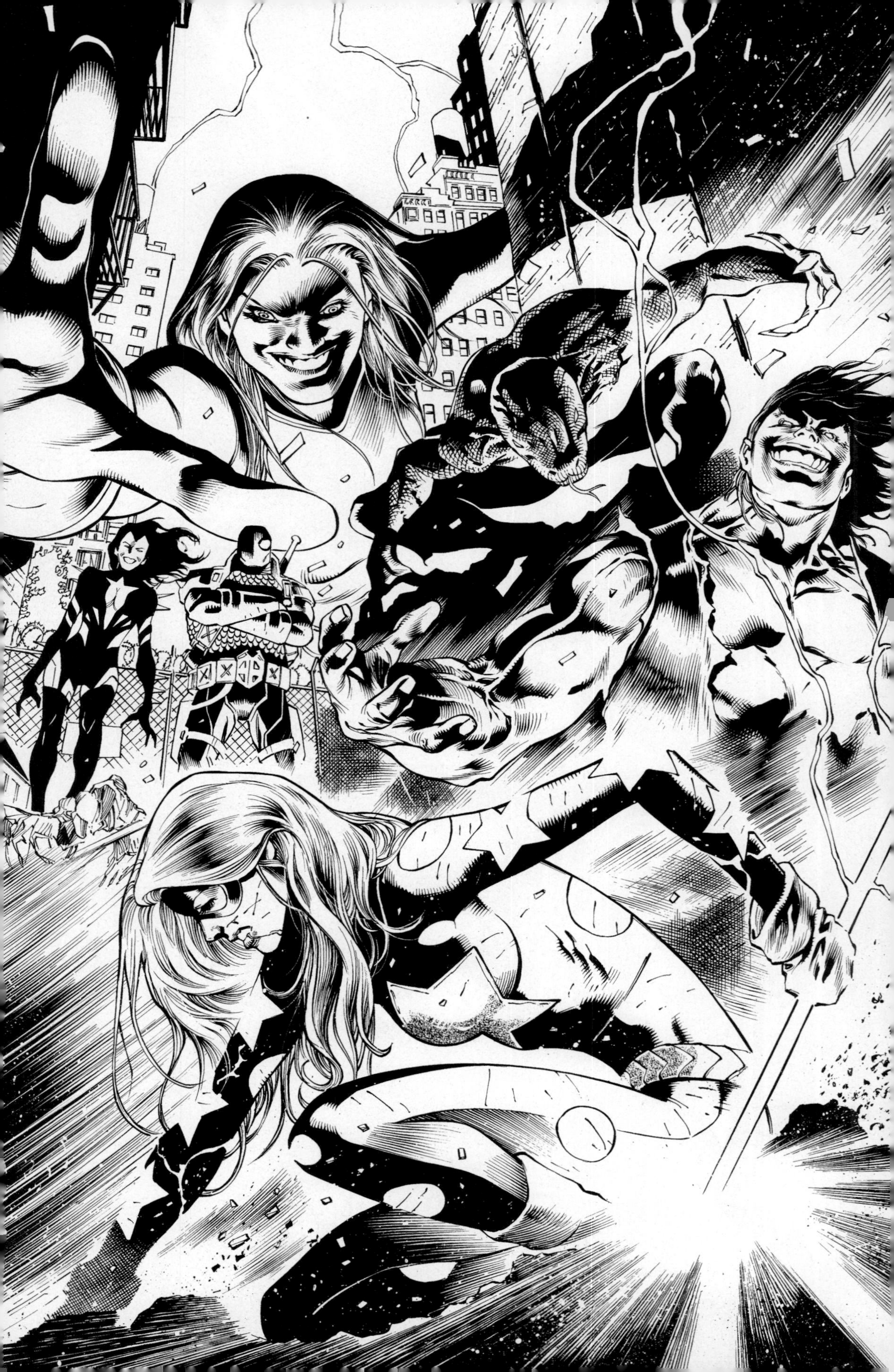

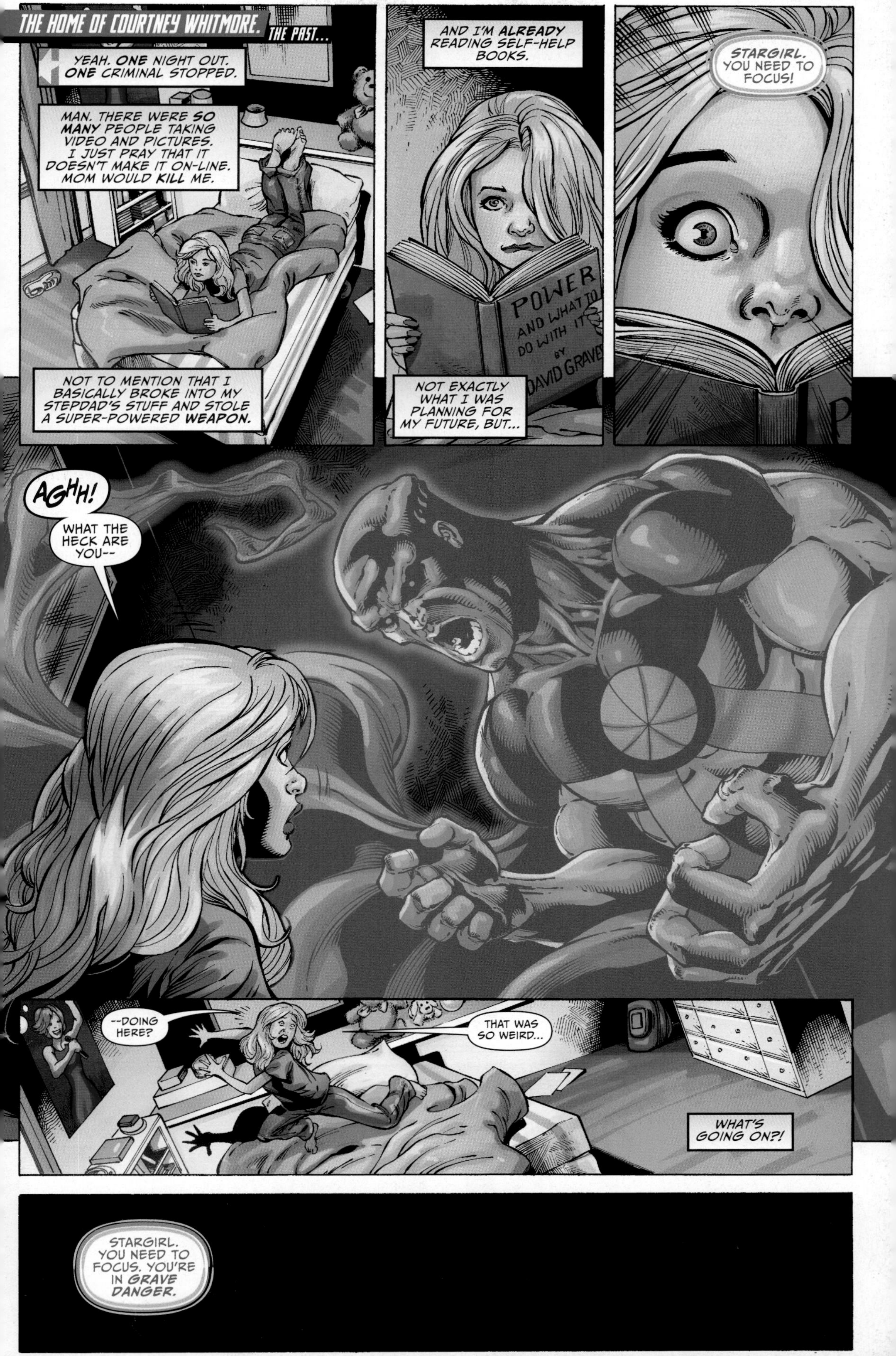
THE HOME OF COURTNEY WHITMORE.
THE PAST...
YEAH. ONE NIGHT OUT. ONE CRIMINAL STOPPED.
MAN. THERE WERE SO MANY PEOPLE TAKING VIDEO AND PICTURES. I JUST PRAY THAT IT DOESN'T MAKE IT ON-LINE. MOM WOULD KILL ME.
NOT TO MENTION THAT I BASICALLY BROKE INTO MY STEPDAD'S STUFF AND STOLE A SUPER-POWERED WEAPON.
AND I'M ALREADY READING SELF-HELP BOOKS.
POWER AND WHAT TO DO WITH IT BY DAVID GRAVES
NOT EXACTLY WHAT I WAS PLANNING FOR MY FUTURE, BUT...
STARGIRL. YOU NEED TO FOCUS!
AGHH!
WHAT THE HECK ARE YOU--
--DOING HERE?
THAT WAS SO WEIRD...
WHAT'S GOING ON?!
STARGIRL. YOU NEED TO FOCUS. YOU'RE IN GRAVE DANGER.

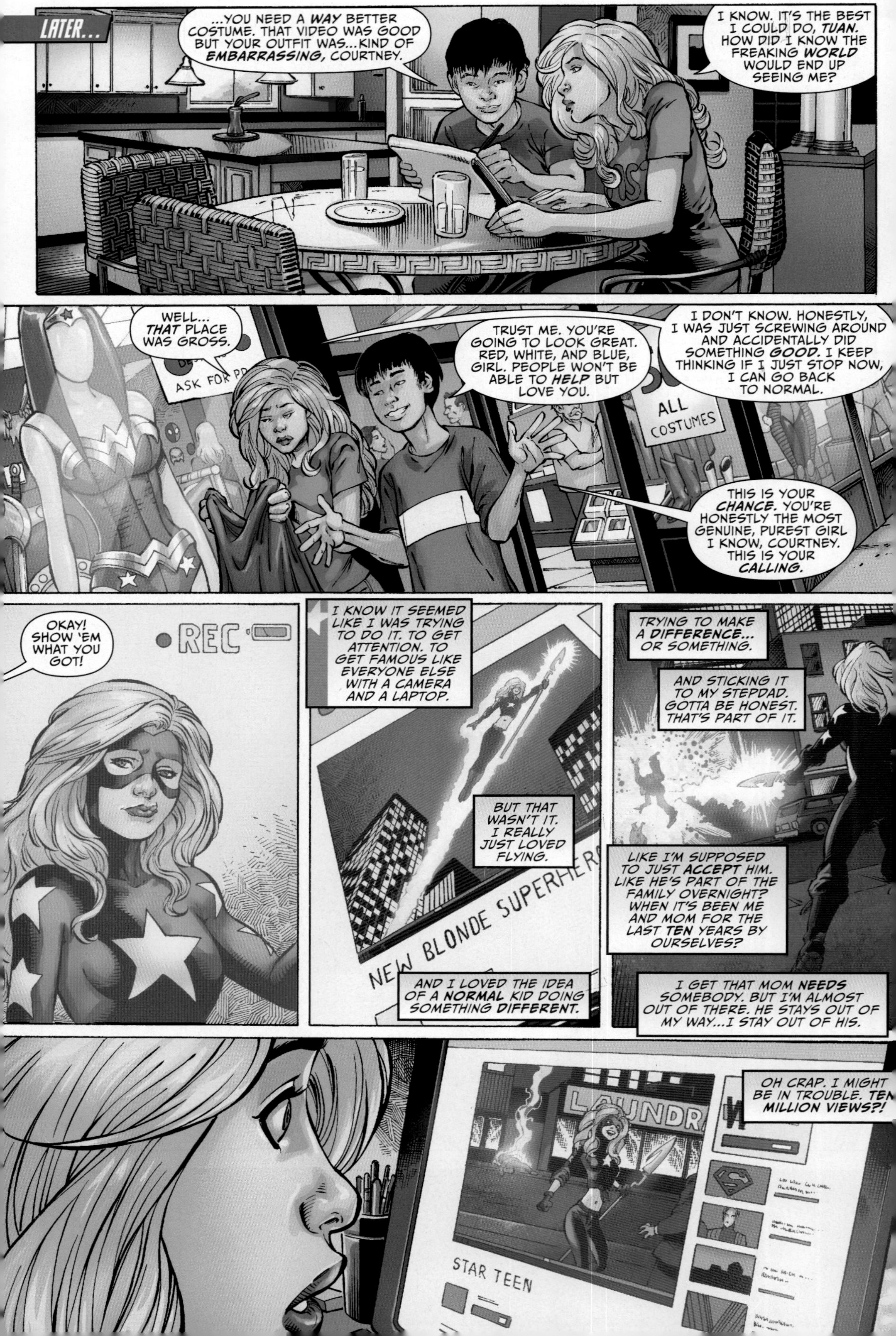
LATER...
...YOU NEED A WAY BETTER COSTUME. THAT VIDEO WAS GOOD BUT YOUR OUTFIT WAS...KIND OF EMBARRASSING, COURTNEY.
I KNOW. IT'S THE BEST I COULD DO, TUAN. HOW DID I KNOW THE FREAKING WORLD WOULD END UP SEEING ME?
ASK FOR
WELL... THAT PLACE WAS GROSS.
TRUST ME. YOU'RE GOING TO LOOK GREAT. RED, WHITE, AND BLUE, GIRL. PEOPLE WON'T BE ABLE TO HELP BUT LOVE YOU.
I DON'T KNOW. HONESTLY, I WAS JUST SCREWING AROUND AND ACCIDENTALLY DID SOMETHING GOOD. I KEEP THINKING IF I JUST STOP NOW, I CAN GO BACK TO NORMAL.
ALL COSTUMES
THIS IS YOUR CHANCE. YOU'RE HONESTLY THE MOST GENUINE, PUREST GIRL I KNOW, COURTNEY. THIS IS YOUR CALLING.
OKAY! SHOW 'EM WHAT YOU GOT!
REC
I KNOW IT SEEMED LIKE I WAS TRYING TO DO IT. TO GET ATTENTION. TO GET FAMOUS LIKE EVERYONE ELSE WITH A CAMERA AND A LAPTOP.
BUT THAT WASN'T IT. I REALLY JUST LOVED FLYING.
NEW BLONDE SUPERHER
AND I LOVED THE IDEA OF A NORMAL KID DOING SOMETHING DIFFERENT.
TRYING TO MAKE A DIFFERENCE... OR SOMETHING.
AND STICKING IT TO MY STEPDAD. GOTTA BE HONEST. THAT'S PART OF IT.
LIKE I'M SUPPOSED TO JUST ACCEPT HIM. LIKE HE'S PART OF THE FAMILY OVERNIGHT? WHEN IT'S BEEN ME AND MOM FOR THE LAST TEN YEARS BY OURSELVES?
I GET THAT MOM NEEDS SOMEBODY. BUT I'M ALMOST OUT OF THERE. HE STAYS OUT OF MY WAY...I STAY OUT OF HIS.
LAUNDR
STAR TEEN
OH CRAP. I MIGHT BE IN TROUBLE. TEN MILLION VIEWS?!

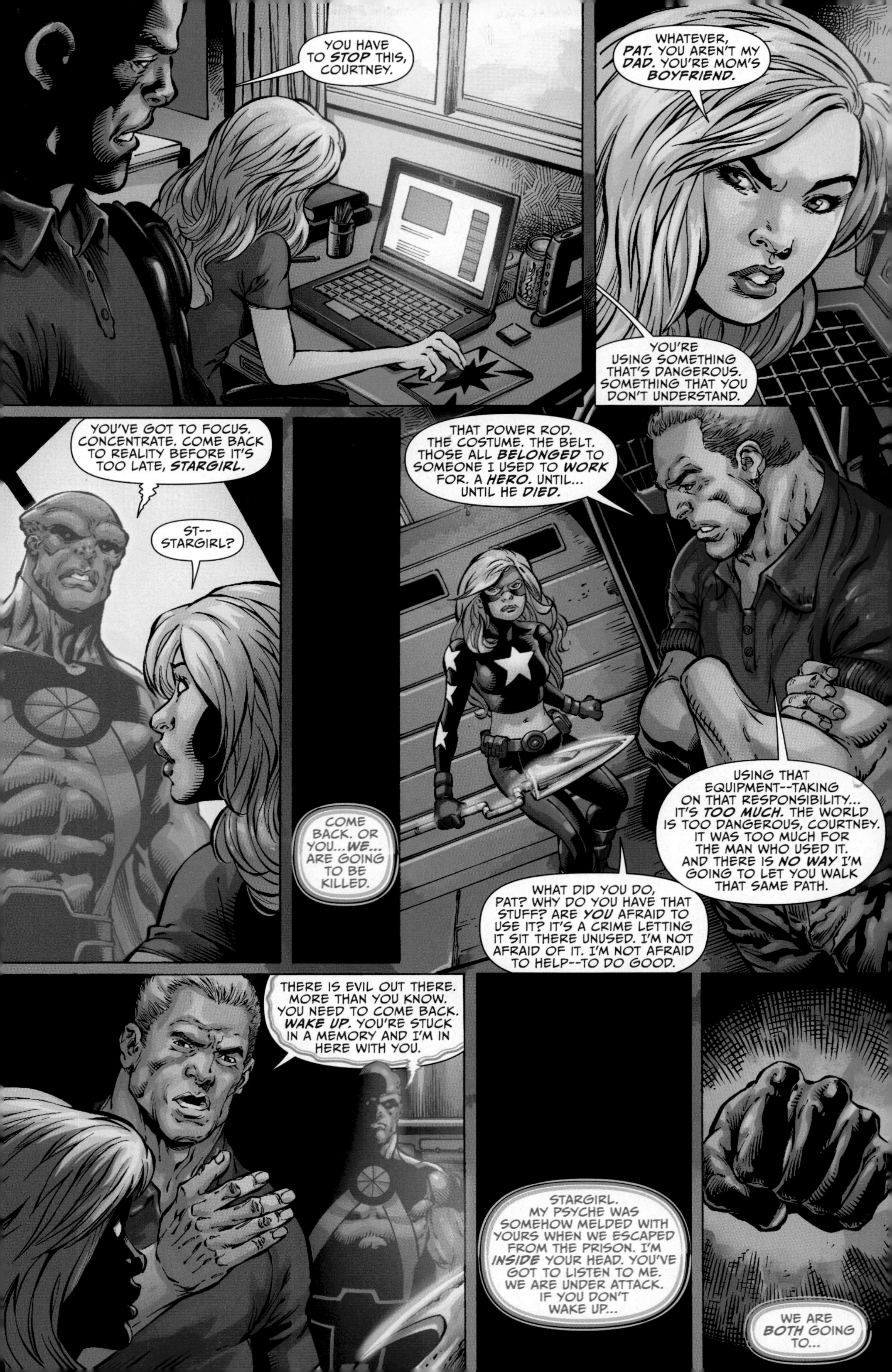
YOU HAVE TO STOP THIS, COURTNEY.
WHATEVER, PAT. YOU AREN'T MY DAD. YOU'RE MOM'S BOYFRIEND.
YOU'RE USING SOMETHING THAT'S DANGEROUS. SOMETHING THAT YOU DON'T UNDERSTAND.
YOU'VE GOT TO FOCUS. CONCENTRATE. COME BACK TO REALITY BEFORE IT'S TOO LATE, STARGIRL.
ST-- STARGIRL?
COME BACK. OR YOU... WE... ARE GOING TO BE KILLED.
THAT POWER ROD. THE COSTUME. THE BELT. THOSE ALL BELONGED TO SOMEONE I USED TO WORK FOR. A HERO. UNTIL... UNTIL HE DIED.
USING THAT EQUIPMENT--TAKING ON THAT RESPONSIBILITY... IT'S TOO MUCH. THE WORLD IS TOO DANGEROUS, COURTNEY. IT WAS TOO MUCH FOR THE MAN WHO USED IT. AND THERE IS NO WAY I'M GOING TO LET YOU WALK THAT SAME PATH.
WHAT DID YOU DO, PAT? WHY DO YOU HAVE THAT STUFF? ARE YOU AFRAID TO USE IT? IT'S A CRIME LETTING IT SIT THERE UNUSED. I'M NOT AFRAID OF IT. I'M NOT AFRAID TO HELP--TO DO GOOD.
THERE IS EVIL OUT THERE. MORE THAN YOU KNOW. YOU NEED TO COME BACK. WAKE UP. YOU'RE STUCK IN A MEMORY AND I'M IN HERE WITH YOU.
STARGIRL. MY PSYCHE WAS SOMEHOW MELDED WITH YOURS WHEN WE ESCAPED FROM THE PRISON. I'M INSIDE YOUR HEAD. YOU'VE GOT TO LISTEN TO ME. WE ARE UNDER ATTACK. IF YOU DON'T WAKE UP...
WE ARE BOTH GOING TO...

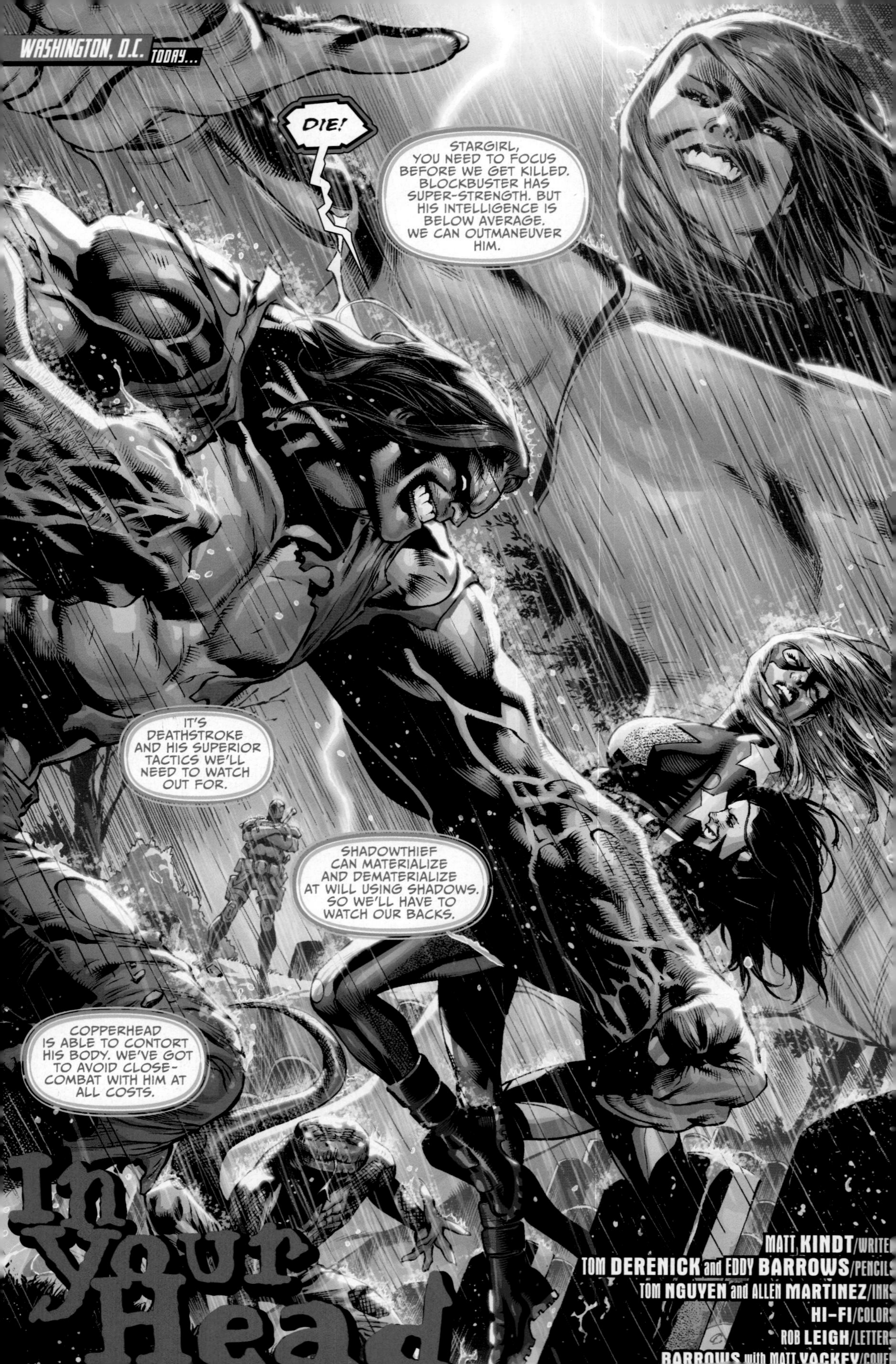
WASHINGTON, D.C. TODAY...
DIE!
STARGIRL, YOU NEED TO FOCUS BEFORE WE GET KILLED. BLOCKBUSTER HAS SUPER-STRENGTH. BUT HIS INTELLIGENCE IS BELOW AVERAGE. WE CAN OUTMANEUVER HIM.
IT'S DEATHSTROKE AND HIS SUPERIOR TACTICS WE'LL NEED TO WATCH OUT FOR.
SHADOWTHIEF CAN MATERIALIZE AND DEMATERIALIZE AT WILL USING SHADOWS. SO WE'LL HAVE TO WATCH OUR BACKS.
COPPERHEAD IS ABLE TO CONTORT HIS BODY. WE'VE GOT TO AVOID CLOSE-COMBAT WITH HIM AT ALL COSTS.
In your Head
MATT KINDT/WRITE
TOM DERENICK and EDDY BARROWS/PENCIL
TOM NGUYEN and ALLEN MARTINEZ/INK
HI-FI/COLOR
ROB LEIGH/LETTER
BARROWS with MATT YACKEY/COVE

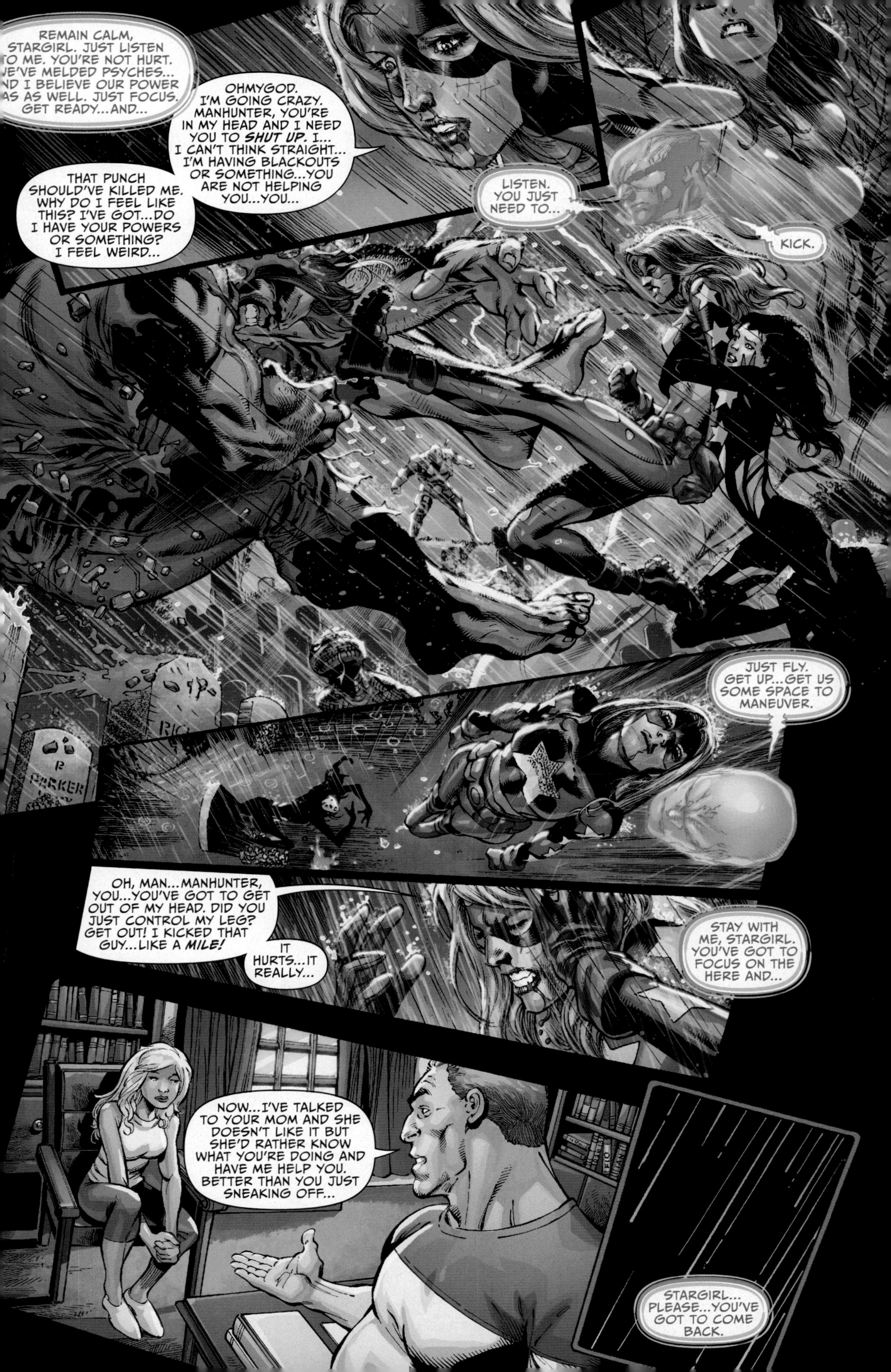
REMAIN CALM, STARGIRL. JUST LISTEN TO ME. YOU'RE NOT HURT. WE'VE MELDED PSYCHES... AND I BELIEVE OUR POWER HAS AS WELL. JUST FOCUS. GET READY...AND...
OHMYGOD. I'M GOING CRAZY. MANHUNTER, YOU'RE IN MY HEAD AND I NEED YOU TO SHUT UP. I... I CAN'T THINK STRAIGHT... I'M HAVING BLACKOUTS OR SOMETHING...YOU ARE NOT HELPING YOU...YOU...
THAT PUNCH SHOULD'VE KILLED ME. WHY DO I FEEL LIKE THIS? I'VE GOT...DO I HAVE YOUR POWERS OR SOMETHING? I FEEL WEIRD...
LISTEN. YOU JUST NEED TO...
KICK.
JUST FLY. GET UP...GET US SOME SPACE TO MANEUVER.
OH, MAN...MANHUNTER, YOU...YOU'VE GOT TO GET OUT OF MY HEAD. DID YOU JUST CONTROL MY LEG? GET OUT! I KICKED THAT GUY...LIKE A MILE!
IT HURTS...IT REALLY...
STAY WITH ME, STARGIRL. YOU'VE GOT TO FOCUS ON THE HERE AND...
NOW...I'VE TALKED TO YOUR MOM AND SHE DOESN'T LIKE IT BUT SHE'D RATHER KNOW WHAT YOU'RE DOING AND HAVE ME HELP YOU. BETTER THAN YOU JUST SNEAKING OFF...
STARGIRL... PLEASE...YOU'VE GOT TO COME BACK.

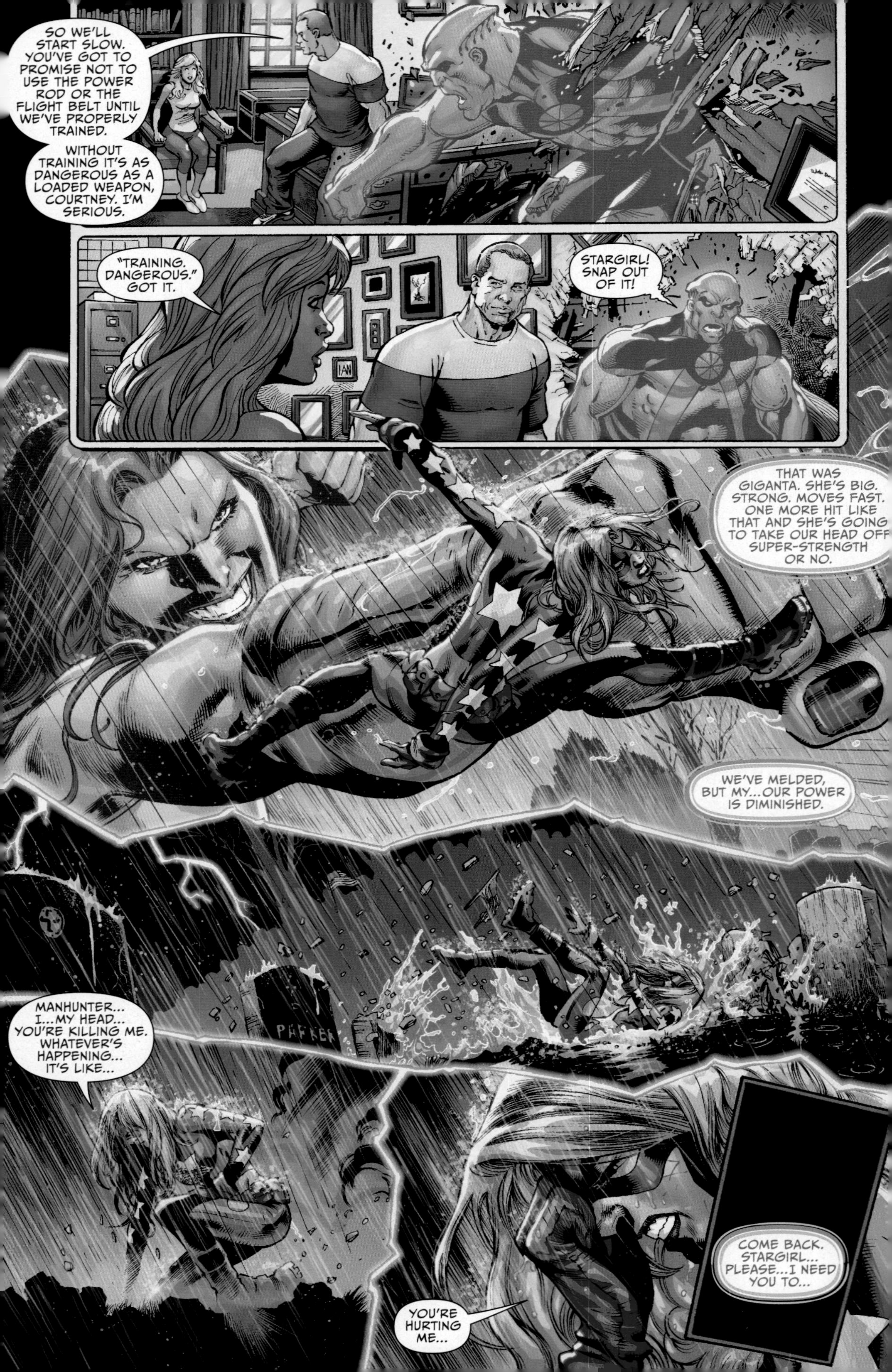

SO WE'LL START SLOW. YOU'VE GOT TO PROMISE NOT TO USE THE POWER ROD OR THE FLIGHT BELT UNTIL WE'VE PROPERLY TRAINED.
WITHOUT TRAINING IT'S AS DANGEROUS AS A LOADED WEAPON, COURTNEY. I'M SERIOUS.
"TRAINING. DANGEROUS." GOT IT.
STARGIRL! SNAP OUT OF IT!
THAT WAS GIGANTA. SHE'S BIG. STRONG. MOVES FAST. ONE MORE HIT LIKE THAT AND SHE'S GOING TO TAKE OUR HEAD OFF SUPER-STRENGTH OR NO.
WE'VE MELDED, BUT MY...OUR POWER IS DIMINISHED.
PARKER
MANHUNTER... I...MY HEAD... YOU'RE KILLING ME. WHATEVER'S HAPPENING... IT'S LIKE...
COME BACK. STARGIRL... PLEASE...I NEED YOU TO...
YOU'RE HURTING ME...

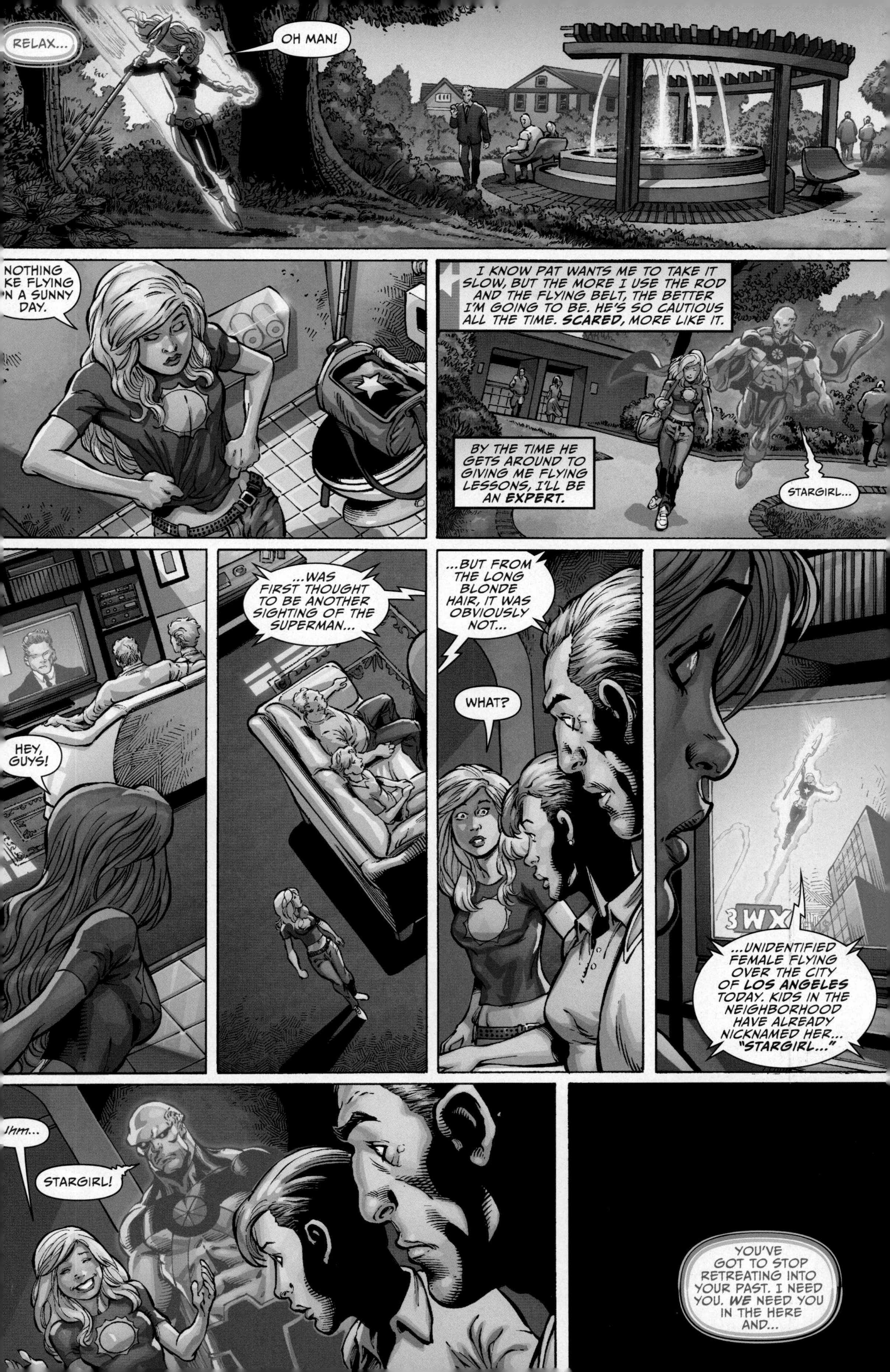

RELAX...
OH MAN!
NOTHING
KE FLYING
N A SUNNY
DAY.
I KNOW PAT WANTS ME TO TAKE IT SLOW, BUT THE MORE I USE THE ROD AND THE FLYING BELT, THE BETTER I'M GOING TO BE. HE'S SO CAUTIOUS ALL THE TIME. SCARED, MORE LIKE IT.
BY THE TIME HE GETS AROUND TO GIVING ME FLYING LESSONS, I'LL BE AN EXPERT.
STARGIRL...
HEY, GUYS!
...WAS FIRST THOUGHT TO BE ANOTHER SIGHTING OF THE SUPERMAN...
...BUT FROM THE LONG BLONDE HAIR, IT WAS OBVIOUSLY NOT...
WHAT?
...UNIDENTIFIED FEMALE FLYING OVER THE CITY OF LOS ANGELES TODAY. KIDS IN THE NEIGHBORHOOD HAVE ALREADY NICKNAMED HER... "STARGIRL..."
hm...
STARGIRL!
YOU'VE GOT TO STOP RETREATING INTO YOUR PAST. I NEED YOU. WE NEED YOU IN THE HERE AND...

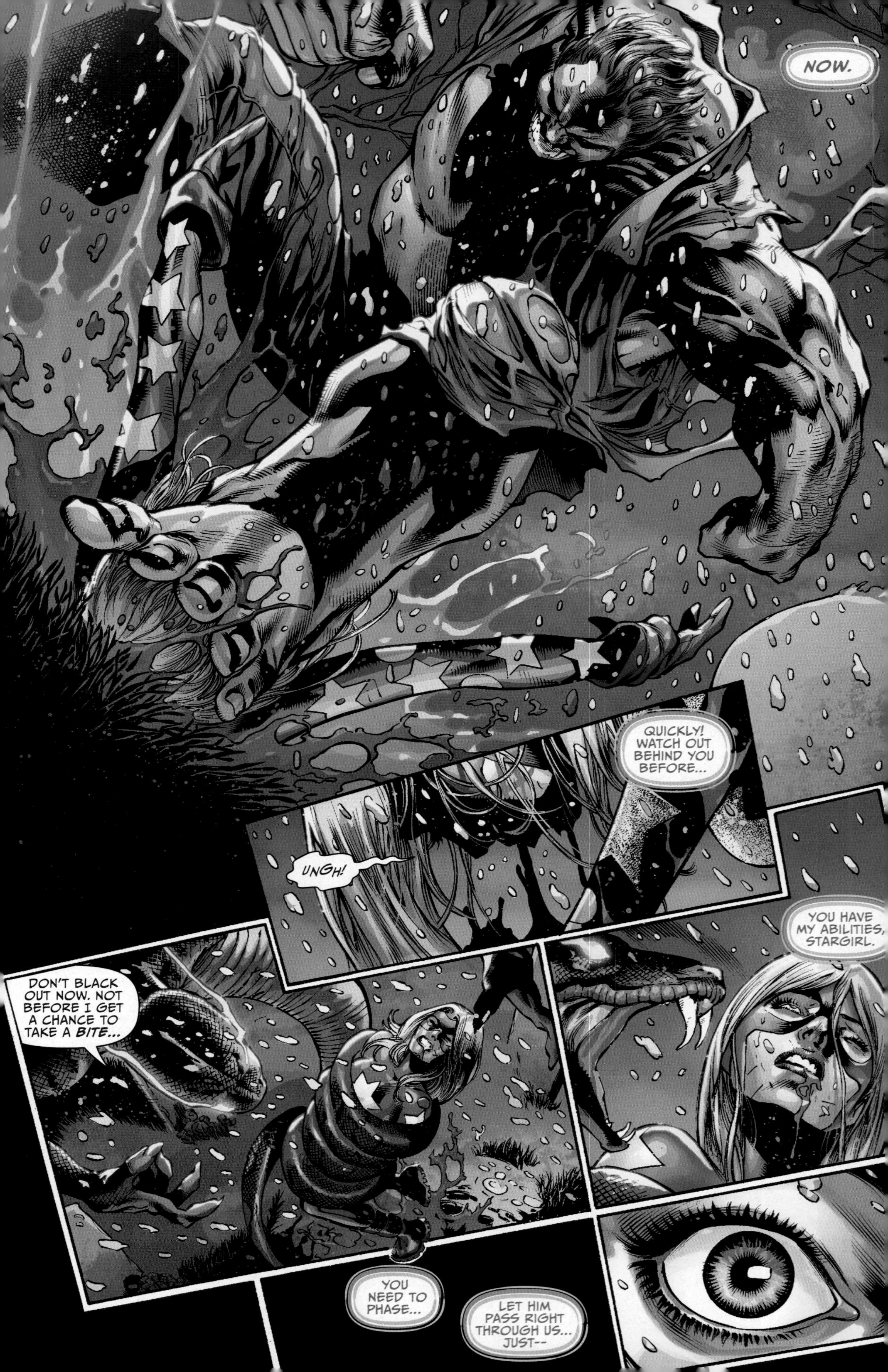
NOW.
QUICKLY! WATCH OUT BEHIND YOU BEFORE...
UNGH!
YOU HAVE MY ABILITIES, STARGIRL.
DON'T BLACK OUT NOW. NOT BEFORE I GET A CHANCE TO TAKE A *BITE*...
YOU NEED TO PHASE...
LET HIM PASS RIGHT THROUGH US... JUST--

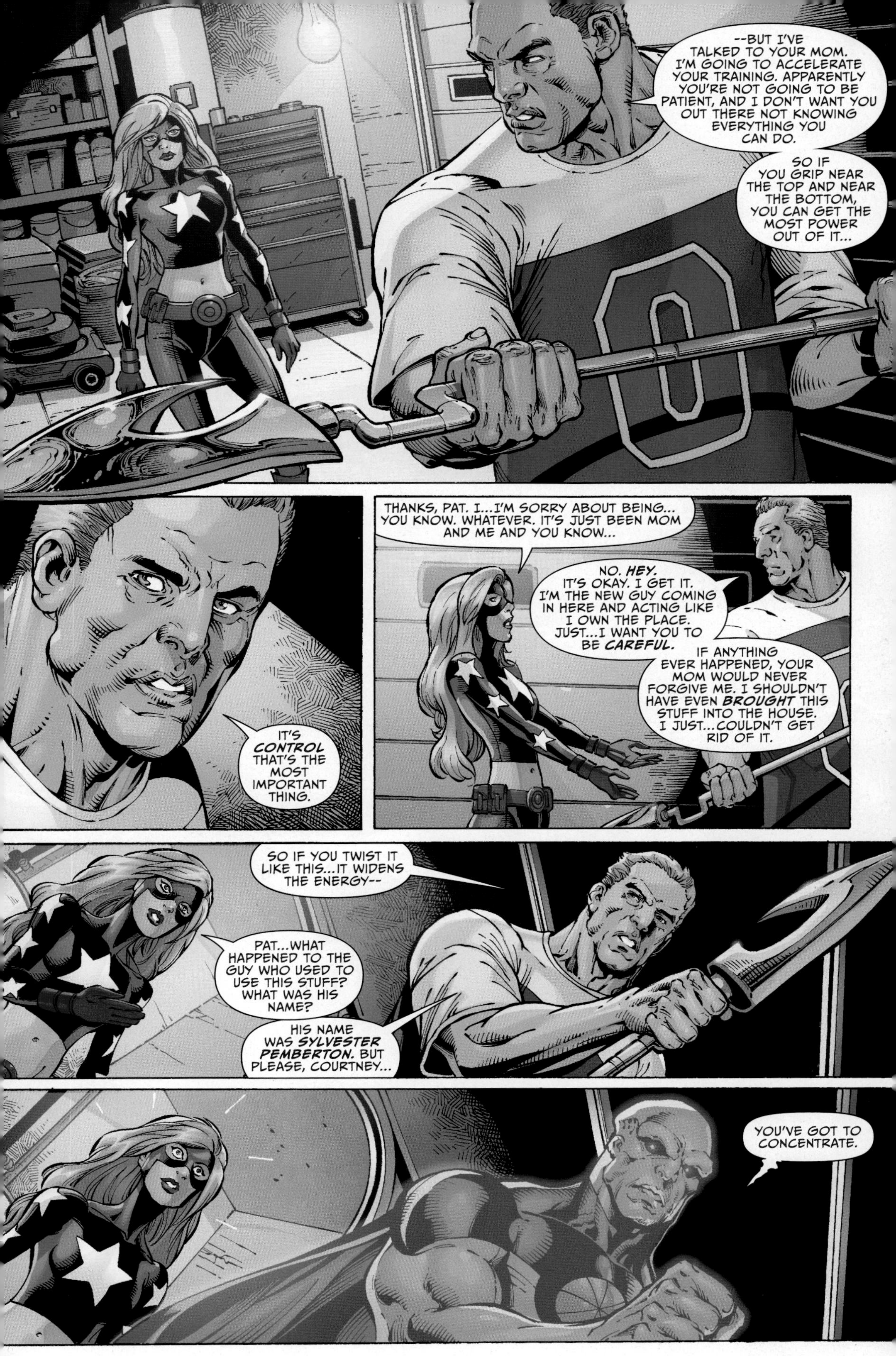
--BUT I'VE TALKED TO YOUR MOM. I'M GOING TO ACCELERATE YOUR TRAINING. APPARENTLY YOU'RE NOT GOING TO BE PATIENT, AND I DON'T WANT YOU OUT THERE NOT KNOWING EVERYTHING YOU CAN DO.
SO IF YOU GRIP NEAR THE TOP AND NEAR THE BOTTOM, YOU CAN GET THE MOST POWER OUT OF IT...
IT'S *CONTROL* THAT'S THE MOST IMPORTANT THING.
THANKS, PAT. I...I'M SORRY ABOUT BEING... YOU KNOW. WHATEVER. IT'S JUST BEEN MOM AND ME AND YOU KNOW...
NO. *HEY.* IT'S OKAY. I GET IT. I'M THE NEW GUY COMING IN HERE AND ACTING LIKE I OWN THE PLACE. JUST...I WANT YOU TO BE *CAREFUL.*
IF ANYTHING EVER HAPPENED, YOUR MOM WOULD NEVER FORGIVE ME. I SHOULDN'T HAVE EVEN *BROUGHT* THIS STUFF INTO THE HOUSE. I JUST...COULDN'T GET RID OF IT.
SO IF YOU TWIST IT LIKE THIS...IT WIDENS THE ENERGY--
PAT...WHAT HAPPENED TO THE GUY WHO USED TO USE THIS STUFF? WHAT WAS HIS NAME?
HIS NAME WAS *SYLVESTER PEMBERTON.* BUT PLEASE, COURTNEY...
YOU'VE GOT TO CONCENTRATE.

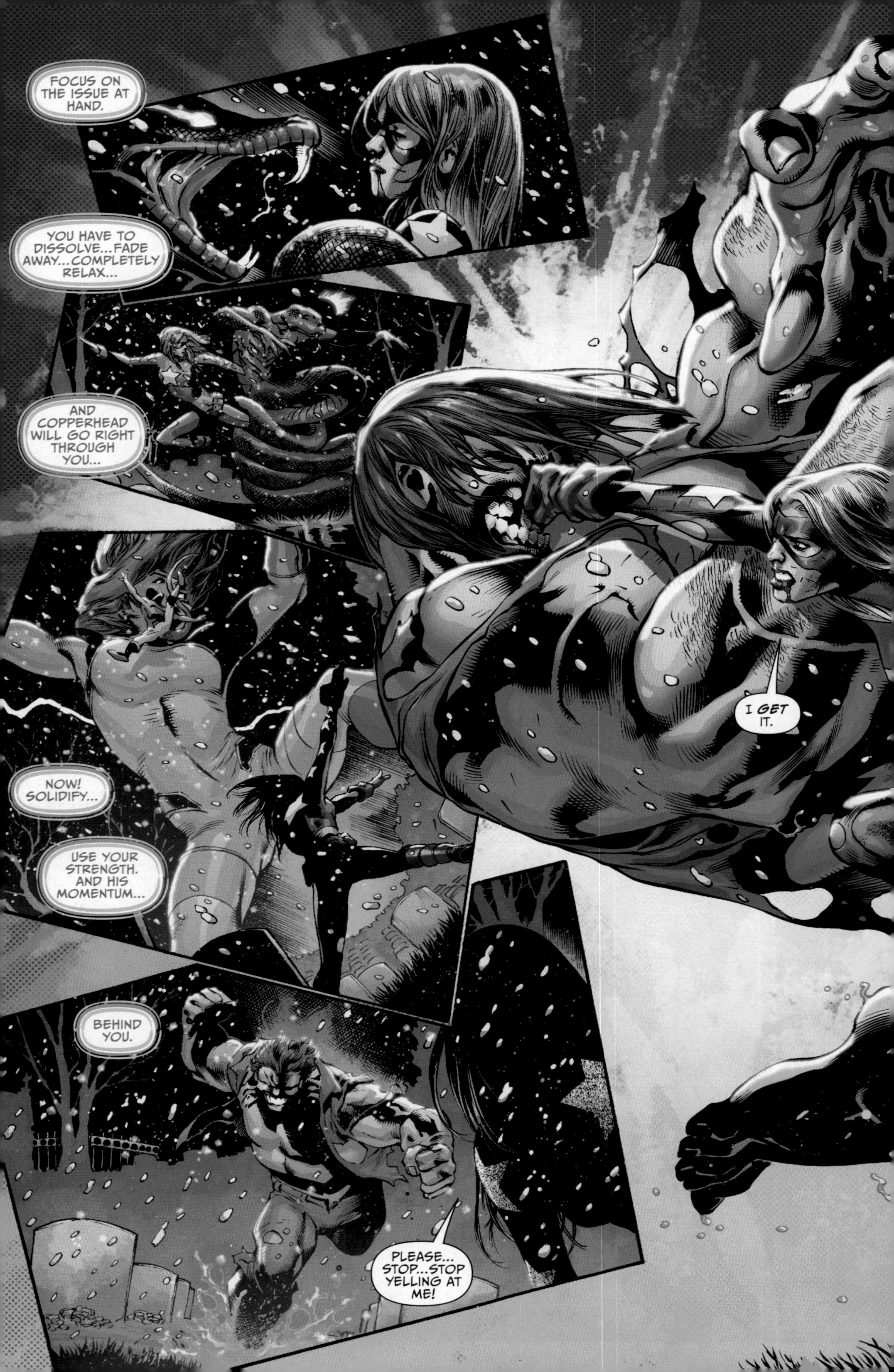
FOCUS ON THE ISSUE AT HAND.
YOU HAVE TO DISSOLVE...FADE AWAY...COMPLETELY RELAX...
AND COPPERHEAD WILL GO RIGHT THROUGH YOU...
I GET IT.
NOW! SOLIDIFY...
USE YOUR STRENGTH. AND HIS MOMENTUM...
BEHIND YOU.
PLEASE... STOP...STOP YELLING AT ME!

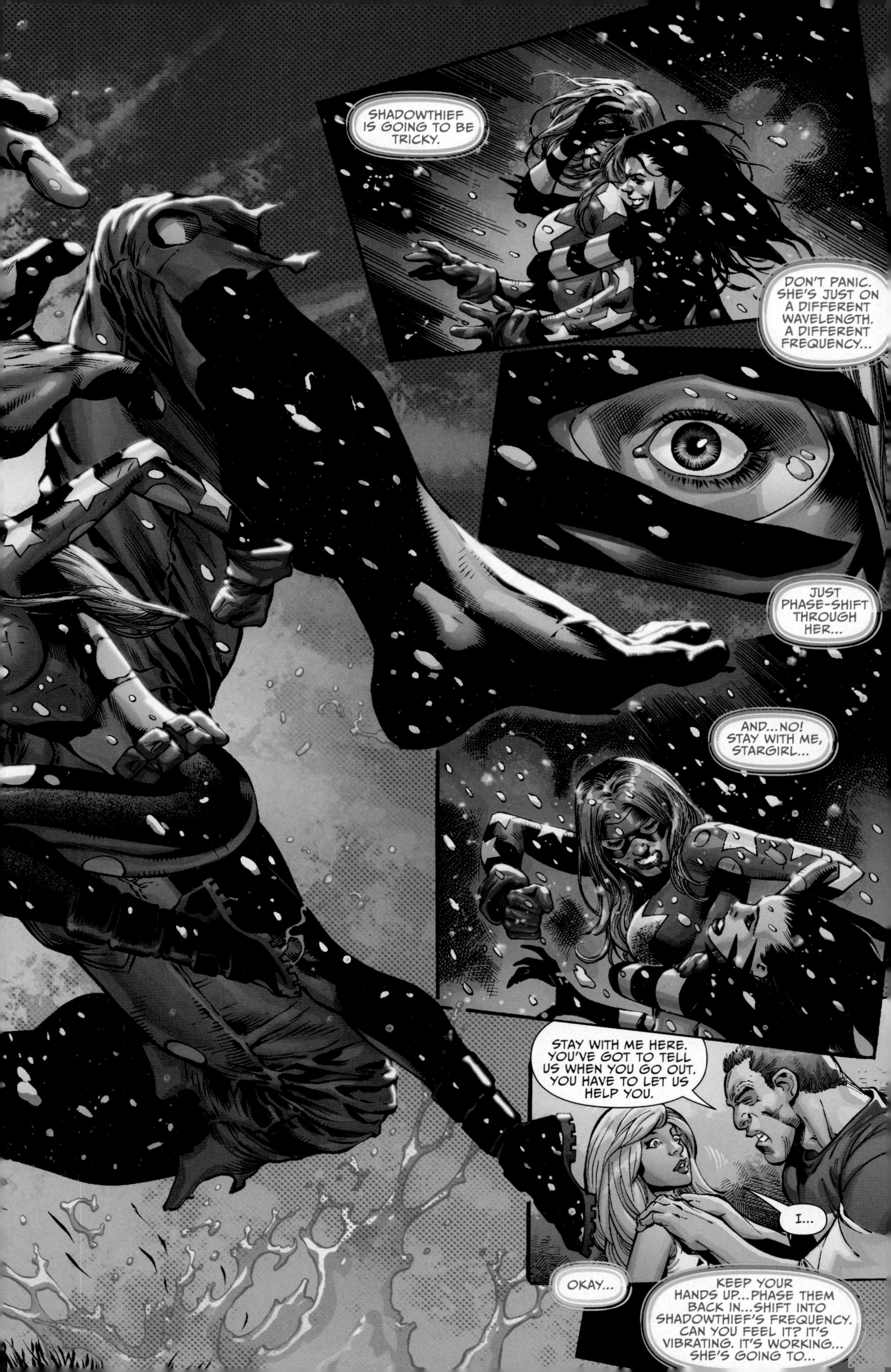
SHADOWTHIEF IS GOING TO BE TRICKY.
DON'T PANIC. SHE'S JUST ON A DIFFERENT WAVELENGTH. A DIFFERENT FREQUENCY...
JUST PHASE-SHIFT THROUGH HER...
AND...NO! STAY WITH ME, STARGIRL...
STAY WITH ME HERE. YOU'VE GOT TO TELL US WHEN YOU GO OUT. YOU HAVE TO LET US HELP YOU.
I...
OKAY...
KEEP YOUR HANDS UP...PHASE THEM BACK IN...SHIFT INTO SHADOWTHIEF'S FREQUENCY. CAN YOU FEEL IT? IT'S VIBRATING. IT'S WORKING... SHE'S GOING TO...

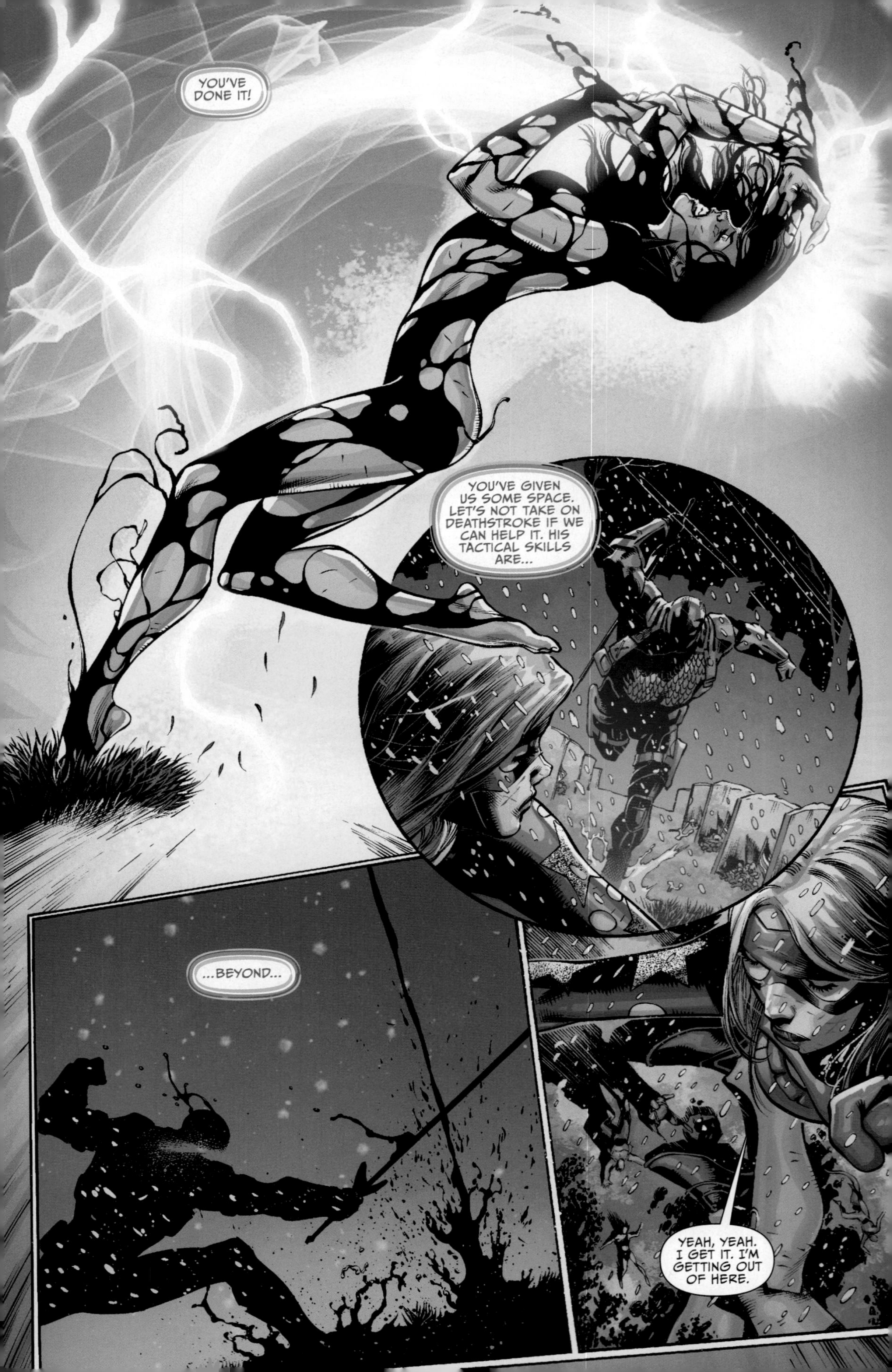
YOU'VE DONE IT!
YOU'VE GIVEN US SOME SPACE. LET'S NOT TAKE ON DEATHSTROKE IF WE CAN HELP IT. HIS TACTICAL SKILLS ARE...
...BEYOND...
YEAH, YEAH. I GET IT. I'M GETTING OUT OF HERE.

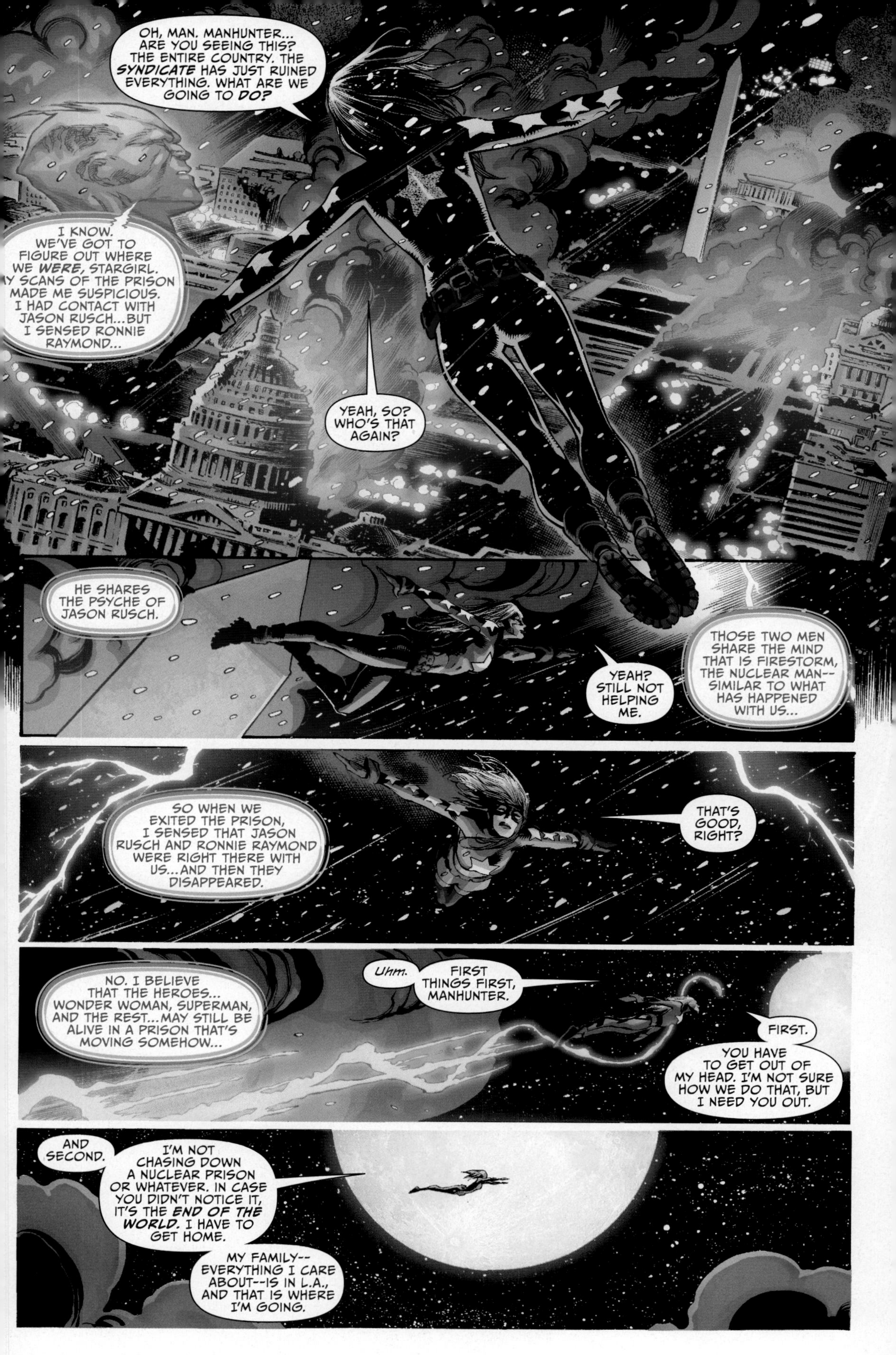
OH, MAN. MANHUNTER... ARE YOU SEEING THIS? THE ENTIRE COUNTRY. THE SYNDICATE HAS JUST RUINED EVERYTHING. WHAT ARE WE GOING TO DO?
I KNOW. WE'VE GOT TO FIGURE OUT WHERE WE WERE, STARGIRL. Y SCANS OF THE PRISON MADE ME SUSPICIOUS. I HAD CONTACT WITH JASON RUSCH...BUT I SENSED RONNIE RAYMOND...
YEAH, SO? WHO'S THAT AGAIN?
HE SHARES THE PSYCHE OF JASON RUSCH.
YEAH? STILL NOT HELPING ME.
THOSE TWO MEN SHARE THE MIND THAT IS FIRESTORM, THE NUCLEAR MAN--SIMILAR TO WHAT HAS HAPPENED WITH US...
SO WHEN WE EXITED THE PRISON, I SENSED THAT JASON RUSCH AND RONNIE RAYMOND WERE RIGHT THERE WITH US...AND THEN THEY DISAPPEARED.
THAT'S GOOD, RIGHT?
NO. I BELIEVE THAT THE HEROES... WONDER WOMAN, SUPERMAN, AND THE REST...MAY STILL BE ALIVE IN A PRISON THAT'S MOVING SOMEHOW...
Uhm.
FIRST THINGS FIRST, MANHUNTER.
FIRST.
YOU HAVE TO GET OUT OF MY HEAD. I'M NOT SURE HOW WE DO THAT, BUT I NEED YOU OUT.
AND SECOND.
I'M NOT CHASING DOWN A NUCLEAR PRISON OR WHATEVER. IN CASE YOU DIDN'T NOTICE IT, IT'S THE END OF THE WORLD. I HAVE TO GET HOME.
MY FAMILY--EVERYTHING I CARE ABOUT--IS IN L.A., AND THAT IS WHERE I'M GOING.

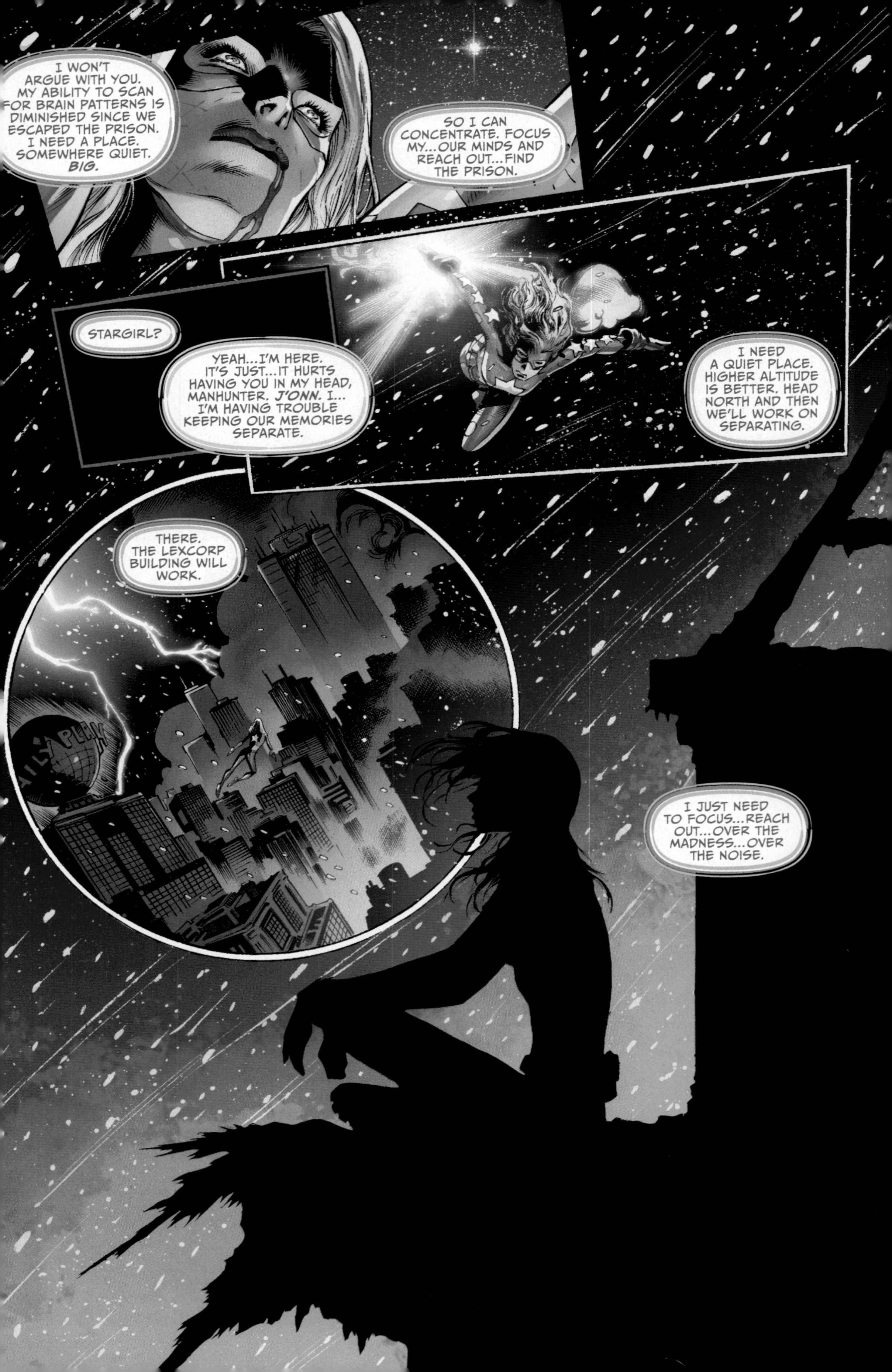
I WON'T ARGUE WITH YOU. MY ABILITY TO SCAN FOR BRAIN PATTERNS IS DIMINISHED SINCE WE ESCAPED THE PRISON. I NEED A PLACE. SOMEWHERE QUIET. *BIG.*
SO I CAN CONCENTRATE. FOCUS MY...OUR MINDS AND REACH OUT...FIND THE PRISON.
STARGIRL?
YEAH...I'M HERE. IT'S JUST...IT HURTS HAVING YOU IN MY HEAD, MANHUNTER. *J'ONN.* I... I'M HAVING TROUBLE KEEPING OUR MEMORIES SEPARATE.
I NEED A QUIET PLACE. HIGHER ALTITUDE IS BETTER. HEAD NORTH AND THEN WE'LL WORK ON SEPARATING.
THERE. THE LEXCORP BUILDING WILL WORK.
I JUST NEED TO FOCUS...REACH OUT...OVER THE MADNESS...OVER THE NOISE.

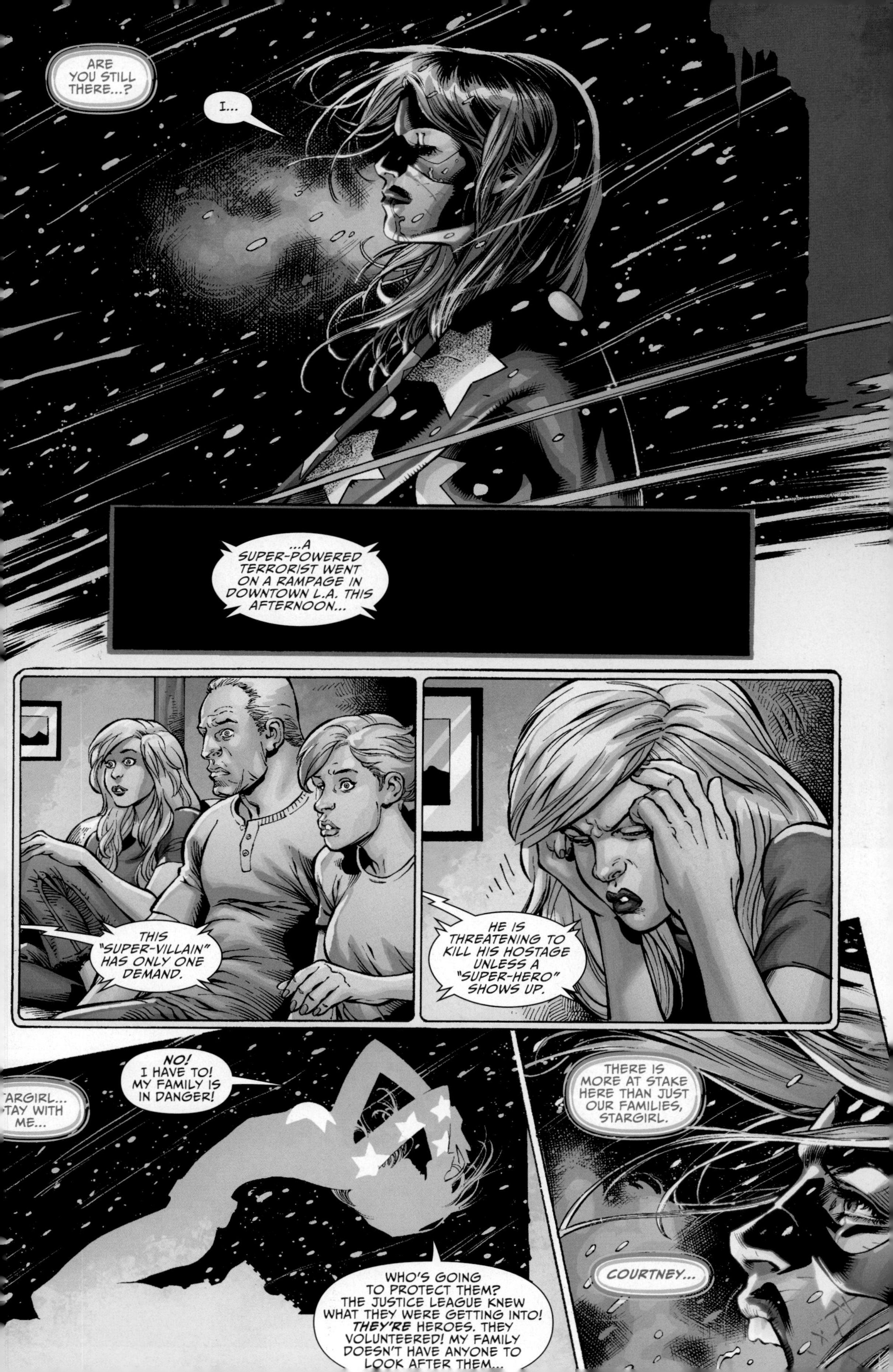

ARE YOU STILL THERE...?
I...
...A SUPER-POWERED TERRORIST WENT ON A RAMPAGE IN DOWNTOWN L.A. THIS AFTERNOON...
THIS "SUPER-VILLAIN" HAS ONLY ONE DEMAND.
HE IS THREATENING TO KILL HIS HOSTAGE UNLESS A "SUPER-HERO" SHOWS UP.
TARGIRL... TAY WITH ME...
NO! I HAVE TO! MY FAMILY IS IN DANGER!
THERE IS MORE AT STAKE HERE THAN JUST OUR FAMILIES, STARGIRL.
WHO'S GOING TO PROTECT THEM? THE JUSTICE LEAGUE KNEW WHAT THEY WERE GETTING INTO! THEY'RE HEROES. THEY VOLUNTEERED! MY FAMILY DOESN'T HAVE ANYONE TO LOOK AFTER THEM...
COURTNEY...

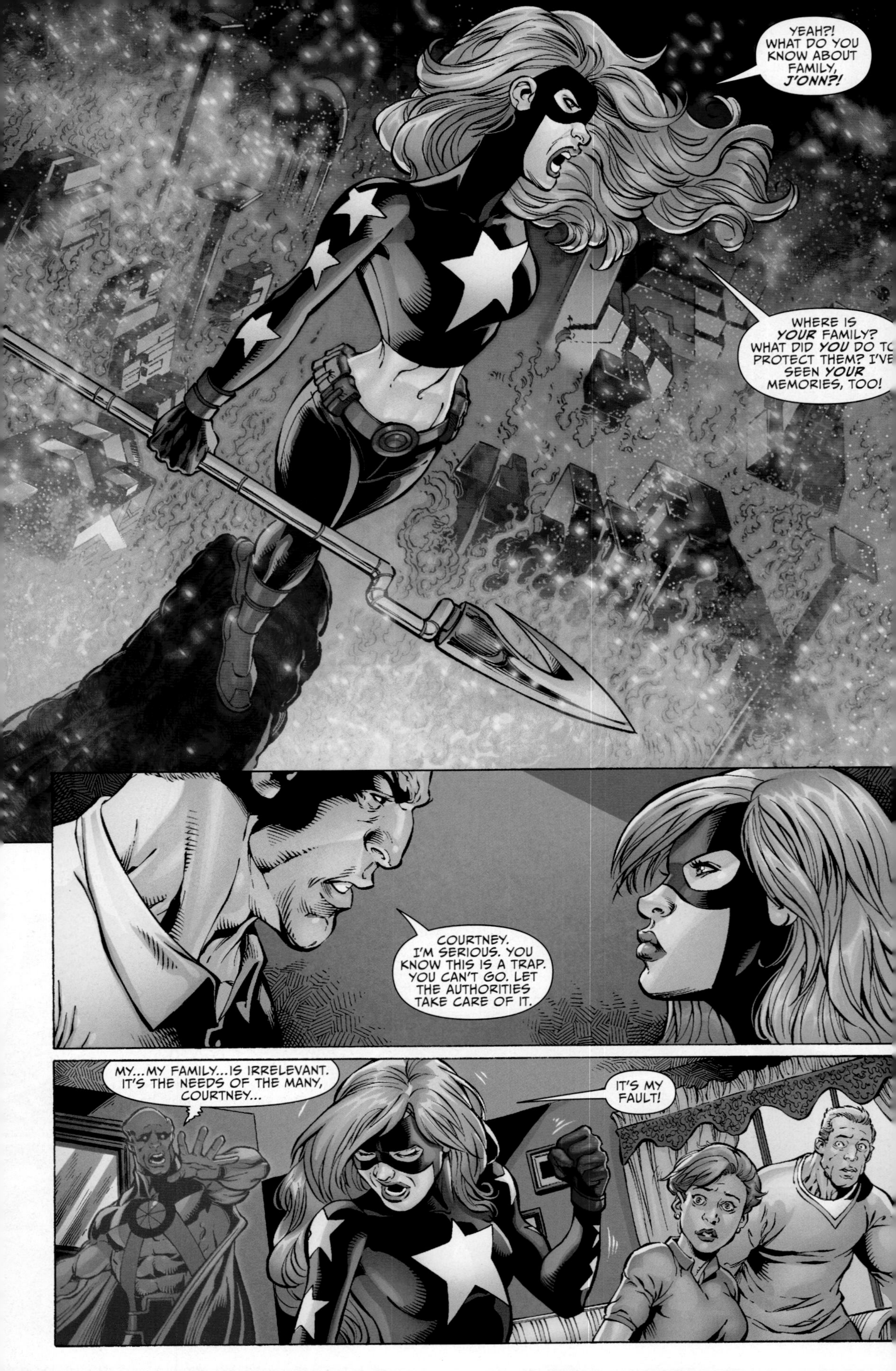

YEAH?! WHAT DO YOU KNOW ABOUT FAMILY, J'ONN?!
WHERE IS YOUR FAMILY? WHAT DID YOU DO TO PROTECT THEM? I'VE SEEN YOUR MEMORIES, TOO!
COURTNEY. I'M SERIOUS. YOU KNOW THIS IS A TRAP. YOU CAN'T GO. LET THE AUTHORITIES TAKE CARE OF IT.
MY...MY FAMILY...IS IRRELEVANT. IT'S THE NEEDS OF THE MANY, COURTNEY...
IT'S MY FAULT!

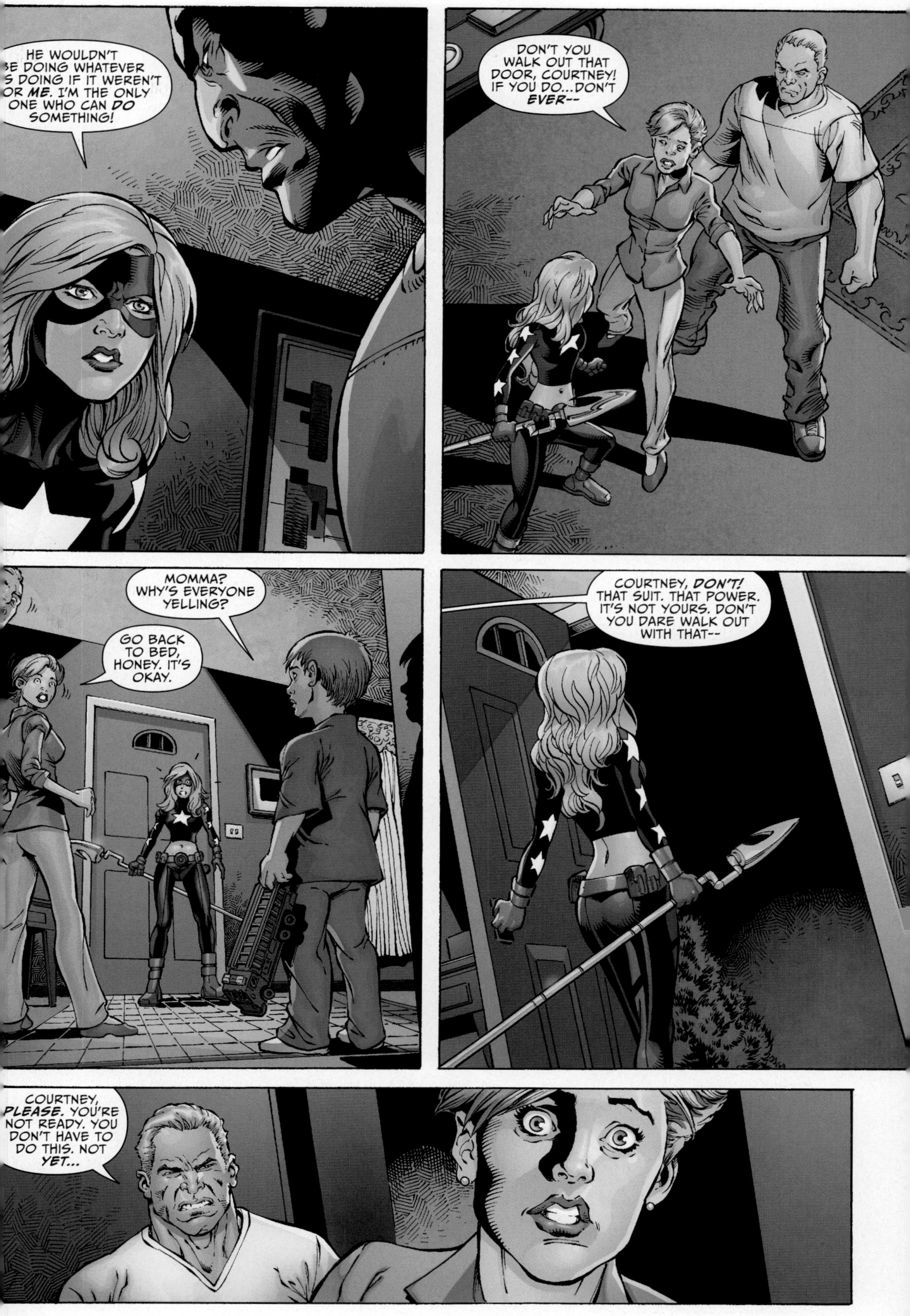

HE WOULDN'T
BE DOING WHATEVER
S DOING IF IT WEREN'T
OR ME. I'M THE ONLY
ONE WHO CAN DO
SOMETHING!
DON'T YOU WALK OUT THAT DOOR, COURTNEY! IF YOU DO...DON'T EVER--
MOMMA? WHY'S EVERYONE YELLING?
GO BACK TO BED, HONEY. IT'S OKAY.
COURTNEY, DON'T! THAT SUIT. THAT POWER. IT'S NOT YOURS. DON'T YOU DARE WALK OUT WITH THAT--
COURTNEY, PLEASE. YOU'RE NOT READY. YOU DON'T HAVE TO DO THIS. NOT YET...

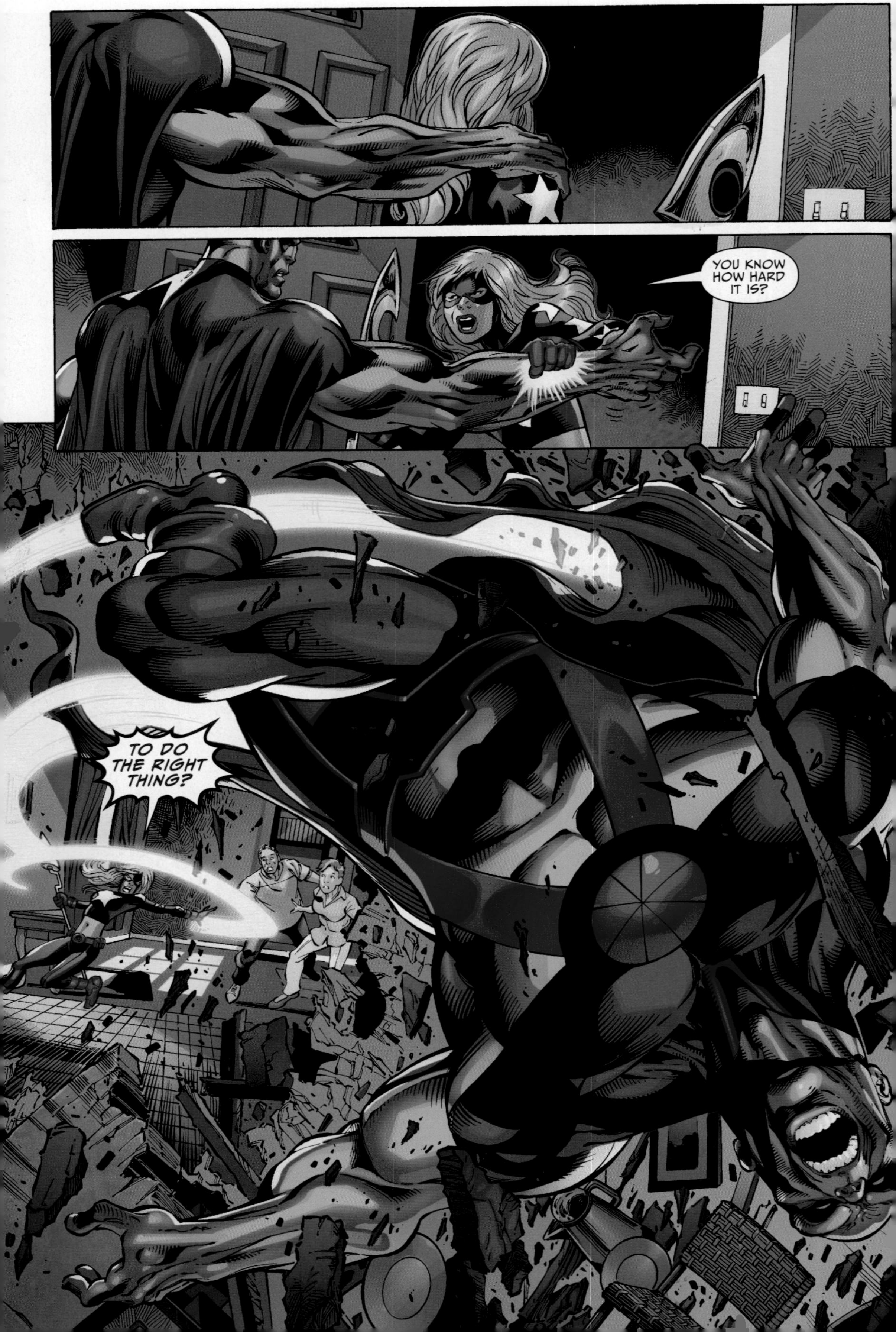
YOU KNOW HOW HARD IT IS?
TO DO THE RIGHT THING?

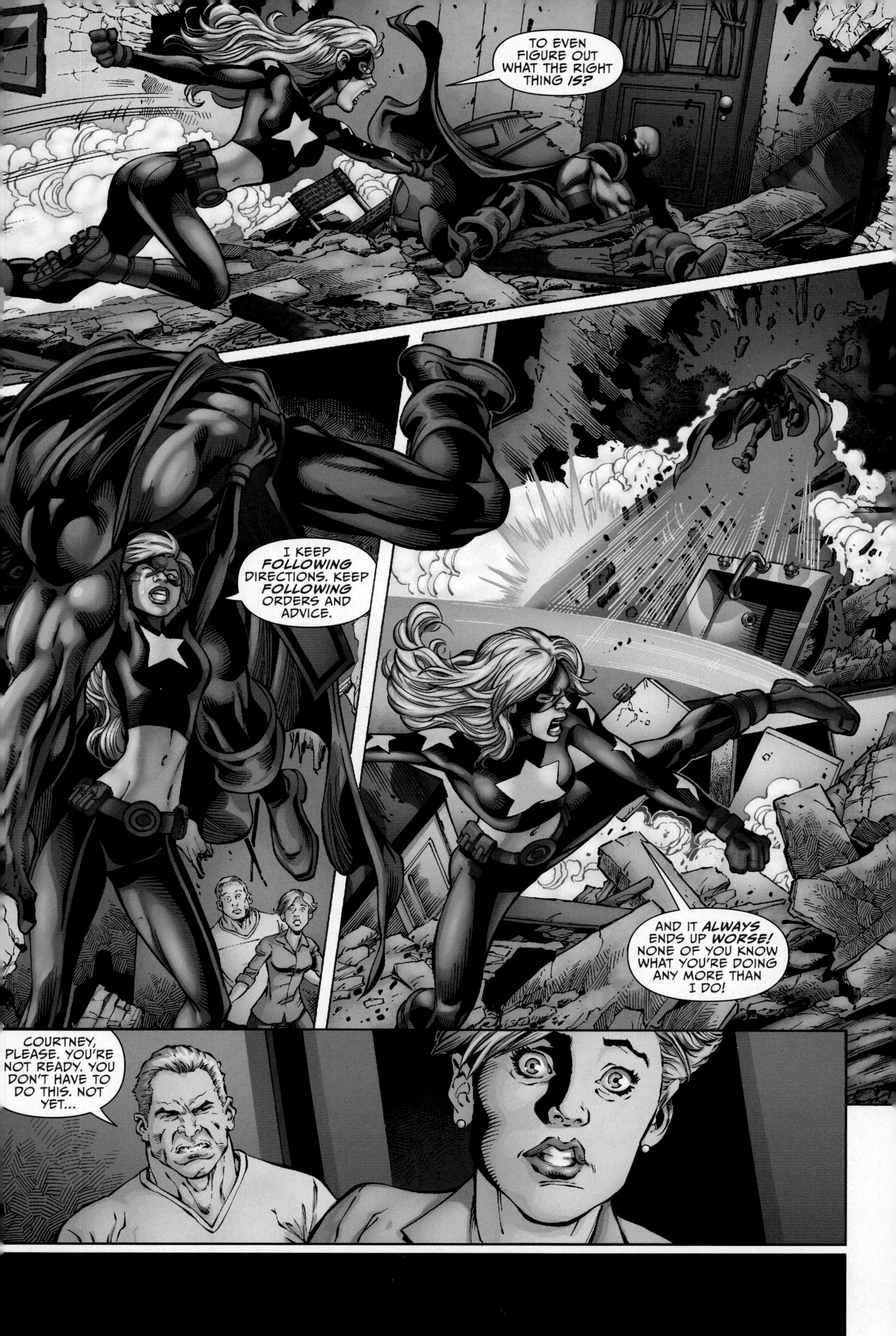
TO EVEN FIGURE OUT WHAT THE RIGHT THING IS?
I KEEP FOLLOWING DIRECTIONS. KEEP FOLLOWING ORDERS AND ADVICE.
AND IT ALWAYS ENDS UP WORSE! NONE OF YOU KNOW WHAT YOU'RE DOING ANY MORE THAN I DO!
COURTNEY, PLEASE. YOU'RE NOT READY. YOU DON'T HAVE TO DO THIS. NOT YET...

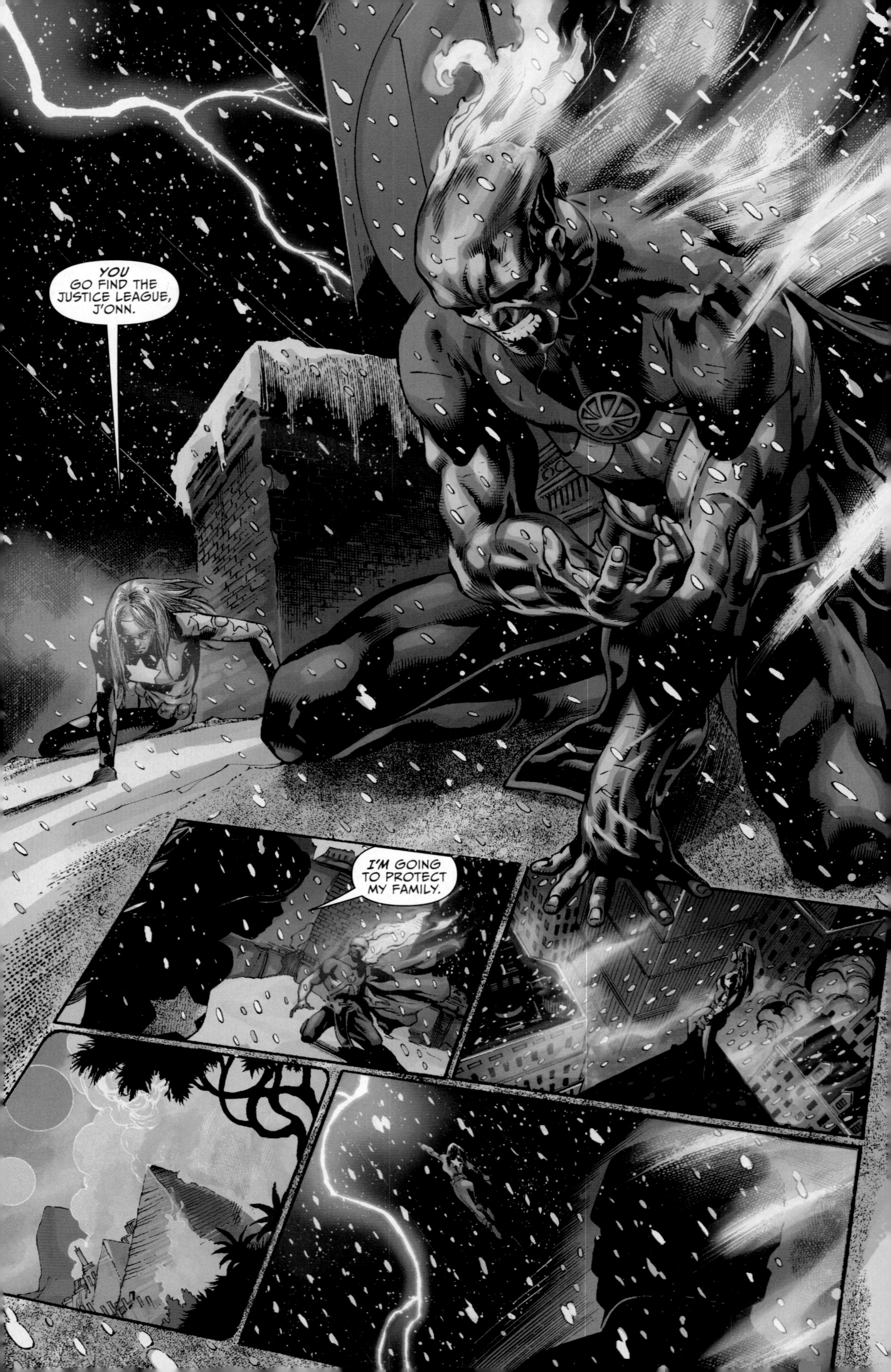
YOU GO FIND THE JUSTICE LEAGUE, J'ONN.
I'M GOING TO PROTECT MY FAMILY.

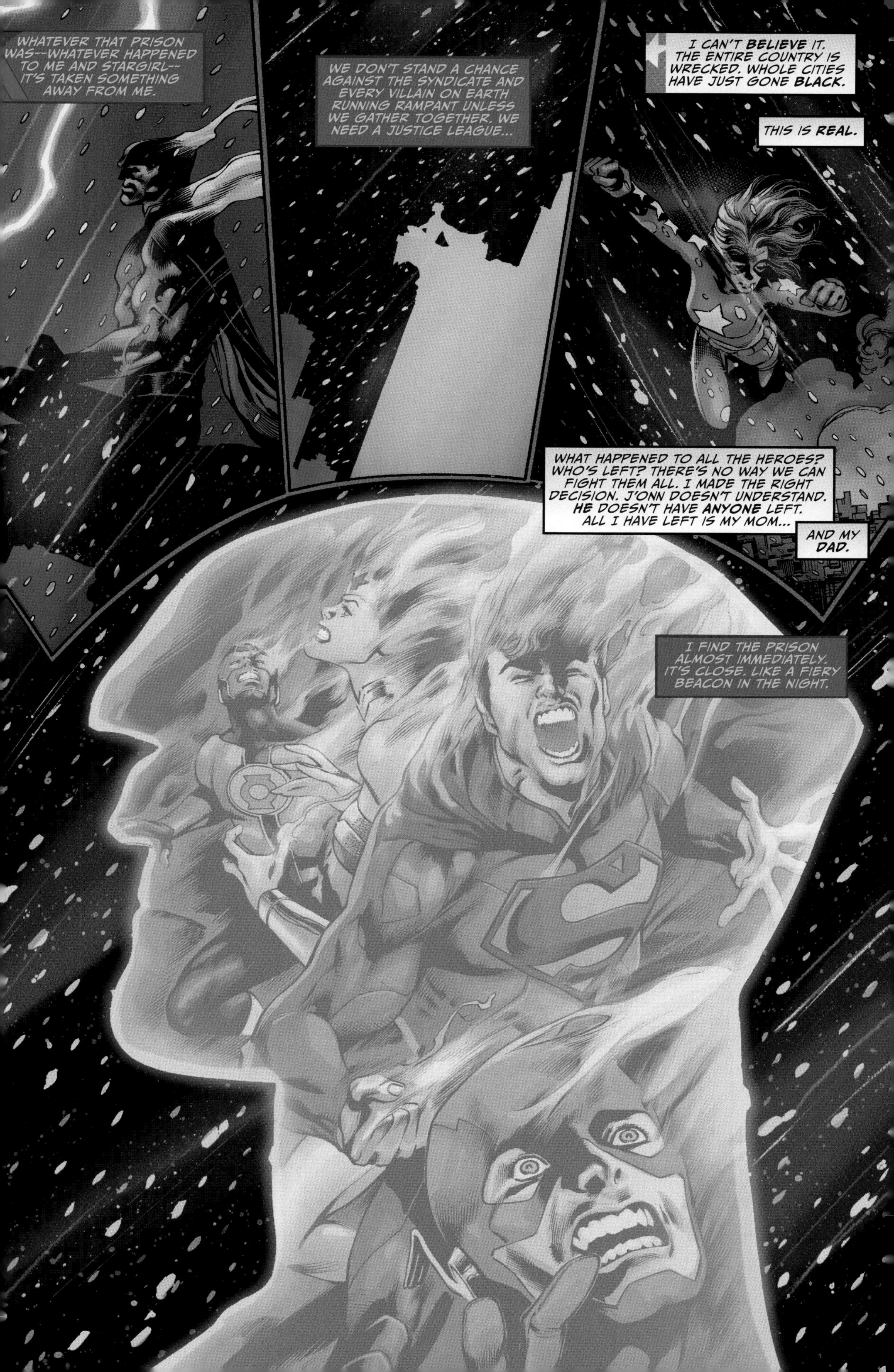
WHATEVER THAT PRISON WAS--WHATEVER HAPPENED TO ME AND STARGIRL--IT'S TAKEN SOMETHING AWAY FROM ME.
WE DON'T STAND A CHANCE AGAINST THE SYNDICATE AND EVERY VILLAIN ON EARTH RUNNING RAMPANT UNLESS WE GATHER TOGETHER. WE NEED A JUSTICE LEAGUE...
I CAN'T BELIEVE IT. THE ENTIRE COUNTRY IS WRECKED. WHOLE CITIES HAVE JUST GONE BLACK.
THIS IS REAL.
WHAT HAPPENED TO ALL THE HEROES? WHO'S LEFT? THERE'S NO WAY WE CAN FIGHT THEM ALL. I MADE THE RIGHT DECISION. J'ONN DOESN'T UNDERSTAND. HE DOESN'T HAVE ANYONE LEFT. ALL I HAVE LEFT IS MY MOM...
AND MY DAD.
I FIND THE PRISON ALMOST IMMEDIATELY. IT'S CLOSE. LIKE A FIERY BEACON IN THE NIGHT.

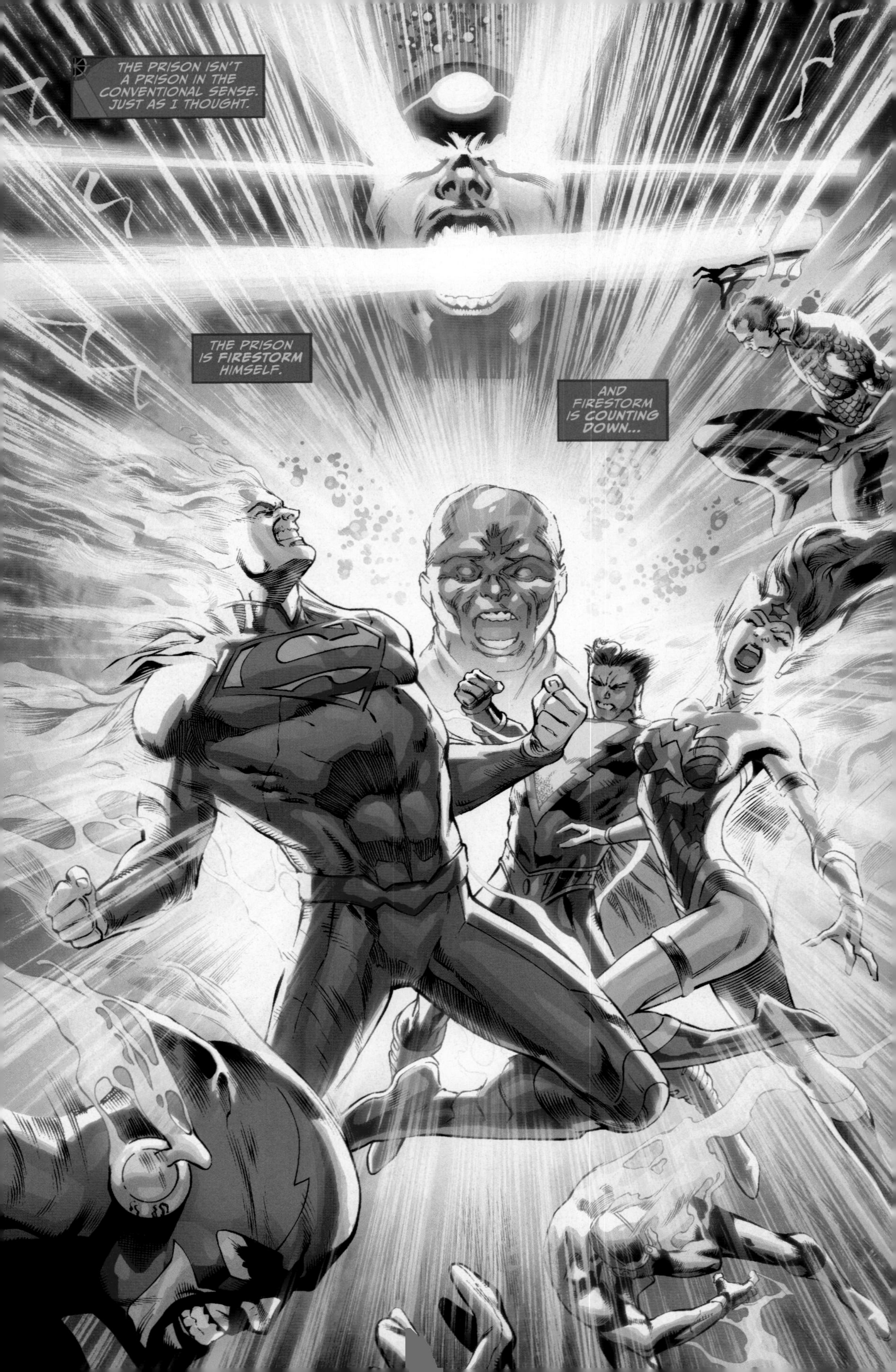
THE PRISON ISN'T A PRISON IN THE CONVENTIONAL SENSE. JUST AS I THOUGHT.
THE PRISON IS FIRESTORM HIMSELF.
AND FIRESTORM IS COUNTING DOWN...

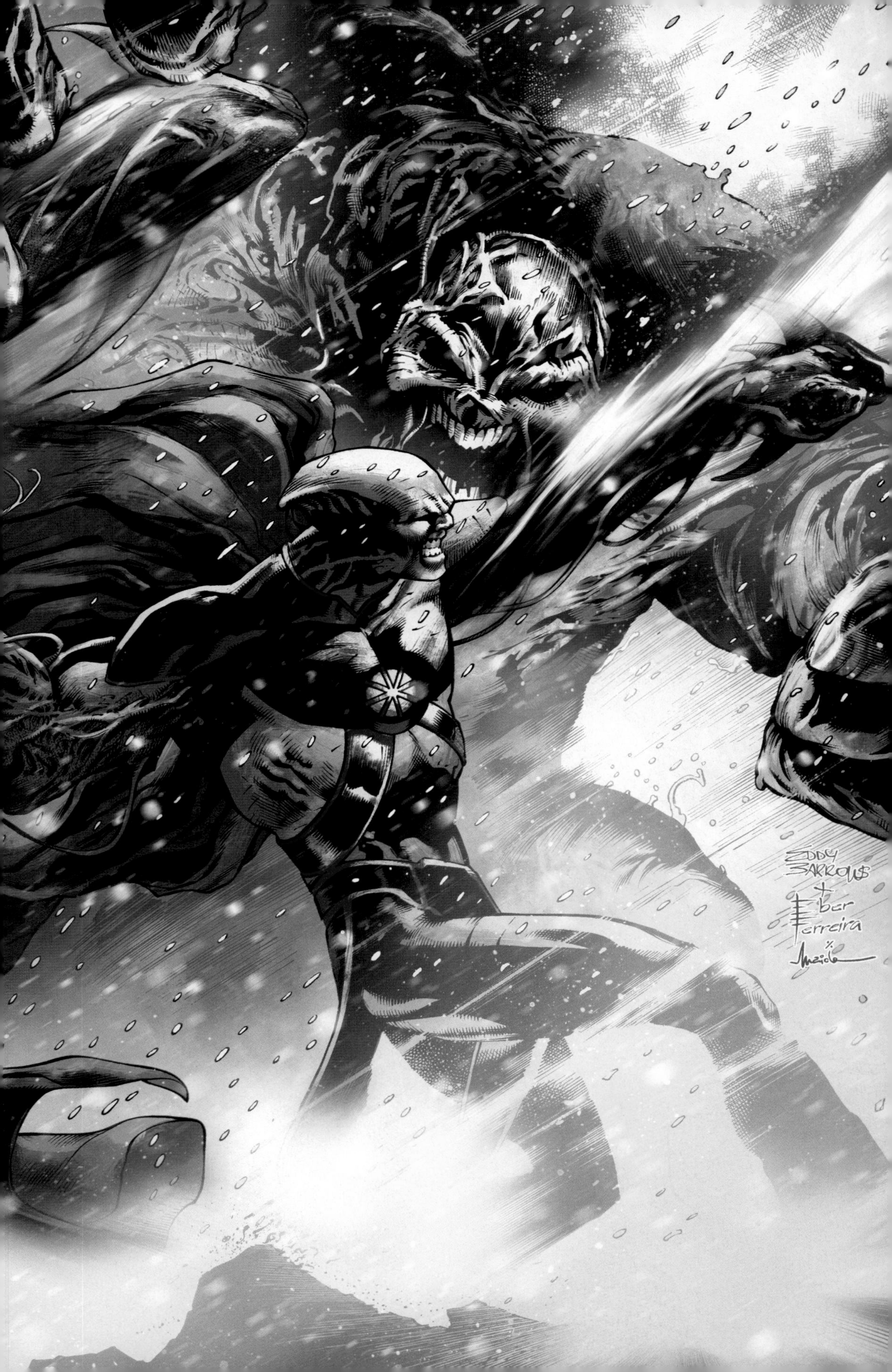
EDDY BARROWS
Eber Ferreira

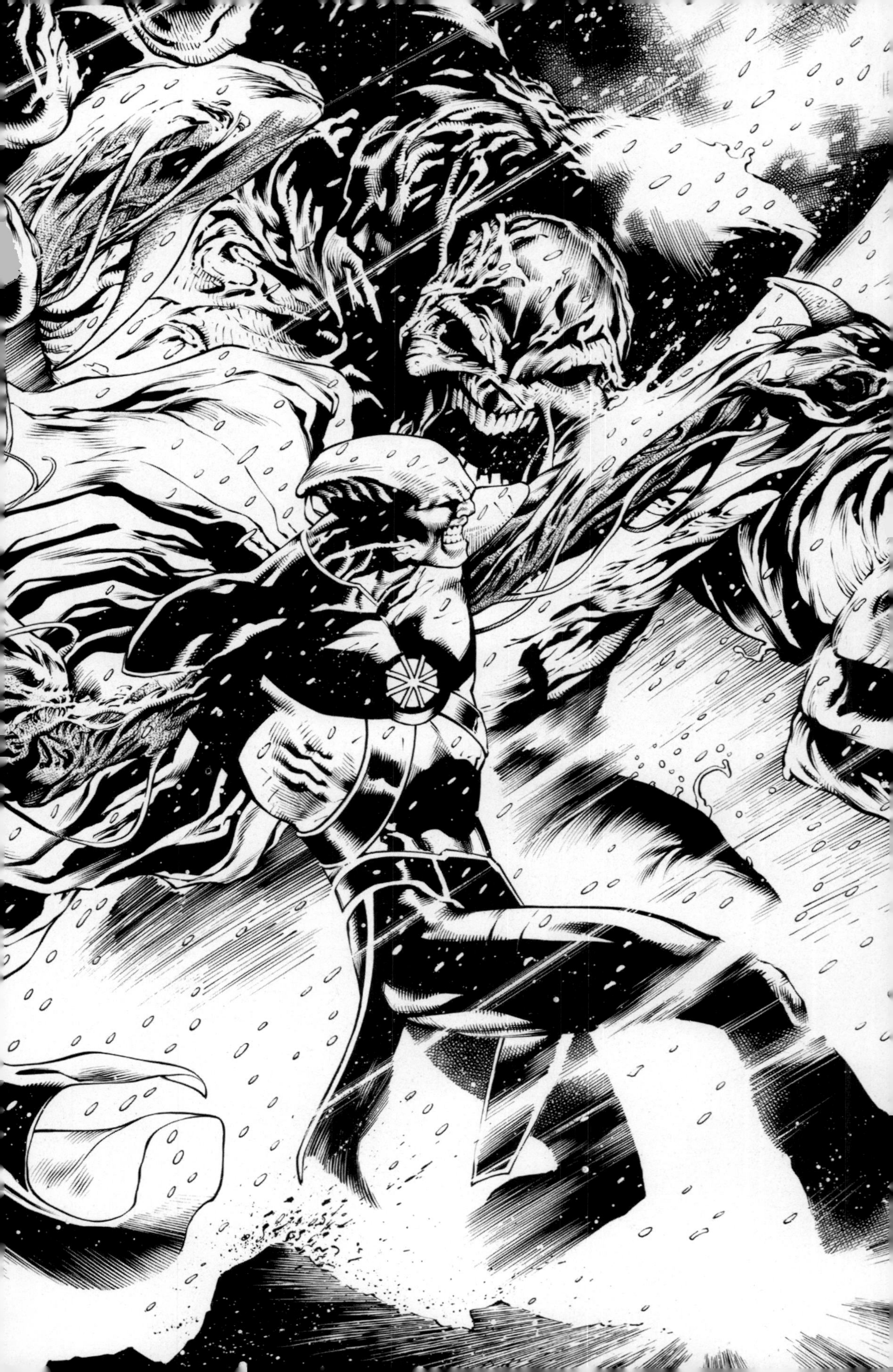

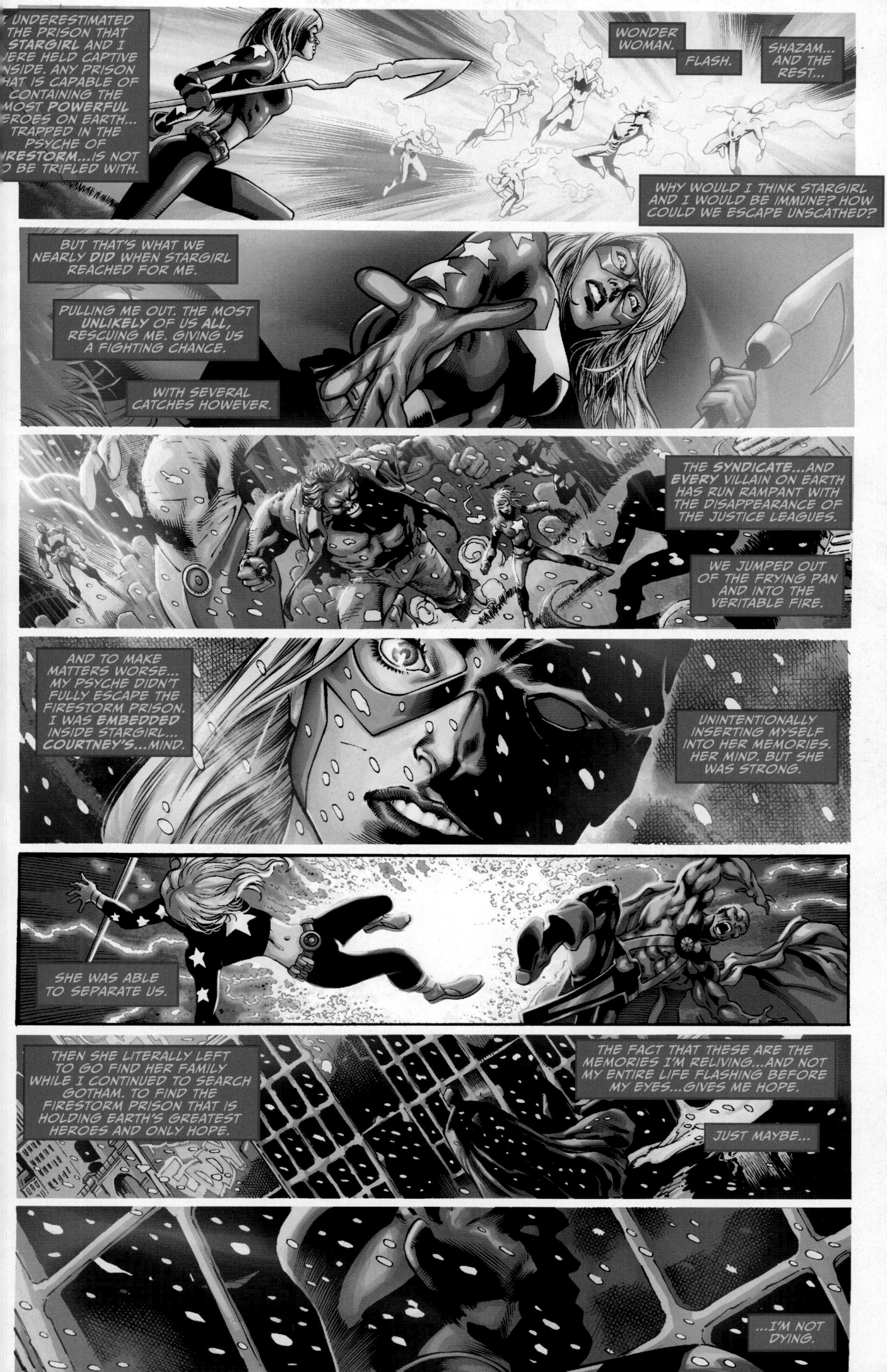

UNDERESTIMATED THE PRISON THAT STARGIRL AND I WERE HELD CAPTIVE INSIDE. ANY PRISON THAT IS CAPABLE OF CONTAINING THE MOST POWERFUL HEROES ON EARTH... TRAPPED IN THE PSYCHE OF FIRESTORM...IS NOT TO BE TRIFLED WITH.
WONDER WOMAN.
FLASH.
SHAZAM... AND THE REST...
WHY WOULD I THINK STARGIRL AND I WOULD BE IMMUNE? HOW COULD WE ESCAPE UNSCATHED?
BUT THAT'S WHAT WE NEARLY DID WHEN STARGIRL REACHED FOR ME.
PULLING ME OUT. THE MOST UNLIKELY OF US ALL, RESCUING ME. GIVING US A FIGHTING CHANCE.
WITH SEVERAL CATCHES HOWEVER.
THE SYNDICATE...AND EVERY VILLAIN ON EARTH HAS RUN RAMPANT WITH THE DISAPPEARANCE OF THE JUSTICE LEAGUES.
WE JUMPED OUT OF THE FRYING PAN AND INTO THE VERITABLE FIRE.
AND TO MAKE MATTERS WORSE... MY PSYCHE DIDN'T FULLY ESCAPE THE FIRESTORM PRISON. I WAS EMBEDDED INSIDE STARGIRL... COURTNEY'S...MIND.
UNINTENTIONALLY INSERTING MYSELF INTO HER MEMORIES. HER MIND. BUT SHE WAS STRONG.
SHE WAS ABLE TO SEPARATE US.
THEN SHE LITERALLY LEFT TO GO FIND HER FAMILY WHILE I CONTINUED TO SEARCH GOTHAM. TO FIND THE FIRESTORM PRISON THAT IS HOLDING EARTH'S GREATEST HEROES AND ONLY HOPE.
THE FACT THAT THESE ARE THE MEMORIES I'M RELIVING...AND NOT MY ENTIRE LIFE FLASHING BEFORE MY EYES...GIVES ME HOPE.
JUST MAYBE...
...I'M NOT DYING.

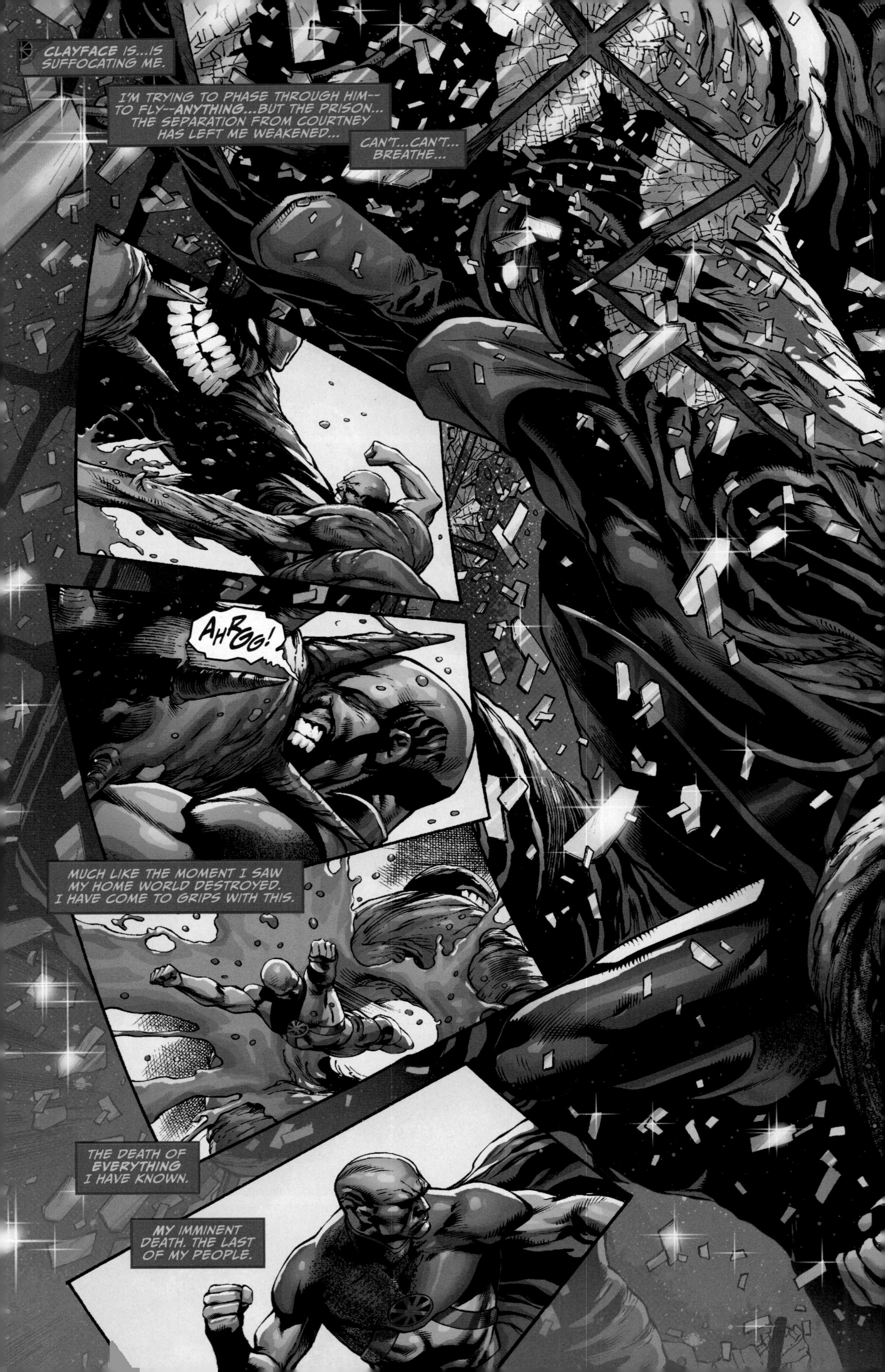
CLAYFACE IS...IS SUFFOCATING ME.
I'M TRYING TO PHASE THROUGH HIM--TO FLY--ANYTHING...BUT THE PRISON... THE SEPARATION FROM COURTNEY HAS LEFT ME WEAKENED...
CAN'T...CAN'T... BREATHE...
AHRGG!
MUCH LIKE THE MOMENT I SAW MY HOME WORLD DESTROYED. I HAVE COME TO GRIPS WITH THIS.
THE DEATH OF EVERYTHING I HAVE KNOWN.
MY IMMINENT DEATH. THE LAST OF MY PEOPLE.

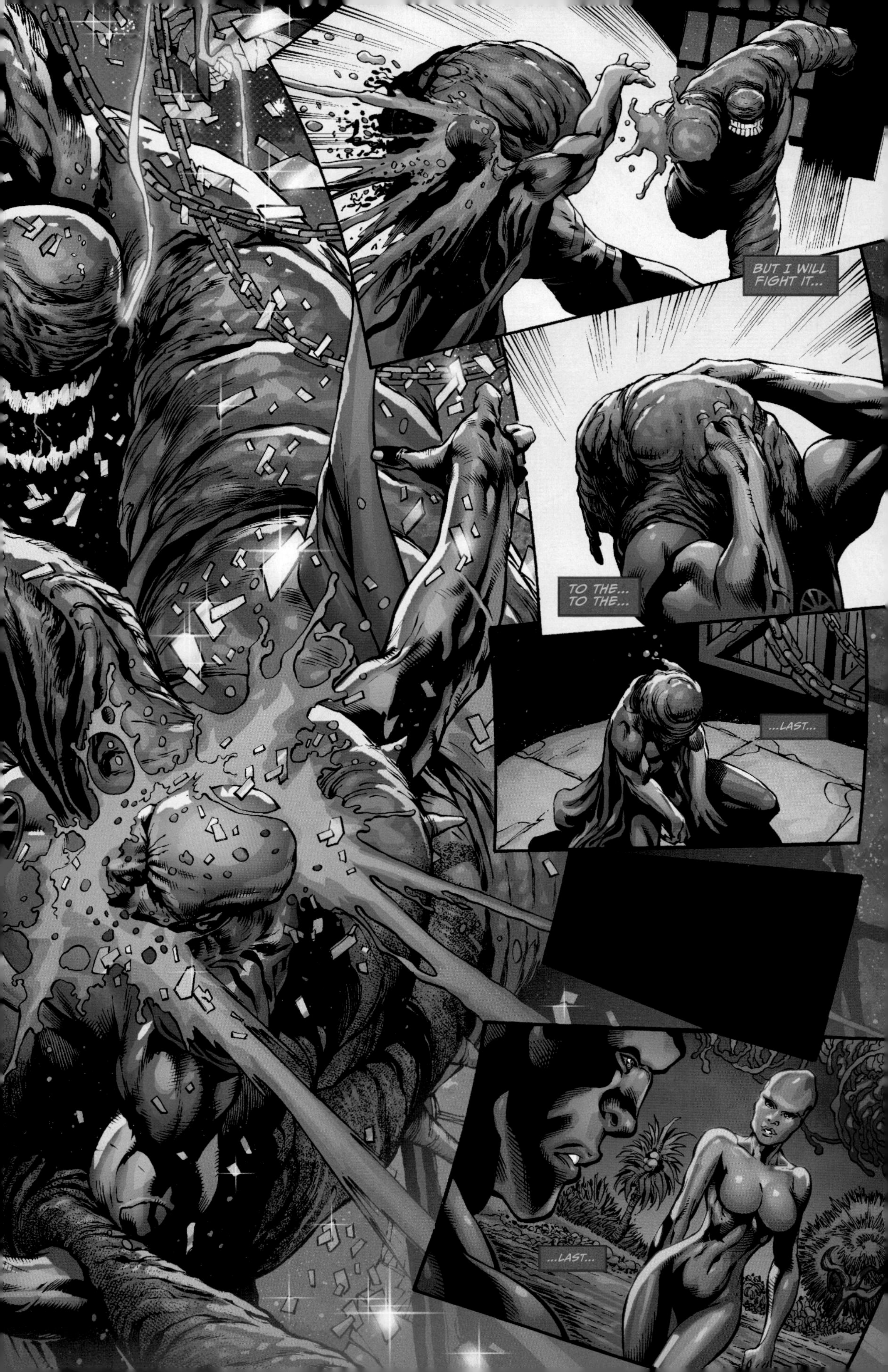
BUT I WILL FIGHT IT...
TO THE... TO THE...
...LAST...
...LAST...

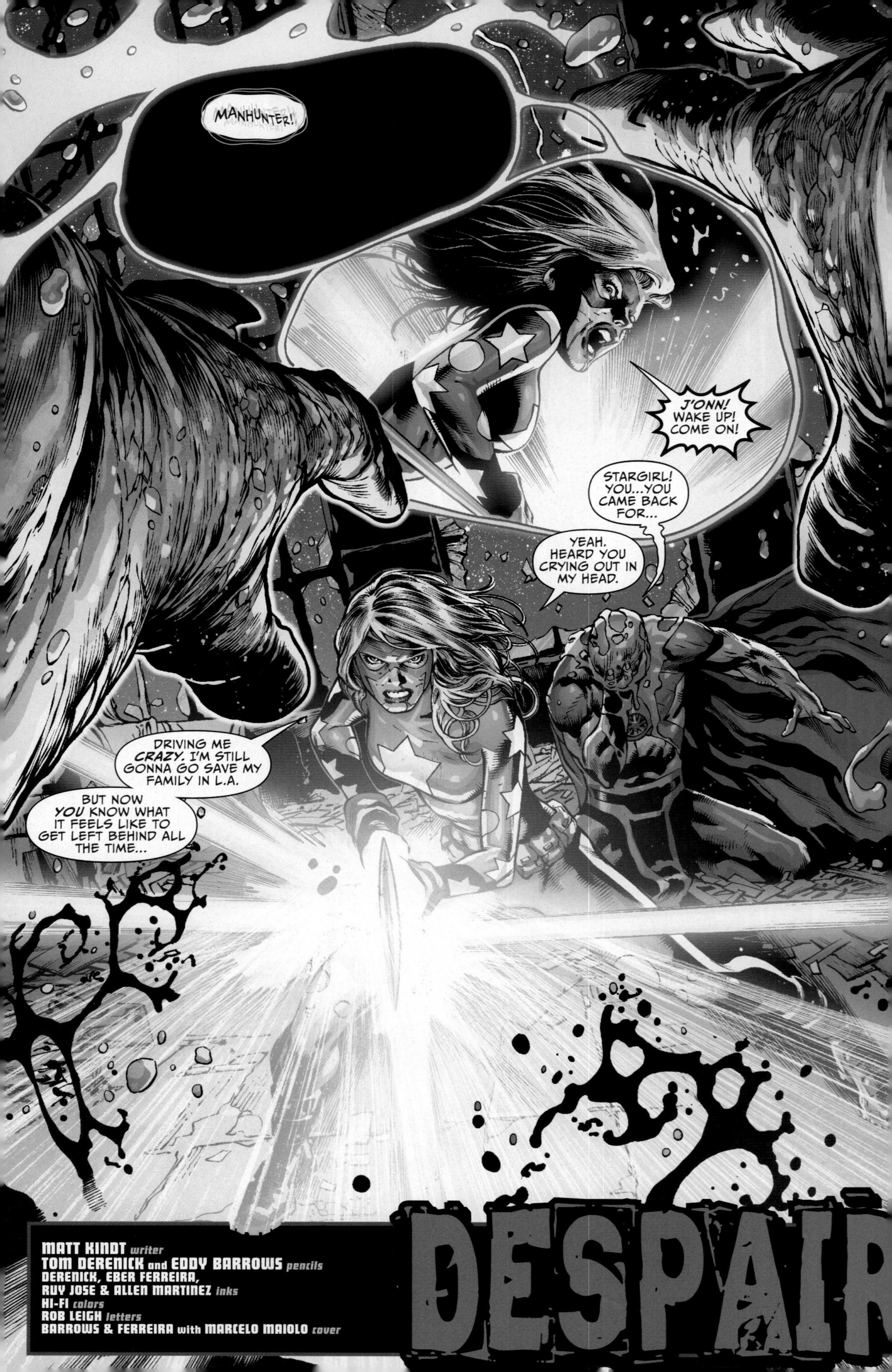

MANHUNTER!
J'ONN! WAKE UP! COME ON!
STARGIRL! YOU...YOU CAME BACK FOR...
YEAH. HEARD YOU CRYING OUT IN MY HEAD.
DRIVING ME CRAZY. I'M STILL GONNA GO SAVE MY FAMILY IN L.A.
BUT NOW YOU KNOW WHAT IT FEELS LIKE TO GET LEFT BEHIND ALL THE TIME...
DESPAIR
MATT KINDT writer
TOM DERENICK and EDDY BARROWS pencils
DERENICK, EBER FERREIRA, RUY JOSE & ALLEN MARTINEZ inks
HI-FI colors
ROB LEIGH letters
BARROWS & FERREIRA with MARCELO MAIOLO cover

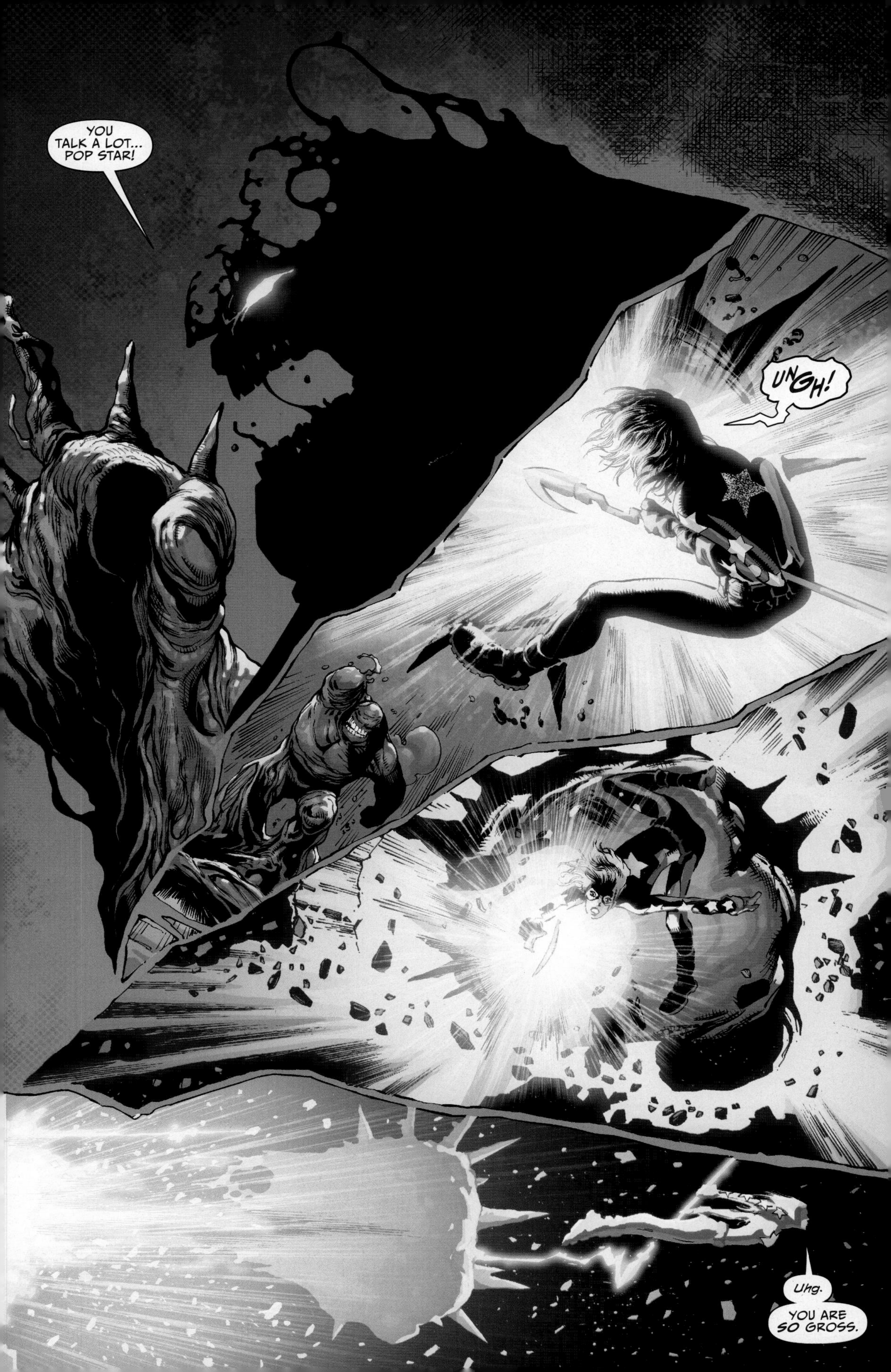
YOU TALK A LOT... POP STAR!
UNGH!
Uhg.
YOU ARE SO GROSS.

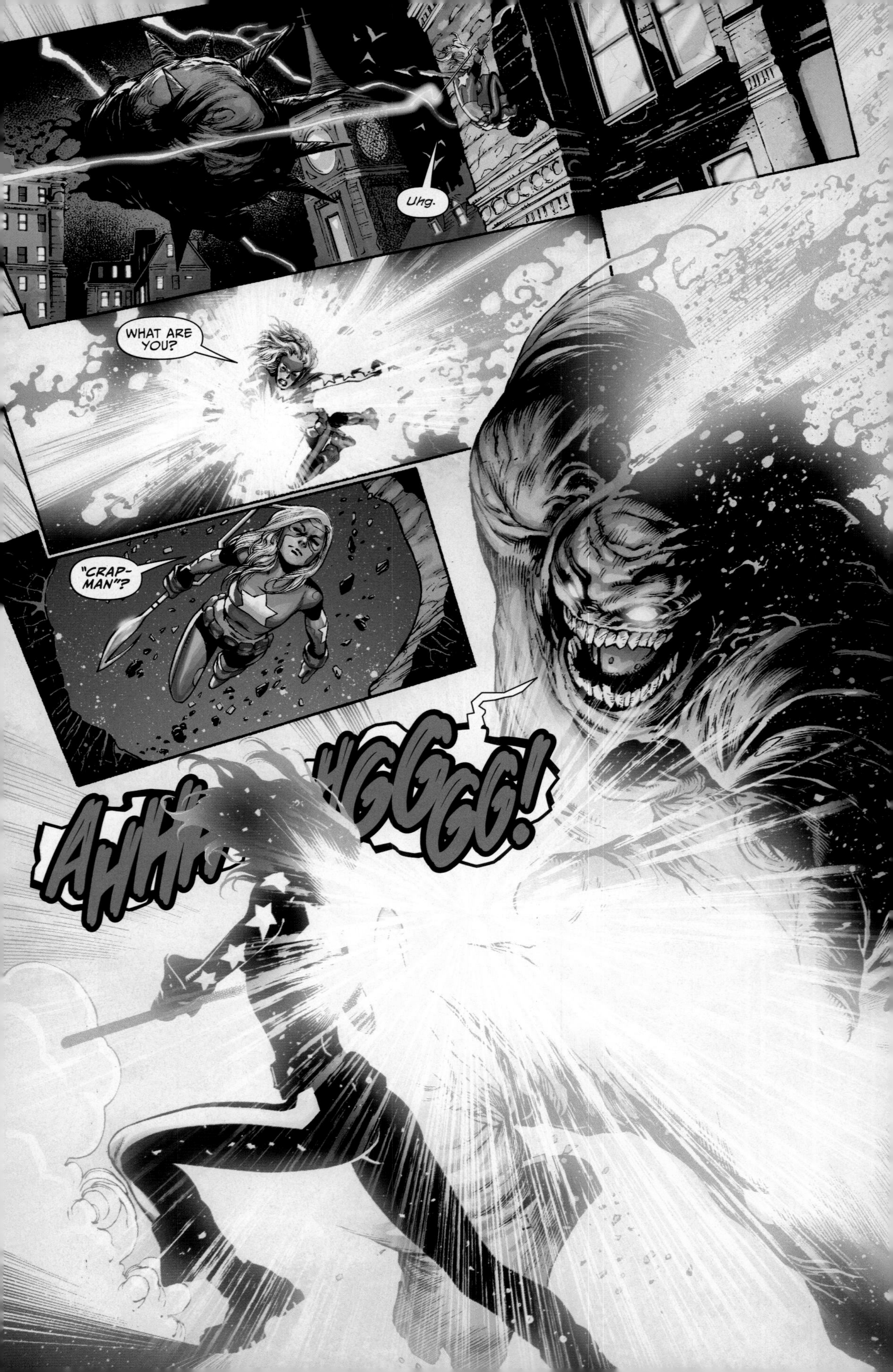
Uhg.
WHAT ARE YOU?
"CRAP-MAN"?
AHHH HGGGG!

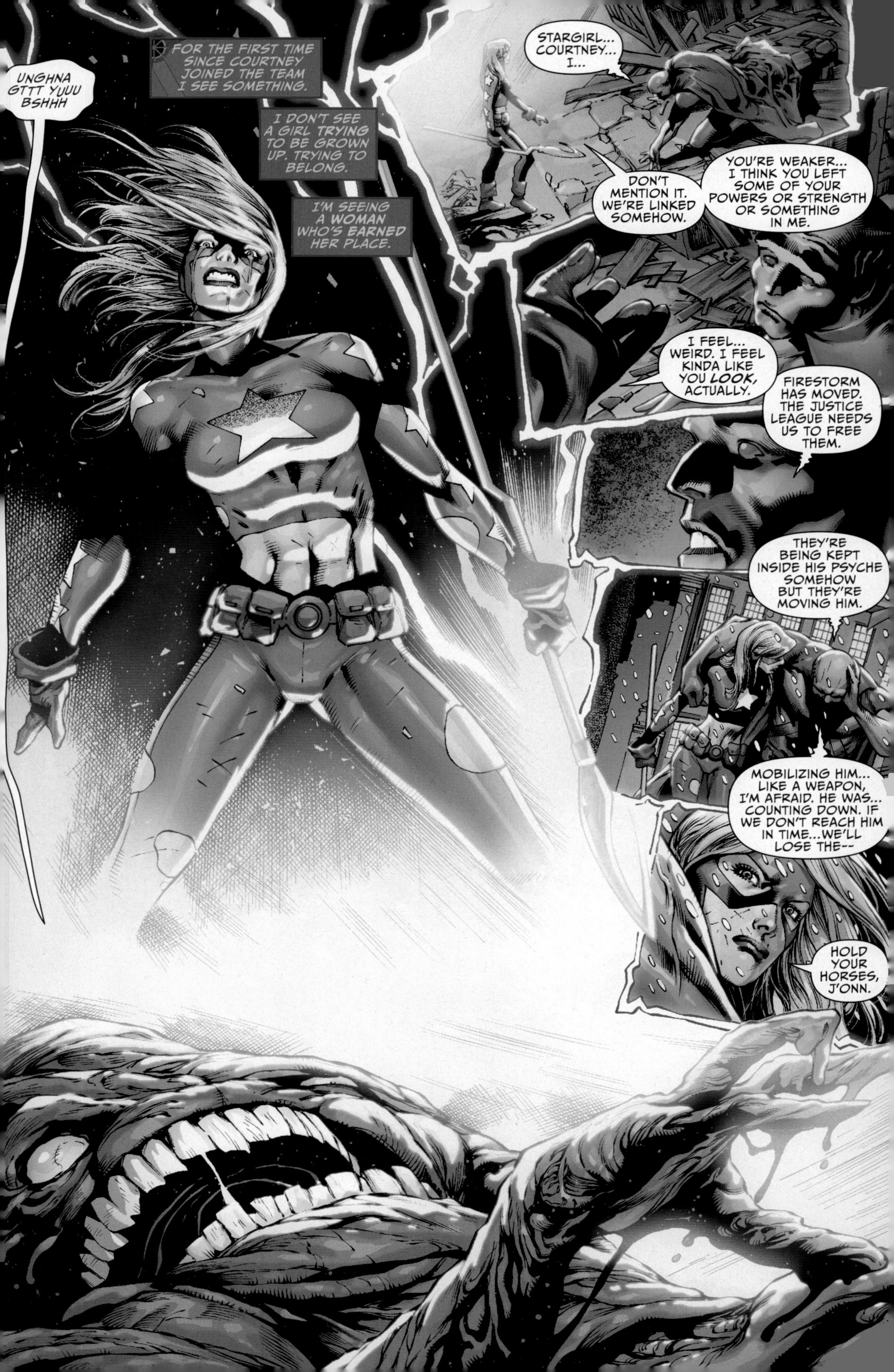
UNGHNA GTTT YUUU BSHHH
FOR THE FIRST TIME SINCE COURTNEY JOINED THE TEAM I SEE SOMETHING.
I DON'T SEE A GIRL TRYING TO BE GROWN UP. TRYING TO BELONG.
I'M SEEING A WOMAN WHO'S EARNED HER PLACE.
STARGIRL... COURTNEY... I...
DON'T MENTION IT. WE'RE LINKED SOMEHOW.
YOU'RE WEAKER... I THINK YOU LEFT SOME OF YOUR POWERS OR STRENGTH OR SOMETHING IN ME.
I FEEL... WEIRD. I FEEL KINDA LIKE YOU LOOK, ACTUALLY.
FIRESTORM HAS MOVED. THE JUSTICE LEAGUE NEEDS US TO FREE THEM.
THEY'RE BEING KEPT INSIDE HIS PSYCHE SOMEHOW BUT THEY'RE MOVING HIM.
MOBILIZING HIM... LIKE A WEAPON, I'M AFRAID. HE WAS... COUNTING DOWN. IF WE DON'T REACH HIM IN TIME...WE'LL LOSE THE--
HOLD YOUR HORSES, J'ONN.

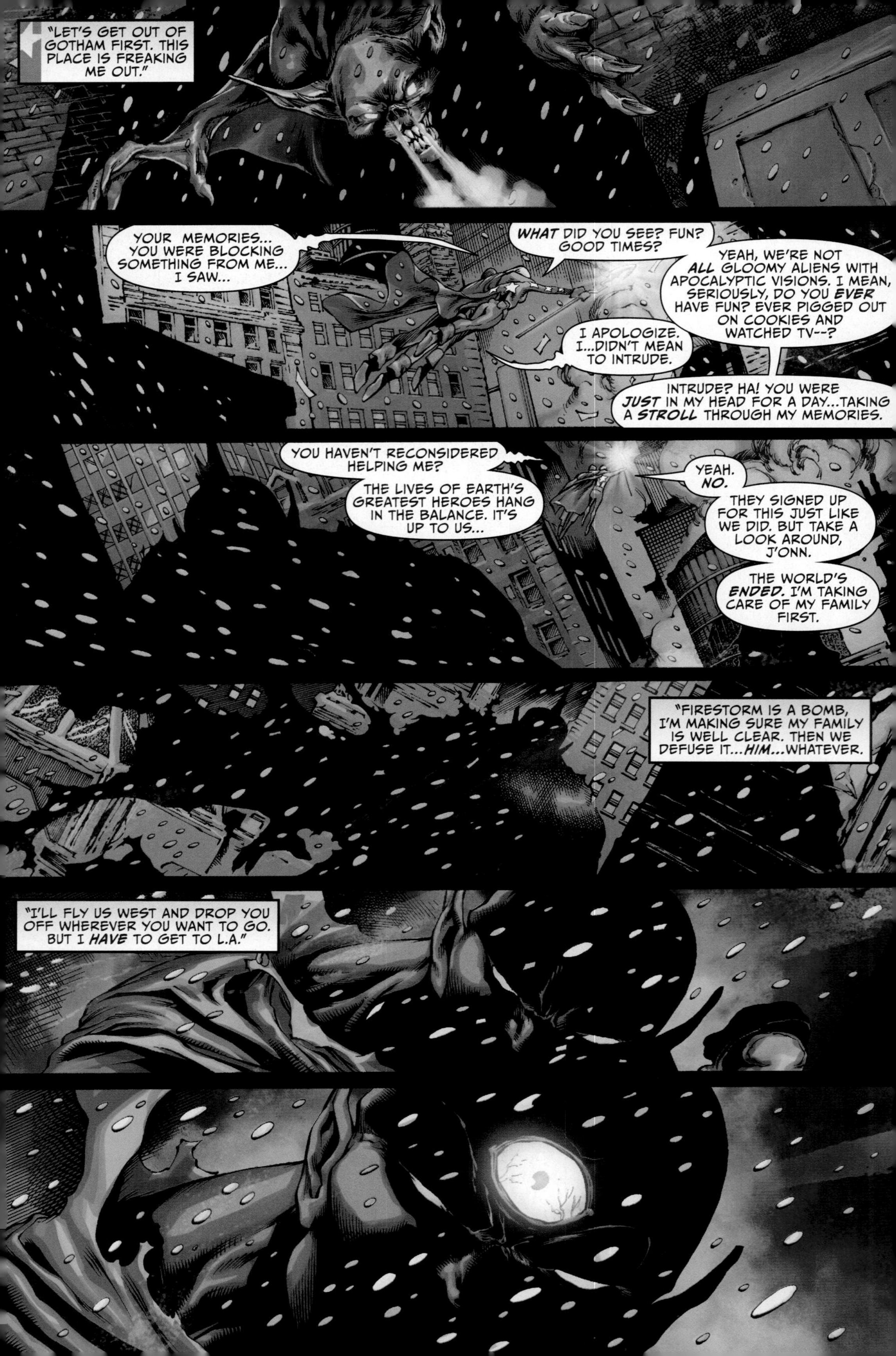
"LET'S GET OUT OF GOTHAM FIRST. THIS PLACE IS FREAKING ME OUT."
YOUR MEMORIES... YOU WERE BLOCKING SOMETHING FROM ME... I SAW...
WHAT DID YOU SEE? FUN? GOOD TIMES?
YEAH, WE'RE NOT ALL GLOOMY ALIENS WITH APOCALYPTIC VISIONS. I MEAN, SERIOUSLY, DO YOU EVER HAVE FUN? EVER PIGGED OUT ON COOKIES AND WATCHED TV--?
I APOLOGIZE. I...DIDN'T MEAN TO INTRUDE.
INTRUDE? HA! YOU WERE JUST IN MY HEAD FOR A DAY...TAKING A STROLL THROUGH MY MEMORIES.
YOU HAVEN'T RECONSIDERED HELPING ME?
THE LIVES OF EARTH'S GREATEST HEROES HANG IN THE BALANCE. IT'S UP TO US...
YEAH. NO.
THEY SIGNED UP FOR THIS JUST LIKE WE DID. BUT TAKE A LOOK AROUND, J'ONN.
THE WORLD'S ENDED. I'M TAKING CARE OF MY FAMILY FIRST.
"FIRESTORM IS A BOMB, I'M MAKING SURE MY FAMILY IS WELL CLEAR. THEN WE DEFUSE IT...HIM...WHATEVER.
"I'LL FLY US WEST AND DROP YOU OFF WHEREVER YOU WANT TO GO. BUT I HAVE TO GET TO L.A."

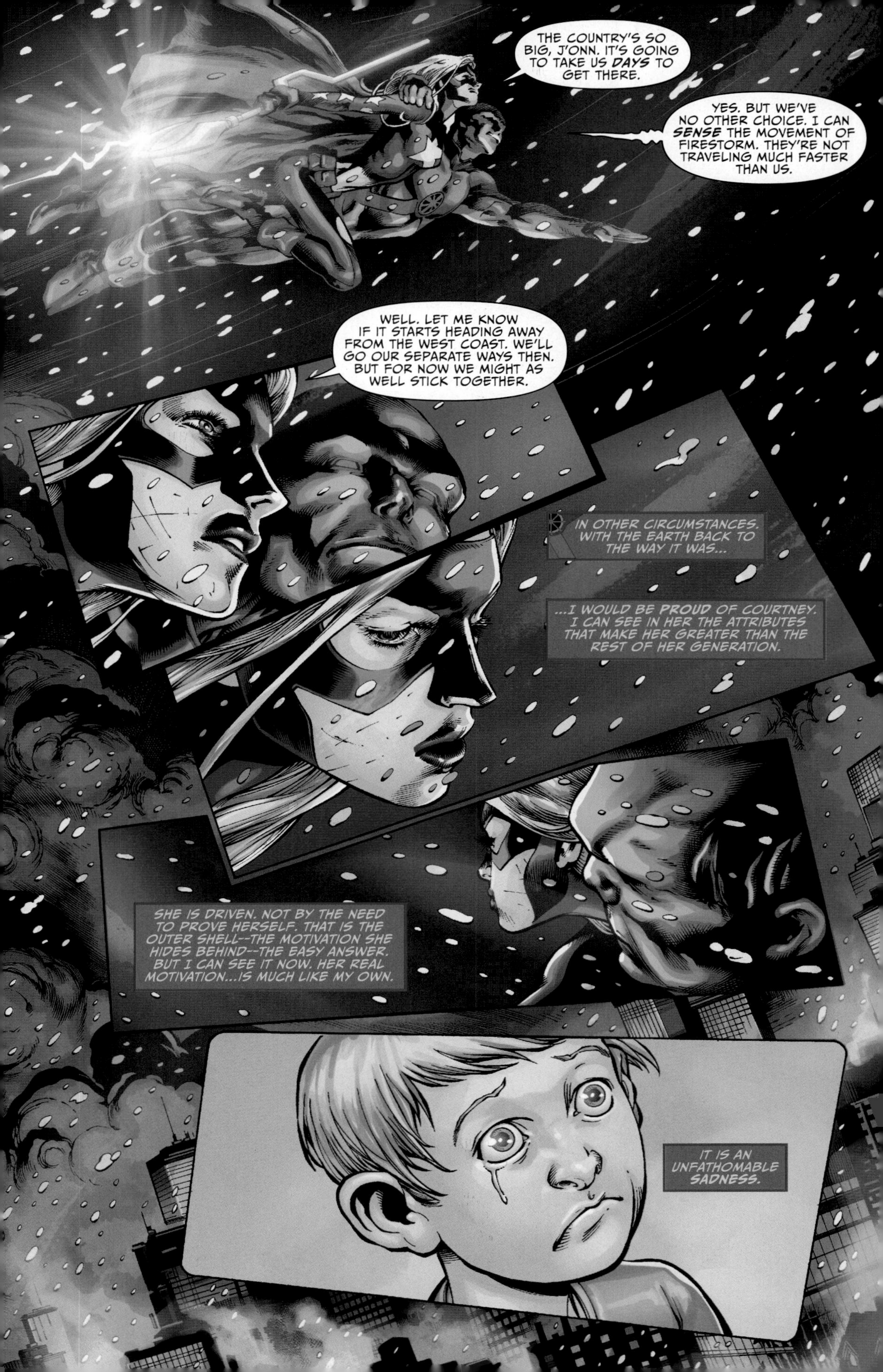

THE COUNTRY'S SO BIG, J'ONN. IT'S GOING TO TAKE US *DAYS* TO GET THERE.
YES. BUT WE'VE NO OTHER CHOICE. I CAN *SENSE* THE MOVEMENT OF FIRESTORM. THEY'RE NOT TRAVELING MUCH FASTER THAN US.
WELL. LET ME KNOW IF IT STARTS HEADING AWAY FROM THE WEST COAST. WE'LL GO OUR SEPARATE WAYS THEN. BUT FOR NOW WE MIGHT AS WELL STICK TOGETHER.
IN OTHER CIRCUMSTANCES. WITH THE EARTH BACK TO THE WAY IT WAS...
...I WOULD BE *PROUD* OF COURTNEY. I CAN SEE IN HER THE ATTRIBUTES THAT MAKE HER GREATER THAN THE REST OF HER GENERATION.
SHE IS DRIVEN. NOT BY THE NEED TO PROVE HERSELF. THAT IS THE OUTER SHELL--THE MOTIVATION SHE HIDES BEHIND--THE EASY ANSWER. BUT I CAN SEE IT NOW. HER REAL MOTIVATION...IS MUCH LIKE MY OWN.
IT IS AN UNFATHOMABLE *SADNESS.*

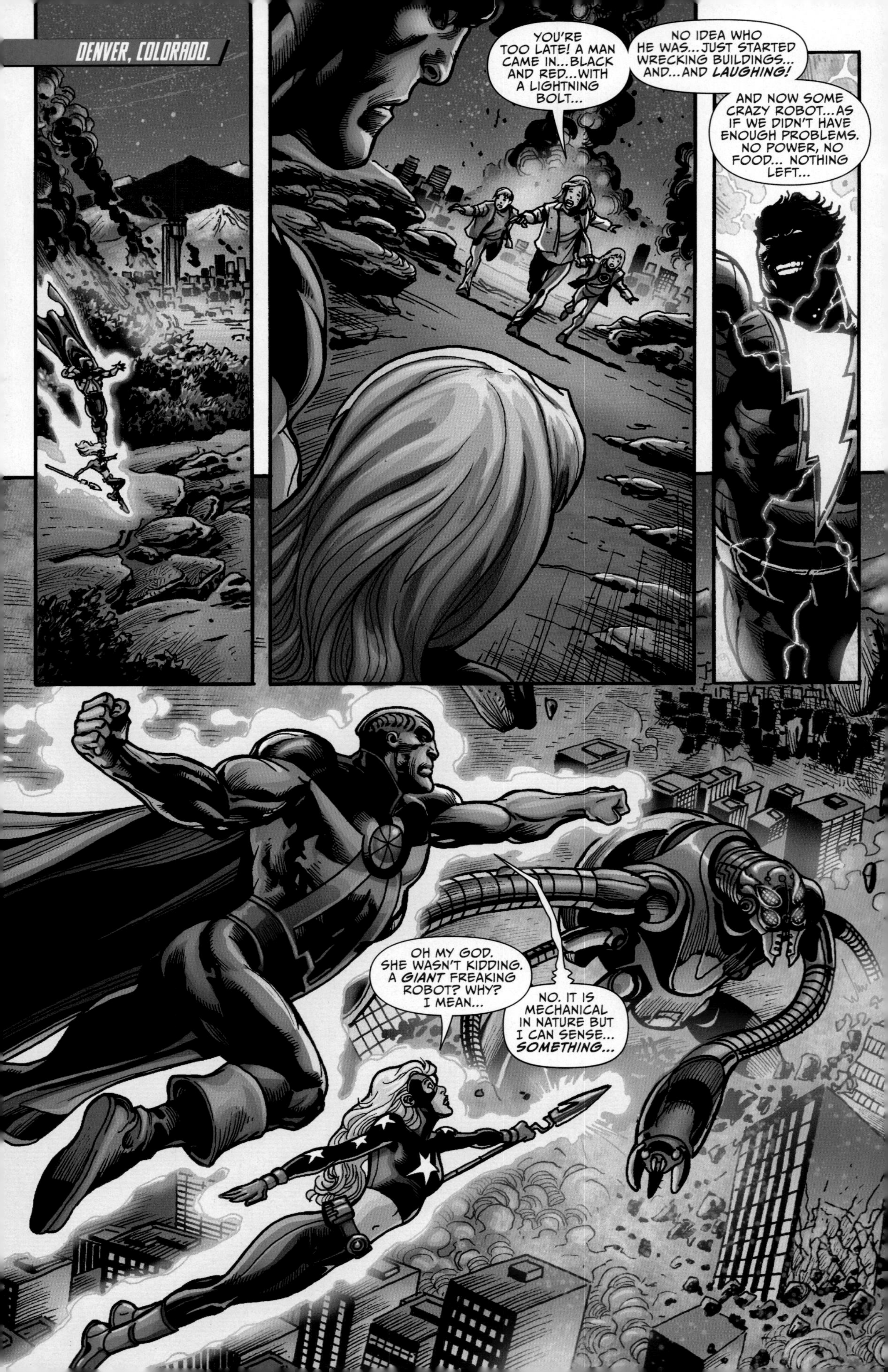
DENVER, COLORADO.
YOU'RE TOO LATE! A MAN CAME IN...BLACK AND RED...WITH A LIGHTNING BOLT...
NO IDEA WHO HE WAS...JUST STARTED WRECKING BUILDINGS... AND...AND LAUGHING!
AND NOW SOME CRAZY ROBOT...AS IF WE DIDN'T HAVE ENOUGH PROBLEMS. NO POWER, NO FOOD... NOTHING LEFT...
OH MY GOD. SHE WASN'T KIDDING. A GIANT FREAKING ROBOT? WHY? I MEAN...
NO. IT IS MECHANICAL IN NATURE BUT I CAN SENSE... SOMETHING...

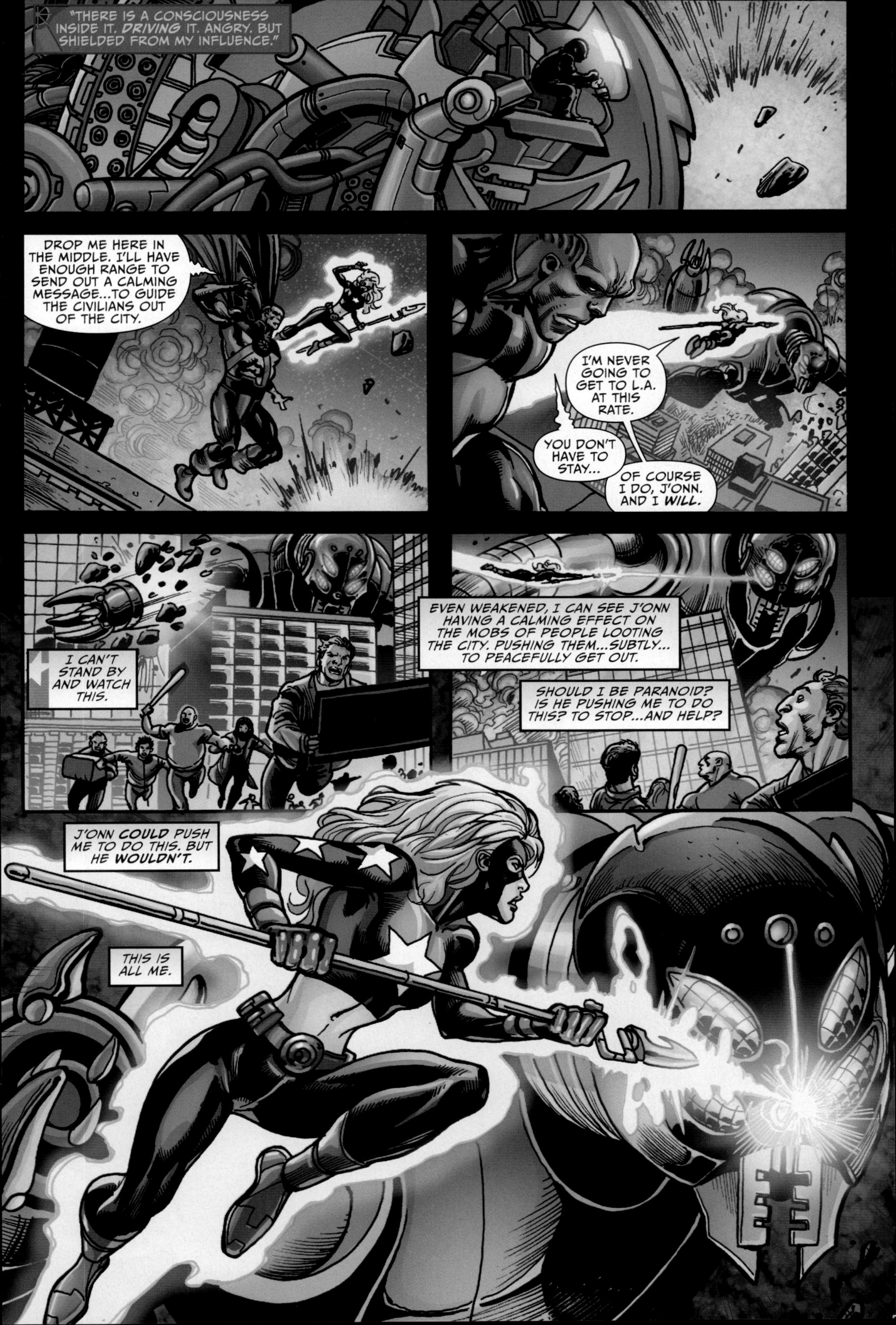
"THERE IS A CONSCIOUSNESS INSIDE IT. DRIVING IT. ANGRY. BUT SHIELDED FROM MY INFLUENCE."
DROP ME HERE IN THE MIDDLE. I'LL HAVE ENOUGH RANGE TO SEND OUT A CALMING MESSAGE...TO GUIDE THE CIVILIANS OUT OF THE CITY.
I'M NEVER GOING TO GET TO L.A. AT THIS RATE.
YOU DON'T HAVE TO STAY...
OF COURSE I DO, J'ONN. AND I WILL.
I CAN'T STAND BY AND WATCH THIS.
EVEN WEAKENED, I CAN SEE J'ONN HAVING A CALMING EFFECT ON THE MOBS OF PEOPLE LOOTING THE CITY. PUSHING THEM...SUBTLY... TO PEACEFULLY GET OUT.
SHOULD I BE PARANOID? IS HE PUSHING ME TO DO THIS? TO STOP...AND HELP?
J'ONN COULD PUSH ME TO DO THIS. BUT HE WOULDN'T.
THIS IS ALL ME.

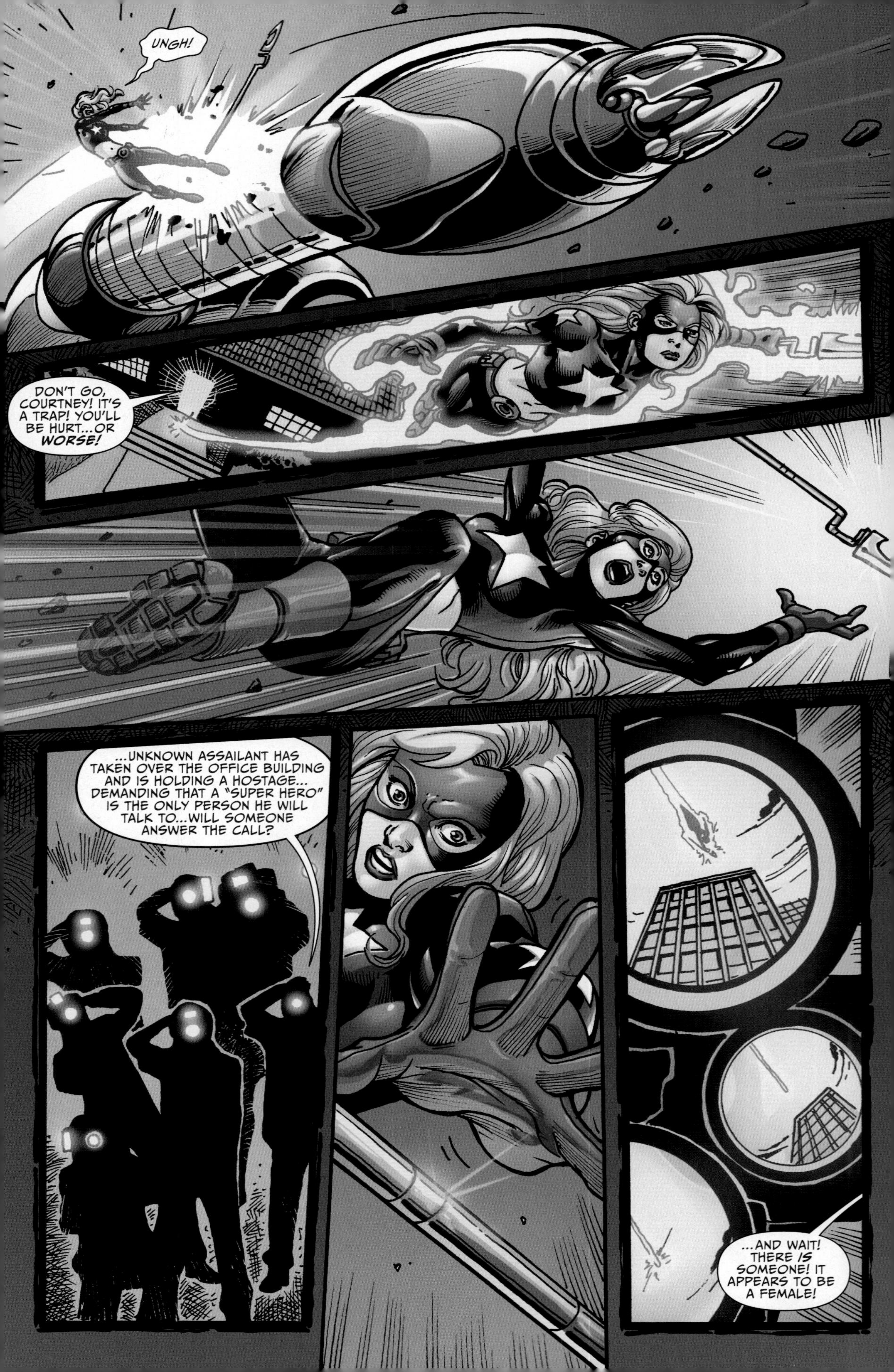
UNGH!
DON'T GO, COURTNEY! IT'S A TRAP! YOU'LL BE HURT...OR WORSE!
...UNKNOWN ASSAILANT HAS TAKEN OVER THE OFFICE BUILDING AND IS HOLDING A HOSTAGE... DEMANDING THAT A "SUPER HERO" IS THE ONLY PERSON HE WILL TALK TO...WILL SOMEONE ANSWER THE CALL?
...AND WAIT! THERE IS SOMEONE! IT APPEARS TO BE A FEMALE!

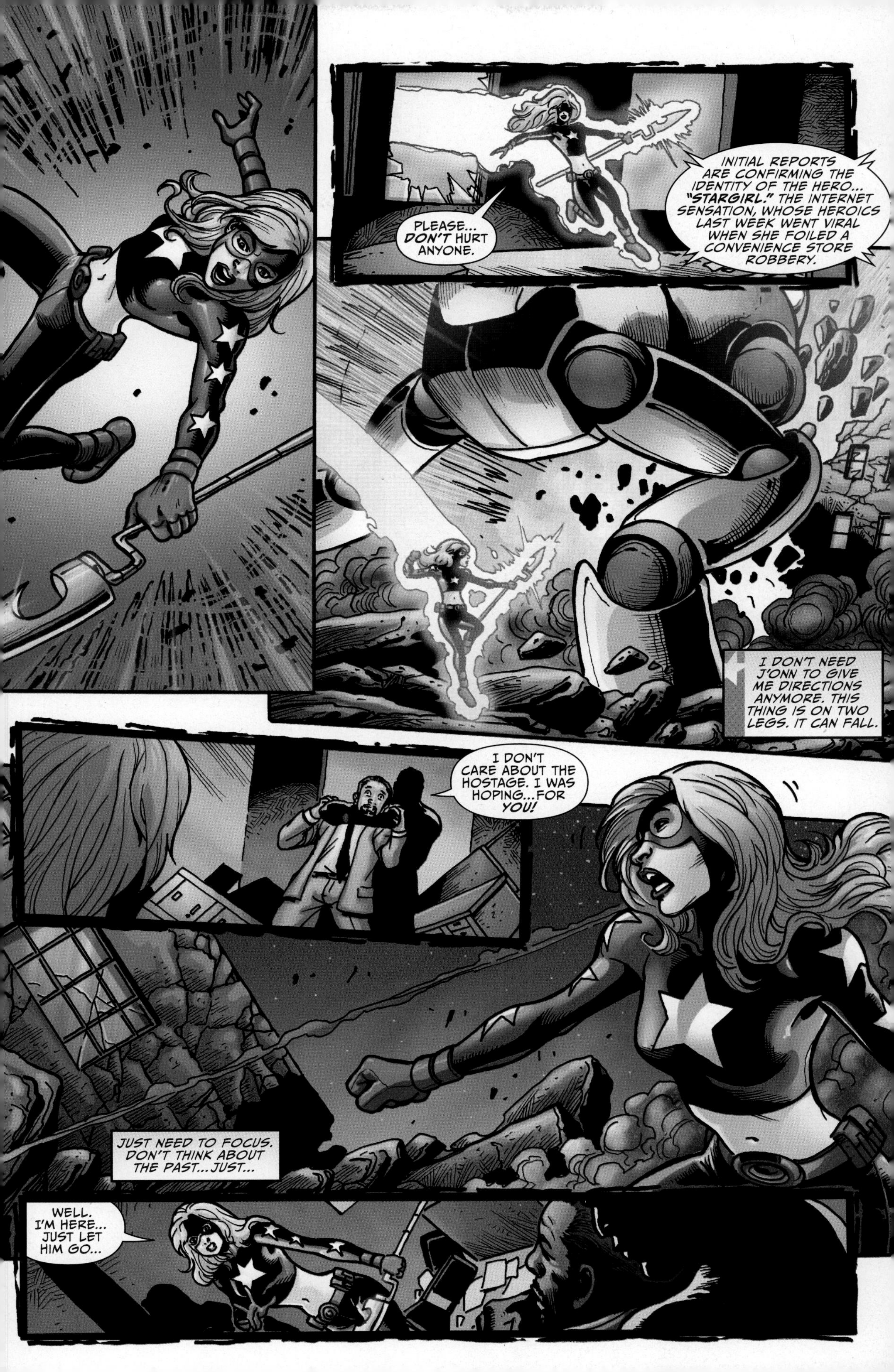
PLEASE... DON'T HURT ANYONE.
INITIAL REPORTS ARE CONFIRMING THE IDENTITY OF THE HERO... "STARGIRL." THE INTERNET SENSATION, WHOSE HEROICS LAST WEEK WENT VIRAL WHEN SHE FOILED A CONVENIENCE STORE ROBBERY.
I DON'T NEED J'ONN TO GIVE ME DIRECTIONS ANYMORE. THIS THING IS ON TWO LEGS. IT CAN FALL.
I DON'T CARE ABOUT THE HOSTAGE. I WAS HOPING...FOR YOU!
JUST NEED TO FOCUS. DON'T THINK ABOUT THE PAST...JUST...
WELL. I'M HERE... JUST LET HIM GO...

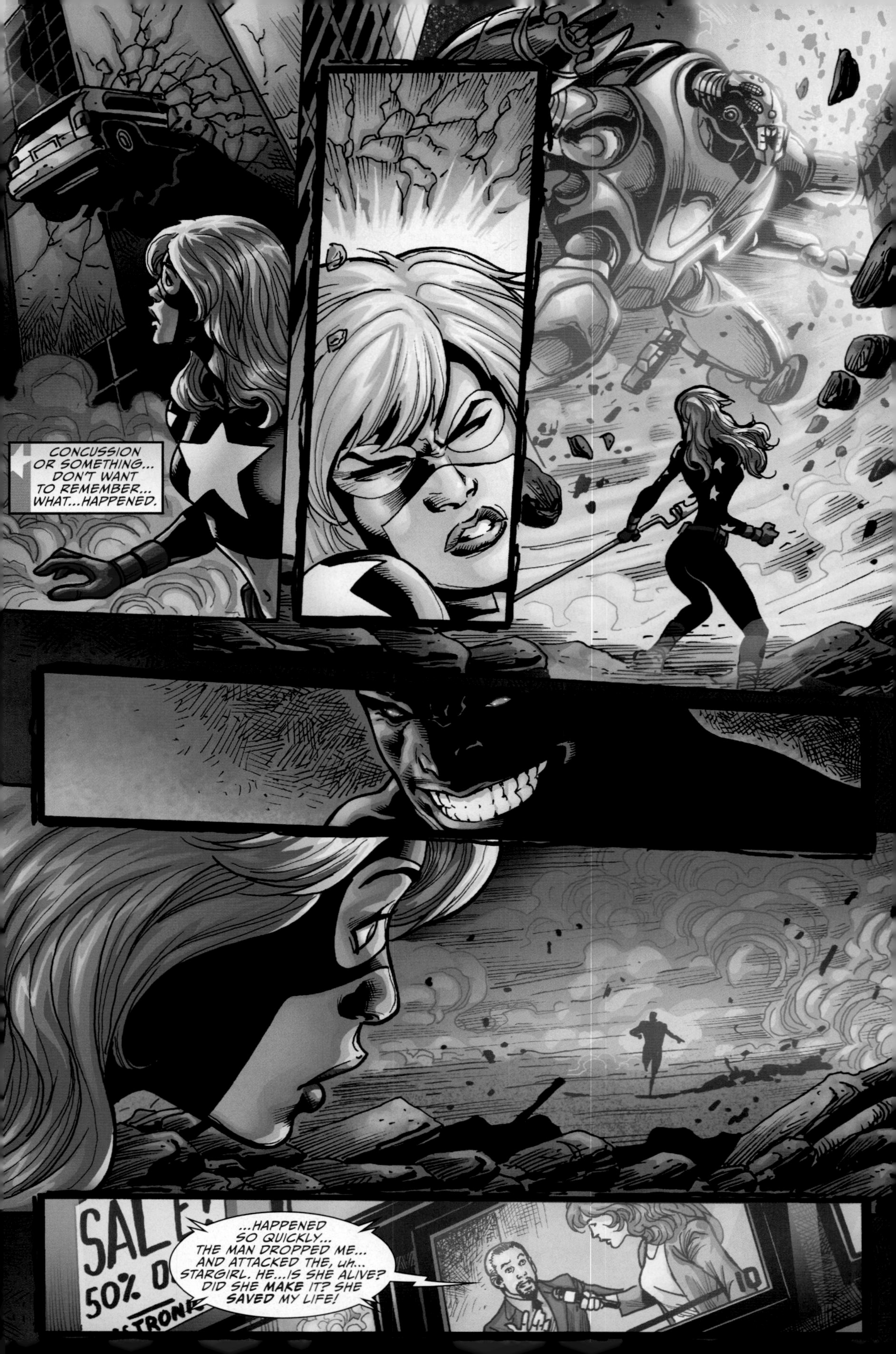
CONCUSSION OR SOMETHING... DON'T WANT TO REMEMBER... WHAT...HAPPENED.
SALE!
50% O
...HAPPENED SO QUICKLY... THE MAN DROPPED ME... AND ATTACKED THE, uh... STARGIRL. HE...IS SHE ALIVE? DID SHE MAKE IT? SHE SAVED MY LIFE!

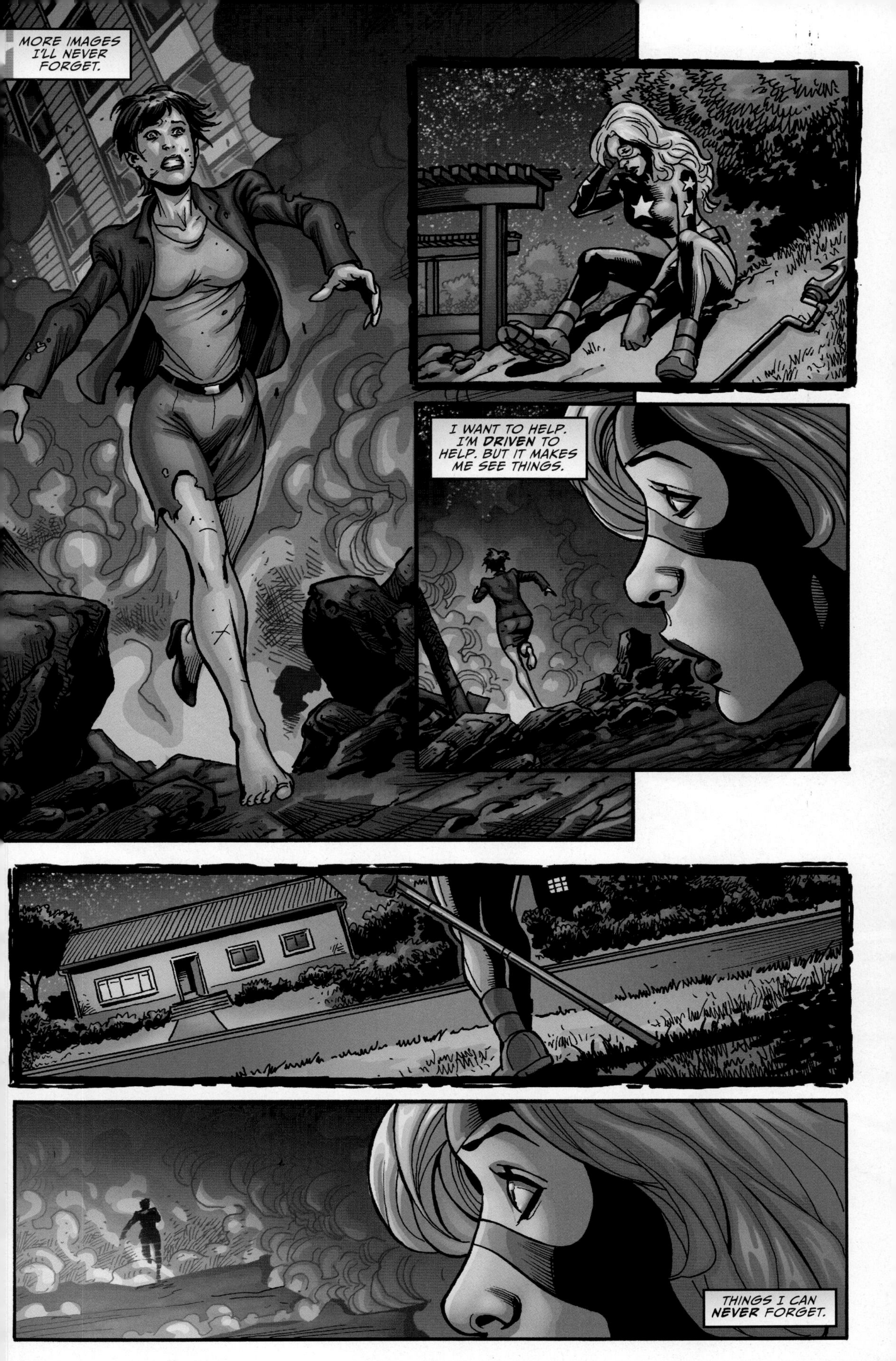
MORE IMAGES I'LL NEVER FORGET.
I WANT TO HELP. I'M DRIVEN TO HELP. BUT IT MAKES ME SEE THINGS.
THINGS I CAN NEVER FORGET.

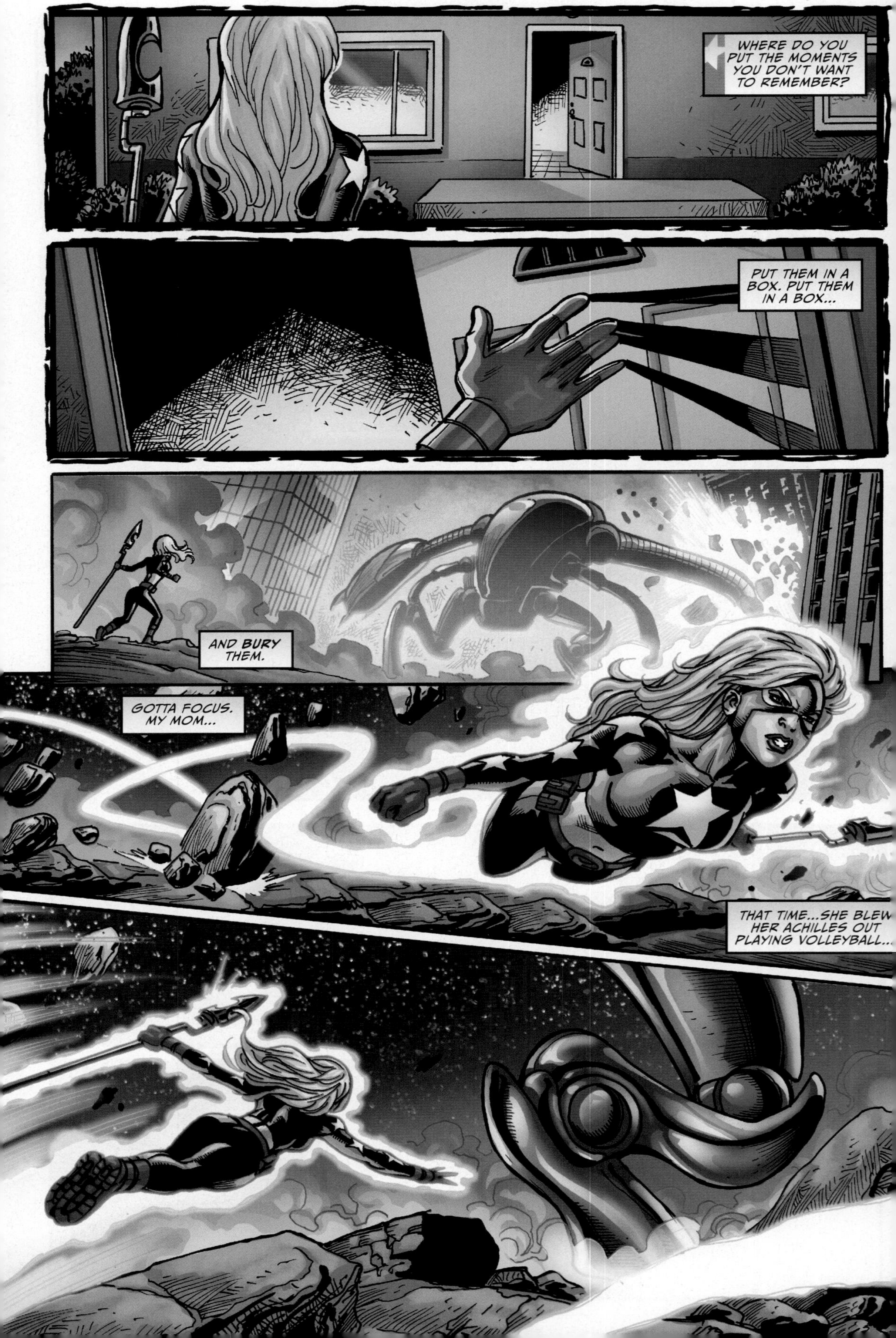
WHERE DO YOU PUT THE MOMENTS YOU DON'T WANT TO REMEMBER?
PUT THEM IN A BOX. PUT THEM IN A BOX...
AND BURY THEM.
GOTTA FOCUS. MY MOM...
THAT TIME...SHE BLEW HER ACHILLES OUT PLAYING VOLLEYBALL...

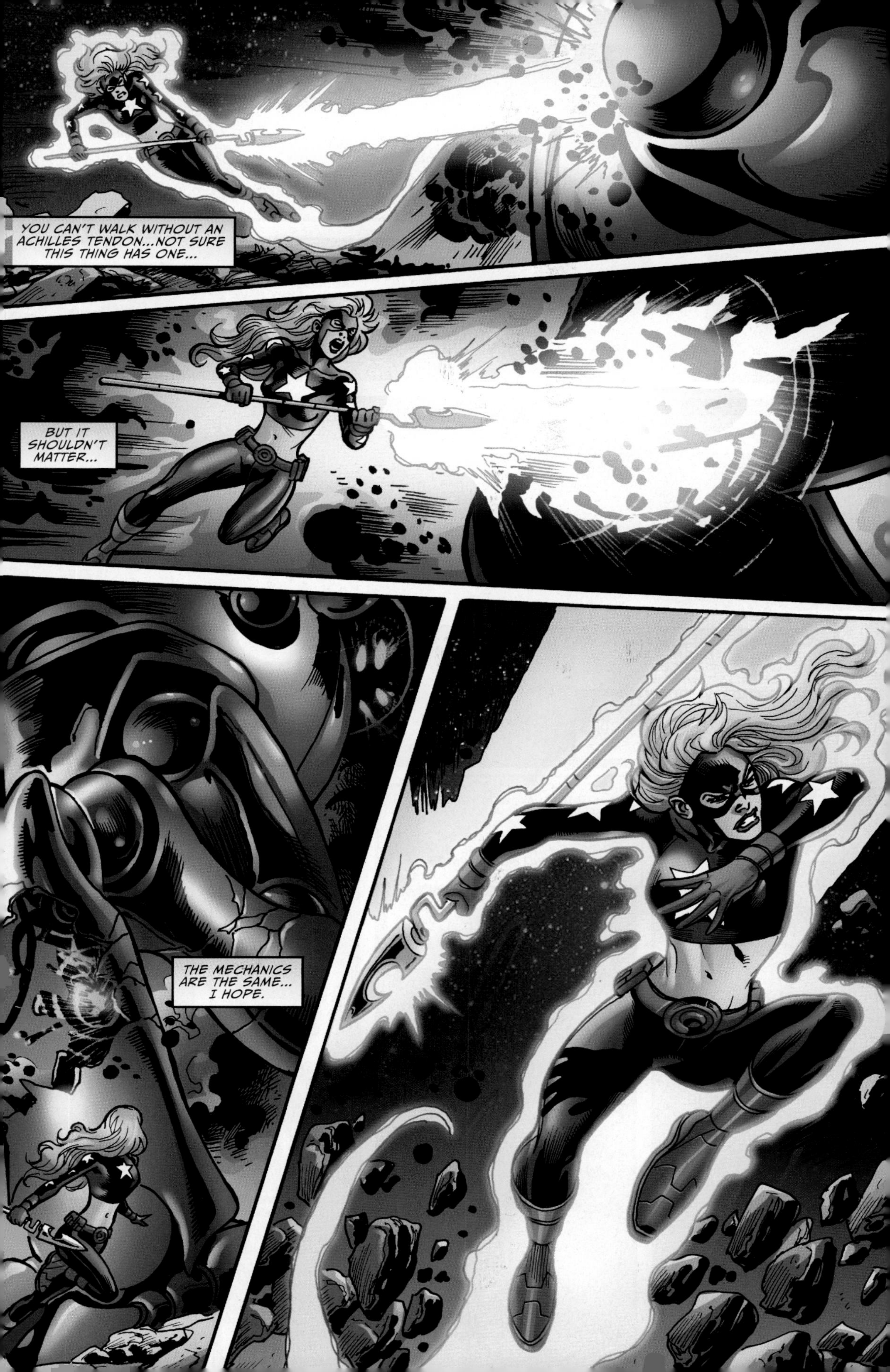
YOU CAN'T WALK WITHOUT AN ACHILLES TENDON...NOT SURE THIS THING HAS ONE...
BUT IT SHOULDN'T MATTER...
THE MECHANICS ARE THE SAME... I HOPE.

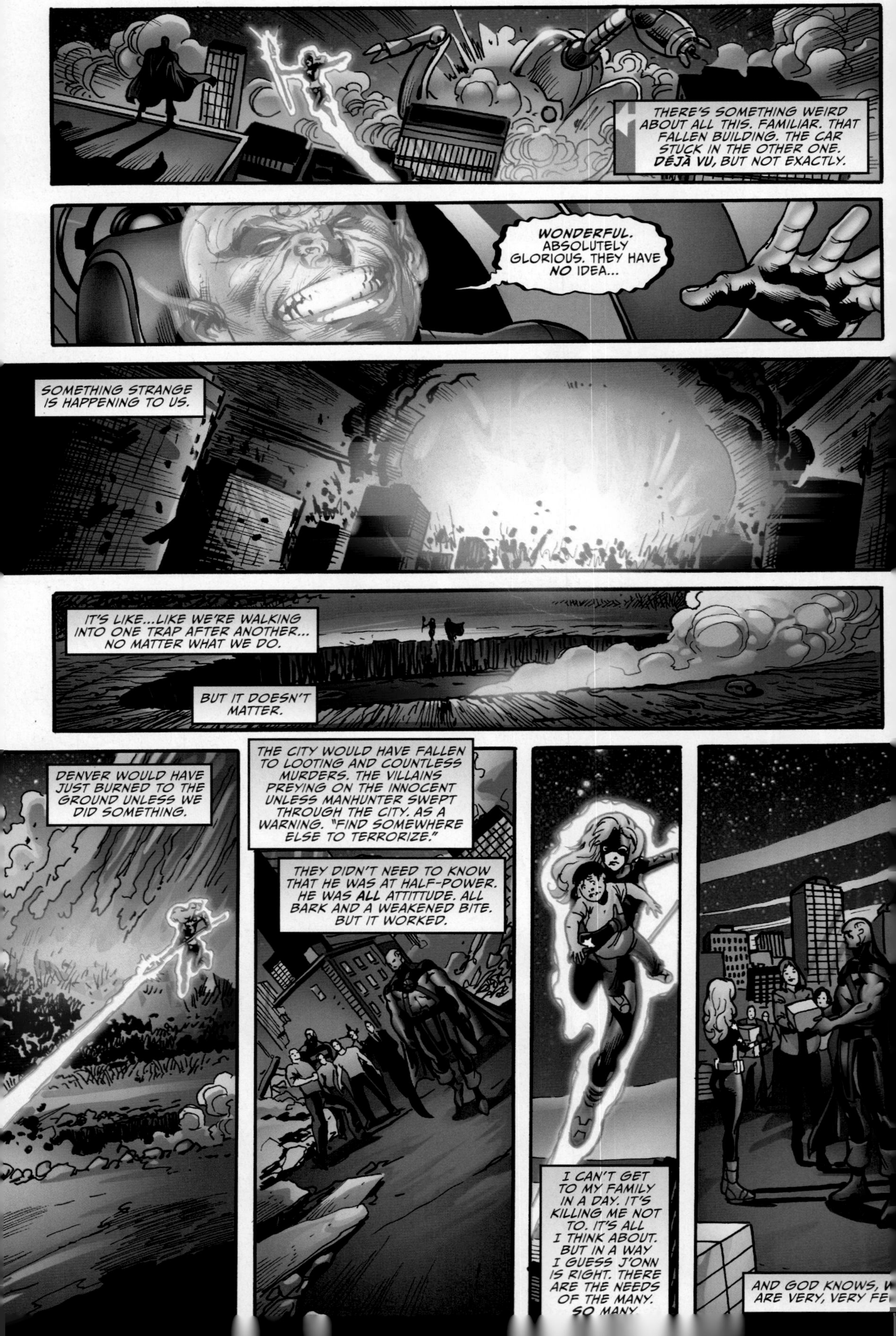

THERE'S SOMETHING WEIRD ABOUT ALL THIS. FAMILIAR. THAT FALLEN BUILDING. THE CAR STUCK IN THE OTHER ONE. DÉJÀ VU, BUT NOT EXACTLY.
WONDERFUL. ABSOLUTELY GLORIOUS. THEY HAVE NO IDEA...
SOMETHING STRANGE IS HAPPENING TO US.
IT'S LIKE...LIKE WE'RE WALKING INTO ONE TRAP AFTER ANOTHER... NO MATTER WHAT WE DO.
BUT IT DOESN'T MATTER.
DENVER WOULD HAVE JUST BURNED TO THE GROUND UNLESS WE DID SOMETHING.
THE CITY WOULD HAVE FALLEN TO LOOTING AND COUNTLESS MURDERS. THE VILLAINS PREYING ON THE INNOCENT UNLESS MANHUNTER SWEPT THROUGH THE CITY. AS A WARNING. "FIND SOMEWHERE ELSE TO TERRORIZE."
THEY DIDN'T NEED TO KNOW THAT HE WAS AT HALF-POWER. HE WAS ALL ATTITTUDE. ALL BARK AND A WEAKENED BITE. BUT IT WORKED.
I CAN'T GET TO MY FAMILY IN A DAY. IT'S KILLING ME NOT TO. IT'S ALL I THINK ABOUT. BUT IN A WAY I GUESS J'ONN IS RIGHT. THERE ARE THE NEEDS OF THE MANY. SO MANY.
AND GOD KNOWS, W ARE VERY, VERY FE

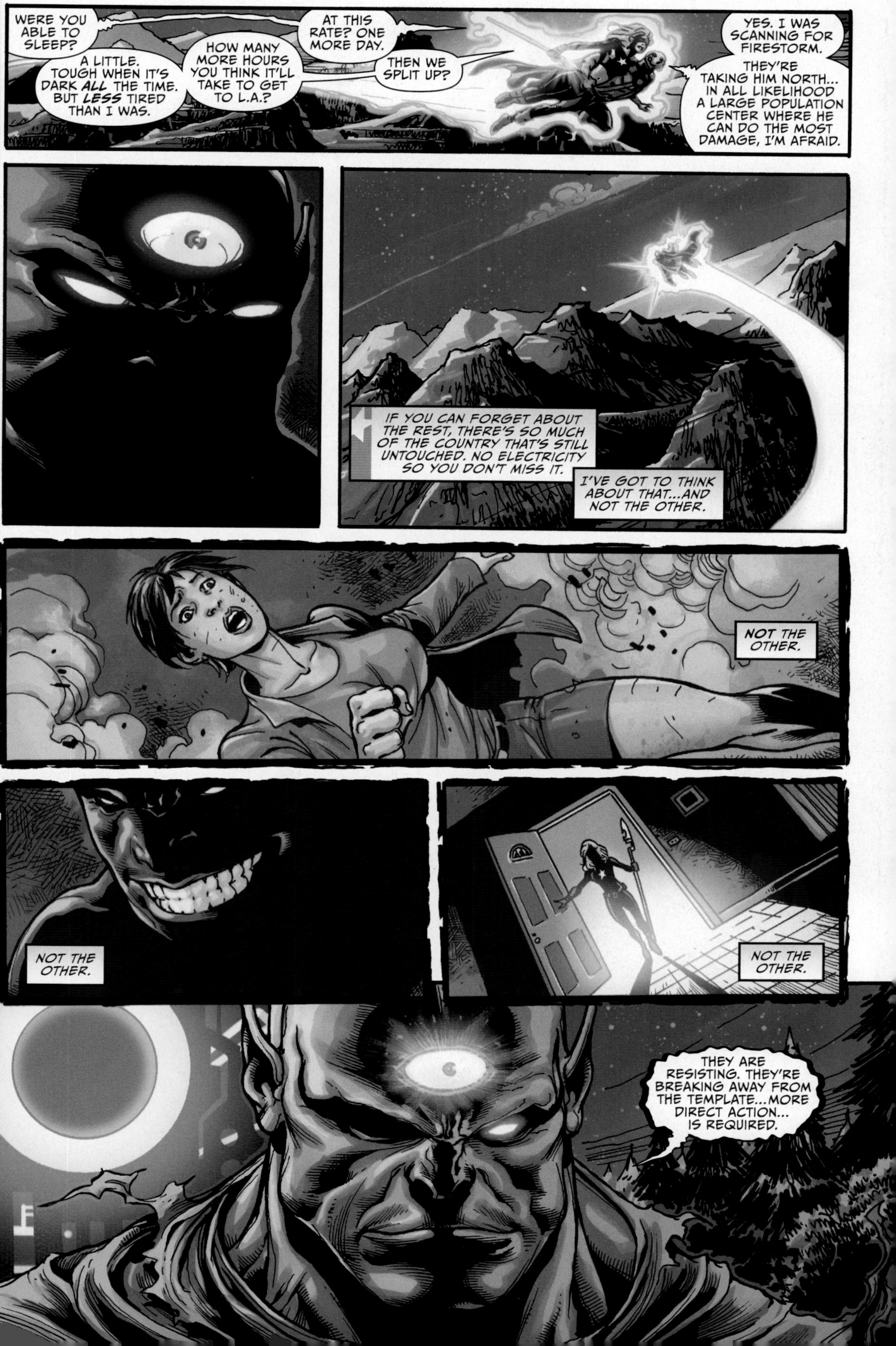
WERE YOU ABLE TO SLEEP?
A LITTLE. TOUGH WHEN IT'S DARK *ALL* THE TIME. BUT *LESS* TIRED THAN I WAS.
HOW MANY MORE HOURS YOU THINK IT'LL TAKE TO GET TO L.A.?
AT THIS RATE? ONE MORE DAY.
THEN WE SPLIT UP?
YES. I WAS SCANNING FOR FIRESTORM.
THEY'RE TAKING HIM NORTH... IN ALL LIKELIHOOD A LARGE POPULATION CENTER WHERE HE CAN DO THE MOST DAMAGE, I'M AFRAID.
IF YOU CAN FORGET ABOUT THE REST, THERE'S SO MUCH OF THE COUNTRY THAT'S STILL UNTOUCHED. NO ELECTRICITY SO YOU DON'T MISS IT.
I'VE GOT TO THINK ABOUT THAT...AND NOT THE OTHER.
NOT THE OTHER.
NOT THE OTHER.
NOT THE OTHER.
THEY ARE RESISTING. THEY'RE BREAKING AWAY FROM THE TEMPLATE...MORE DIRECT ACTION... IS REQUIRED.

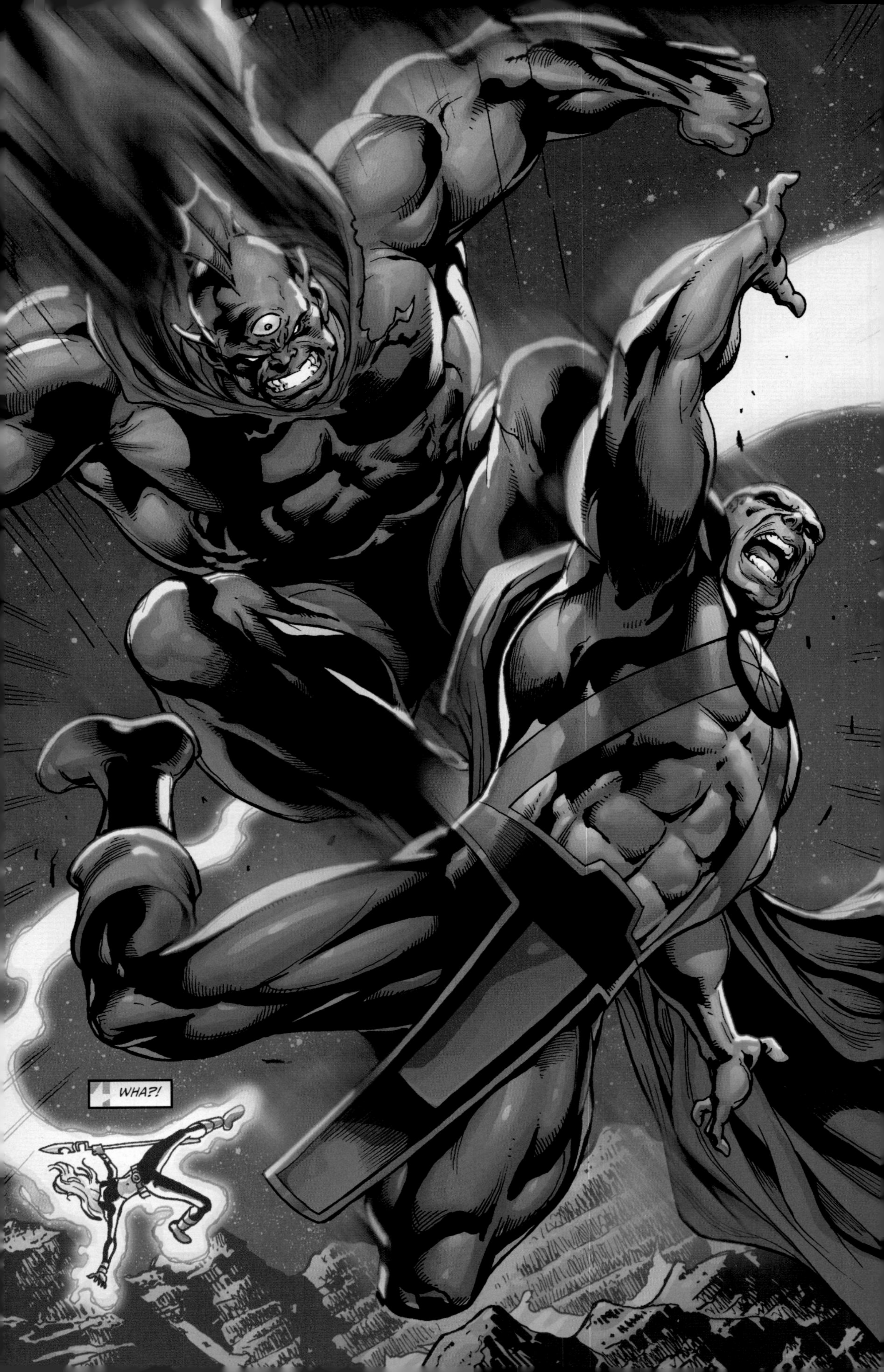
WHA?!

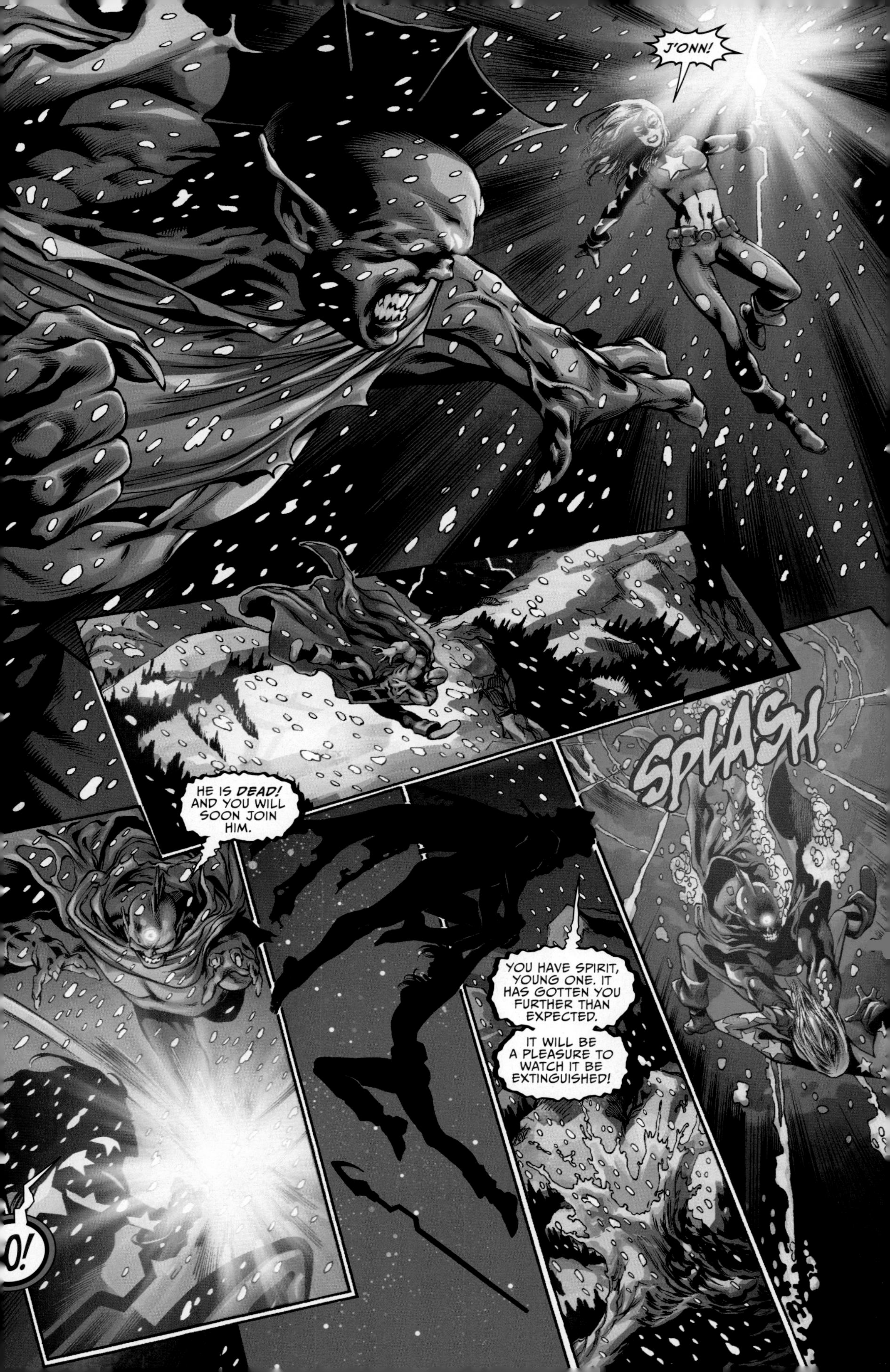
J'ONN!
HE IS DEAD! AND YOU WILL SOON JOIN HIM.
SPLASH
YOU HAVE SPIRIT, YOUNG ONE. IT HAS GOTTEN YOU FURTHER THAN EXPECTED.
IT WILL BE A PLEASURE TO WATCH IT BE EXTINGUISHED!

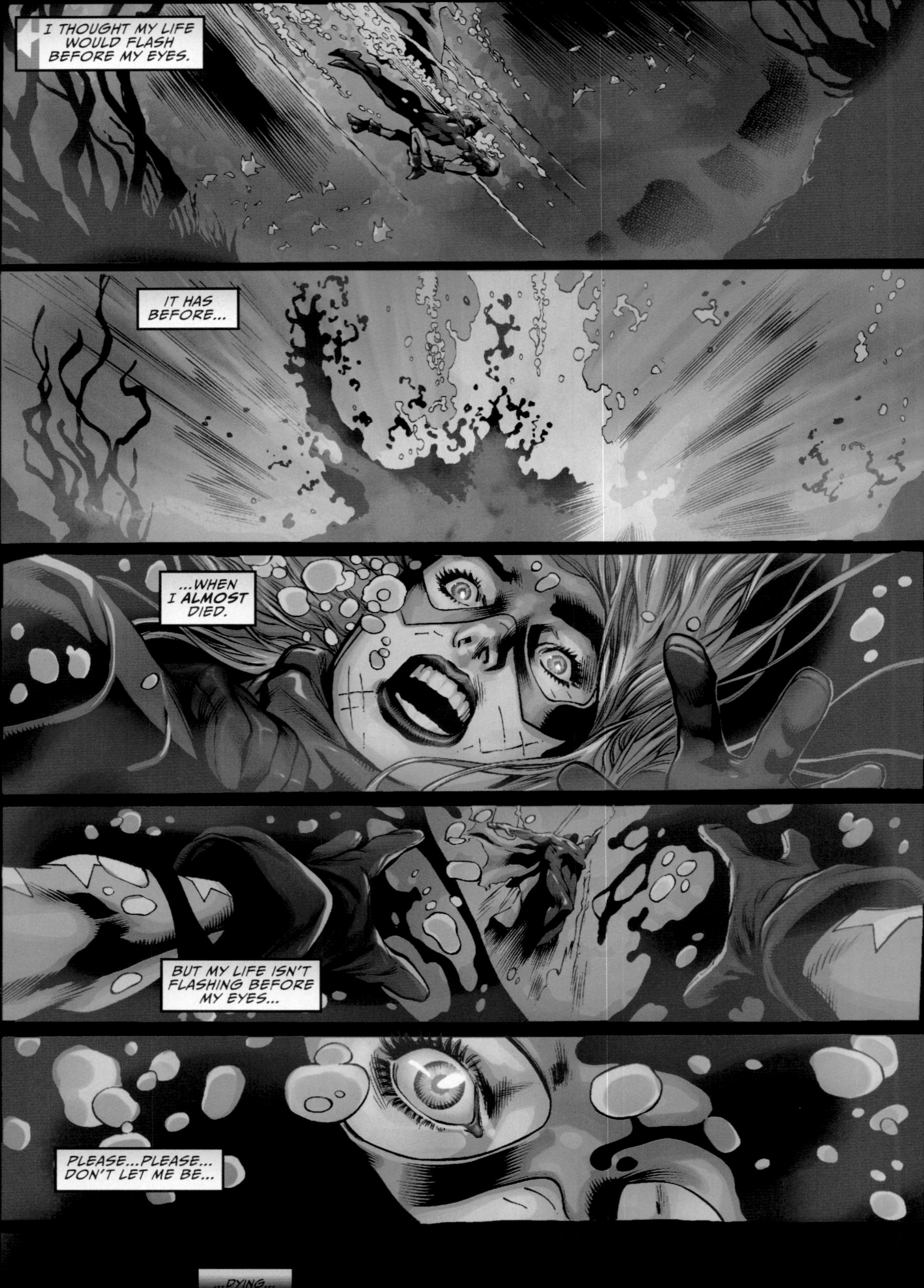
I THOUGHT MY LIFE WOULD FLASH BEFORE MY EYES.
IT HAS BEFORE...
...WHEN I ALMOST DIED.
BUT MY LIFE ISN'T FLASHING BEFORE MY EYES...
PLEASE...PLEASE... DON'T LET ME BE...
...DYING...

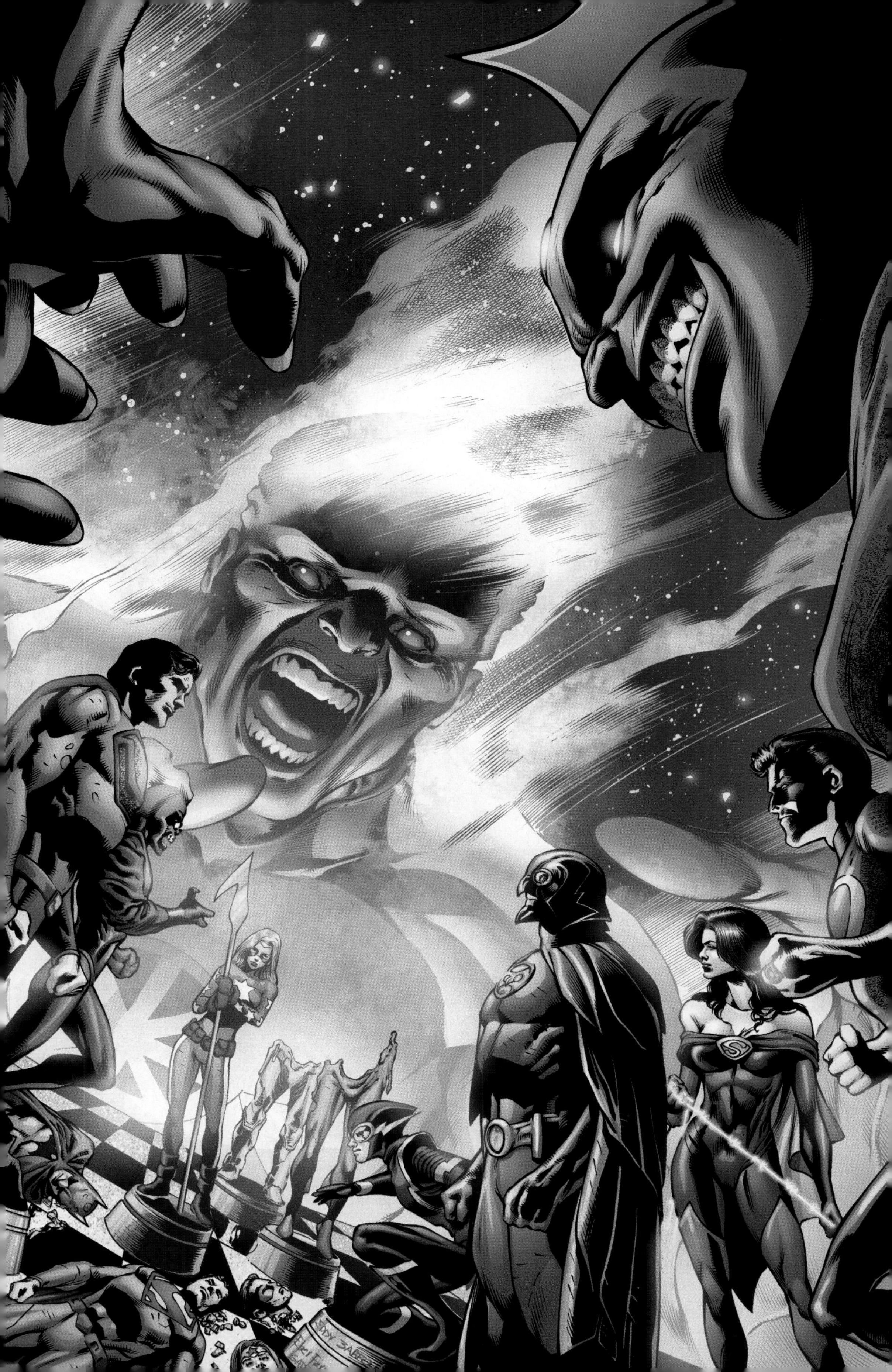

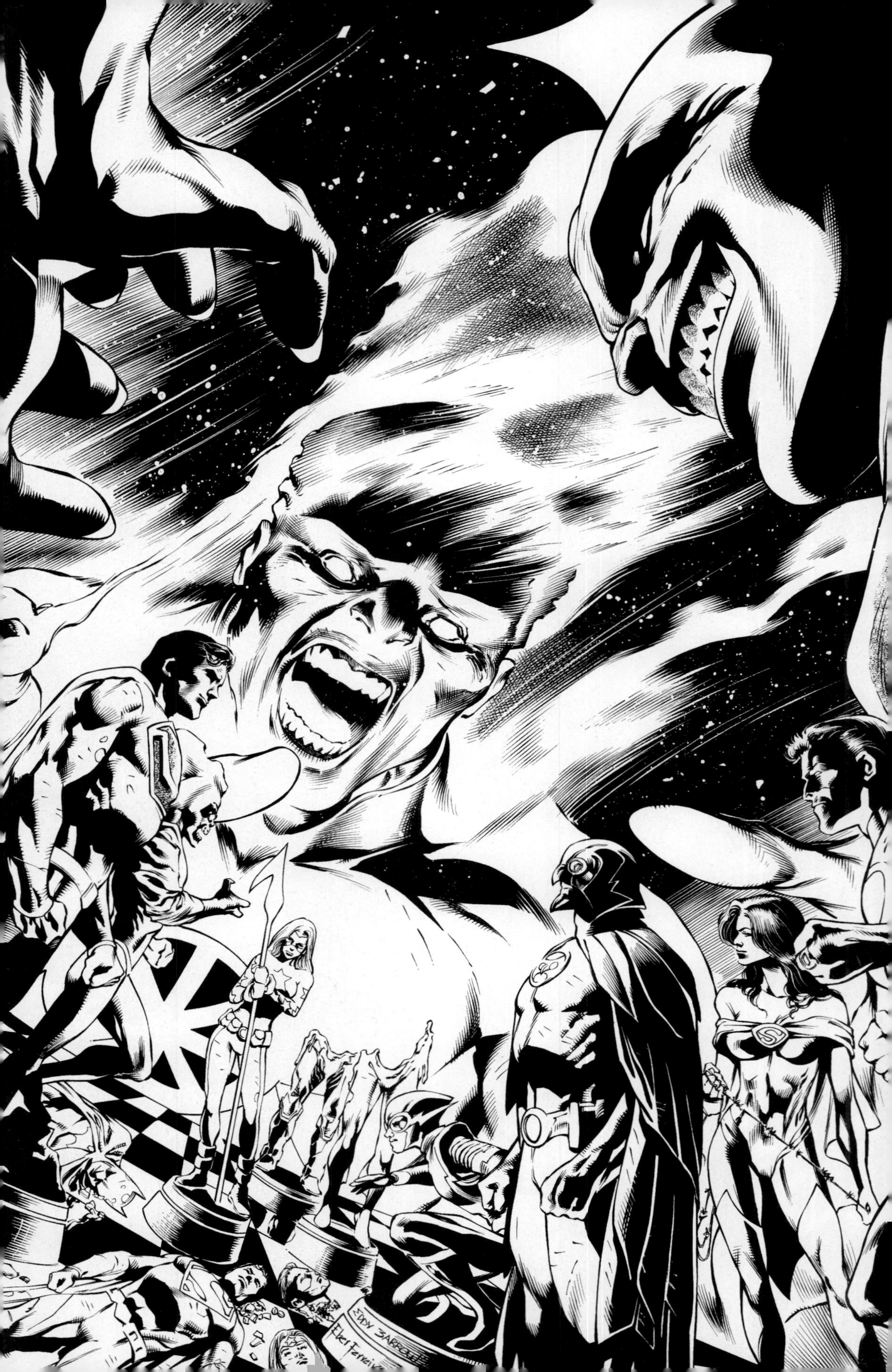

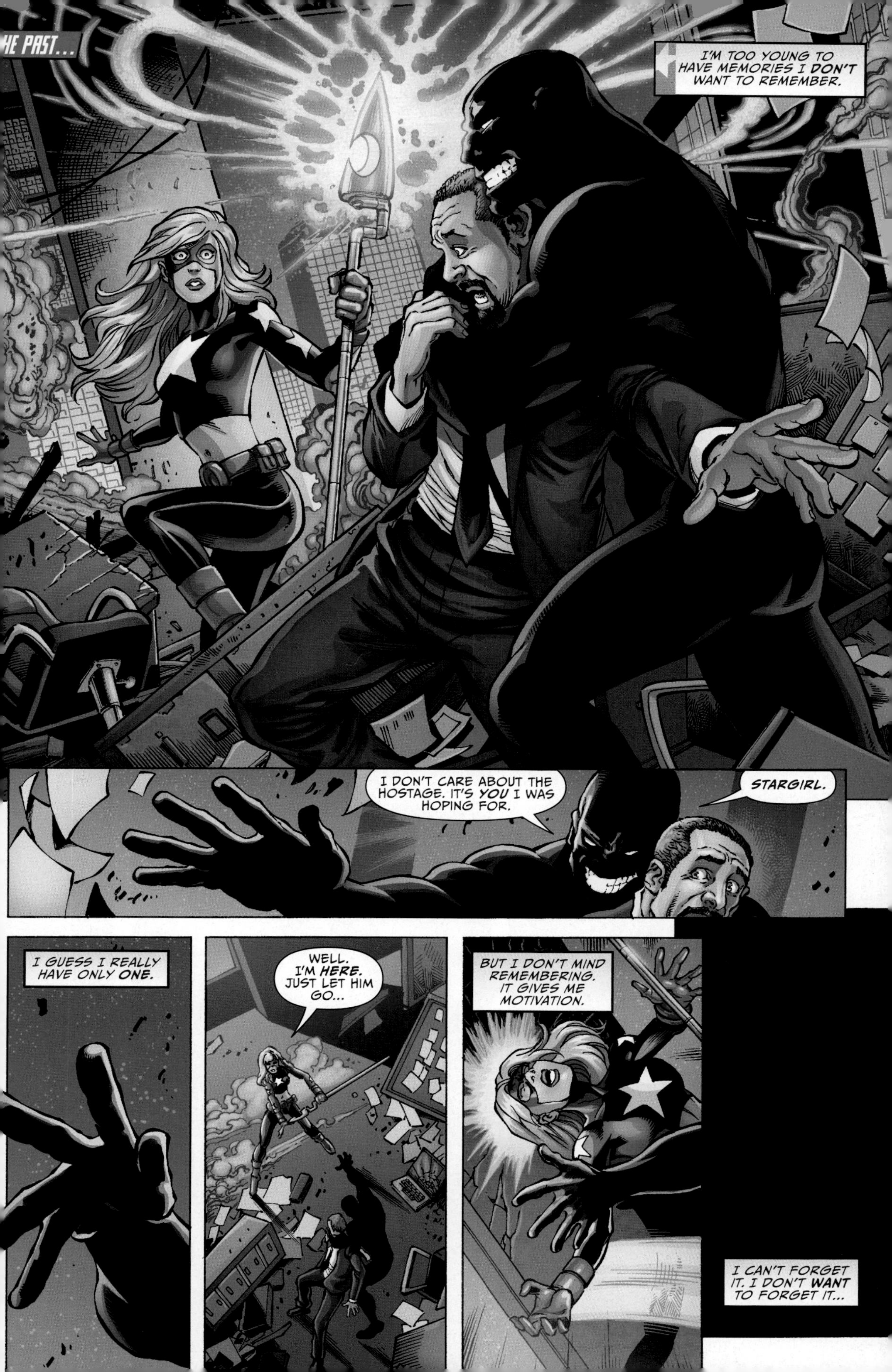
HE PAST...
I'M TOO YOUNG TO HAVE MEMORIES I DON'T WANT TO REMEMBER.
I DON'T CARE ABOUT THE HOSTAGE. IT'S YOU I WAS HOPING FOR.
STARGIRL.
I GUESS I REALLY HAVE ONLY ONE.
WELL. I'M HERE. JUST LET HIM GO...
BUT I DON'T MIND REMEMBERING. IT GIVES ME MOTIVATION.
I CAN'T FORGET IT. I DON'T WANT TO FORGET IT...

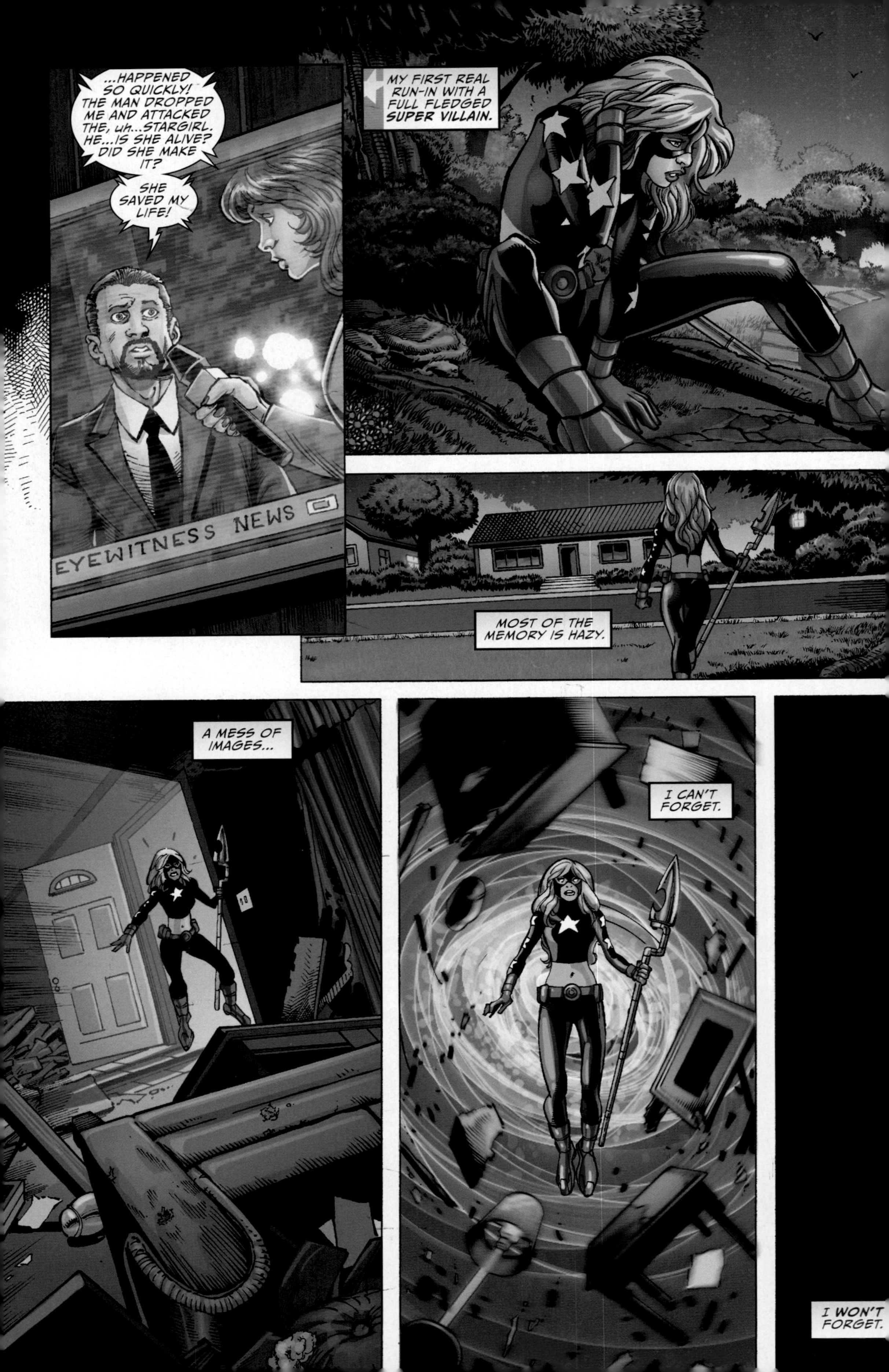
...HAPPENED SO QUICKLY! THE MAN DROPPED ME AND ATTACKED THE, uh...STARGIRL. HE...IS SHE ALIVE? DID SHE MAKE IT?
SHE SAVED MY LIFE!
EYEWITNESS NEWS
MY FIRST REAL RUN-IN WITH A FULL FLEDGED SUPER VILLAIN.
MOST OF THE MEMORY IS HAZY.
A MESS OF IMAGES...
I CAN'T FORGET.
I WON'T FORGET.

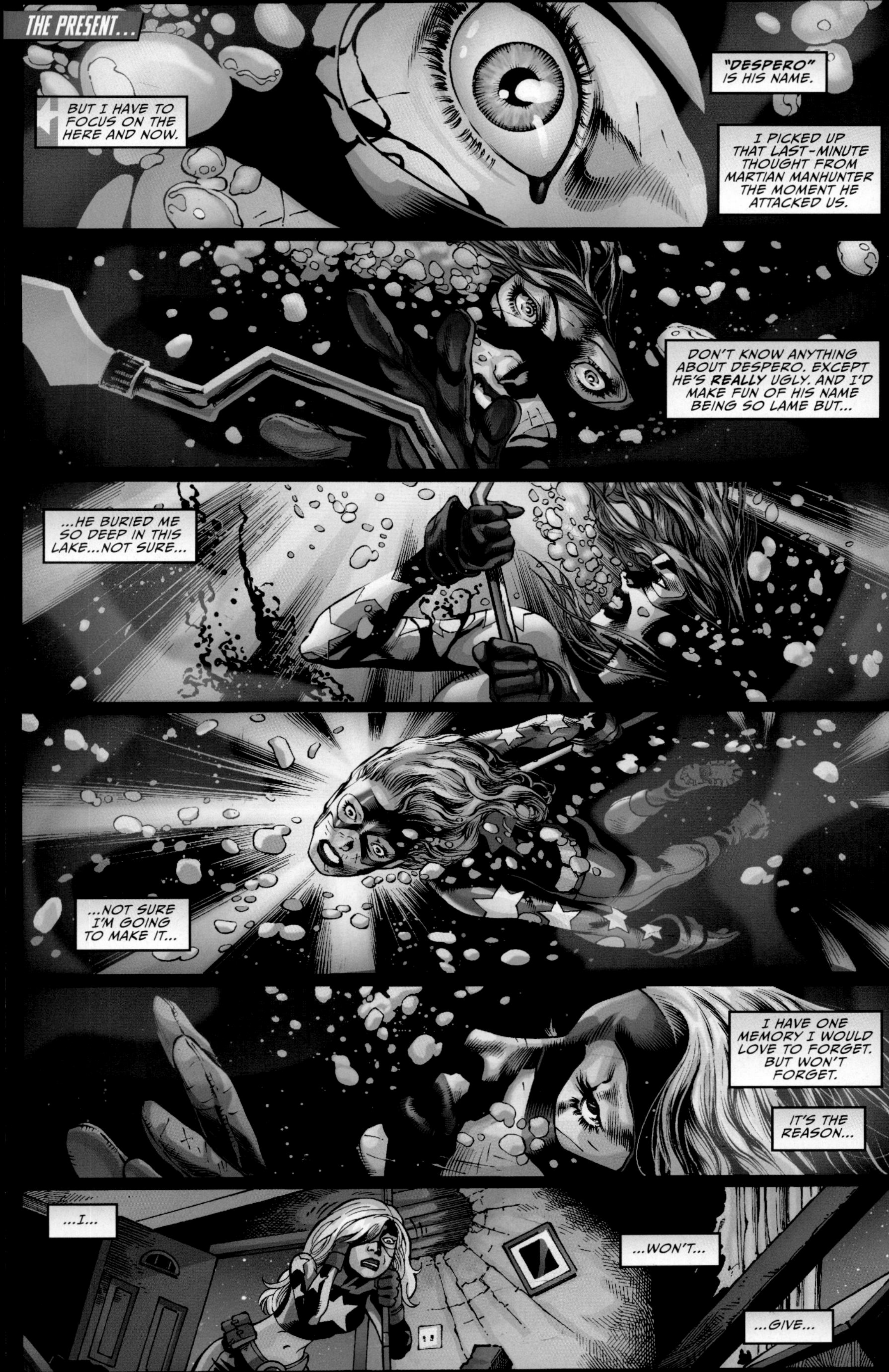
THE PRESENT...
BUT I HAVE TO FOCUS ON THE HERE AND NOW.
"DESPERO" IS HIS NAME.
I PICKED UP THAT LAST-MINUTE THOUGHT FROM MARTIAN MANHUNTER THE MOMENT HE ATTACKED US.
DON'T KNOW ANYTHING ABOUT DESPERO. EXCEPT HE'S **REALLY** UGLY. AND I'D MAKE FUN OF HIS NAME BEING SO LAME BUT...
...HE BURIED ME SO DEEP IN THIS LAKE...NOT SURE...
...NOT SURE I'M GOING TO MAKE IT...
I HAVE ONE MEMORY I WOULD LOVE TO FORGET. BUT WON'T FORGET.
IT'S THE REASON...
...I...
...WON'T...
...GIVE...

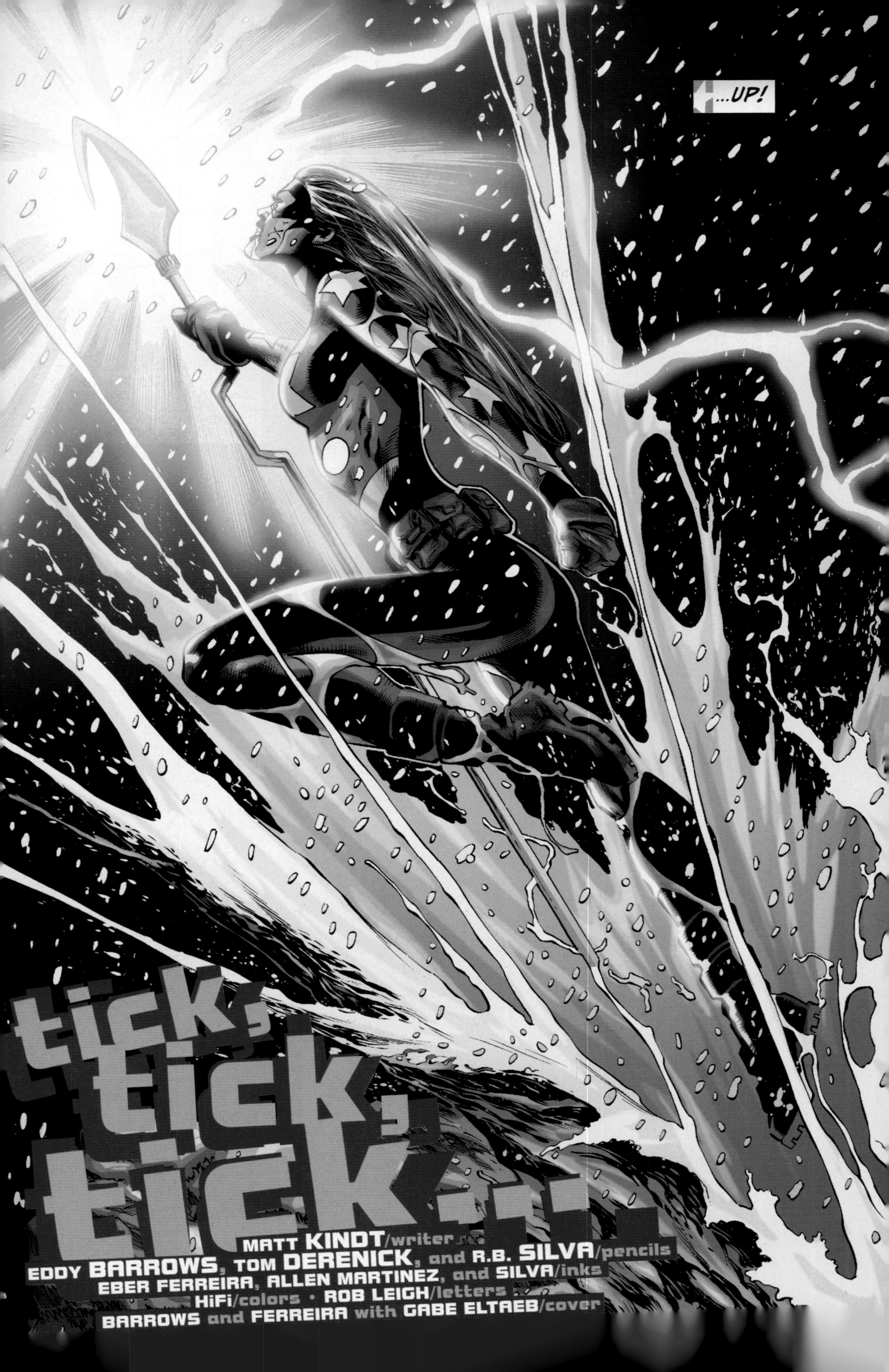
...UP!
tick, tick, tick...
MATT KINDT/writer
EDDY BARROWS, TOM DERENICK, and R.B. SILVA/pencils
EBER FERREIRA, ALLEN MARTINEZ, and SILVA/inks
HiFi/colors · ROB LEIGH/letters
BARROWS and FERREIRA with GABE ELTAEB/cover

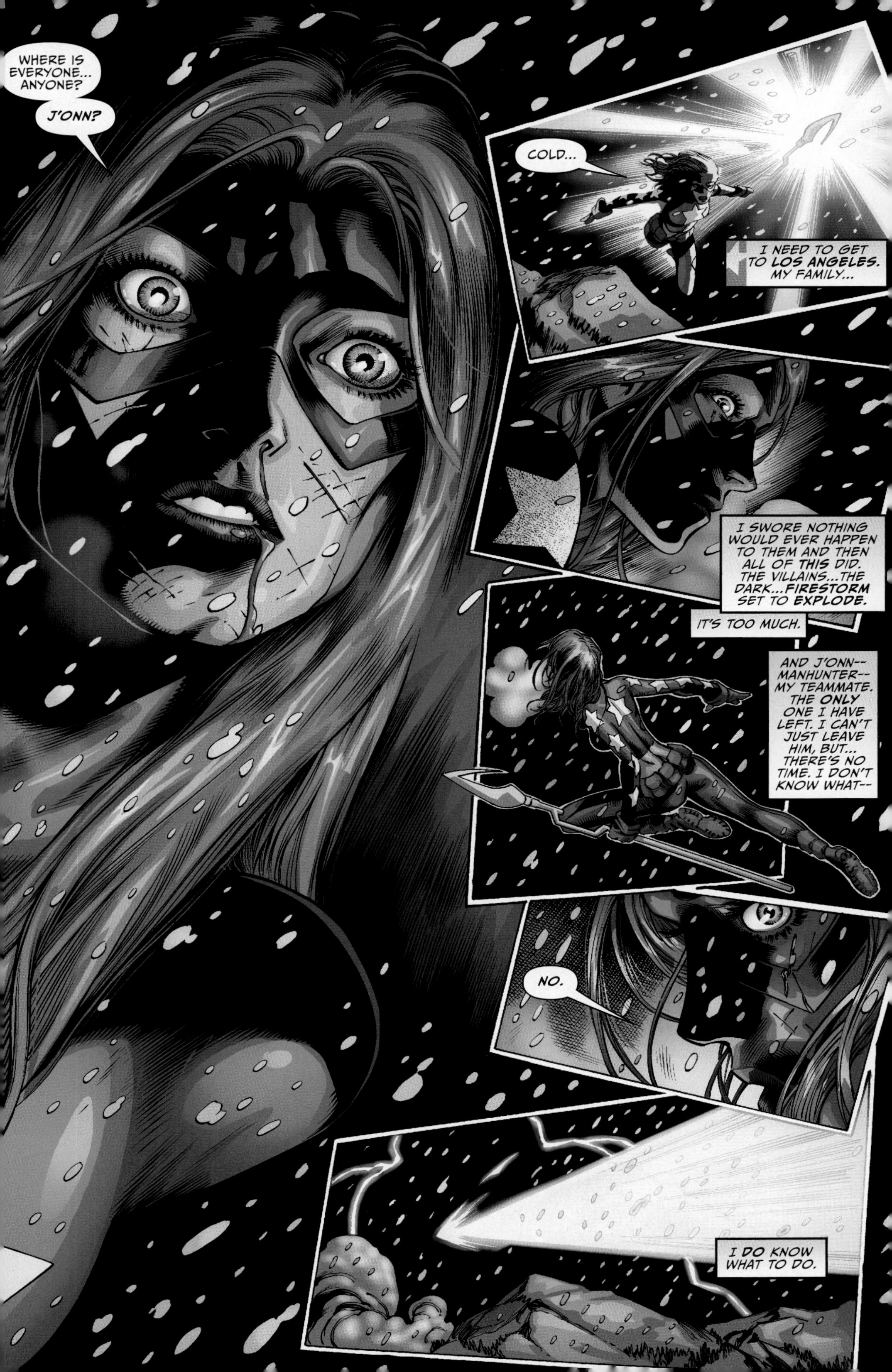
WHERE IS EVERYONE... ANYONE?
J'ONN?
COLD...
I NEED TO GET TO **LOS ANGELES.** MY FAMILY...
I SWORE NOTHING WOULD EVER HAPPEN TO THEM AND THEN ALL OF **THIS** DID. THE VILLAINS...THE DARK...**FIRESTORM** SET TO **EXPLODE.**
IT'S TOO MUCH.
AND J'ONN-- MANHUNTER-- MY TEAMMATE. THE **ONLY** ONE I HAVE LEFT. I CAN'T JUST LEAVE HIM, BUT... THERE'S NO TIME. I DON'T KNOW WHAT--
NO.
I **DO** KNOW WHAT TO DO.

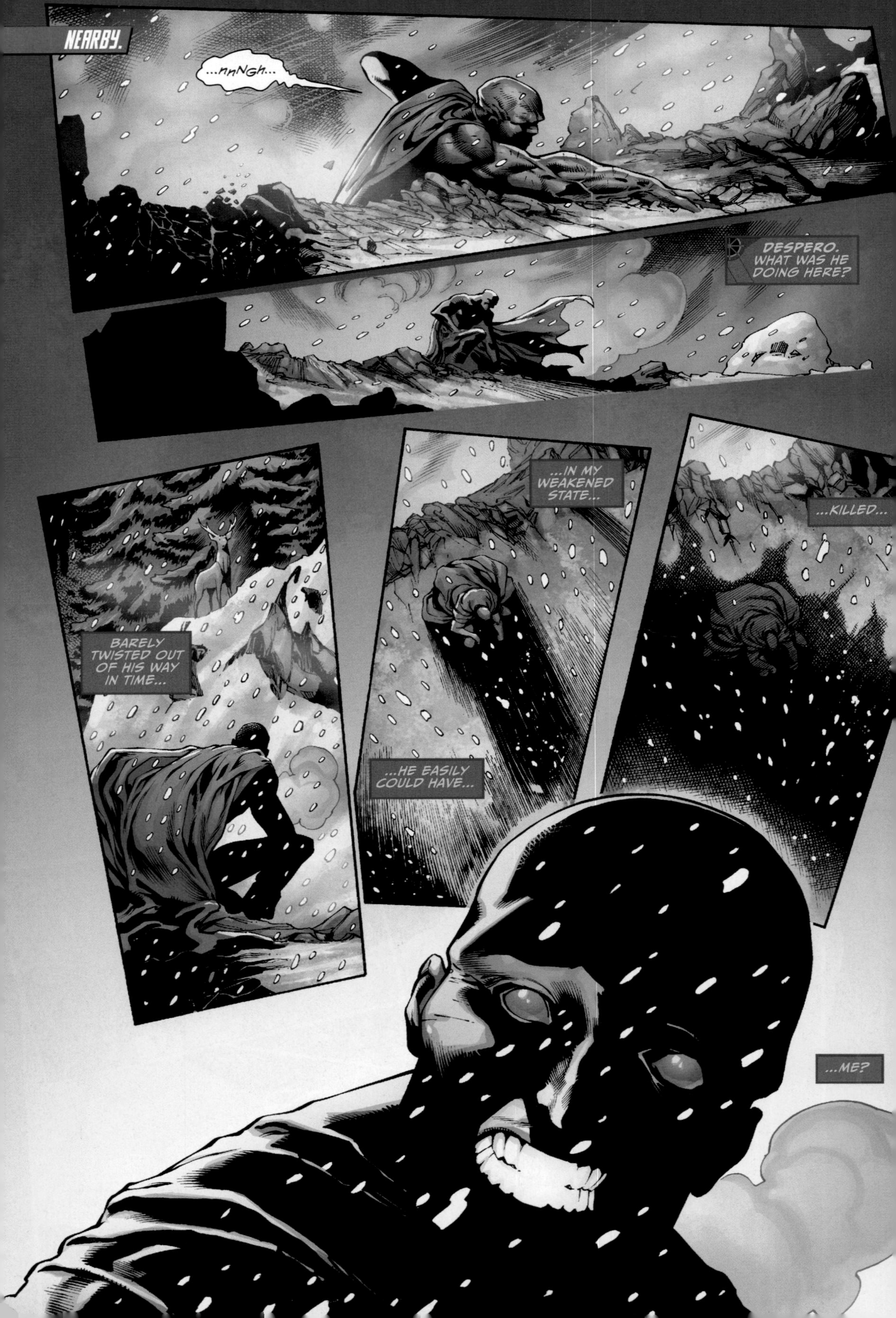
NEARBY.
...nnNGh...
DESPERO. WHAT WAS HE DOING HERE?
BARELY TWISTED OUT OF HIS WAY IN TIME...
...IN MY WEAKENED STATE...
...HE EASILY COULD HAVE...
...KILLED...
...ME?

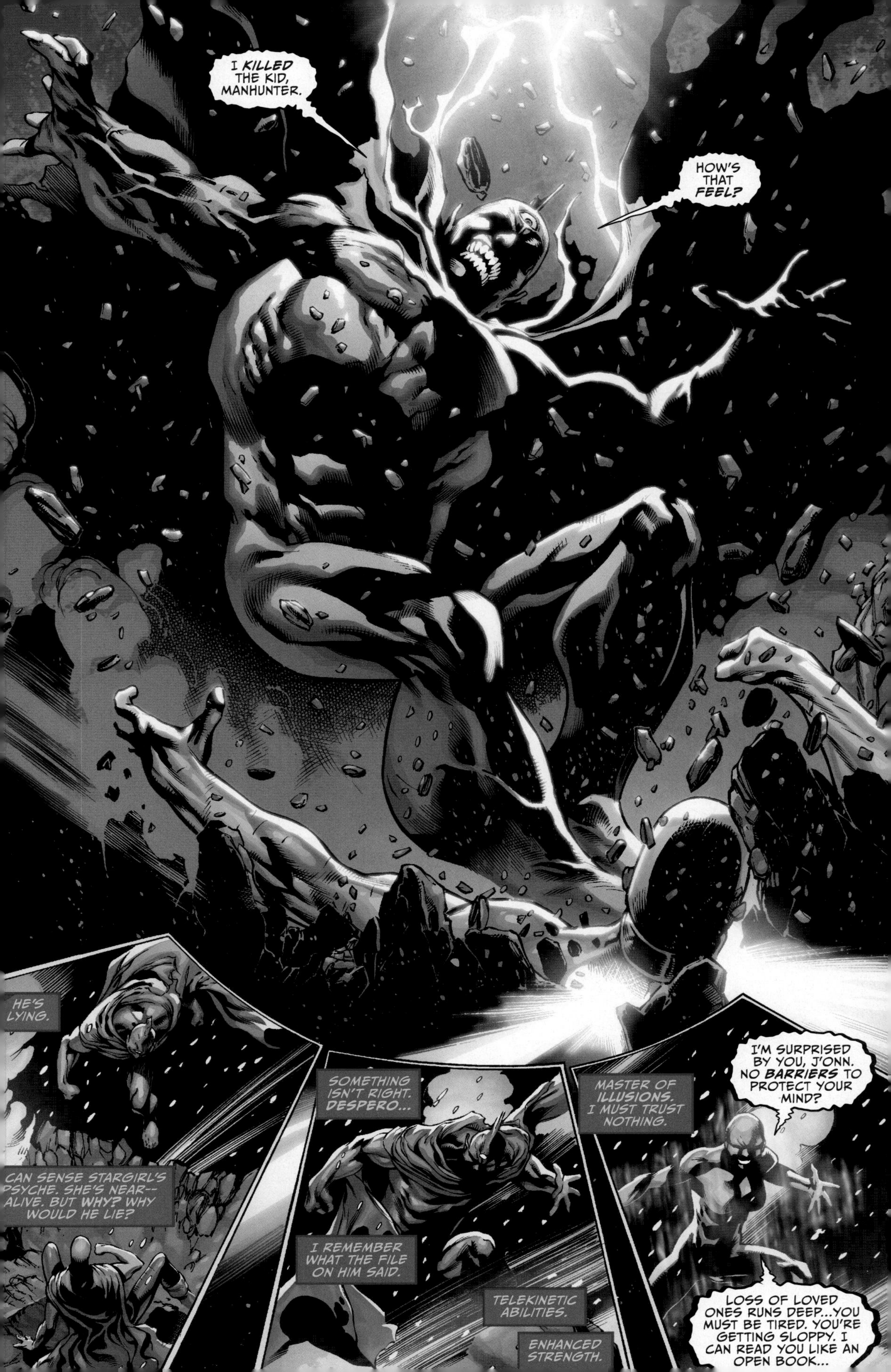

I KILLED THE KID, MANHUNTER.
HOW'S THAT FEEL?
HE'S LYING.
CAN SENSE STARGIRL'S PSYCHE. SHE'S NEAR-- ALIVE. BUT WHY? WHY WOULD HE LIE?
SOMETHING ISN'T RIGHT. DESPERO...
I REMEMBER WHAT THE FILE ON HIM SAID.
TELEKINETIC ABILITIES.
ENHANCED STRENGTH.
MASTER OF ILLUSIONS. I MUST TRUST NOTHING.
I'M SURPRISED BY YOU, J'ONN. NO BARRIERS TO PROTECT YOUR MIND?
LOSS OF LOVED ONES RUNS DEEP...YOU MUST BE TIRED. YOU'RE GETTING SLOPPY. I CAN READ YOU LIKE AN OPEN BOOK...

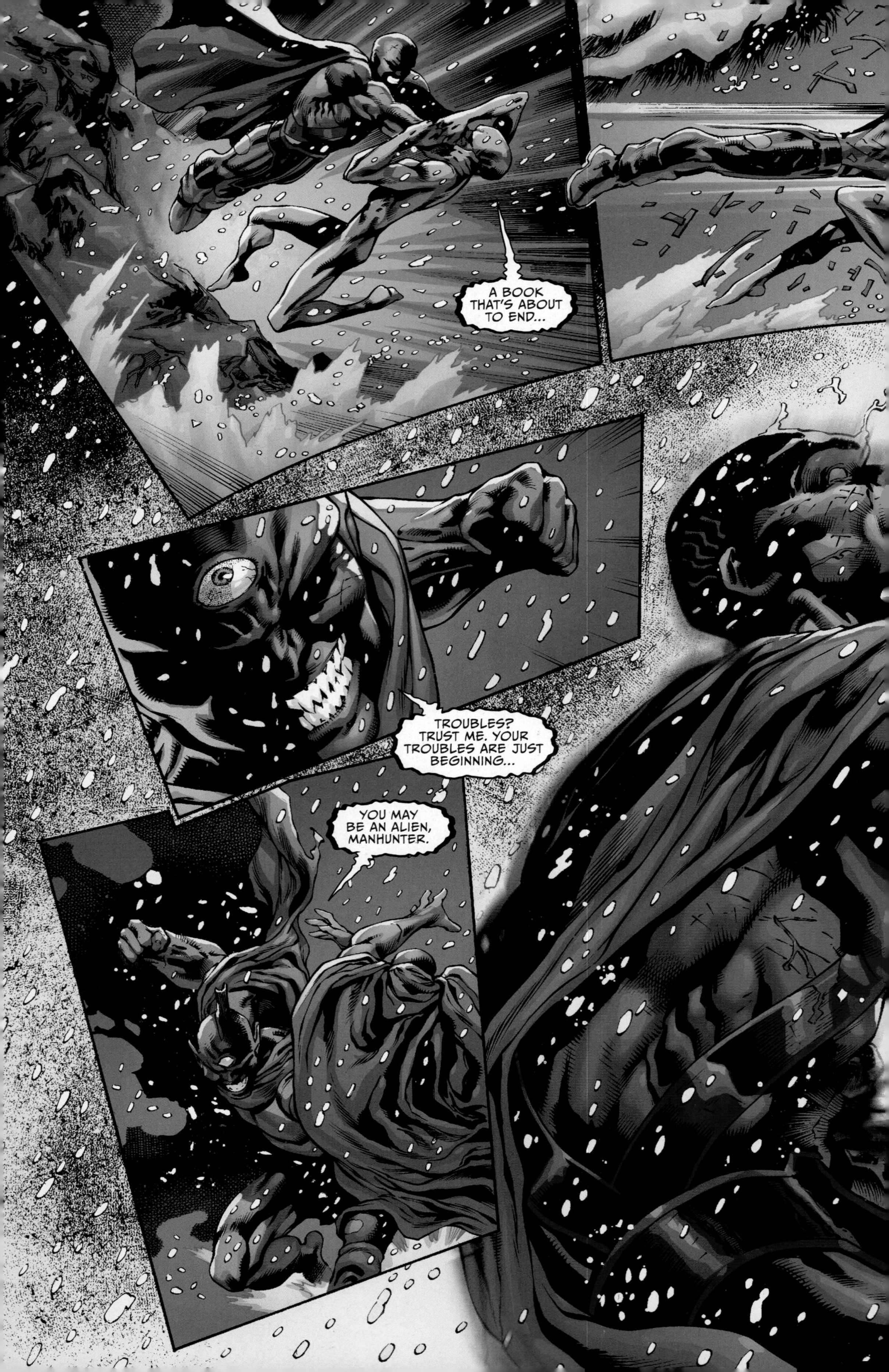
A BOOK THAT'S ABOUT TO END...
TROUBLES? TRUST ME. YOUR TROUBLES ARE JUST BEGINNING...
YOU MAY BE AN ALIEN, MANHUNTER.

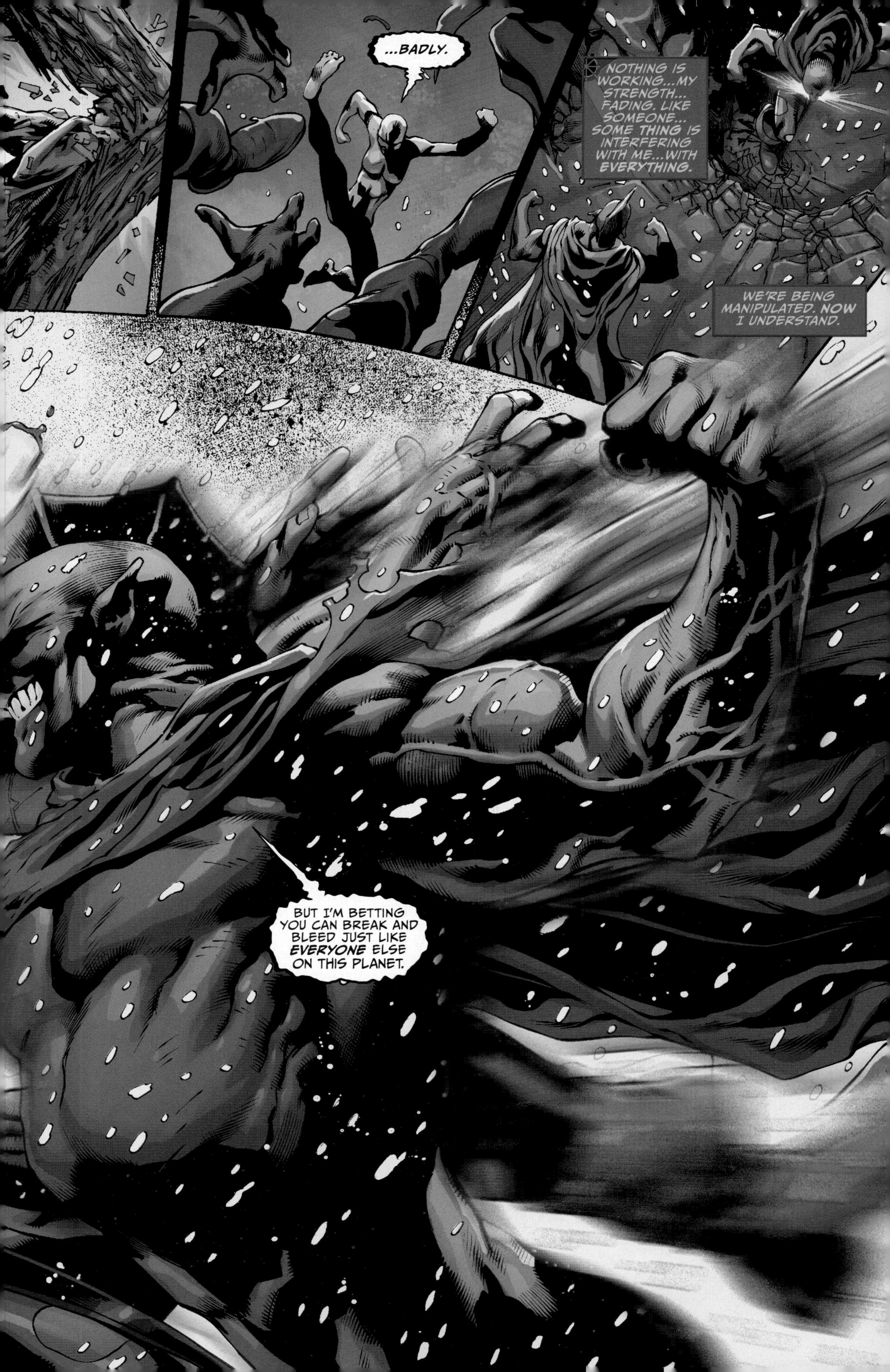
...BADLY.
NOTHING IS WORKING...MY STRENGTH... FADING. LIKE SOMEONE... SOME THING IS INTERFERING WITH ME...WITH EVERYTHING.
WE'RE BEING MANIPULATED. NOW I UNDERSTAND.
BUT I'M BETTING YOU CAN BREAK AND BLEED JUST LIKE EVERYONE ELSE ON THIS PLANET.

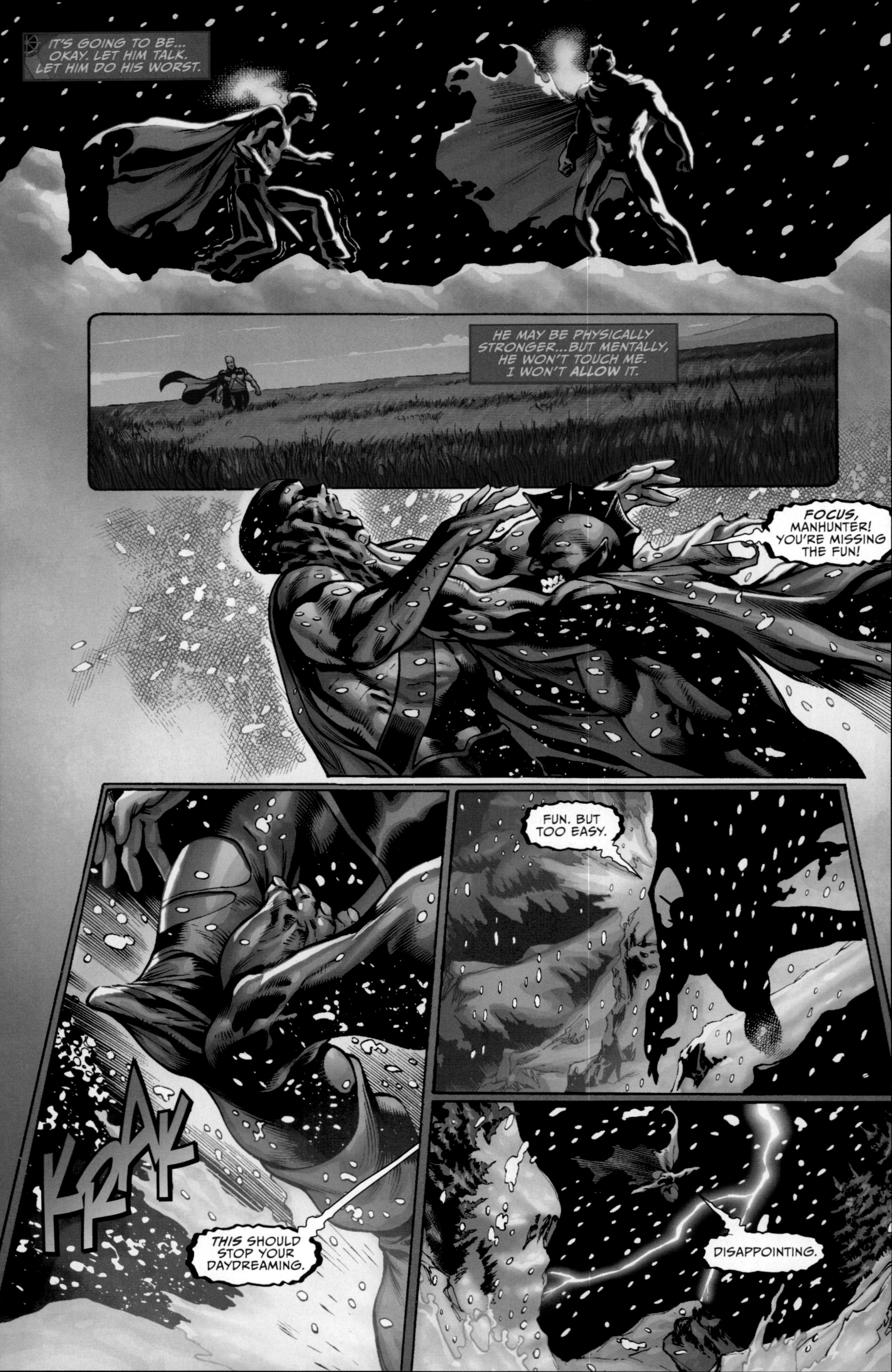

IT'S GOING TO BE... OKAY. LET HIM TALK. LET HIM DO HIS WORST.
HE MAY BE PHYSICALLY STRONGER...BUT MENTALLY, HE WON'T TOUCH ME. I WON'T ALLOW IT.
FOCUS, MANHUNTER! YOU'RE MISSING THE FUN!
KRAK
THIS SHOULD STOP YOUR DAYDREAMING.
FUN. BUT TOO EASY.
DISAPPOINTING.

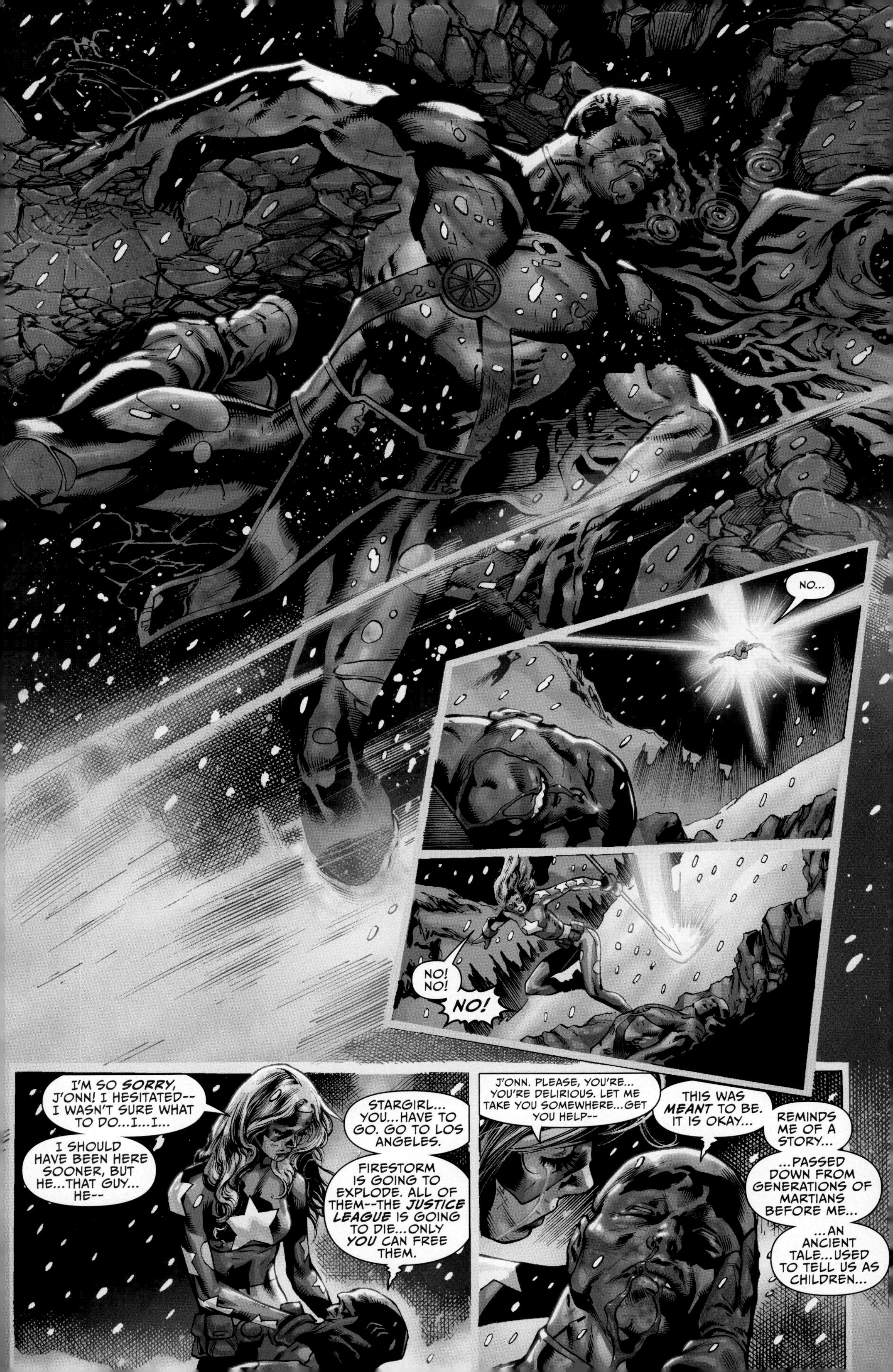
NO...
NO!
NO!
NO!
I'M SO SORRY, J'ONN! I HESITATED-- I WASN'T SURE WHAT TO DO...I...I...
I SHOULD HAVE BEEN HERE SOONER, BUT HE...THAT GUY... HE--
STARGIRL... YOU...HAVE TO GO. GO TO LOS ANGELES.
FIRESTORM IS GOING TO EXPLODE. ALL OF THEM--THE JUSTICE LEAGUE IS GOING TO DIE...ONLY YOU CAN FREE THEM.
J'ONN. PLEASE, YOU'RE... YOU'RE DELIRIOUS. LET ME TAKE YOU SOMEWHERE...GET YOU HELP--
THIS WAS MEANT TO BE. IT IS OKAY...
REMINDS ME OF A STORY...
...PASSED DOWN FROM GENERATIONS OF MARTIANS BEFORE ME...
...AN ANCIENT TALE...USED TO TELL US AS CHILDREN...

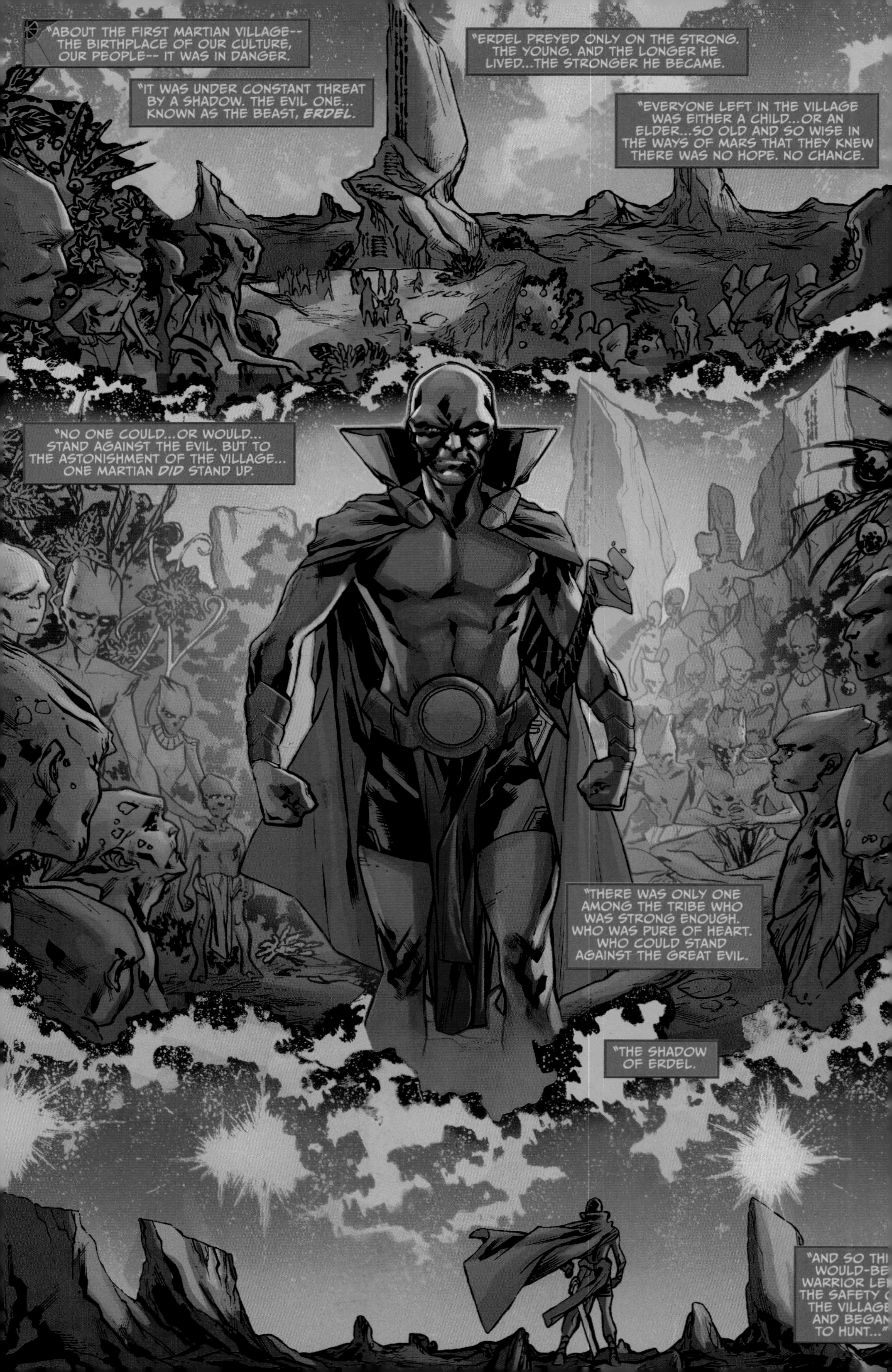
"ABOUT THE FIRST MARTIAN VILLAGE-- THE BIRTHPLACE OF OUR CULTURE, OUR PEOPLE-- IT WAS IN DANGER.
"IT WAS UNDER CONSTANT THREAT BY A SHADOW. THE EVIL ONE... KNOWN AS THE BEAST, *ERDEL*.
"ERDEL PREYED ONLY ON THE STRONG. THE YOUNG. AND THE LONGER HE LIVED...THE STRONGER HE BECAME.
"EVERYONE LEFT IN THE VILLAGE WAS EITHER A CHILD...OR AN ELDER...SO OLD AND SO WISE IN THE WAYS OF MARS THAT THEY KNEW THERE WAS NO HOPE. NO CHANCE.
"NO ONE COULD...OR WOULD... STAND AGAINST THE EVIL. BUT TO THE ASTONISHMENT OF THE VILLAGE... ONE MARTIAN *DID* STAND UP.
"THERE WAS ONLY ONE AMONG THE TRIBE WHO WAS STRONG ENOUGH. WHO WAS PURE OF HEART. WHO COULD STAND AGAINST THE GREAT EVIL.
"THE SHADOW OF ERDEL.
"AND SO THI WOULD-BE WARRIOR LE THE SAFETY THE VILLAGE AND BEGA TO HUNT..."

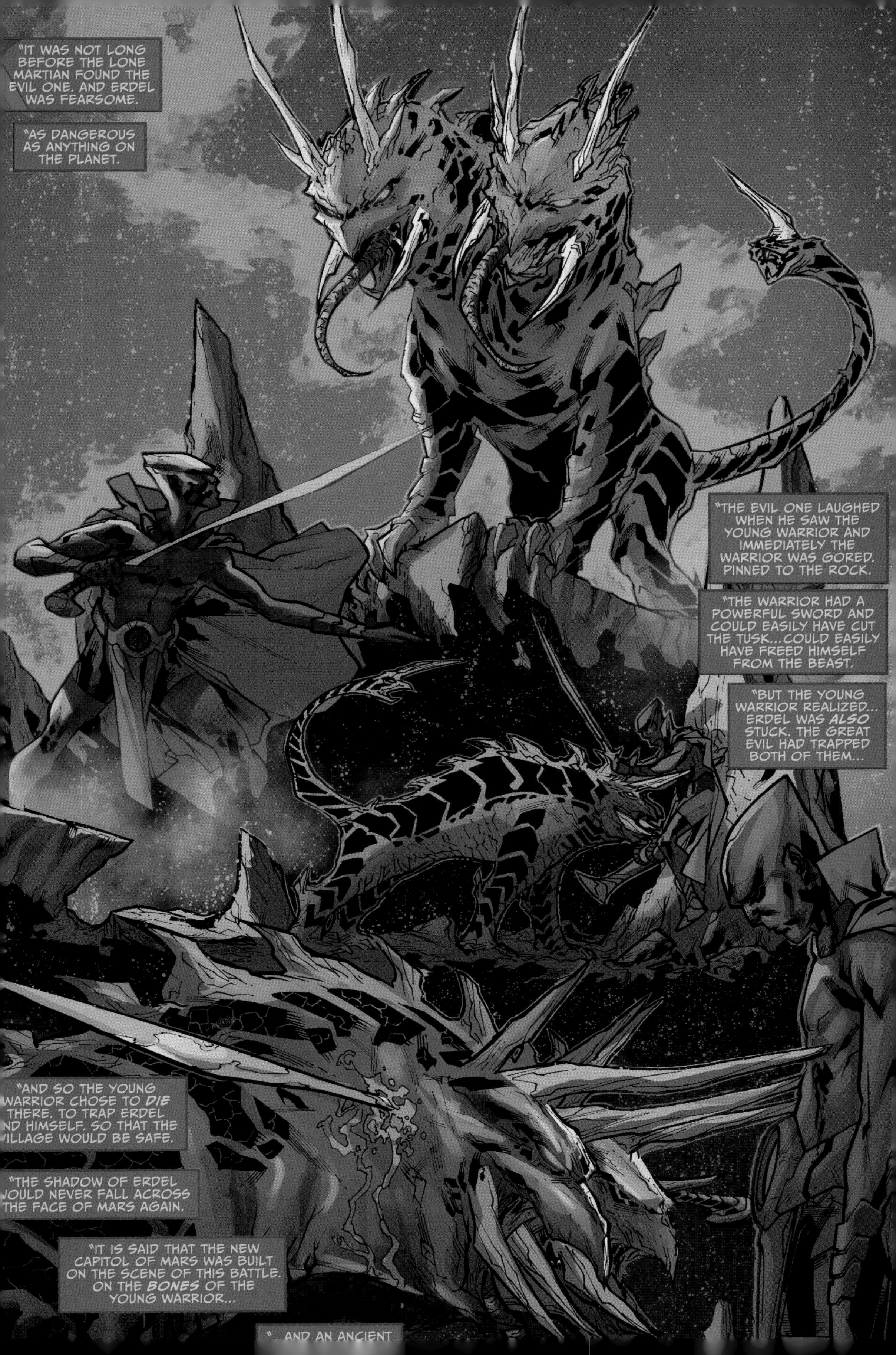
"IT WAS NOT LONG BEFORE THE LONE MARTIAN FOUND THE EVIL ONE. AND ERDEL WAS FEARSOME.
"AS DANGEROUS AS ANYTHING ON THE PLANET.
"THE EVIL ONE LAUGHED WHEN HE SAW THE YOUNG WARRIOR AND IMMEDIATELY THE WARRIOR WAS GORED. PINNED TO THE ROCK.
"THE WARRIOR HAD A POWERFUL SWORD AND COULD EASILY HAVE CUT THE TUSK...COULD EASILY HAVE FREED HIMSELF FROM THE BEAST.
"BUT THE YOUNG WARRIOR REALIZED... ERDEL WAS *ALSO* STUCK. THE GREAT EVIL HAD TRAPPED BOTH OF THEM...
"AND SO THE YOUNG WARRIOR CHOSE TO *DIE* THERE. TO TRAP ERDEL ND HIMSELF. SO THAT THE VILLAGE WOULD BE SAFE.
"THE SHADOW OF ERDEL WOULD NEVER FALL ACROSS THE FACE OF MARS AGAIN.
"IT IS SAID THAT THE NEW CAPITOL OF MARS WAS BUILT ON THE SCENE OF THIS BATTLE. ON THE *BONES* OF THE YOUNG WARRIOR...
"...AND AN ANCIENT

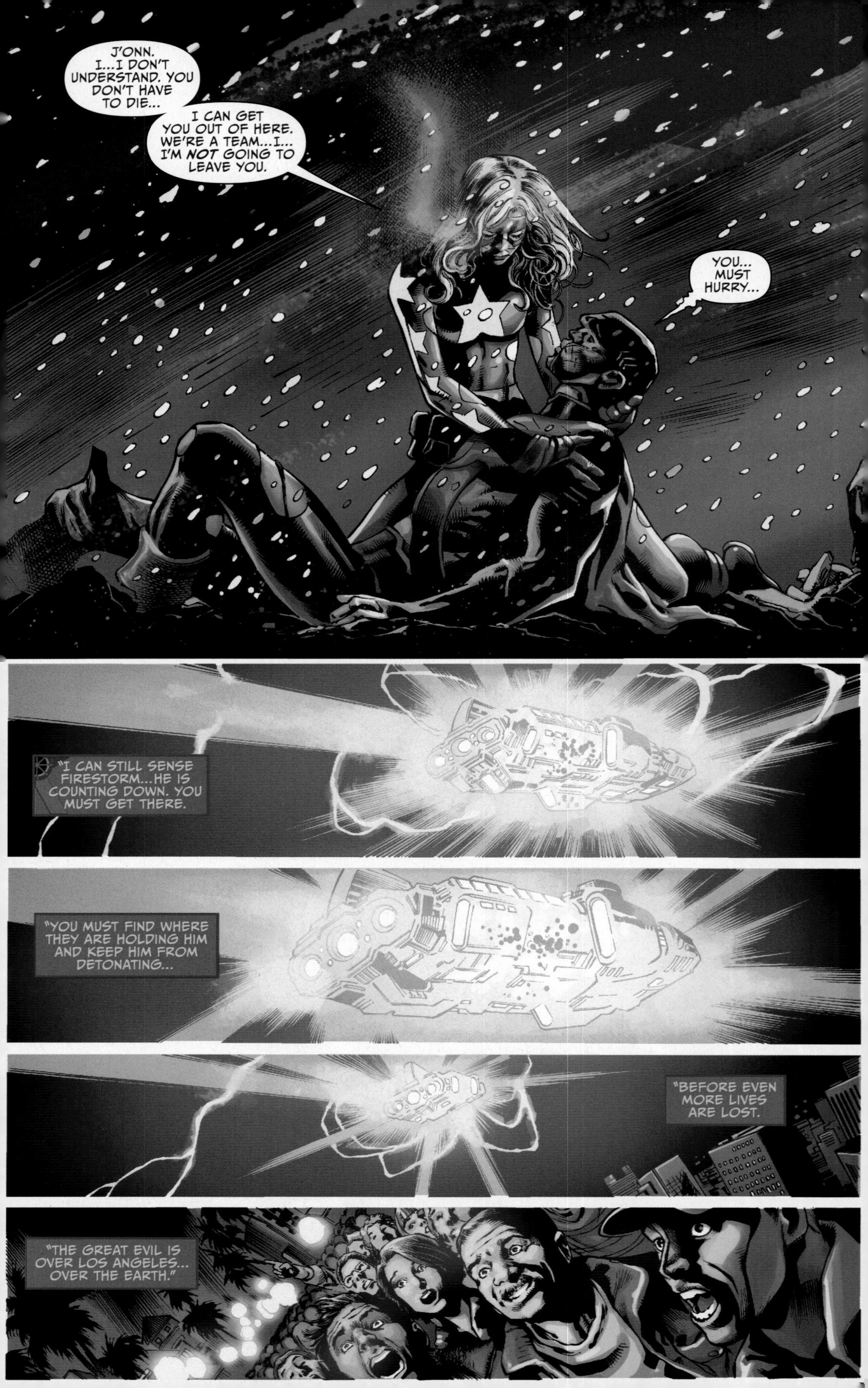
J'ONN. I...I DON'T UNDERSTAND. YOU DON'T HAVE TO DIE...
I CAN GET YOU OUT OF HERE. WE'RE A TEAM...I... I'M NOT GOING TO LEAVE YOU.
YOU... MUST HURRY...
"I CAN STILL SENSE FIRESTORM...HE IS COUNTING DOWN. YOU MUST GET THERE.
"YOU MUST FIND WHERE THEY ARE HOLDING HIM AND KEEP HIM FROM DETONATING...
"BEFORE EVEN MORE LIVES ARE LOST.
"THE GREAT EVIL IS OVER LOS ANGELES... OVER THE EARTH."

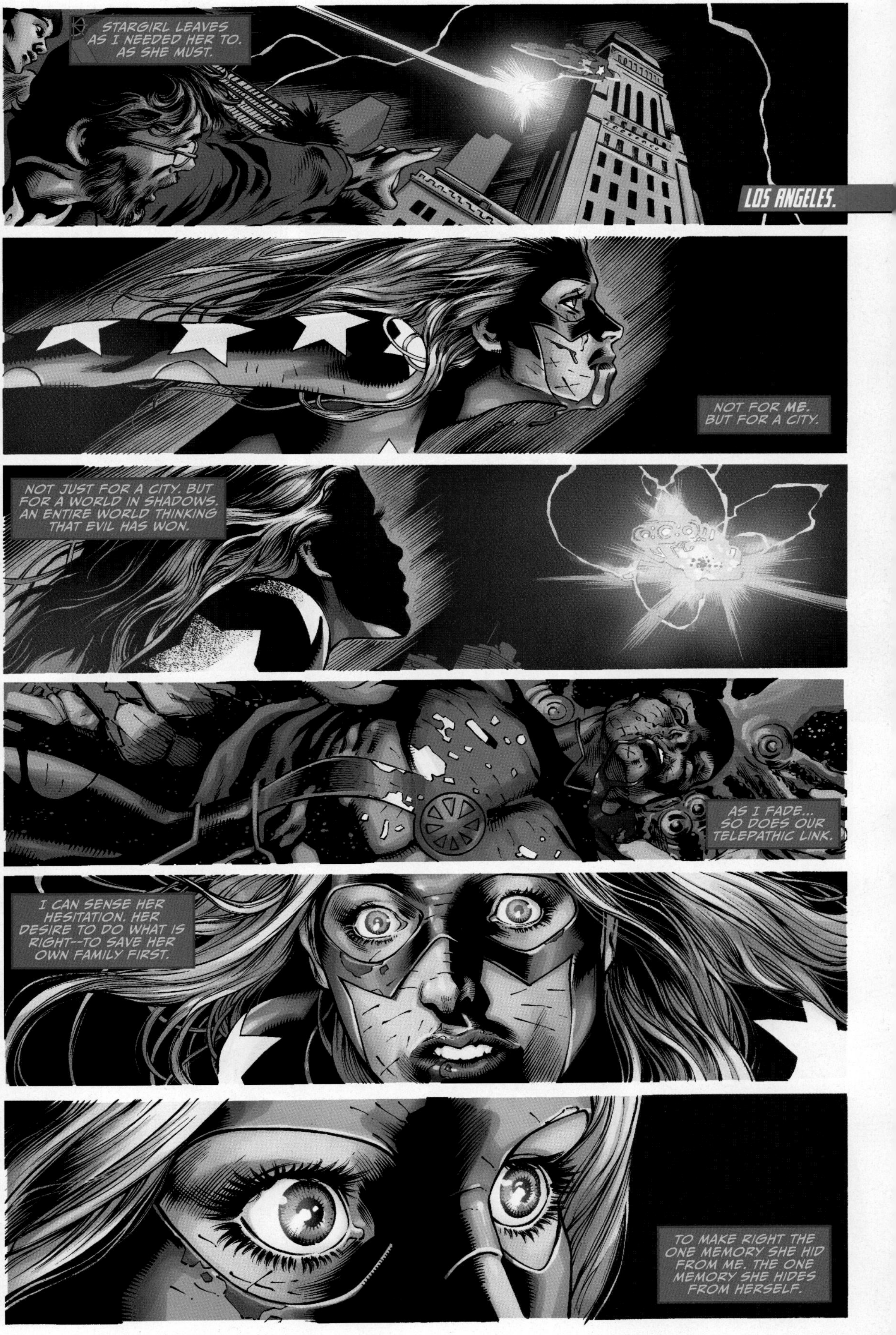
STARGIRL LEAVES AS I NEEDED HER TO. AS SHE MUST.
LOS ANGELES.
NOT FOR ME. BUT FOR A CITY.
NOT JUST FOR A CITY. BUT FOR A WORLD IN SHADOWS. AN ENTIRE WORLD THINKING THAT EVIL HAS WON.
AS I FADE... SO DOES OUR TELEPATHIC LINK.
I CAN SENSE HER HESITATION. HER DESIRE TO DO WHAT IS RIGHT--TO SAVE HER OWN FAMILY FIRST.
TO MAKE RIGHT THE ONE MEMORY SHE HID FROM ME. THE ONE MEMORY SHE HIDES FROM HERSELF.

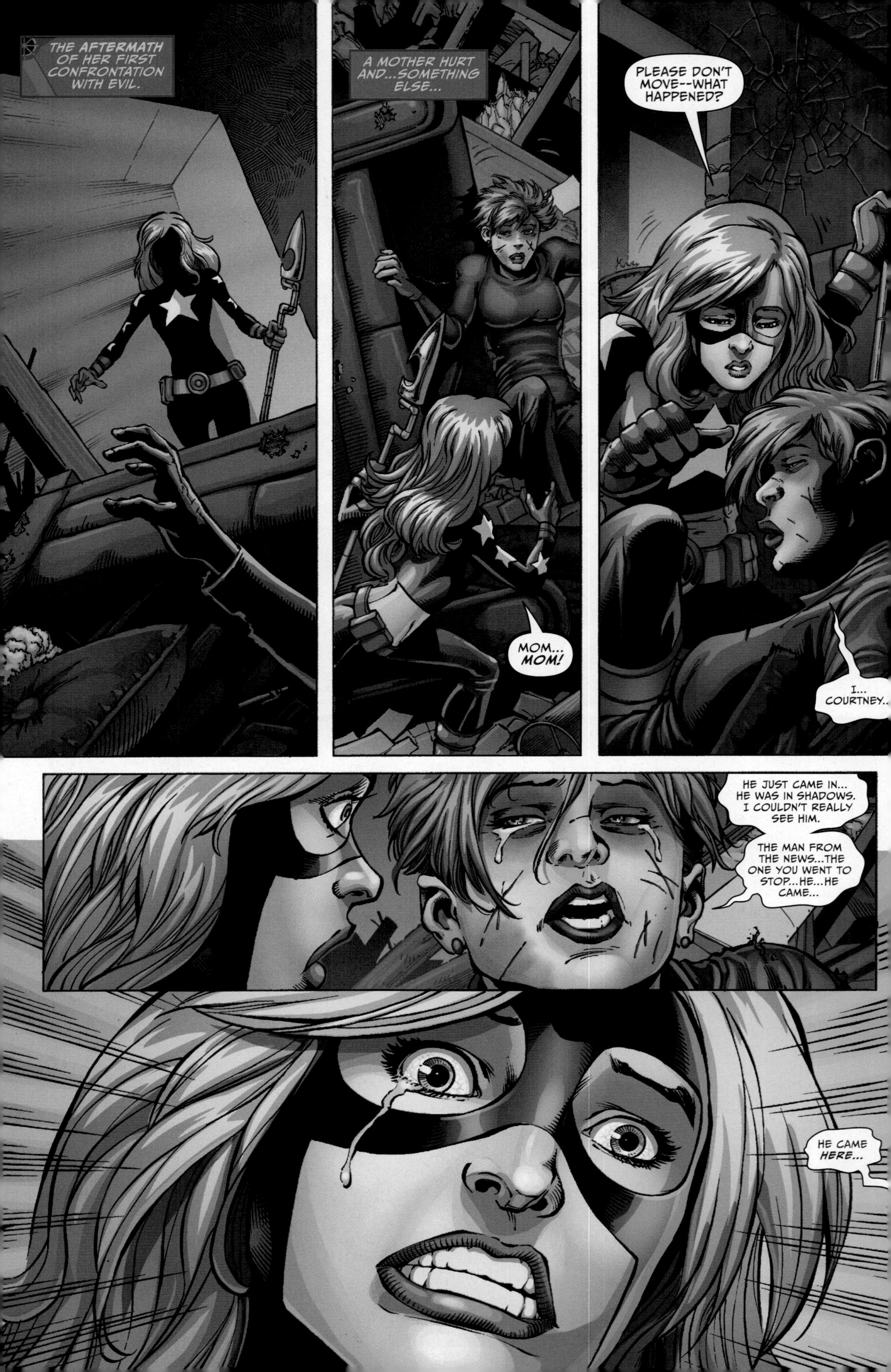
THE AFTERMATH OF HER FIRST CONFRONTATION WITH EVIL.
A MOTHER HURT AND...SOMETHING ELSE...
MOM... MOM!
PLEASE DON'T MOVE--WHAT HAPPENED?
I... COURTNEY...
HE JUST CAME IN... HE WAS IN SHADOWS. I COULDN'T REALLY SEE HIM.
THE MAN FROM THE NEWS...THE ONE YOU WENT TO STOP...HE...HE CAME...
HE CAME HERE...

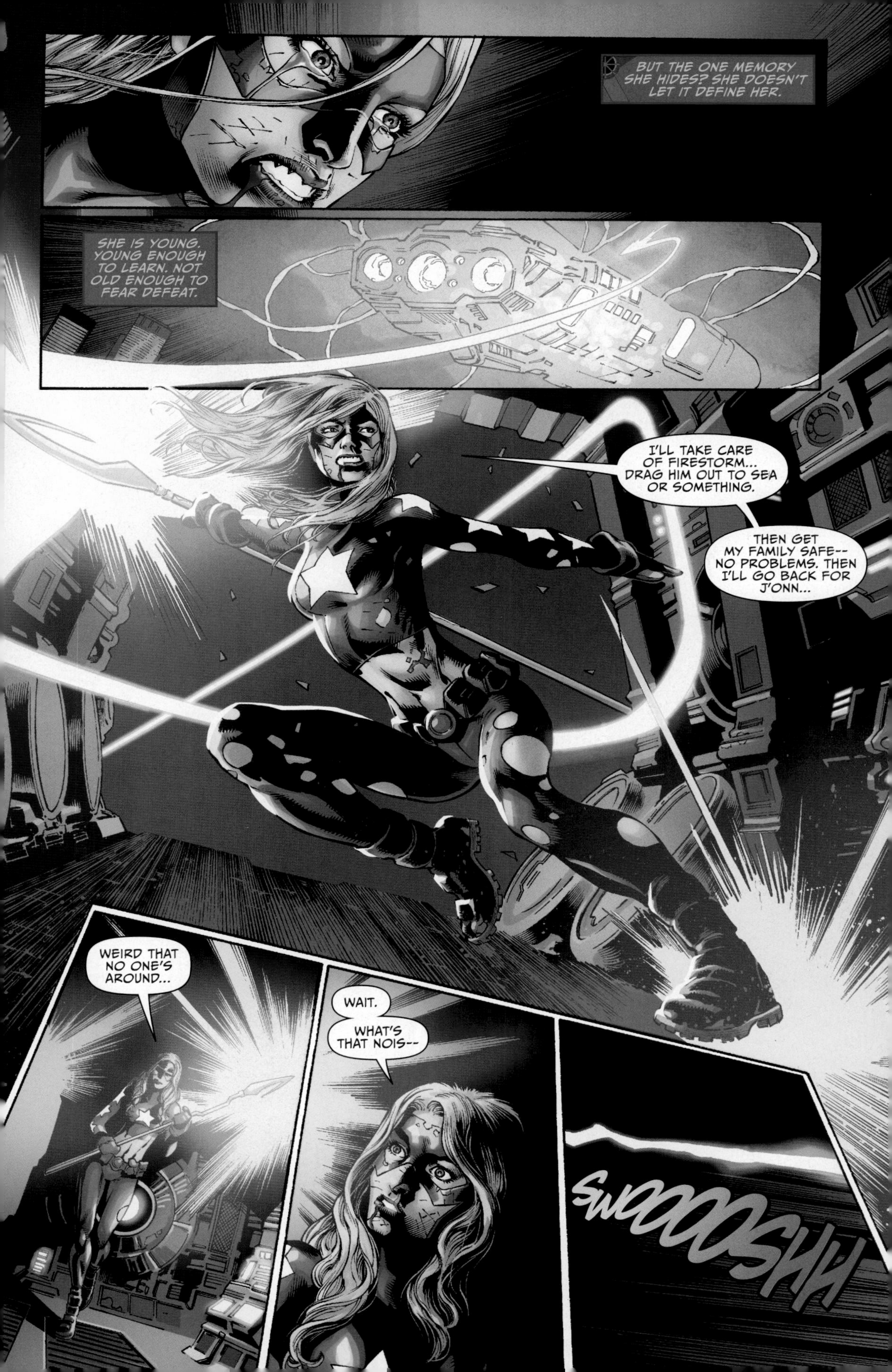
BUT THE ONE MEMORY SHE HIDES? SHE DOESN'T LET IT DEFINE HER.
SHE IS YOUNG. YOUNG ENOUGH TO LEARN. NOT OLD ENOUGH TO FEAR DEFEAT.
I'LL TAKE CARE OF FIRESTORM... DRAG HIM OUT TO SEA OR SOMETHING.
THEN GET MY FAMILY SAFE-- NO PROBLEMS. THEN I'LL GO BACK FOR J'ONN...
WEIRD THAT NO ONE'S AROUND...
WAIT.
WHAT'S THAT NOIS--
SWOOOOSHH

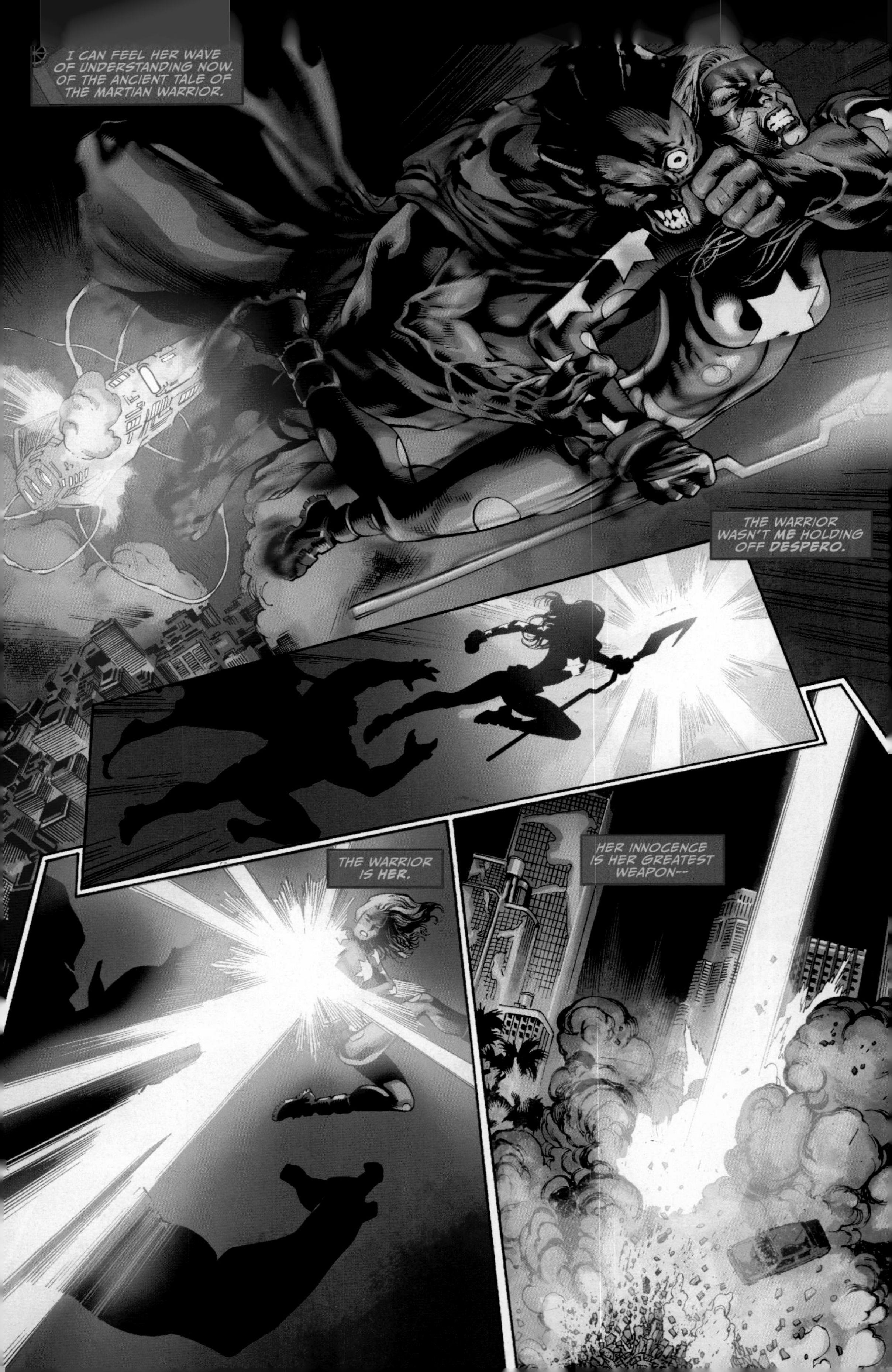
I CAN FEEL HER WAVE OF UNDERSTANDING NOW. OF THE ANCIENT TALE OF THE MARTIAN WARRIOR.
THE WARRIOR WASN'T ME HOLDING OFF DESPERO.
THE WARRIOR IS HER.
HER INNOCENCE IS HER GREATEST WEAPON--

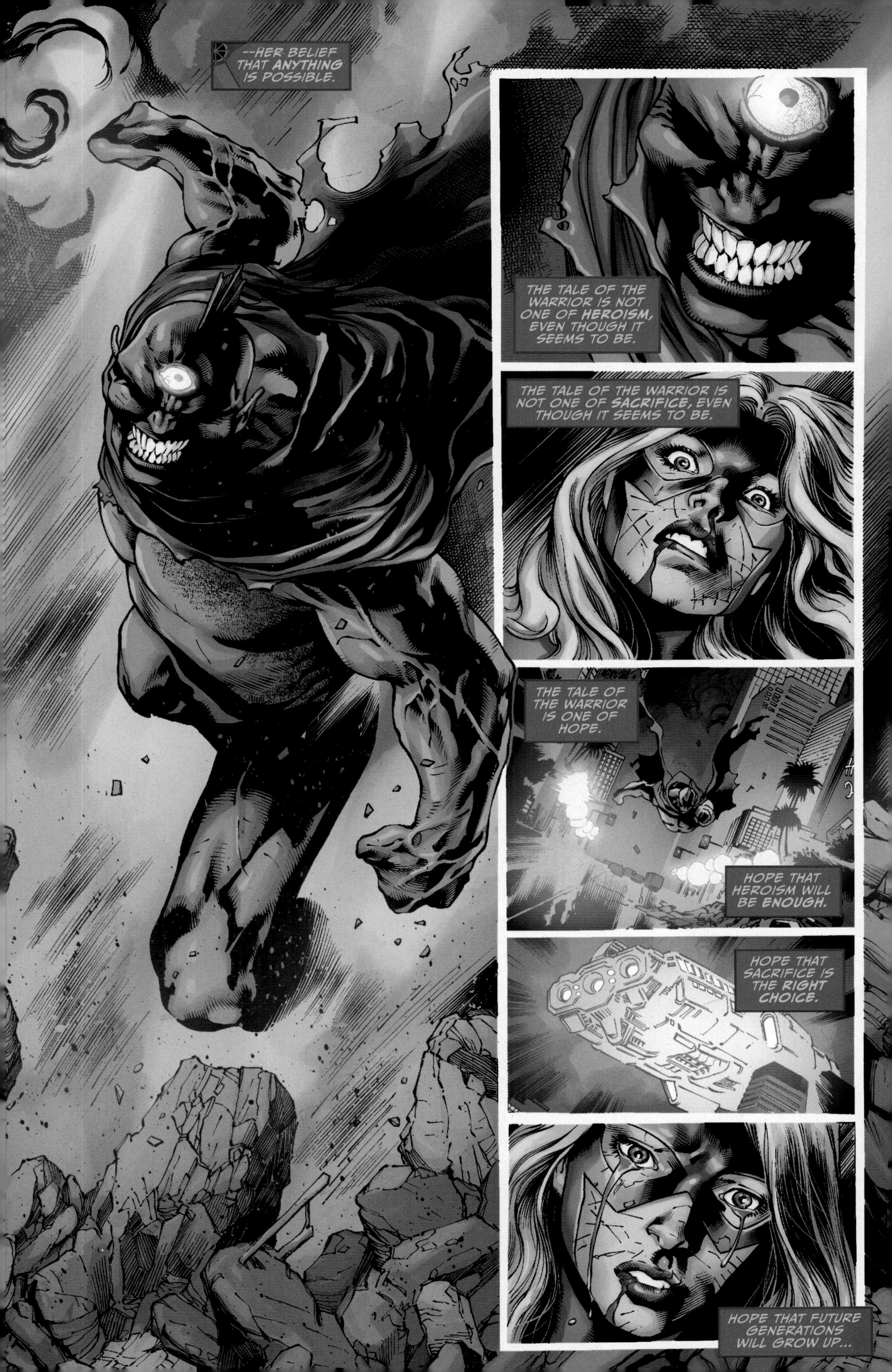
--HER BELIEF THAT ANYTHING IS POSSIBLE.
THE TALE OF THE WARRIOR IS NOT ONE OF HEROISM, EVEN THOUGH IT SEEMS TO BE.
THE TALE OF THE WARRIOR IS NOT ONE OF SACRIFICE, EVEN THOUGH IT SEEMS TO BE.
THE TALE OF THE WARRIOR IS ONE OF HOPE.
HOPE THAT HEROISM WILL BE ENOUGH.
HOPE THAT SACRIFICE IS THE RIGHT CHOICE.
HOPE THAT FUTURE GENERATIONS WILL GROW UP...

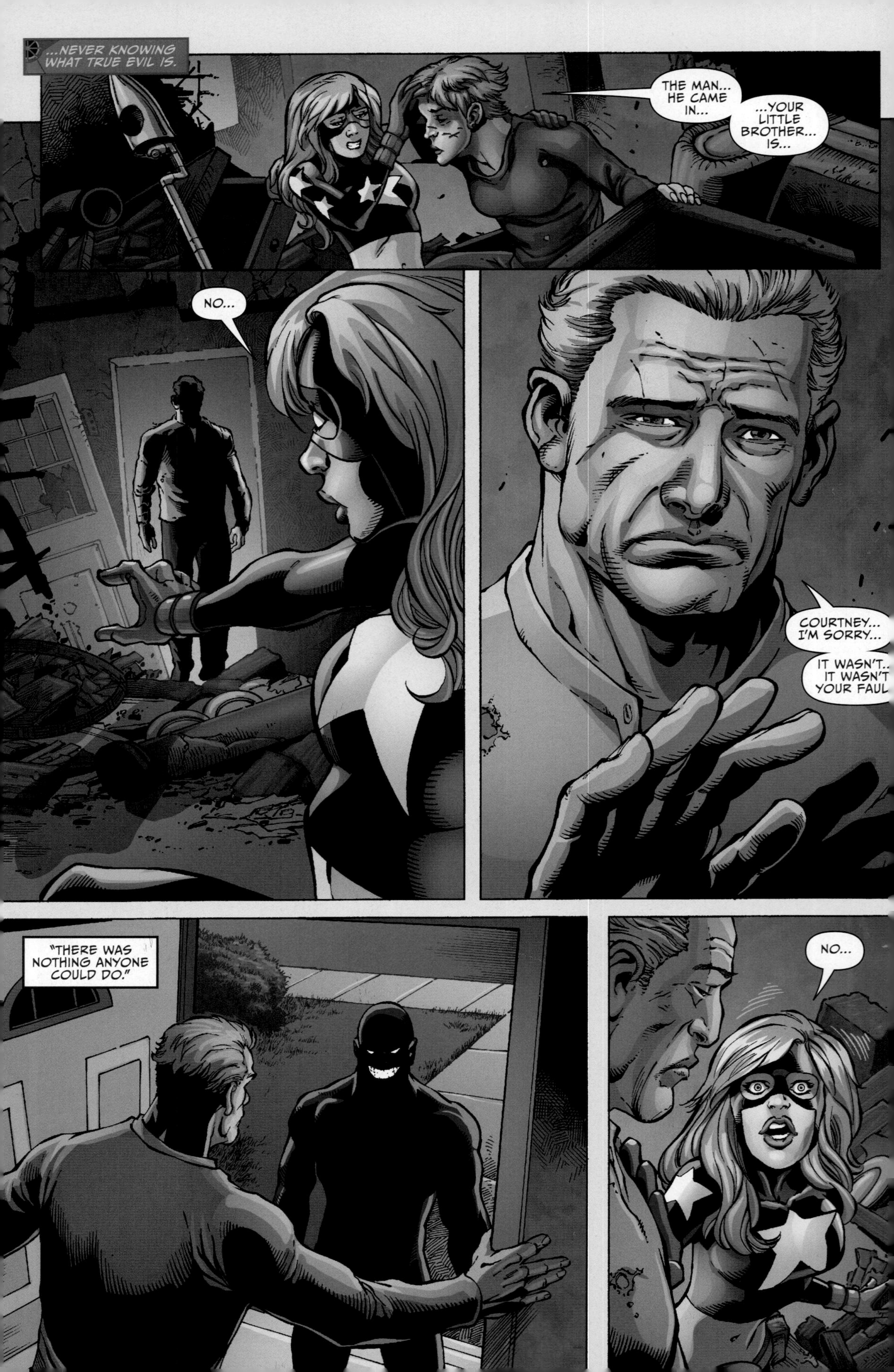

...NEVER KNOWING WHAT TRUE EVIL IS.
THE MAN... HE CAME IN...
...YOUR LITTLE BROTHER... IS...
NO...
COURTNEY... I'M SORRY...
IT WASN'T... IT WASN'T YOUR FAUL
"THERE WAS NOTHING ANYONE COULD DO."
NO...

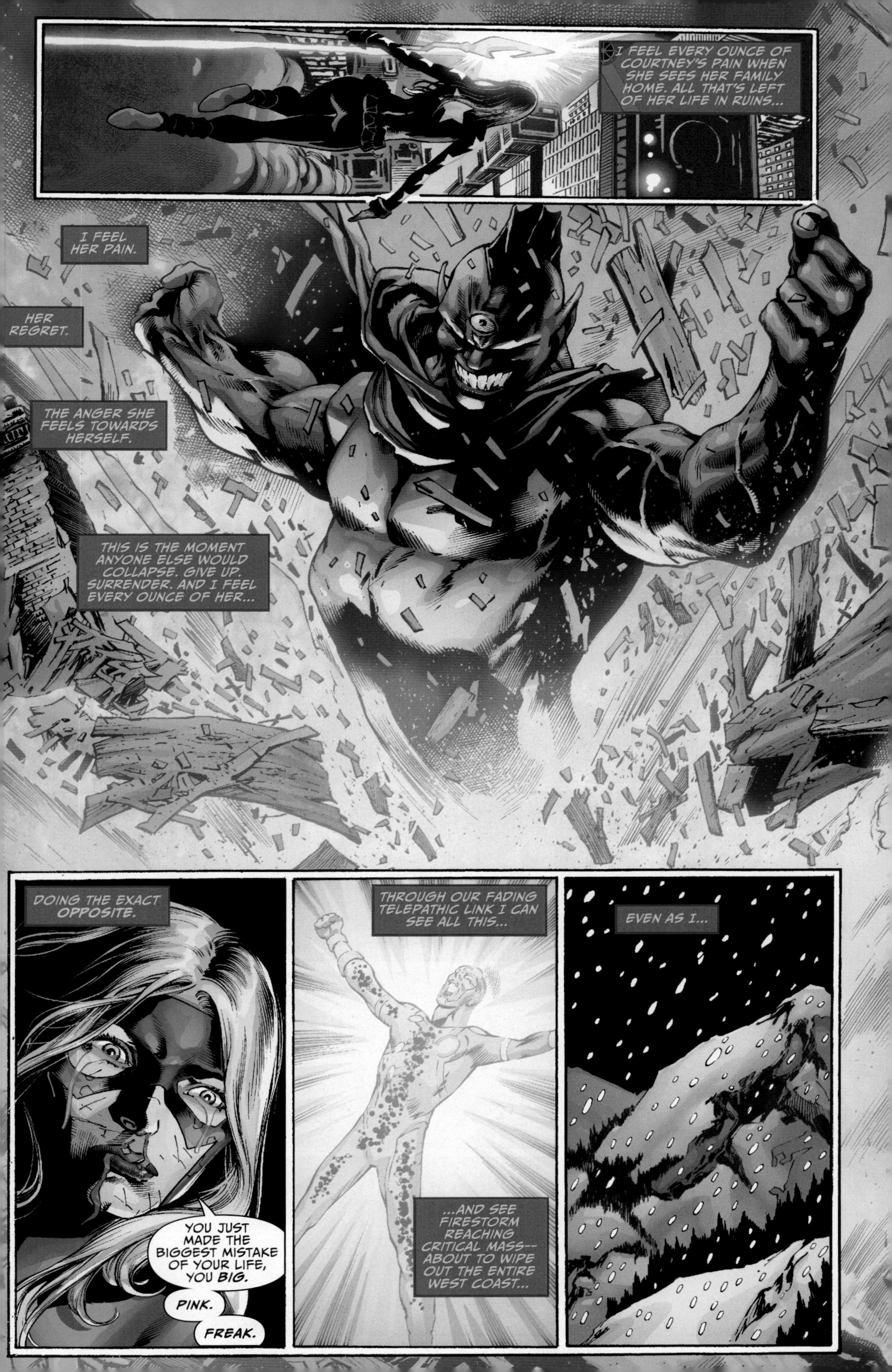
I FEEL EVERY OUNCE OF COURTNEY'S PAIN WHEN SHE SEES HER FAMILY HOME. ALL THAT'S LEFT OF HER LIFE IN RUINS...
I FEEL HER PAIN.
HER REGRET.
THE ANGER SHE FEELS TOWARDS HERSELF.
THIS IS THE MOMENT ANYONE ELSE WOULD COLLAPSE. GIVE UP. SURRENDER. AND I FEEL EVERY OUNCE OF HER...
DOING THE EXACT OPPOSITE.
YOU JUST MADE THE BIGGEST MISTAKE OF YOUR LIFE, YOU BIG.
PINK.
FREAK.
THROUGH OUR FADING TELEPATHIC LINK I CAN SEE ALL THIS...
...AND SEE FIRESTORM REACHING CRITICAL MASS--ABOUT TO WIPE OUT THE ENTIRE WEST COAST...
EVEN AS I...

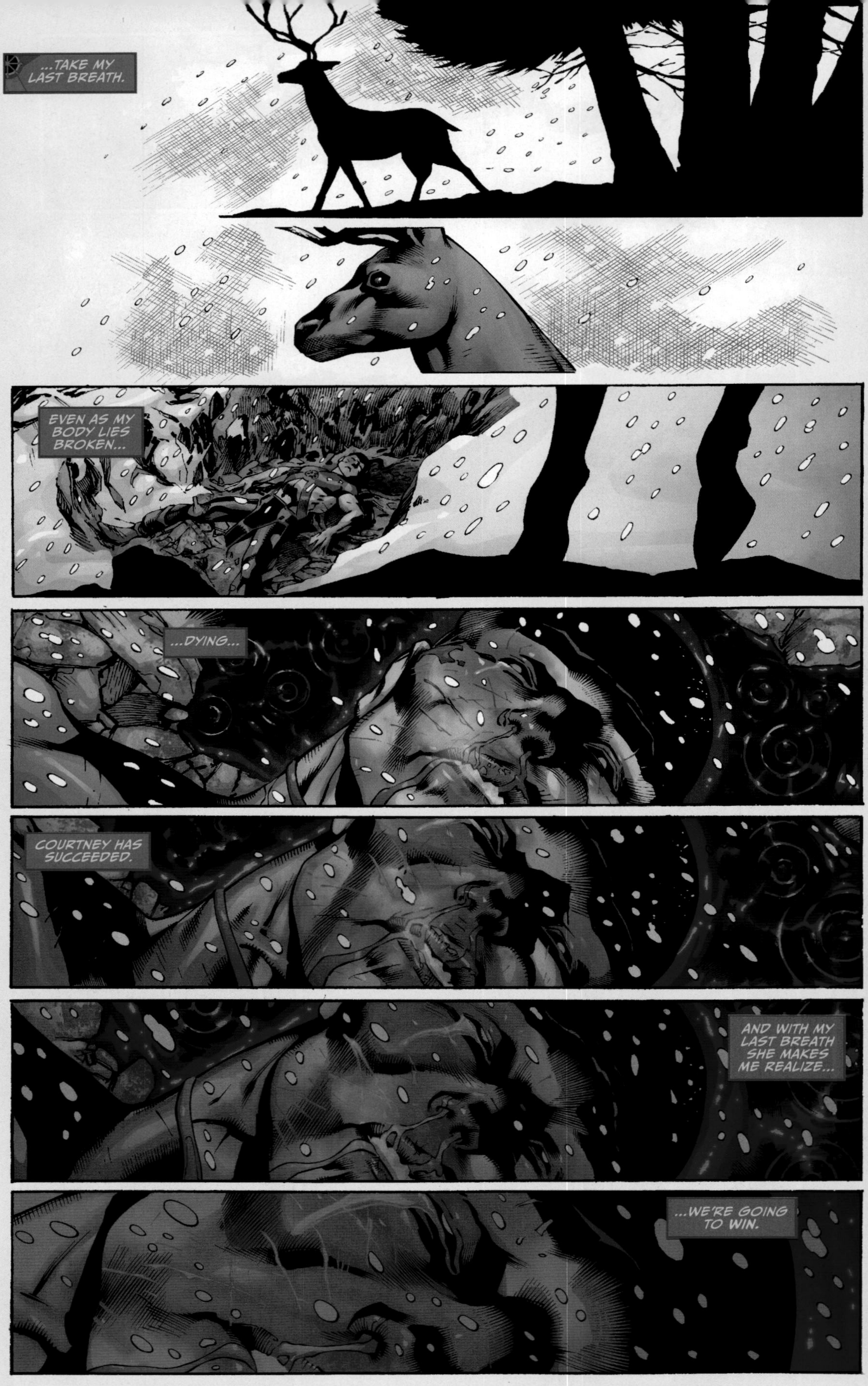
...TAKE MY LAST BREATH.
EVEN AS MY BODY LIES BROKEN...
...DYING...
COURTNEY HAS SUCCEEDED.
AND WITH MY LAST BREATH SHE MAKES ME REALIZE...
...WE'RE GOING TO WIN.

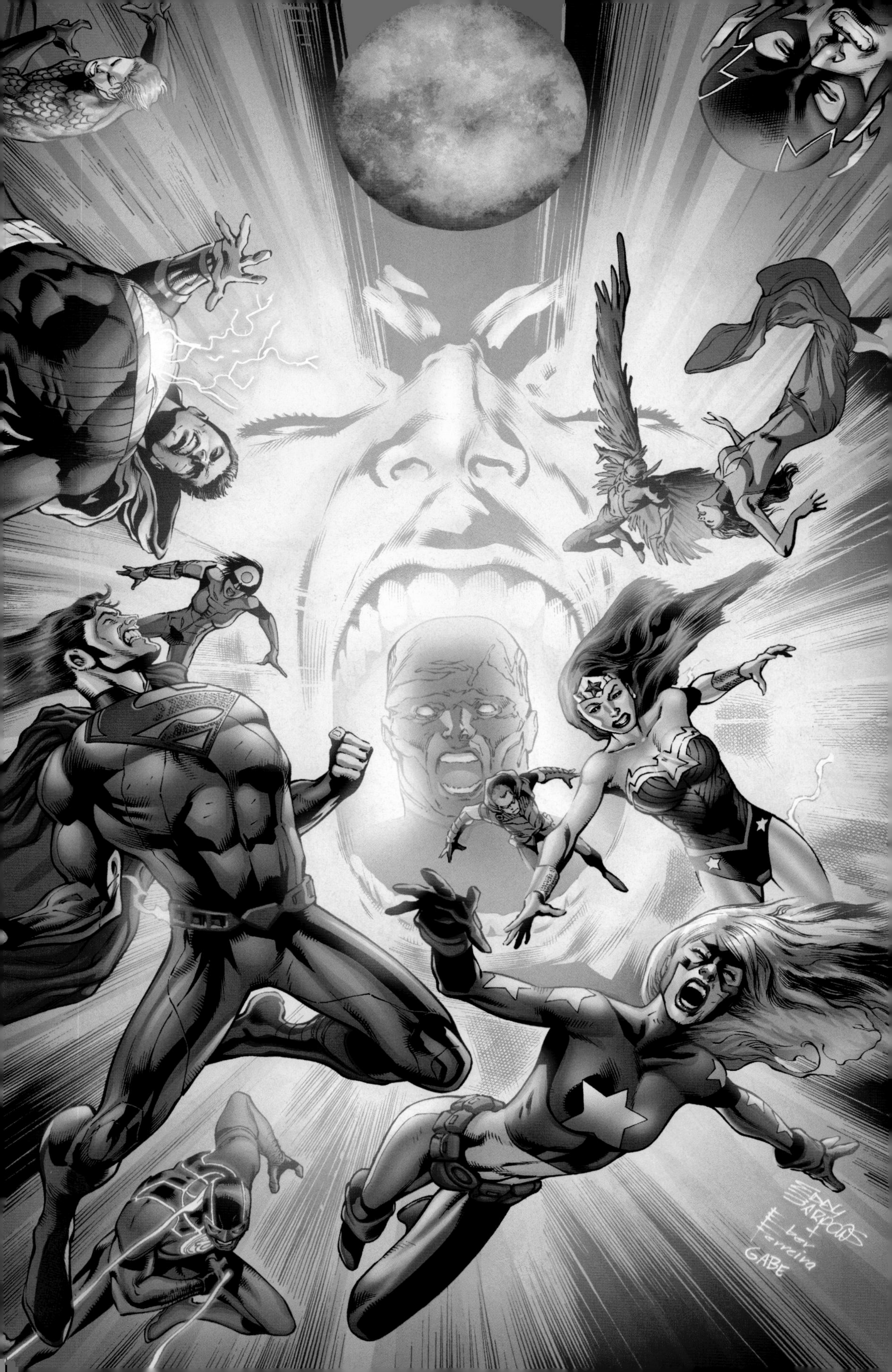

Ferreira
GABE

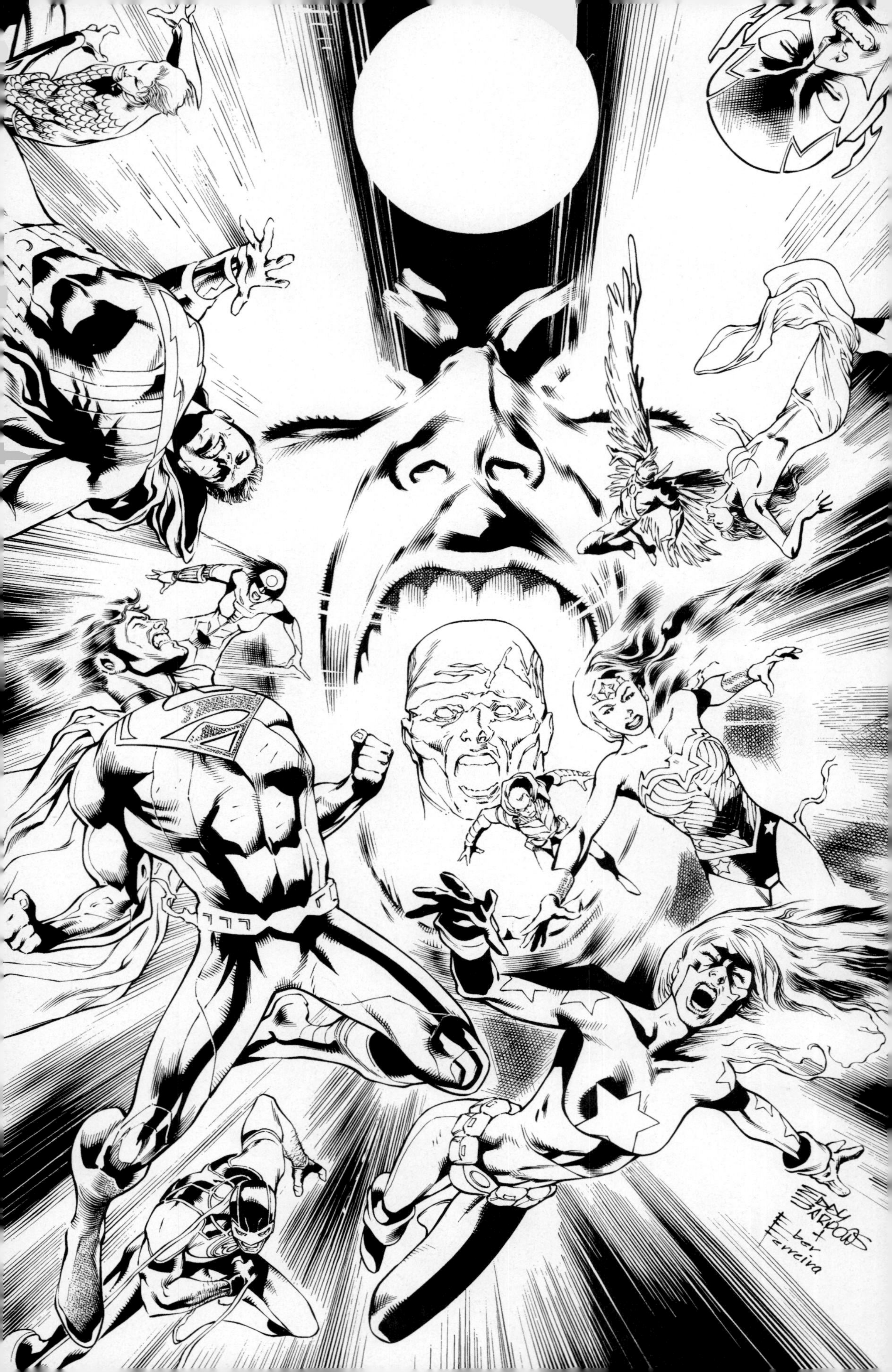
EDDY BARROWS
+
Eber Ferreira

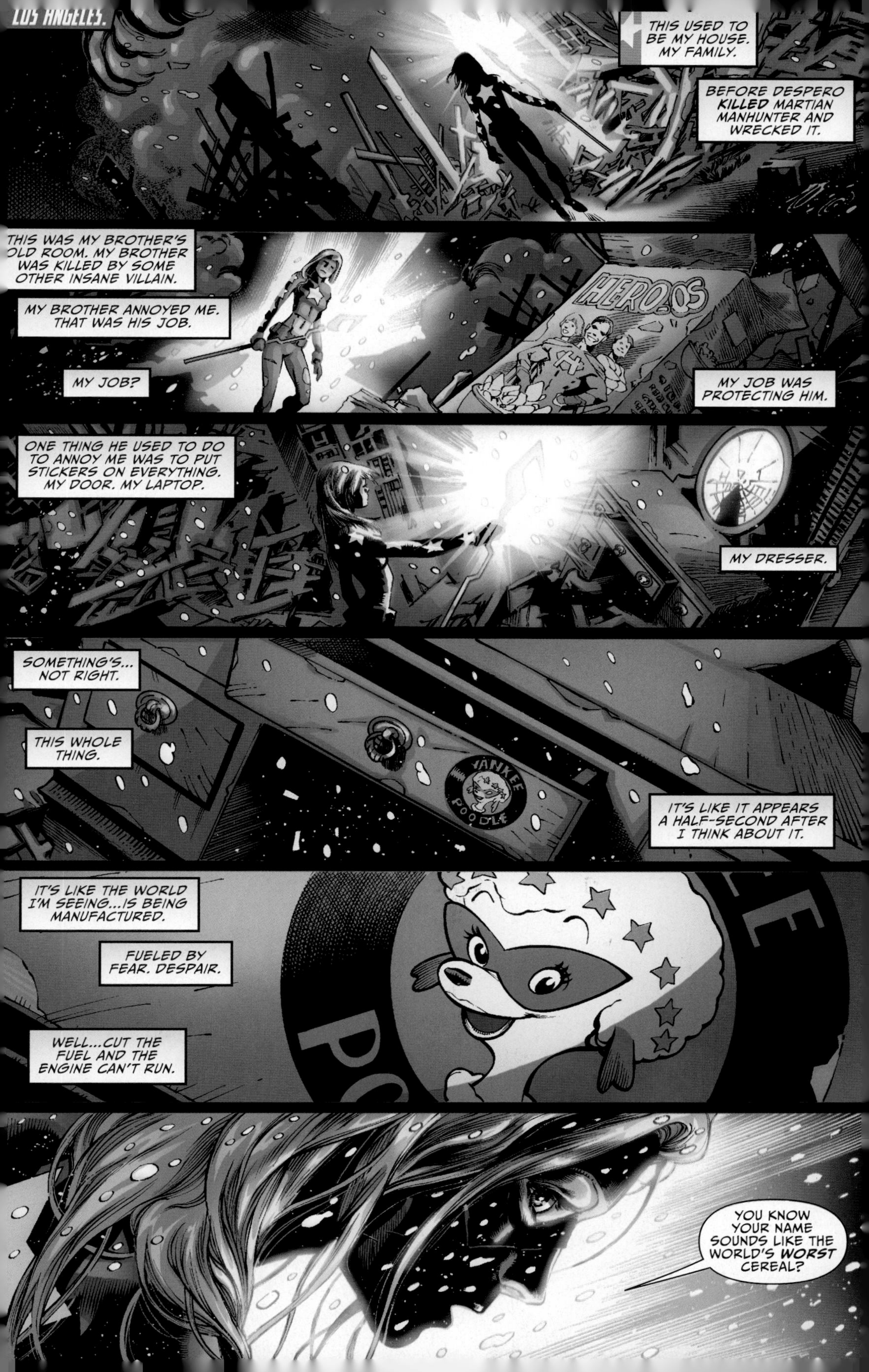
LOS ANGELES.
THIS USED TO BE MY HOUSE. MY FAMILY.
BEFORE DESPERO KILLED MARTIAN MANHUNTER AND WRECKED IT.
THIS WAS MY BROTHER'S OLD ROOM. MY BROTHER WAS KILLED BY SOME OTHER INSANE VILLAIN.
MY BROTHER ANNOYED ME. THAT WAS HIS JOB.
MY JOB?
HERO-OS
MY JOB WAS PROTECTING HIM.
ONE THING HE USED TO DO TO ANNOY ME WAS TO PUT STICKERS ON EVERYTHING. MY DOOR. MY LAPTOP.
MY DRESSER.
SOMETHING'S... NOT RIGHT.
THIS WHOLE THING.
YANKEE POODLE
IT'S LIKE IT APPEARS A HALF-SECOND AFTER I THINK ABOUT IT.
IT'S LIKE THE WORLD I'M SEEING...IS BEING MANUFACTURED.
FUELED BY FEAR. DESPAIR.
WELL...CUT THE FUEL AND THE ENGINE CAN'T RUN.
YOU KNOW YOUR NAME SOUNDS LIKE THE WORLD'S WORST CEREAL?

IT'S ALL BEHIND YOU

MATT KINDT
WRITER

EDDY BARROWS and TOM DERENICK
PENCILS

EBER FERREIRA, MARC DEERING and ALLEN MARTINEZ
INKS

HI-FI
COLORS

ROB LEIGH
LETTERER

BARROWS & FERREIRA with GABE ELTAEB
COVER

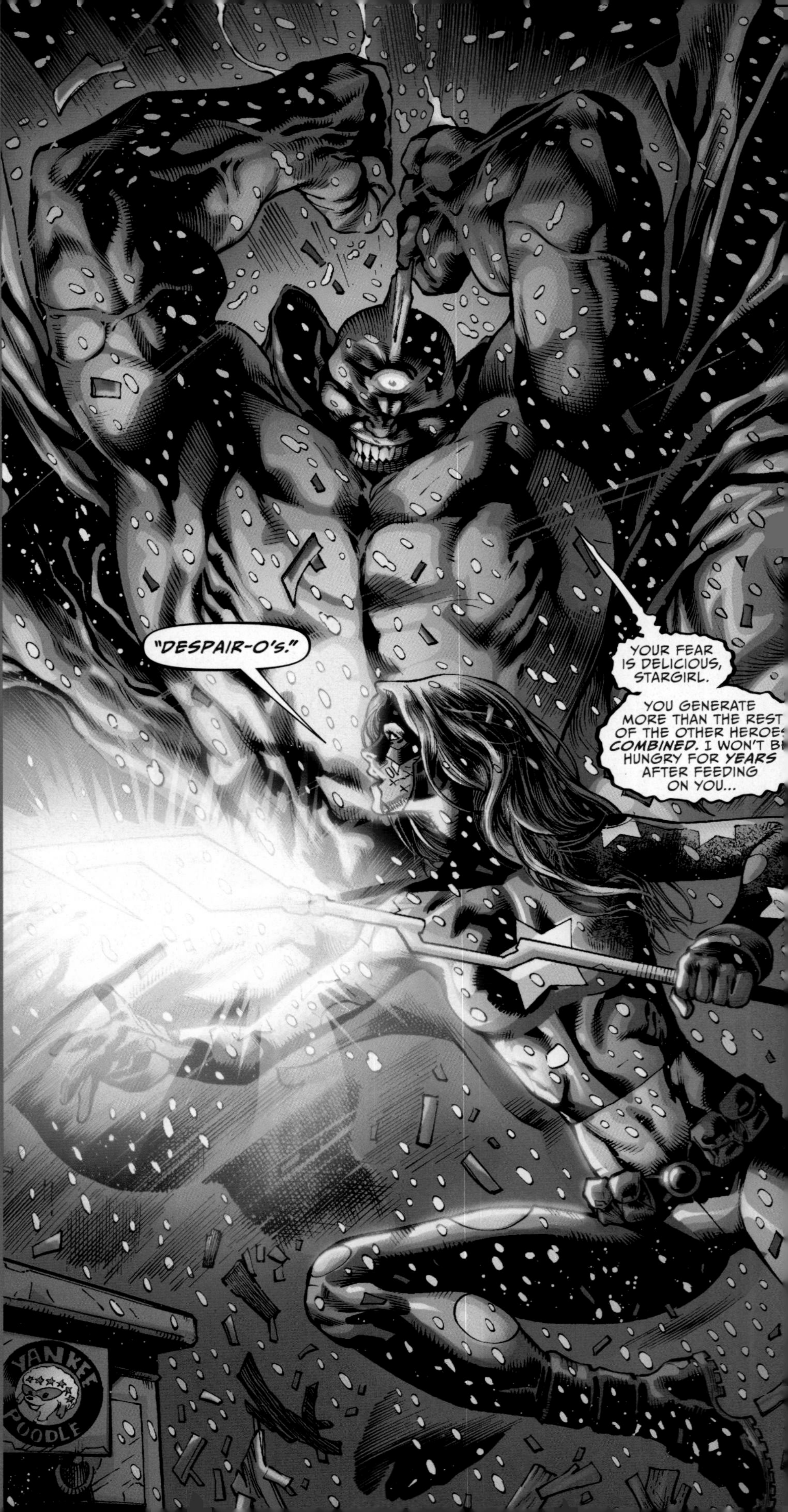
"DESPAIR-O'S."
YOUR FEAR IS DELICIOUS, STARGIRL.
YOU GENERATE MORE THAN THE REST OF THE OTHER HEROES *COMBINED.* I WON'T B HUNGRY FOR *YEARS* AFTER FEEDING ON YOU...
YANKEE POODLE

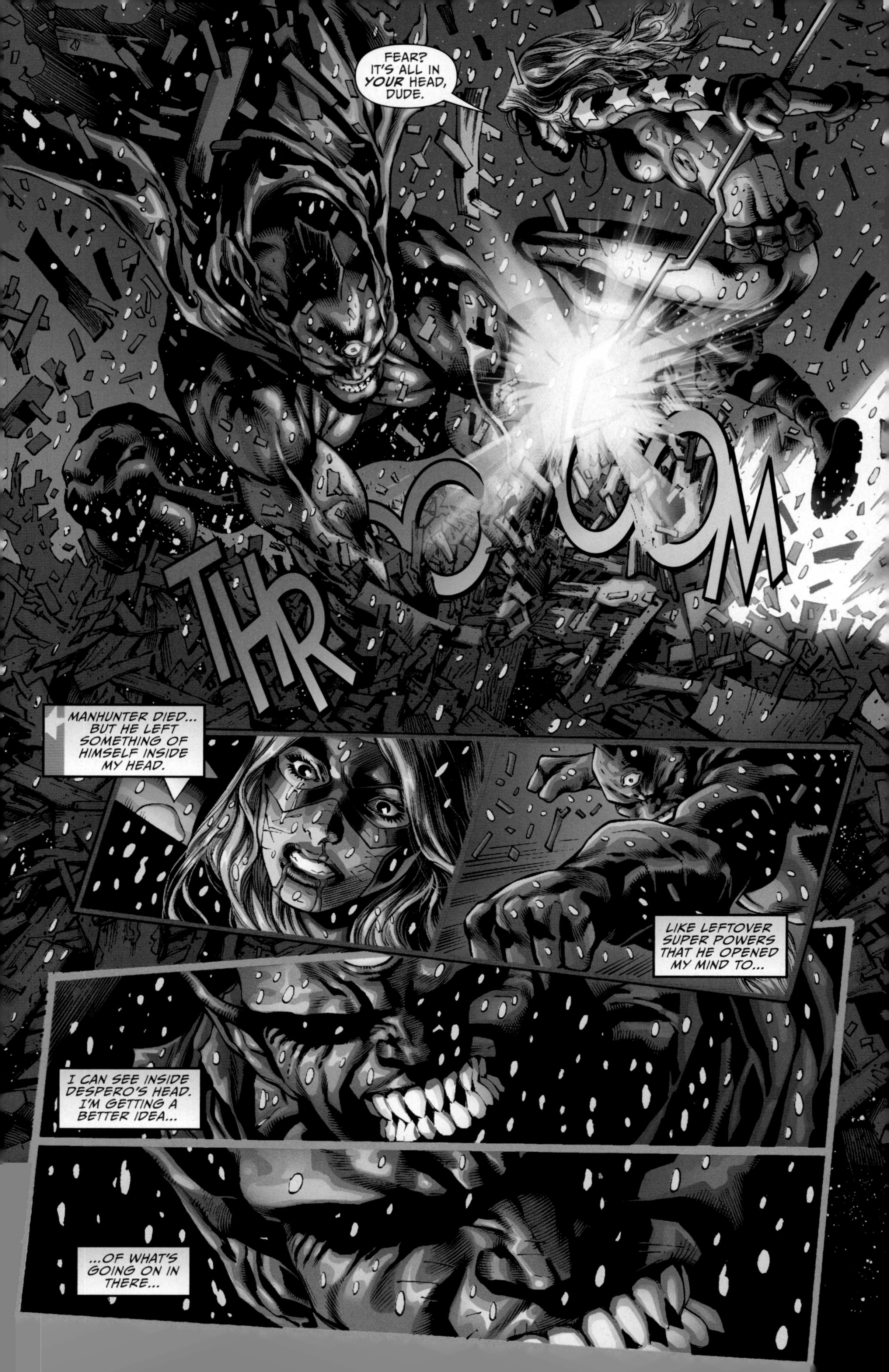
FEAR? IT'S ALL IN YOUR HEAD, DUDE.
THROOOM
MANHUNTER DIED... BUT HE LEFT SOMETHING OF HIMSELF INSIDE MY HEAD.
LIKE LEFTOVER SUPER POWERS THAT HE OPENED MY MIND TO...
I CAN SEE INSIDE DESPERO'S HEAD. I'M GETTING A BETTER IDEA...
...OF WHAT'S GOING ON IN THERE...

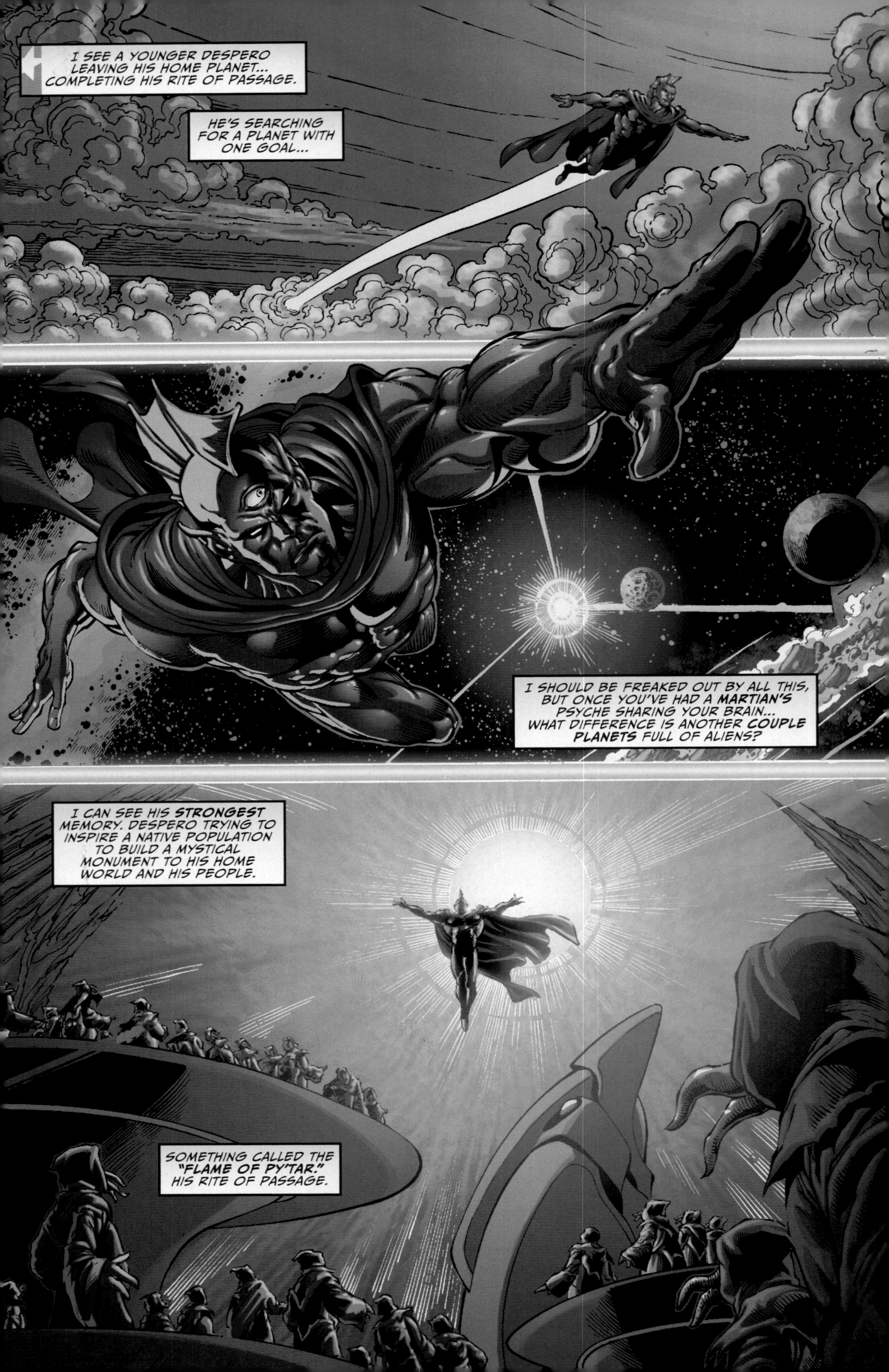
I SEE A YOUNGER DESPERO LEAVING HIS HOME PLANET... COMPLETING HIS RITE OF PASSAGE.
HE'S SEARCHING FOR A PLANET WITH ONE GOAL...
I SHOULD BE FREAKED OUT BY ALL THIS, BUT ONCE YOU'VE HAD A **MARTIAN'S** PSYCHE SHARING YOUR BRAIN... WHAT DIFFERENCE IS ANOTHER **COUPLE PLANETS** FULL OF ALIENS?
I CAN SEE HIS **STRONGEST** MEMORY. DESPERO TRYING TO INSPIRE A NATIVE POPULATION TO BUILD A MYSTICAL MONUMENT TO HIS HOME WORLD AND HIS PEOPLE.
SOMETHING CALLED THE **"FLAME OF PY'TAR."** HIS RITE OF PASSAGE.

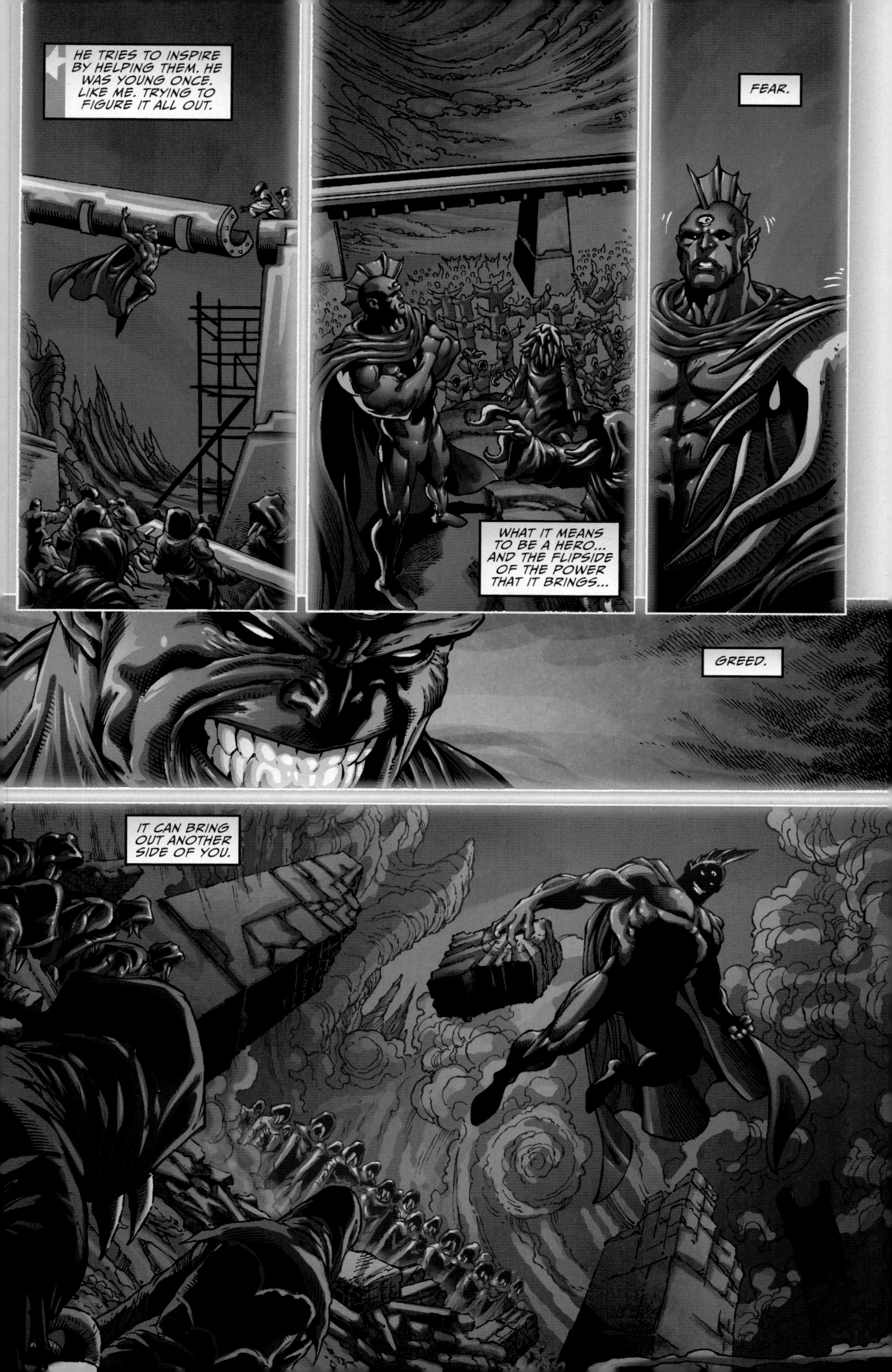
HE TRIES TO INSPIRE BY HELPING THEM. HE WAS YOUNG ONCE. LIKE ME. TRYING TO FIGURE IT ALL OUT.
WHAT IT MEANS TO BE A HERO... AND THE FLIPSIDE OF THE POWER THAT IT BRINGS...
FEAR.
GREED.
IT CAN BRING OUT ANOTHER SIDE OF YOU.

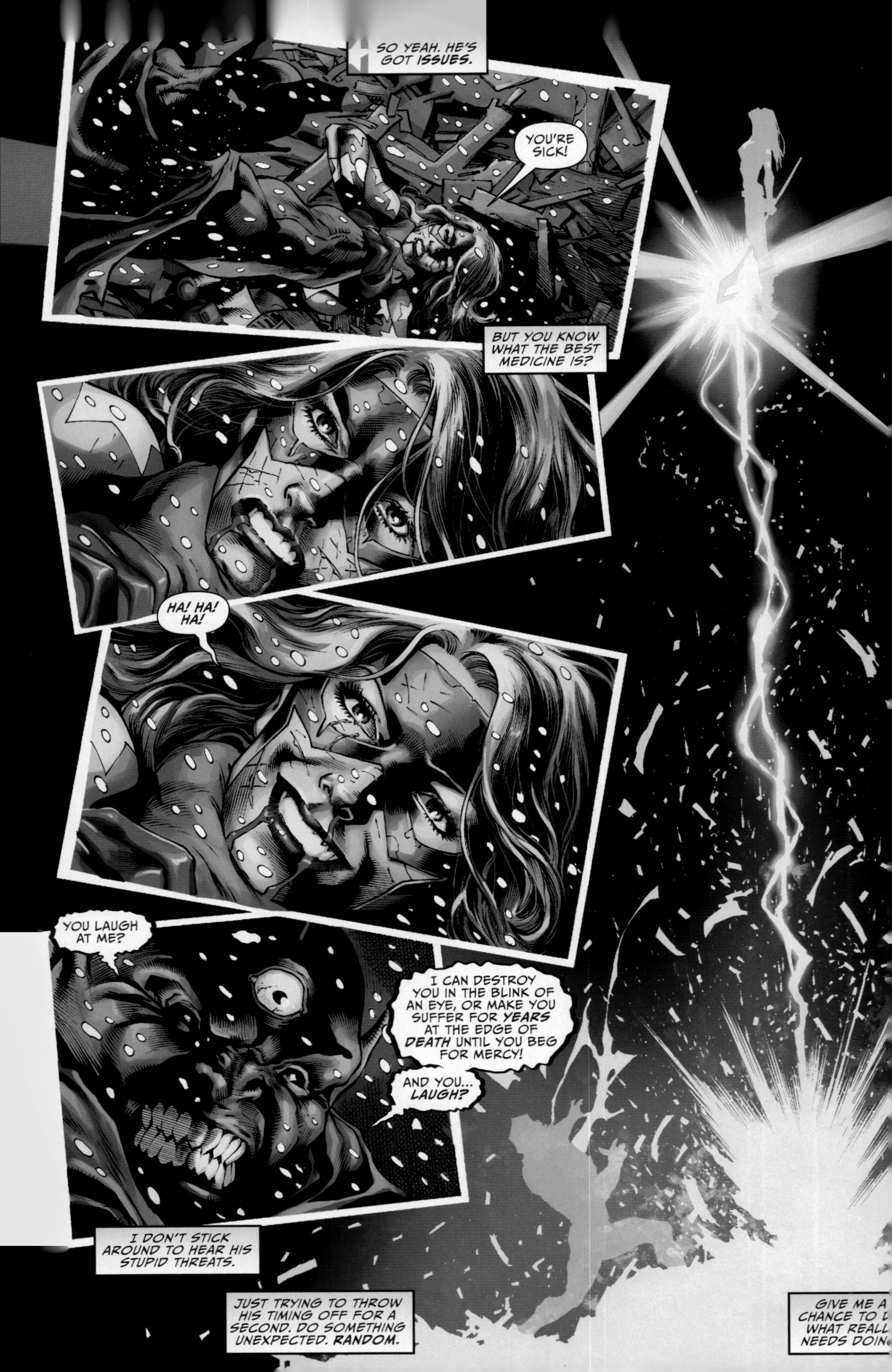
SO YEAH. HE'S GOT ISSUES.
YOU'RE SICK!
BUT YOU KNOW WHAT THE BEST MEDICINE IS?
HA! HA! HA!
YOU LAUGH AT ME?
I CAN DESTROY YOU IN THE BLINK OF AN EYE, OR MAKE YOU SUFFER FOR YEARS AT THE EDGE OF DEATH UNTIL YOU BEG FOR MERCY!
AND YOU... LAUGH?
I DON'T STICK AROUND TO HEAR HIS STUPID THREATS.
JUST TRYING TO THROW HIS TIMING OFF FOR A SECOND. DO SOMETHING UNEXPECTED. RANDOM.
GIVE ME A CHANCE TO
WHAT REALL
NEEDS DOIN

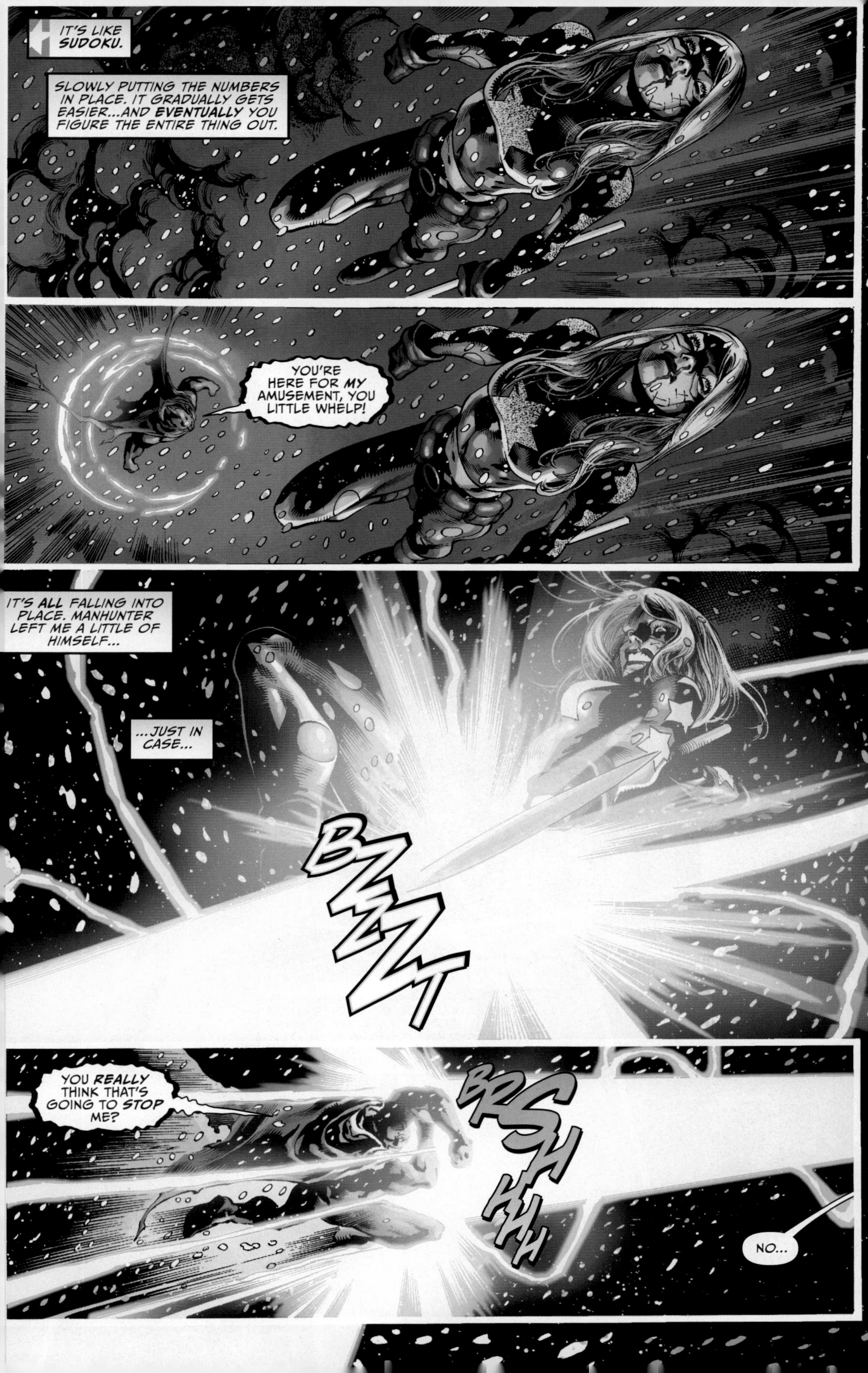
IT'S LIKE SUDOKU.
SLOWLY PUTTING THE NUMBERS IN PLACE. IT GRADUALLY GETS EASIER...AND EVENTUALLY YOU FIGURE THE ENTIRE THING OUT.
YOU'RE HERE FOR MY AMUSEMENT, YOU LITTLE WHELP!
IT'S ALL FALLING INTO PLACE. MANHUNTER LEFT ME A LITTLE OF HIMSELF...
...JUST IN CASE...
BZZZT
YOU REALLY THINK THAT'S GOING TO STOP ME?
BRSHHHH
NO...

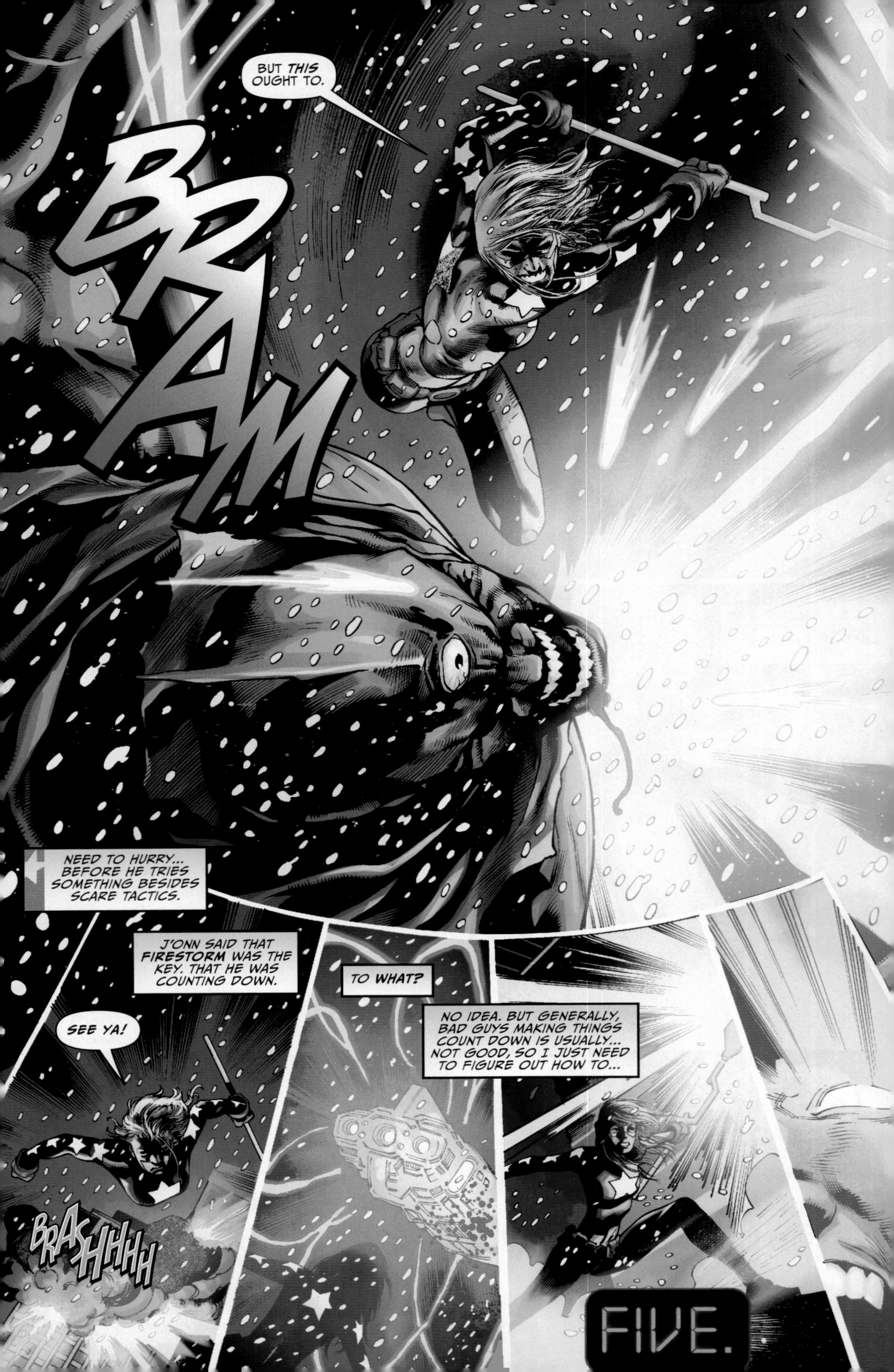
BUT THIS OUGHT TO.
BRAM
NEED TO HURRY... BEFORE HE TRIES SOMETHING BESIDES SCARE TACTICS.
J'ONN SAID THAT FIRESTORM WAS THE KEY. THAT HE WAS COUNTING DOWN.
SEE YA!
BRASHHHH
TO WHAT?
NO IDEA. BUT GENERALLY, BAD GUYS MAKING THINGS COUNT DOWN IS USUALLY... NOT GOOD, SO I JUST NEED TO FIGURE OUT HOW TO...
FIVE.

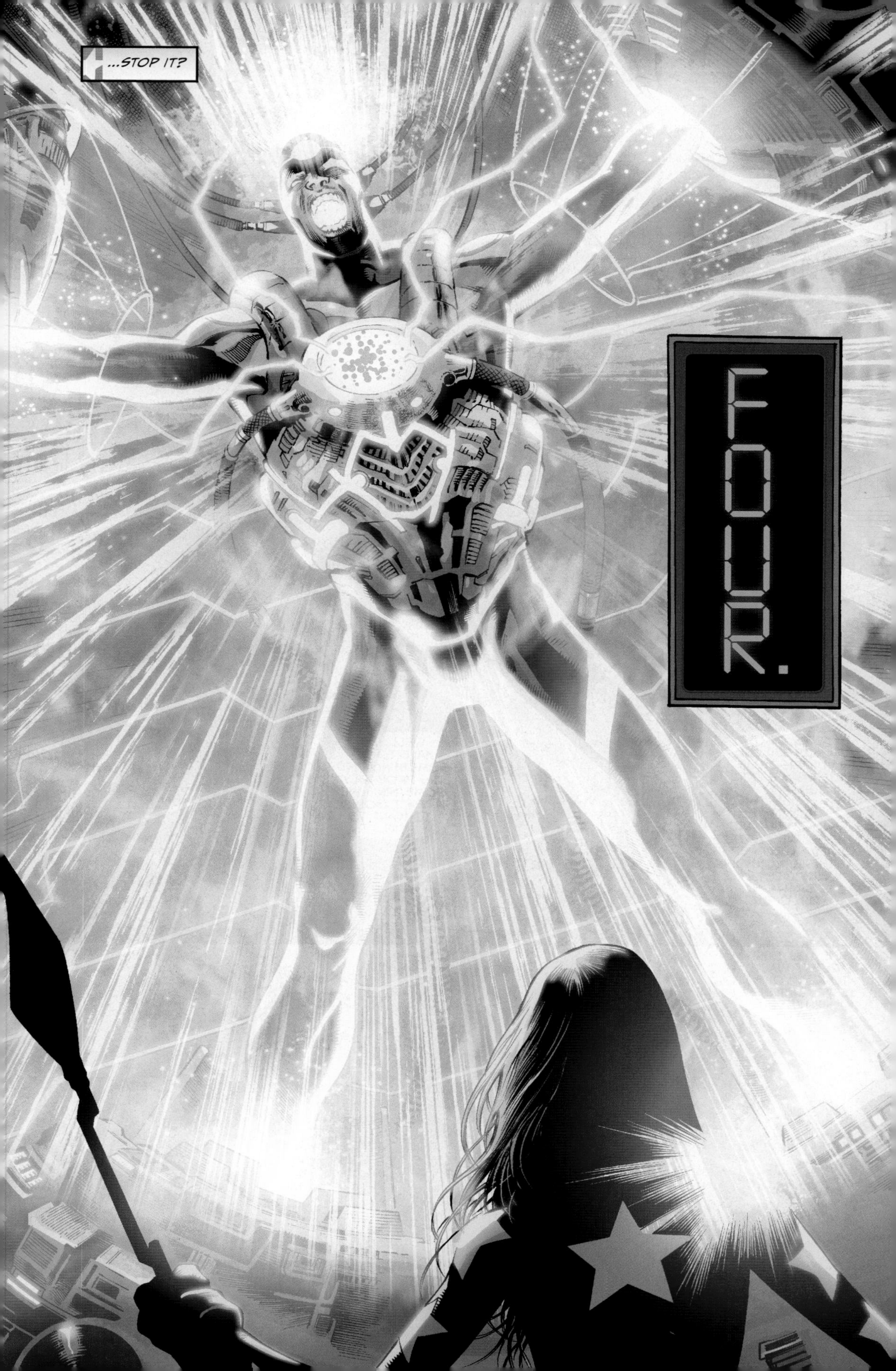
...STOP IT?
FOUR.

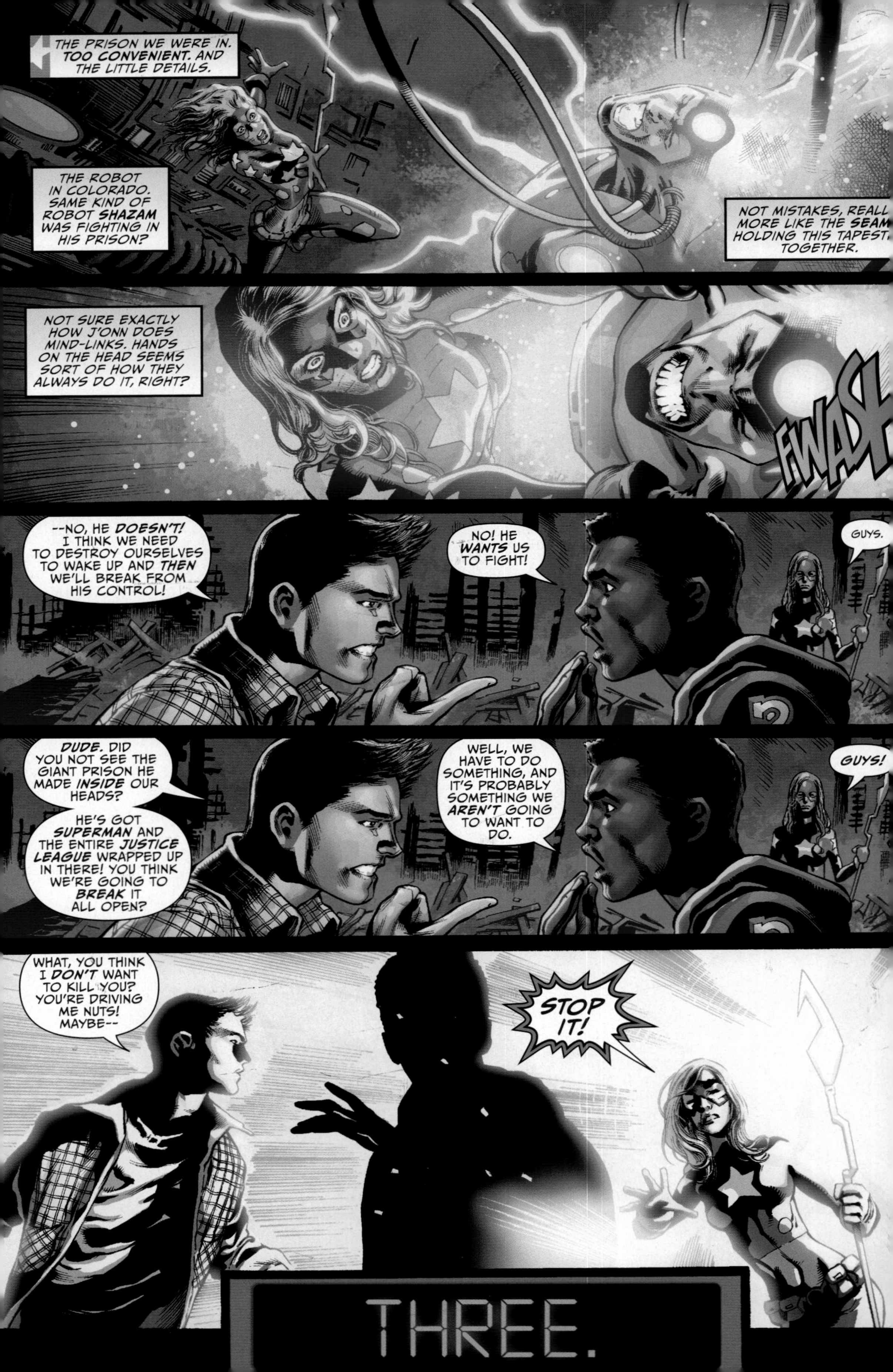
THE PRISON WE WERE IN. TOO CONVENIENT. AND THE LITTLE DETAILS.
THE ROBOT IN COLORADO. SAME KIND OF ROBOT SHAZAM WAS FIGHTING IN HIS PRISON?
NOT MISTAKES, REALL MORE LIKE THE SEAM HOLDING THIS TAPEST TOGETHER.
NOT SURE EXACTLY HOW J'ONN DOES MIND-LINKS. HANDS ON THE HEAD SEEMS SORT OF HOW THEY ALWAYS DO IT, RIGHT?
FWASH
--NO, HE DOESN'T! I THINK WE NEED TO DESTROY OURSELVES TO WAKE UP AND THEN WE'LL BREAK FROM HIS CONTROL!
NO! HE WANTS US TO FIGHT!
GUYS.
DUDE. DID YOU NOT SEE THE GIANT PRISON HE MADE INSIDE OUR HEADS?
HE'S GOT SUPERMAN AND THE ENTIRE JUSTICE LEAGUE WRAPPED UP IN THERE! YOU THINK WE'RE GOING TO BREAK IT ALL OPEN?
WELL, WE HAVE TO DO SOMETHING, AND IT'S PROBABLY SOMETHING WE AREN'T GOING TO WANT TO DO.
GUYS!
WHAT, YOU THINK I DON'T WANT TO KILL YOU? YOU'RE DRIVING ME NUTS! MAYBE--
STOP IT!
THREE.

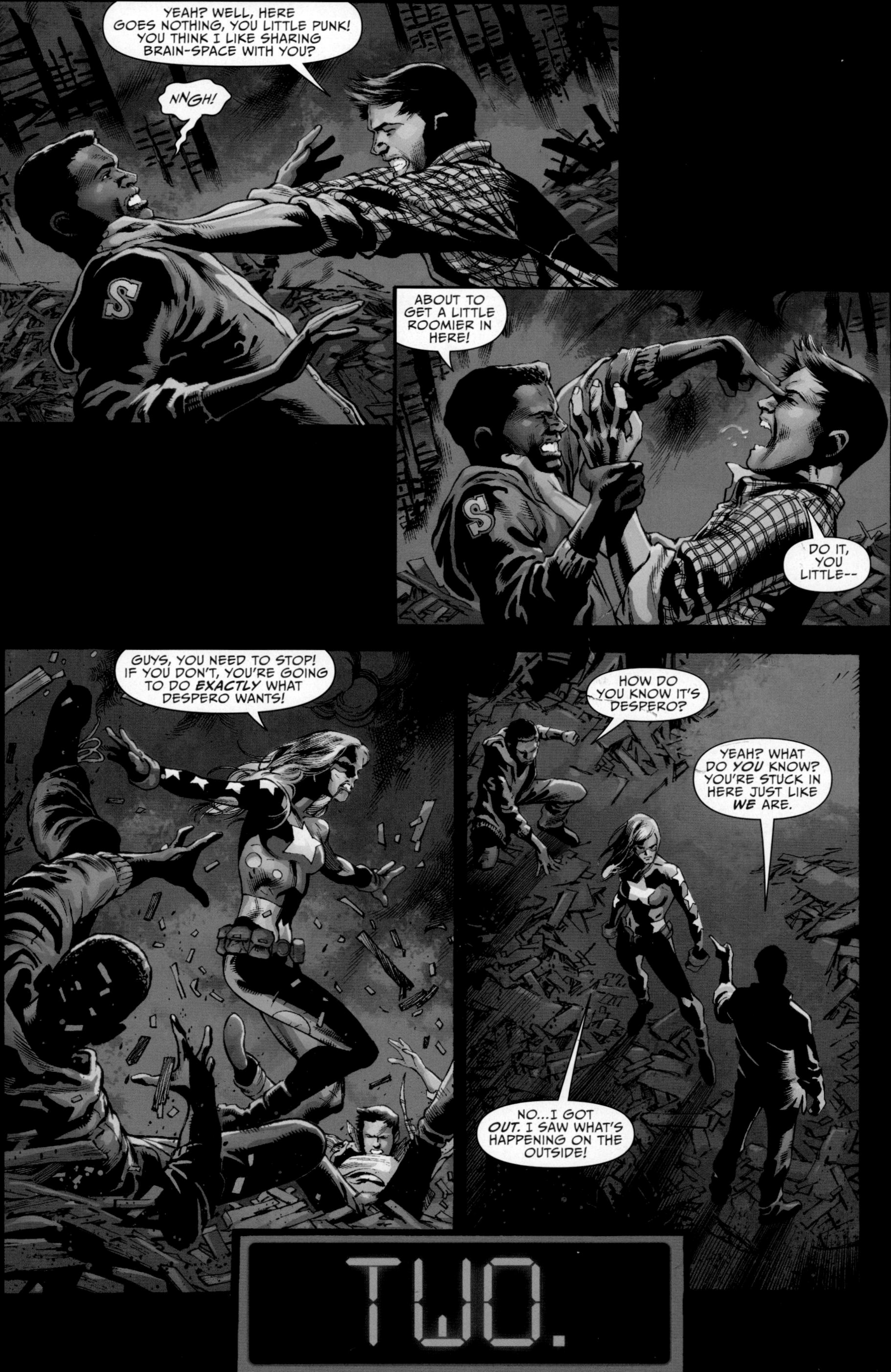
YEAH? WELL, HERE GOES NOTHING, YOU LITTLE PUNK! YOU THINK I LIKE SHARING BRAIN-SPACE WITH YOU?
NNGH!
ABOUT TO GET A LITTLE ROOMIER IN HERE!
DO IT, YOU LITTLE--
GUYS, YOU NEED TO STOP! IF YOU DON'T, YOU'RE GOING TO DO EXACTLY WHAT DESPERO WANTS!
HOW DO YOU KNOW IT'S DESPERO?
YEAH? WHAT DO YOU KNOW? YOU'RE STUCK IN HERE JUST LIKE WE ARE.
NO...I GOT OUT. I SAW WHAT'S HAPPENING ON THE OUTSIDE!
TWO.

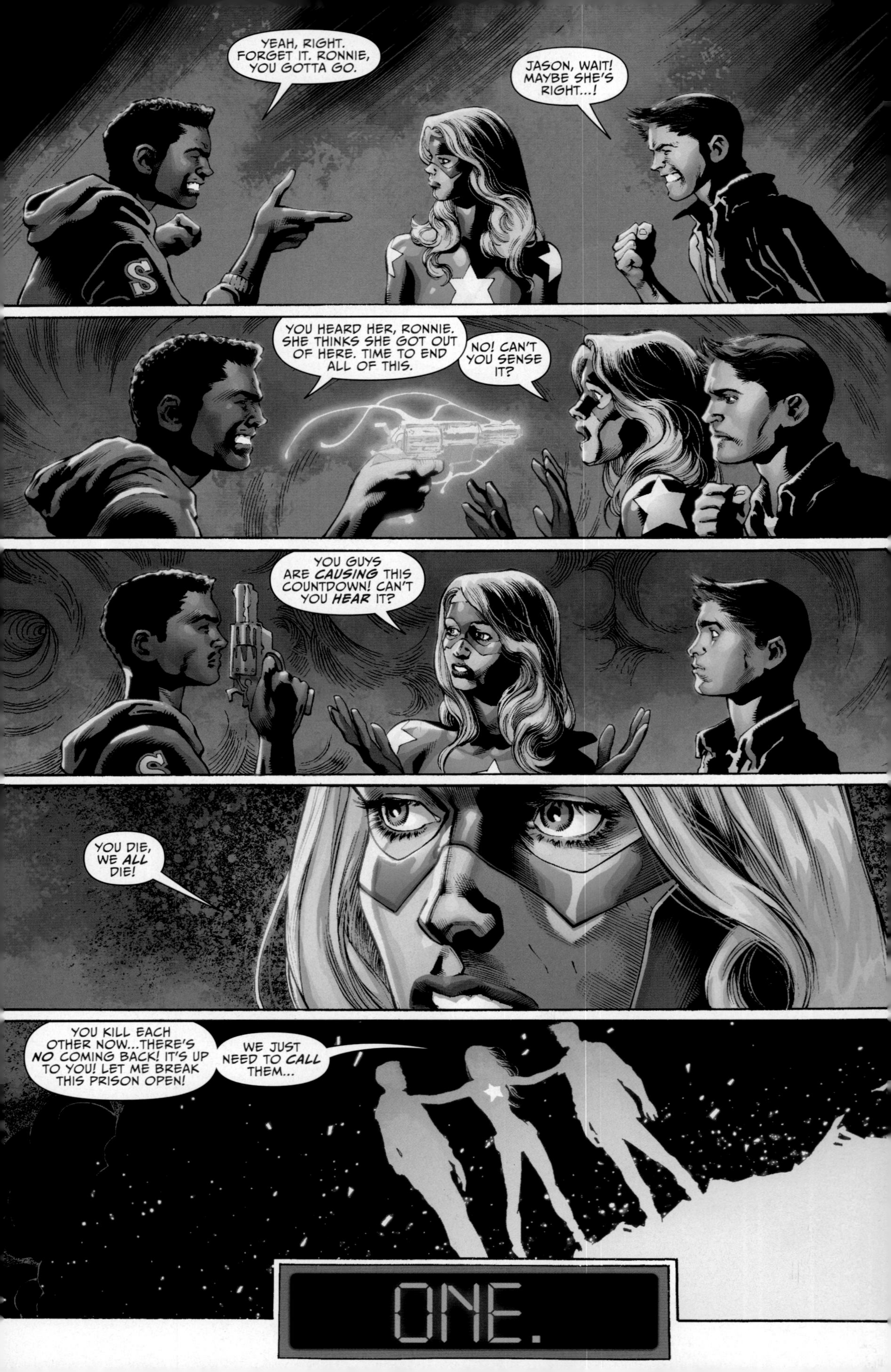
YEAH, RIGHT. FORGET IT. RONNIE, YOU GOTTA GO.
JASON, WAIT! MAYBE SHE'S RIGHT...!
YOU HEARD HER, RONNIE. SHE THINKS SHE GOT OUT OF HERE. TIME TO END ALL OF THIS.
NO! CAN'T YOU SENSE IT?
YOU GUYS ARE CAUSING THIS COUNTDOWN! CAN'T YOU HEAR IT?
YOU DIE, WE ALL DIE!
YOU KILL EACH OTHER NOW...THERE'S NO COMING BACK! IT'S UP TO YOU! LET ME BREAK THIS PRISON OPEN!
WE JUST NEED TO CALL THEM...
ONE.

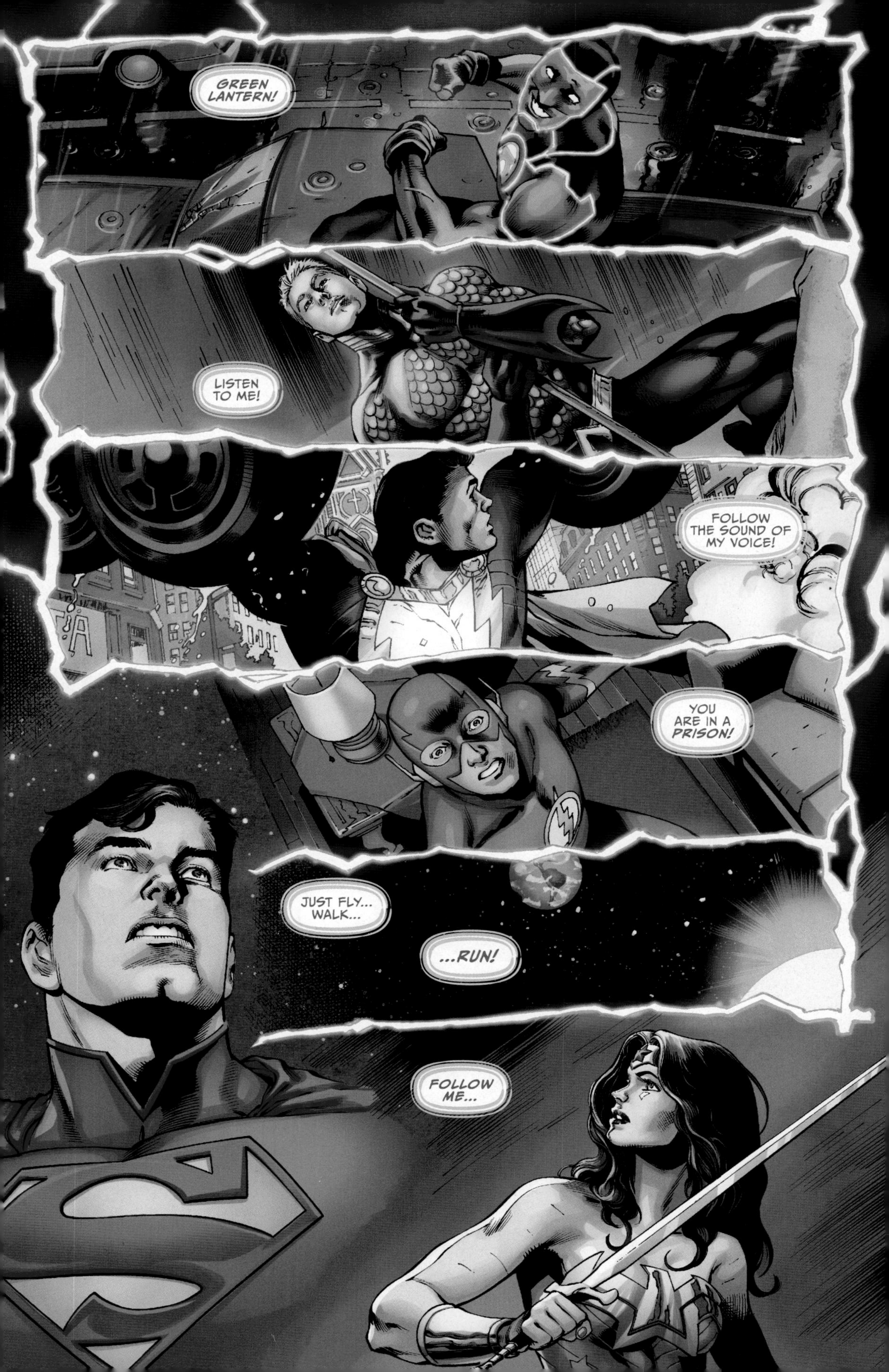
GREEN LANTERN!
LISTEN TO ME!
FOLLOW THE SOUND OF MY VOICE!
YOU ARE IN A PRISON!
JUST FLY... WALK...
...RUN!
FOLLOW ME...

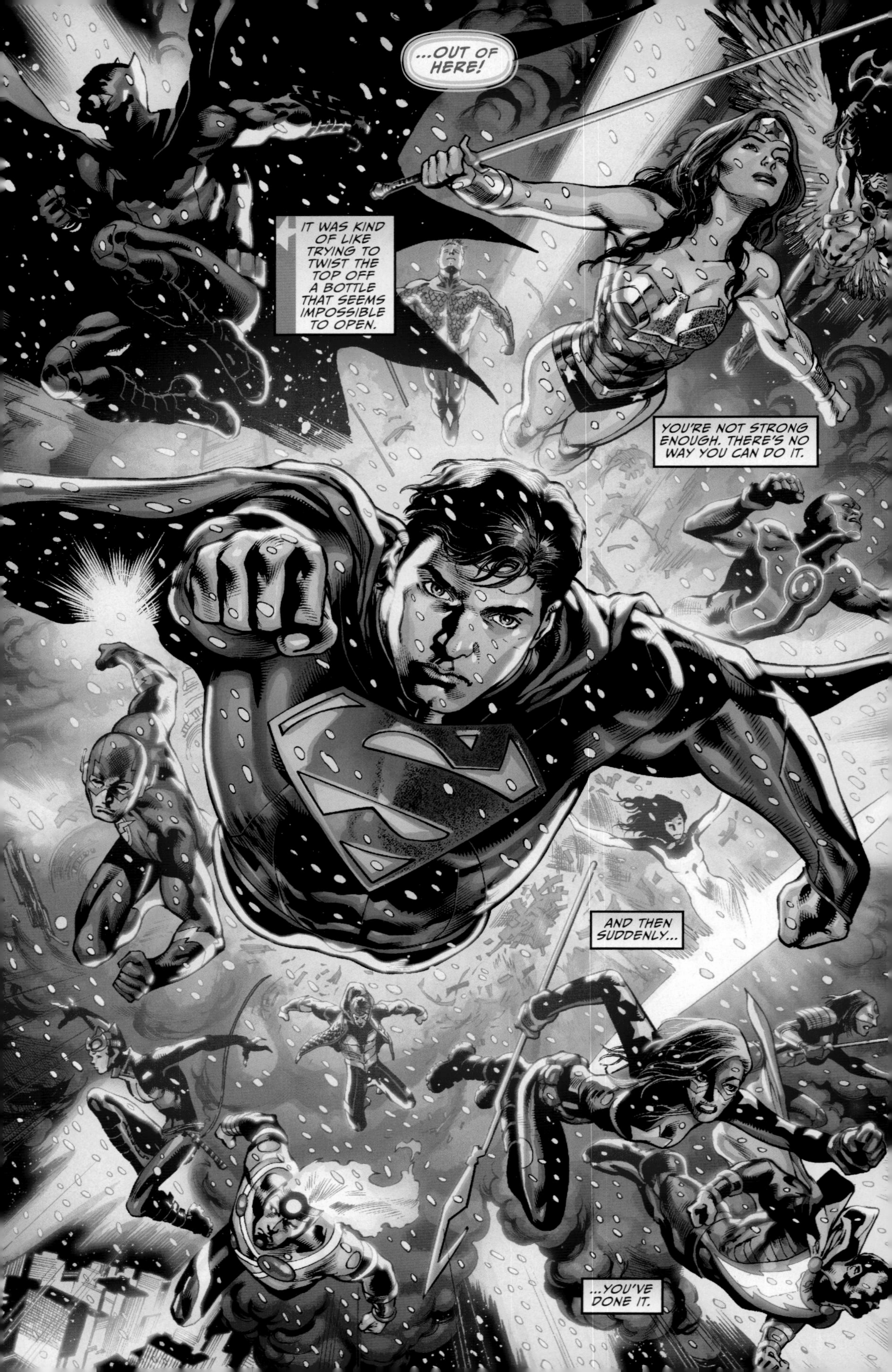
...OUT OF HERE!
IT WAS KIND OF LIKE TRYING TO TWIST THE TOP OFF A BOTTLE THAT SEEMS IMPOSSIBLE TO OPEN.
YOU'RE NOT STRONG ENOUGH. THERE'S NO WAY YOU CAN DO IT.
AND THEN SUDDENLY...
...YOU'VE DONE IT.

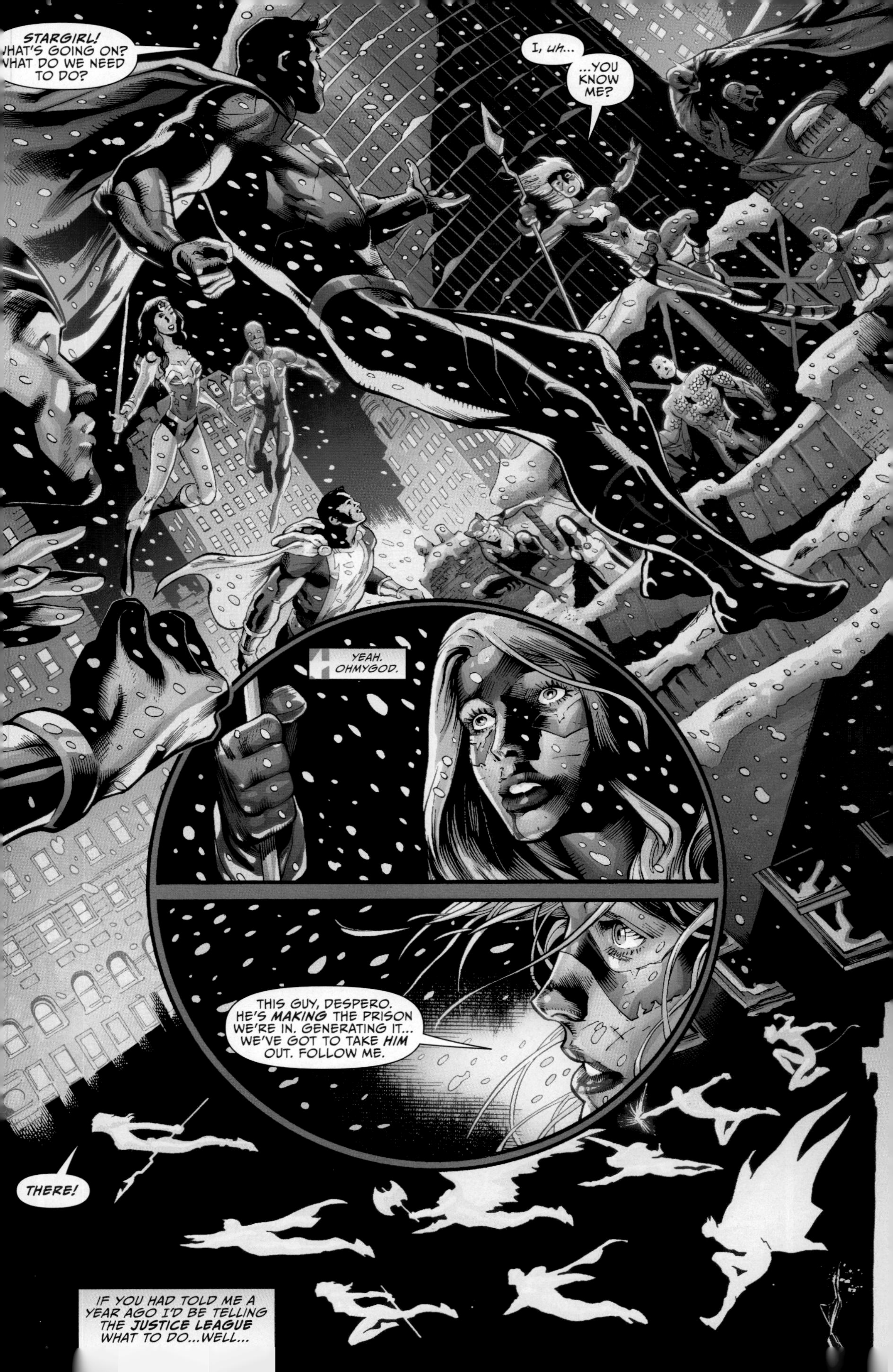
STARGIRL! WHAT'S GOING ON? WHAT DO WE NEED TO DO?
I, uh...
...YOU KNOW ME?
YEAH. OHMYGOD.
THIS GUY, DESPERO. HE'S MAKING THE PRISON WE'RE IN. GENERATING IT... WE'VE GOT TO TAKE HIM OUT. FOLLOW ME.
THERE!
IF YOU HAD TOLD ME A YEAR AGO I'D BE TELLING THE JUSTICE LEAGUE WHAT TO DO...WELL...

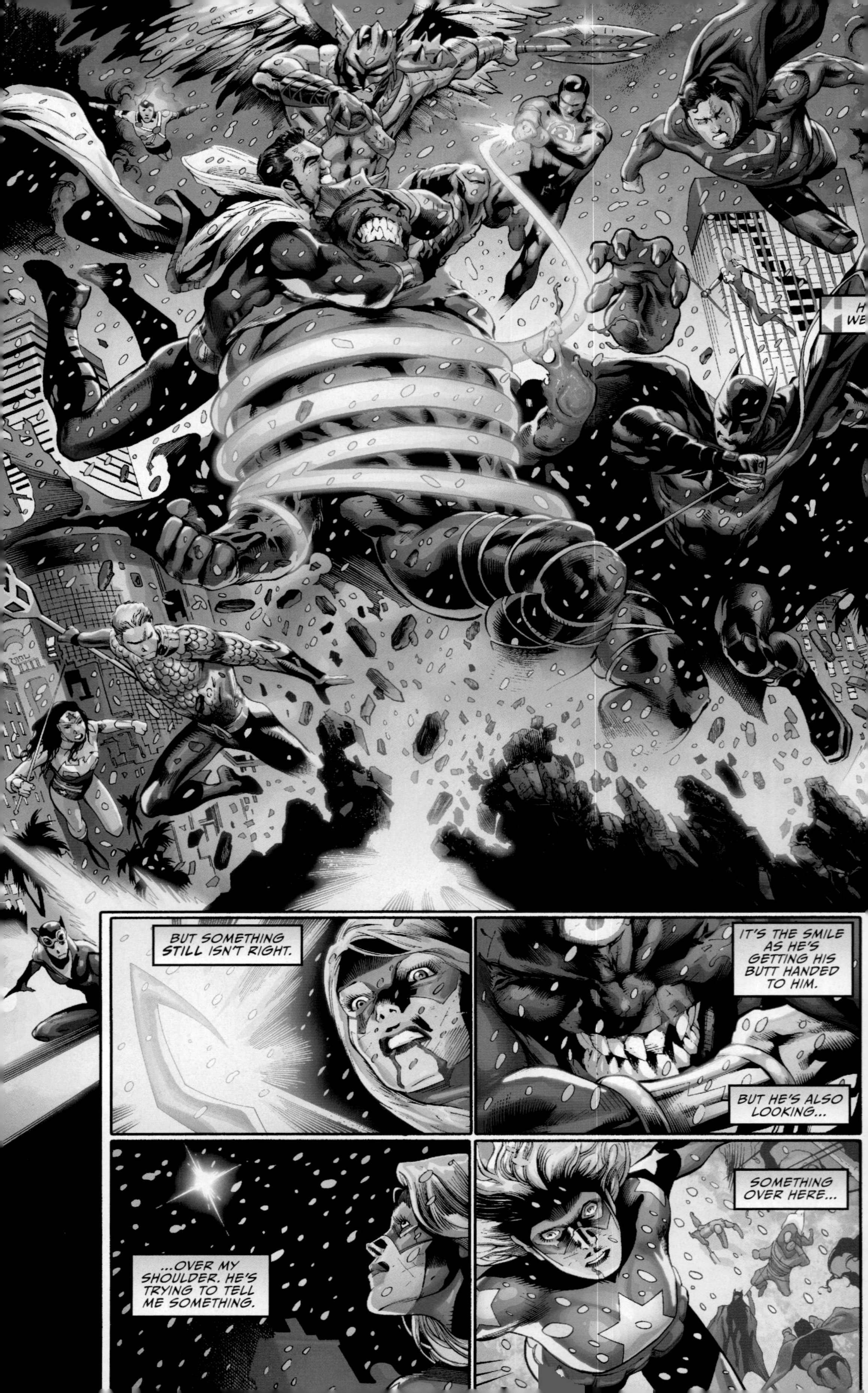
BUT SOMETHING STILL ISN'T RIGHT.
IT'S THE SMILE AS HE'S GETTING HIS BUTT HANDED TO HIM.
BUT HE'S ALSO LOOKING...
...OVER MY SHOULDER. HE'S TRYING TO TELL ME SOMETHING.
SOMETHING OVER HERE...

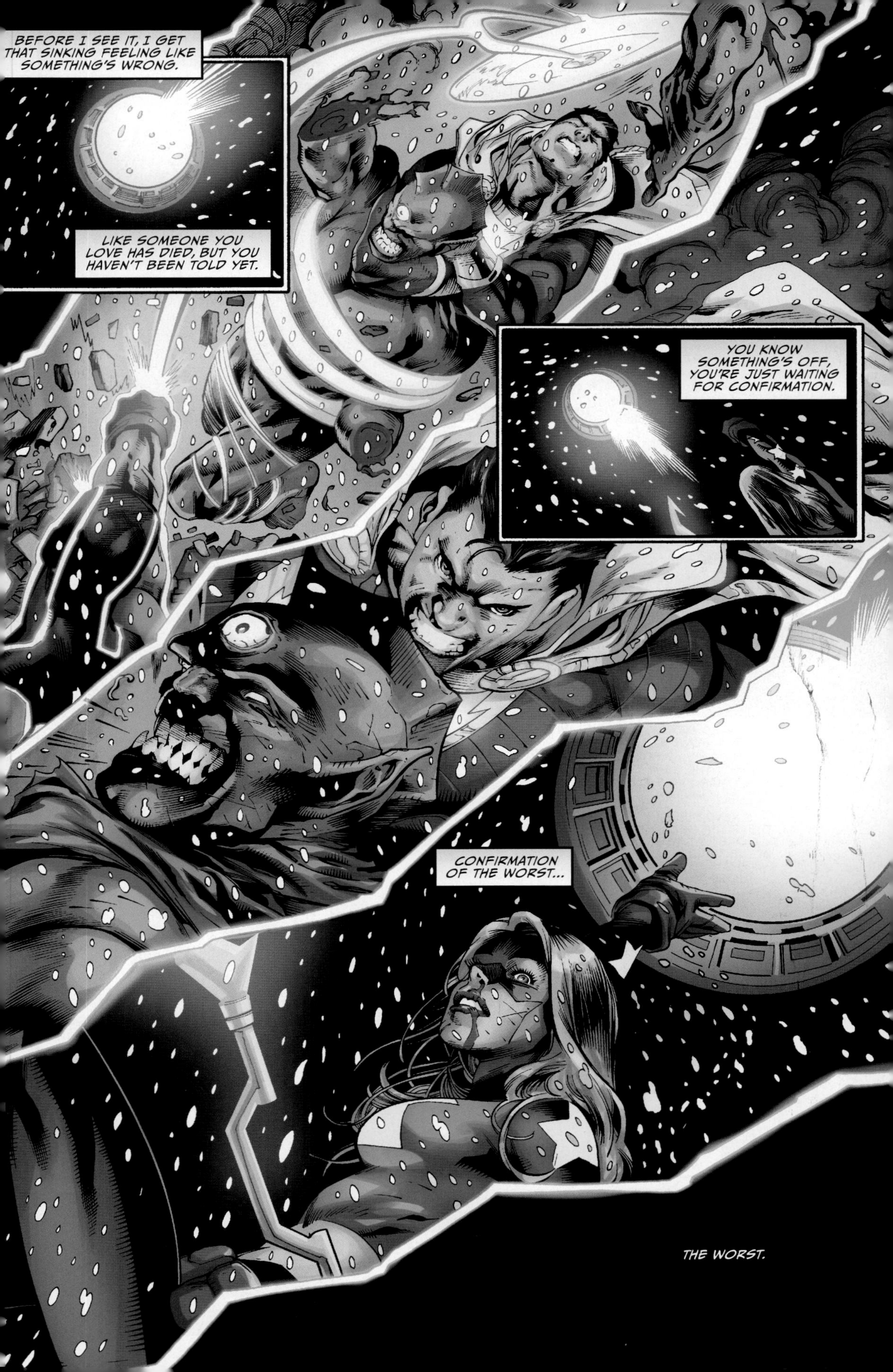
BEFORE I SEE IT, I GET THAT SINKING FEELING LIKE SOMETHING'S WRONG.
LIKE SOMEONE YOU LOVE HAS DIED, BUT YOU HAVEN'T BEEN TOLD YET.
YOU KNOW SOMETHING'S OFF, YOU'RE JUST WAITING FOR CONFIRMATION.
CONFIRMATION OF THE WORST...
THE WORST.

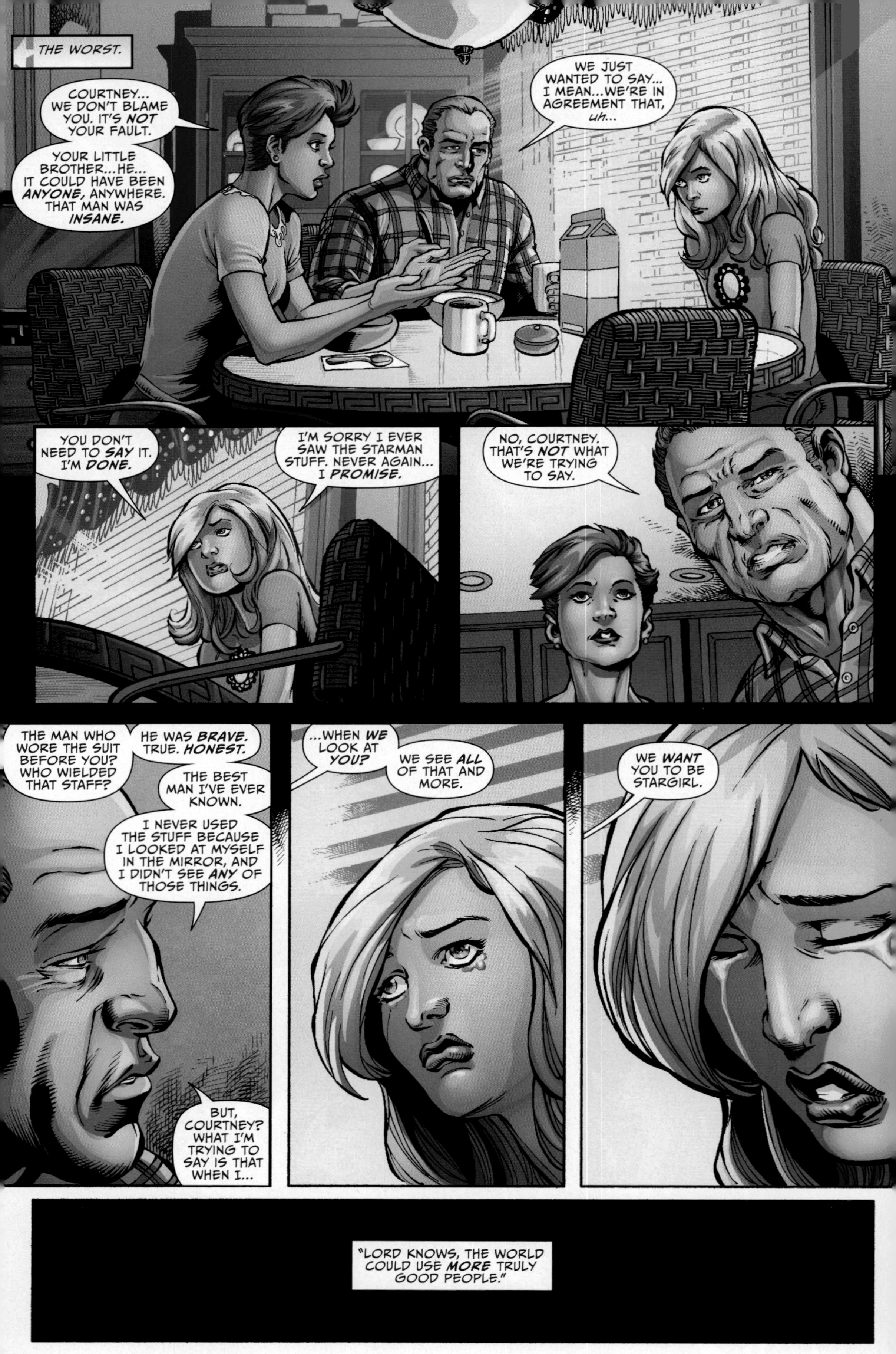
THE WORST.
COURTNEY... WE DON'T BLAME YOU. IT'S NOT YOUR FAULT.
YOUR LITTLE BROTHER...HE... IT COULD HAVE BEEN ANYONE, ANYWHERE. THAT MAN WAS INSANE.
WE JUST WANTED TO SAY... I MEAN...WE'RE IN AGREEMENT THAT, uh...
YOU DON'T NEED TO SAY IT. I'M DONE.
I'M SORRY I EVER SAW THE STARMAN STUFF. NEVER AGAIN... I PROMISE.
NO, COURTNEY. THAT'S NOT WHAT WE'RE TRYING TO SAY.
THE MAN WHO WORE THE SUIT BEFORE YOU? WHO WIELDED THAT STAFF?
HE WAS BRAVE. TRUE. HONEST.
THE BEST MAN I'VE EVER KNOWN.
I NEVER USED THE STUFF BECAUSE I LOOKED AT MYSELF IN THE MIRROR, AND I DIDN'T SEE ANY OF THOSE THINGS.
BUT, COURTNEY? WHAT I'M TRYING TO SAY IS THAT WHEN I...
...WHEN WE LOOK AT YOU?
WE SEE ALL OF THAT AND MORE.
WE WANT YOU TO BE STARGIRL.
"LORD KNOWS, THE WORLD COULD USE MORE TRULY GOOD PEOPLE."

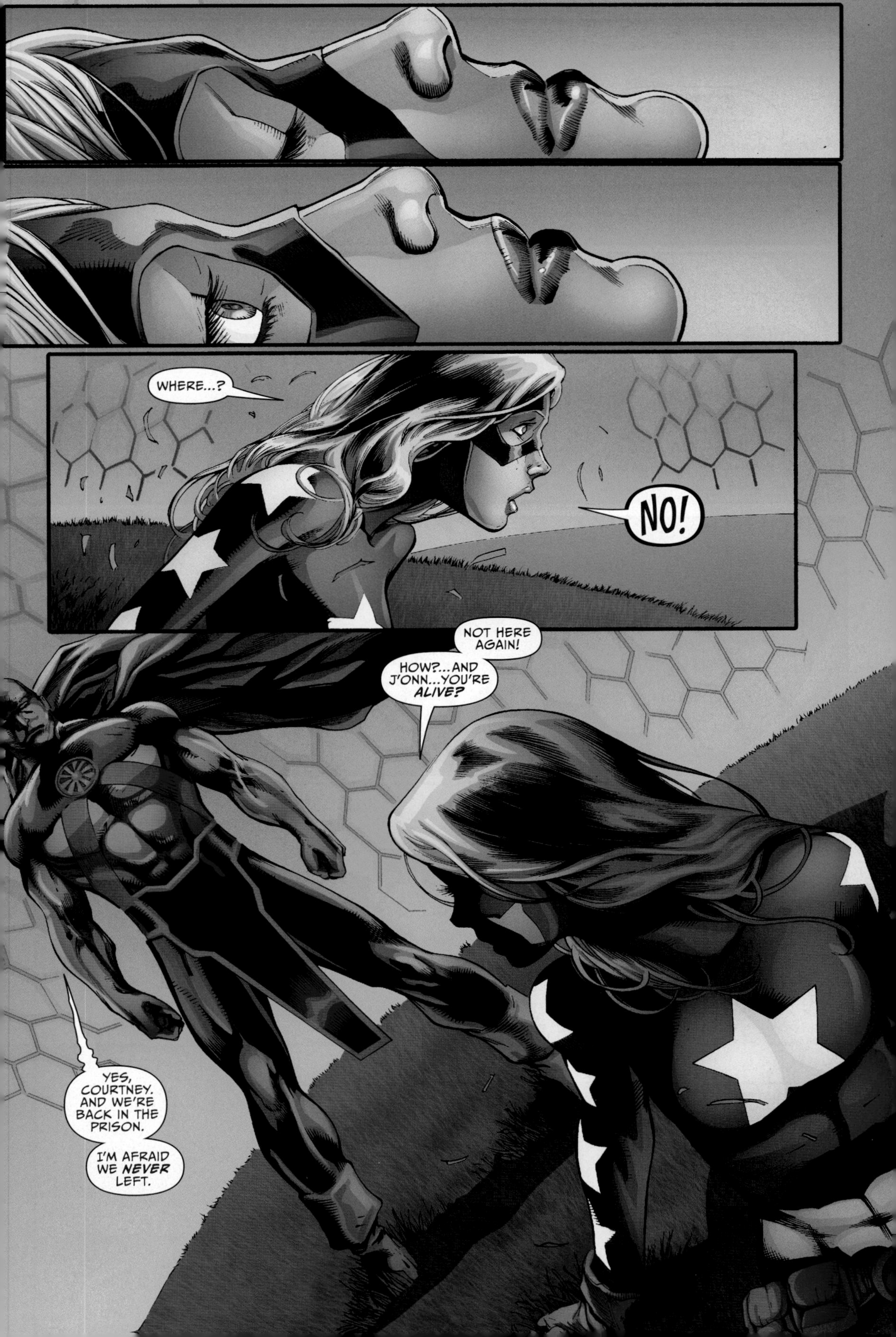
WHERE...?
NO!
NOT HERE AGAIN!
HOW?...AND J'ONN...YOU'RE *ALIVE?*
YES, COURTNEY. AND WE'RE BACK IN THE PRISON.
I'M AFRAID WE *NEVER* LEFT.

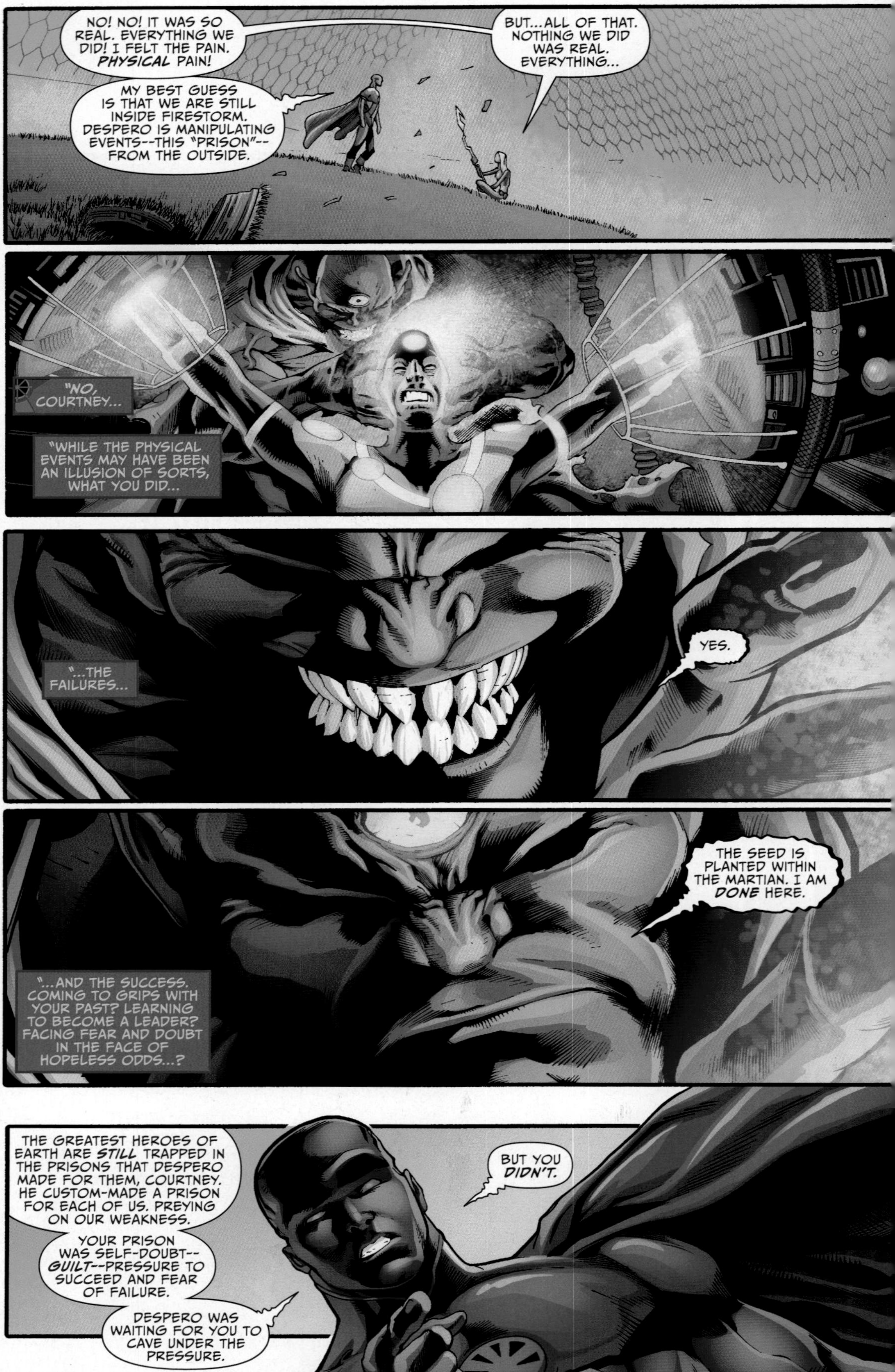
NO! NO! IT WAS SO REAL. EVERYTHING WE DID! I FELT THE PAIN. PHYSICAL PAIN!
BUT...ALL OF THAT. NOTHING WE DID WAS REAL. EVERYTHING...
MY BEST GUESS IS THAT WE ARE STILL INSIDE FIRESTORM. DESPERO IS MANIPULATING EVENTS--THIS "PRISON"--FROM THE OUTSIDE.
"NO, COURTNEY...
"WHILE THE PHYSICAL EVENTS MAY HAVE BEEN AN ILLUSION OF SORTS, WHAT YOU DID...
"...THE FAILURES...
YES.
THE SEED IS PLANTED WITHIN THE MARTIAN. I AM DONE HERE.
"...AND THE SUCCESS. COMING TO GRIPS WITH YOUR PAST? LEARNING TO BECOME A LEADER? FACING FEAR AND DOUBT IN THE FACE OF HOPELESS ODDS...?
THE GREATEST HEROES OF EARTH ARE STILL TRAPPED IN THE PRISONS THAT DESPERO MADE FOR THEM, COURTNEY. HE CUSTOM-MADE A PRISON FOR EACH OF US. PREYING ON OUR WEAKNESS.
YOUR PRISON WAS SELF-DOUBT--GUILT--PRESSURE TO SUCCEED AND FEAR OF FAILURE.
DESPERO WAS WAITING FOR YOU TO CAVE UNDER THE PRESSURE.
BUT YOU DIDN'T.

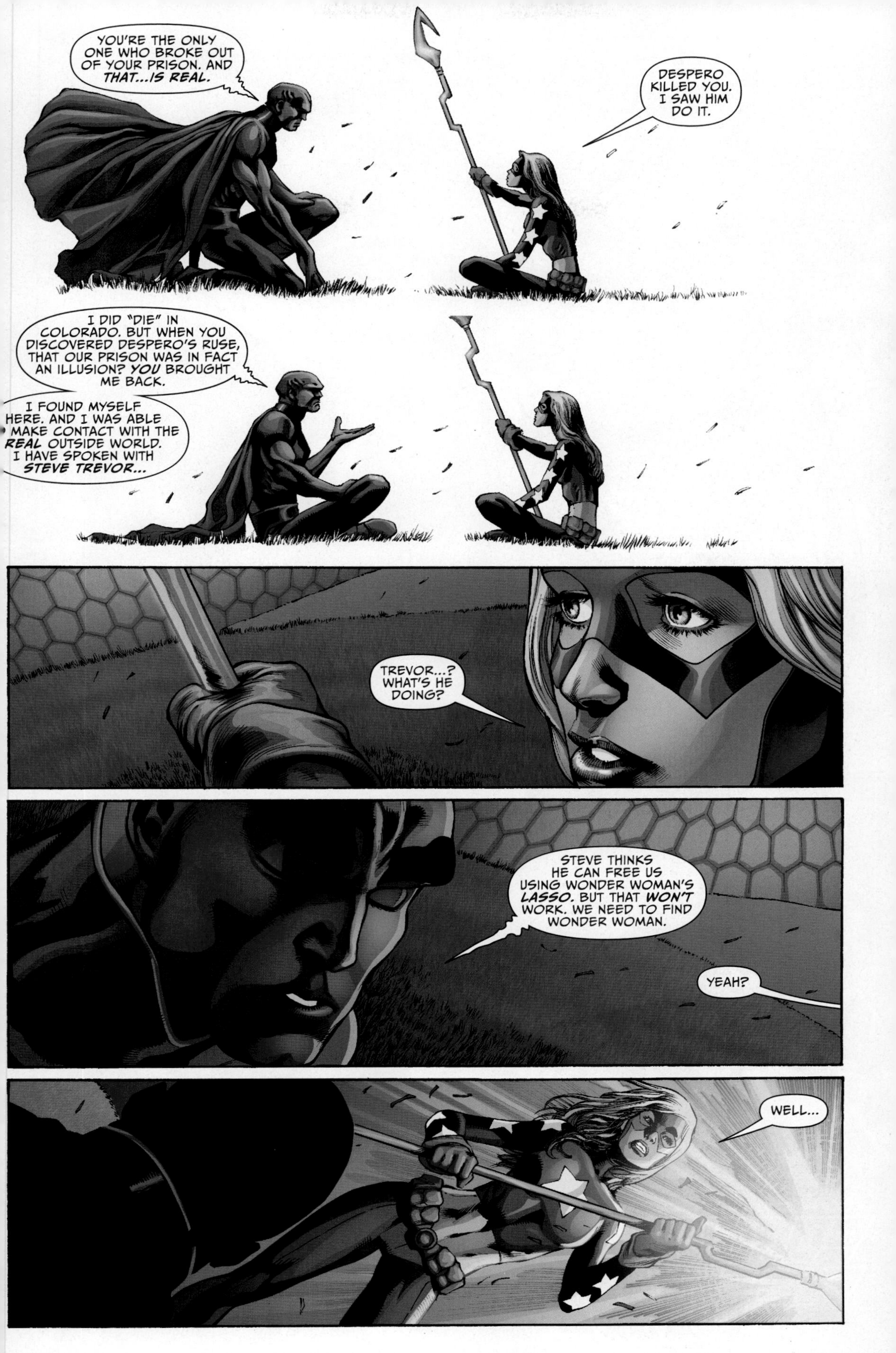
YOU'RE THE ONLY ONE WHO BROKE OUT OF YOUR PRISON. AND THAT...IS REAL.
DESPERO KILLED YOU. I SAW HIM DO IT.
I DID "DIE" IN COLORADO. BUT WHEN YOU DISCOVERED DESPERO'S RUSE, THAT OUR PRISON WAS IN FACT AN ILLUSION? YOU BROUGHT ME BACK.
I FOUND MYSELF HERE. AND I WAS ABLE TO MAKE CONTACT WITH THE REAL OUTSIDE WORLD. I HAVE SPOKEN WITH STEVE TREVOR...
TREVOR...? WHAT'S HE DOING?
STEVE THINKS HE CAN FREE US USING WONDER WOMAN'S LASSO. BUT THAT WON'T WORK. WE NEED TO FIND WONDER WOMAN.
YEAH?
WELL...

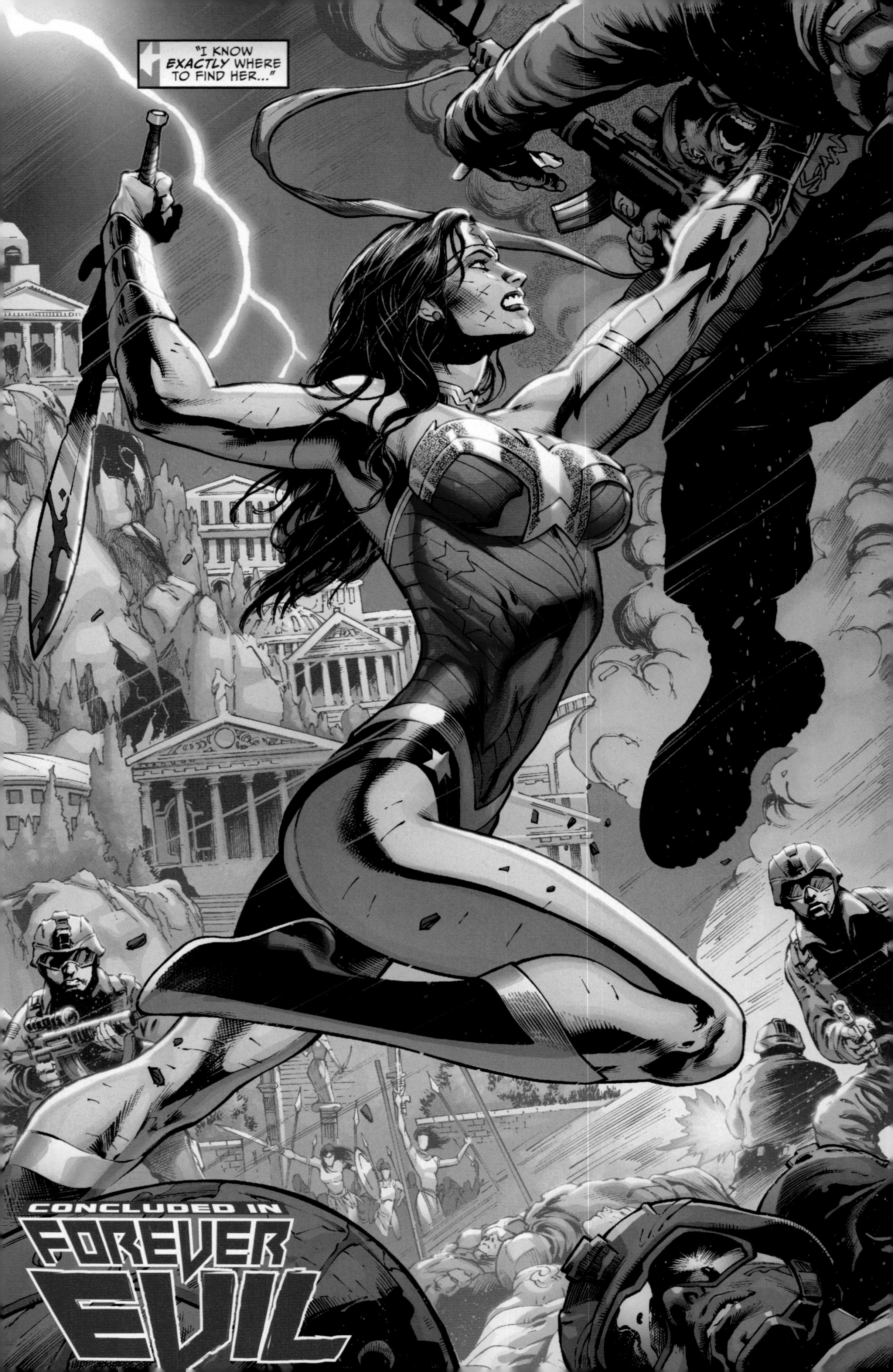
"I KNOW EXACTLY WHERE TO FIND HER..."
CONCLUDED IN
FOREVER EVIL

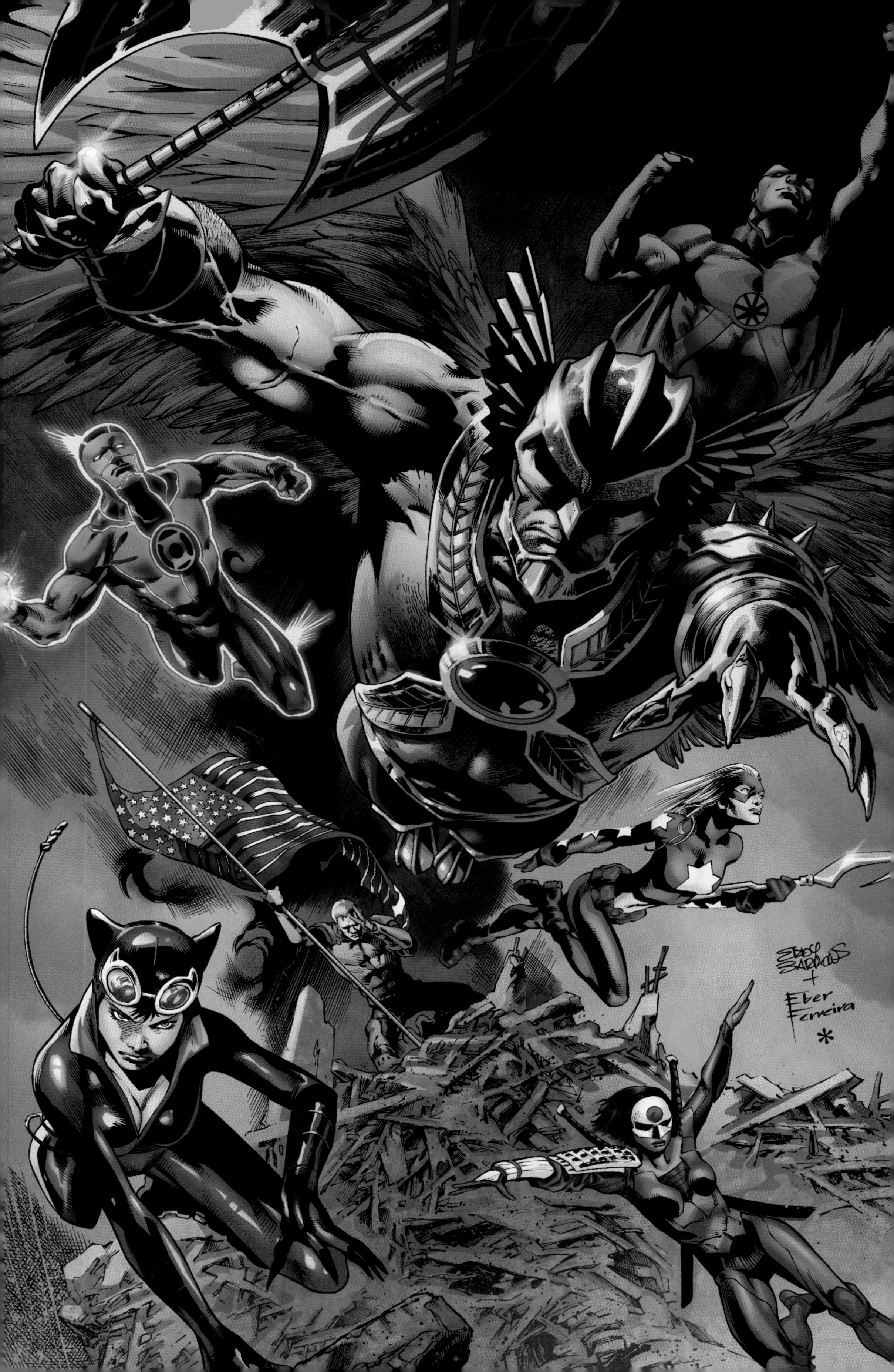
EDDY BARROWS
+
Eber Ferreira

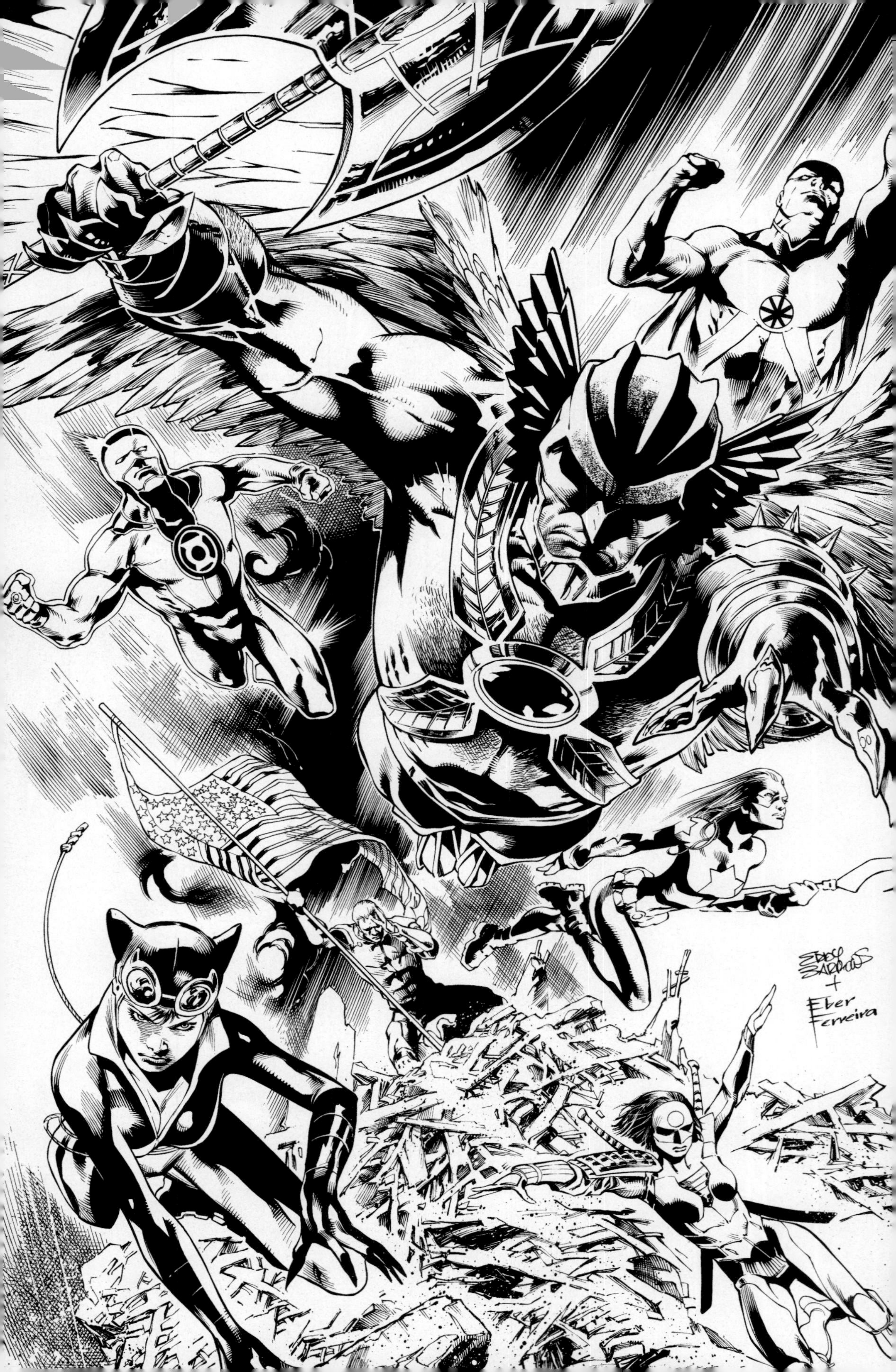

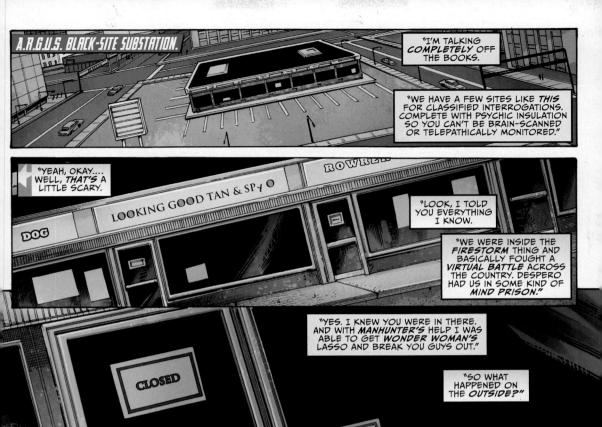

A.R.G.U.S. BLACK-SITE SUBSTATION.

"I'M TALKING *COMPLETELY* OFF THE BOOKS."

"WE HAVE A FEW SITES LIKE *THIS* FOR CLASSIFIED INTERROGATIONS. COMPLETE WITH PSYCHIC INSULATION SO YOU CAN'T BE BRAIN-SCANNED OR TELEPATHICALLY MONITORED."

"YEAH, OKAY.... WELL, *THAT'S* A LITTLE SCARY."

"LOOK, I TOLD YOU EVERYTHING I KNOW."

"WE WERE INSIDE THE *FIRESTORM* THING AND BASICALLY FOUGHT A *VIRTUAL BATTLE* ACROSS THE COUNTRY. DESPERO HAD US IN SOME KIND OF *MIND PRISON*."

"YES. I KNEW YOU WERE IN THERE. AND WITH *MANHUNTER'S* HELP I WAS ABLE TO GET *WONDER WOMAN'S* LASSO AND BREAK YOU GUYS OUT."

"SO WHAT HAPPENED ON THE *OUTSIDE?*"

LOOKING GOOD TAN & SP O

ROWR

DOG

CLOSED

WELL...

MOST OF THAT IS GOING TO BE FOREVER CLASSIFIED. AND THE REST YOU'VE HEARD ON THE NEWS ANYWAY.

THE *GRID* WENT DOWN AND THE *VILLAINS* RAN ROUGHSHOD OVER THE ENTIRE EARTH.

I WON'T BORE YOU WITH THE DETAILS, SINCE MOST OF THAT IS NEED-TO-KNOW, ANYWAY.

IT'S A TWO-WAY STREET, HERE, *MR. TREVOR.* YOU KNOW THE *HELL* I'VE LITERALLY BEEN THROUGH.

STARGIRL.

COURTNEY?

IF I TOLD YOU...

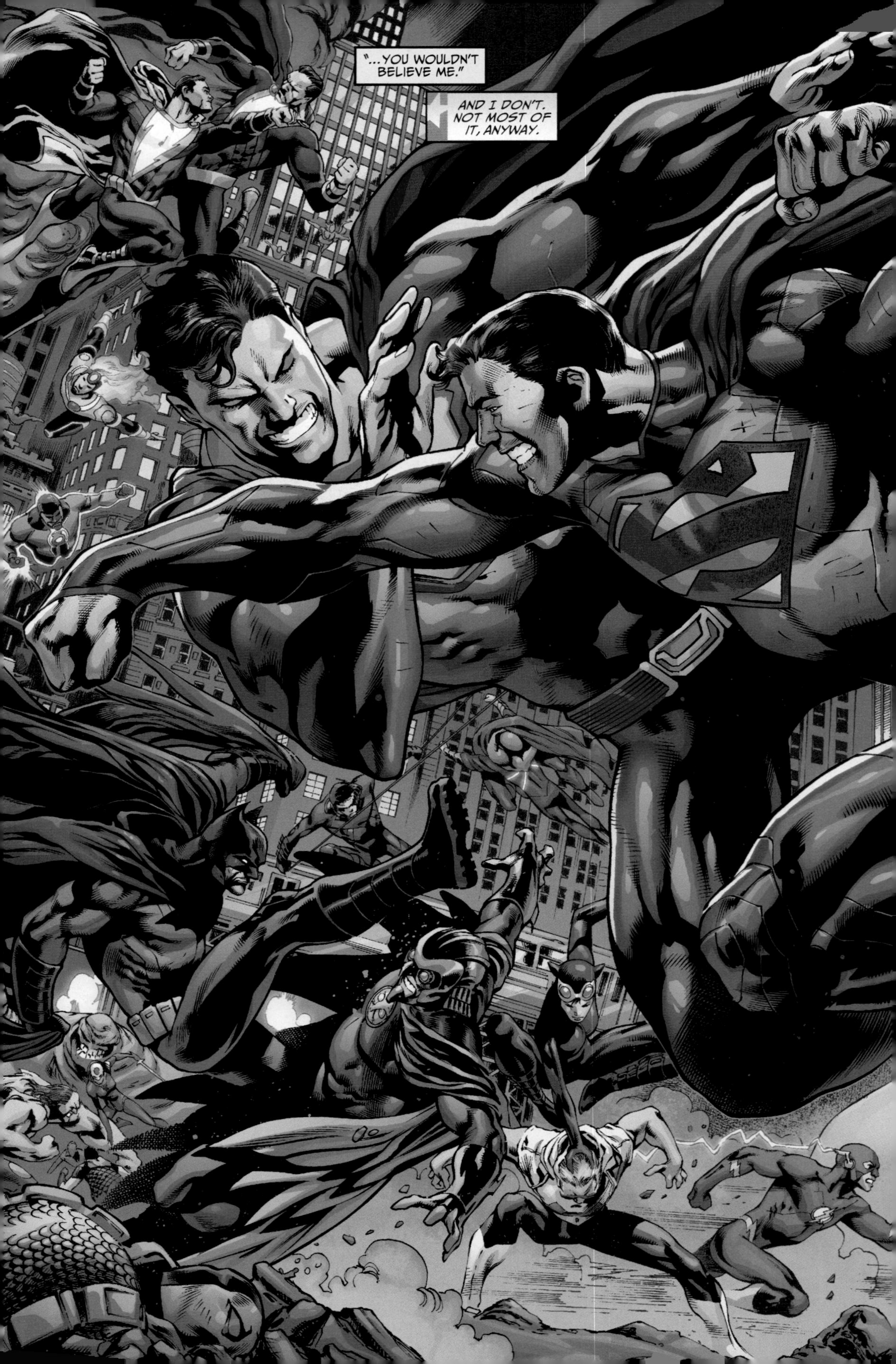
"...YOU WOULDN'T BELIEVE ME."
AND I DON'T. NOT MOST OF IT, ANYWAY.

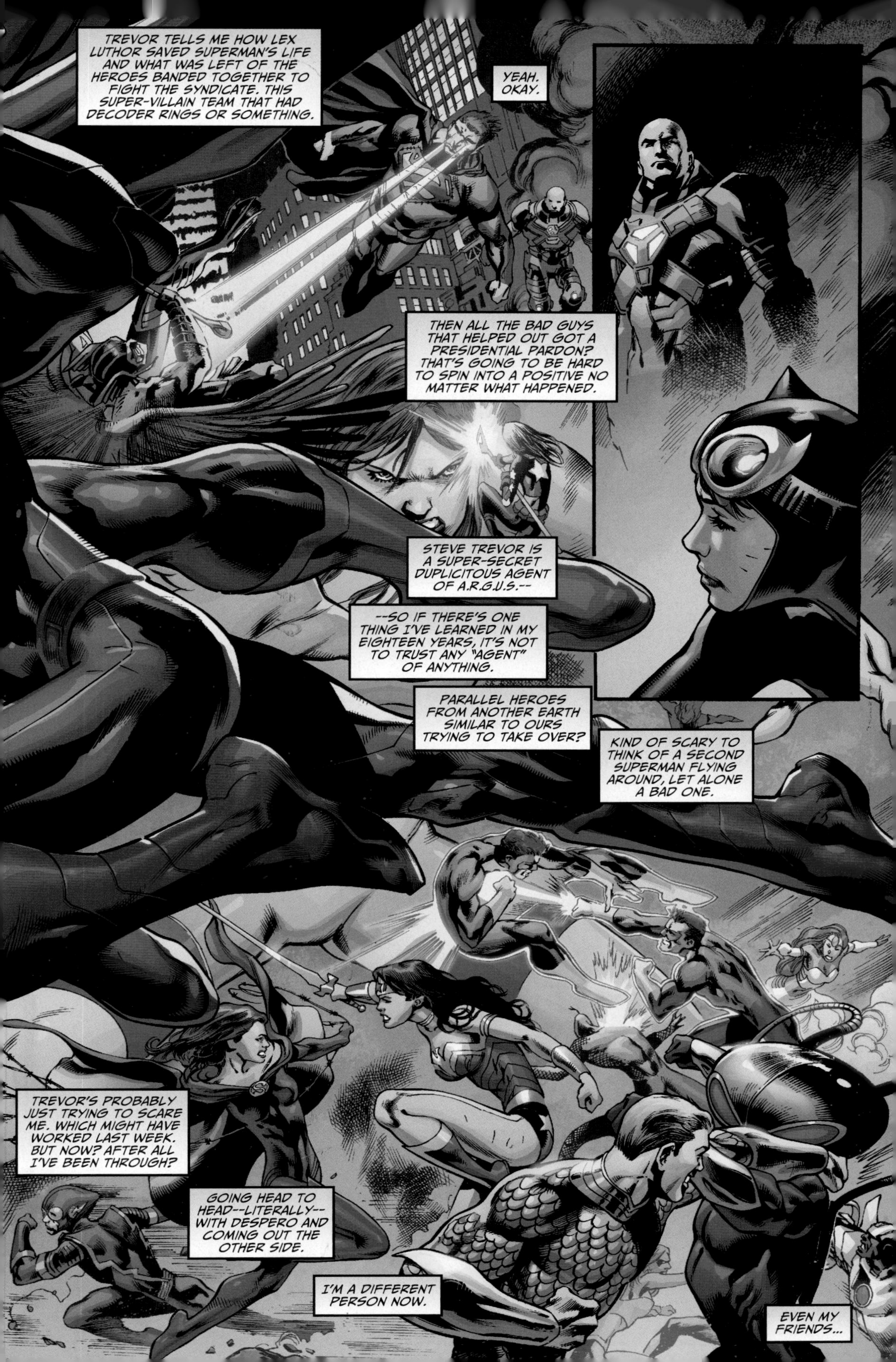
TREVOR TELLS ME HOW LEX LUTHOR SAVED SUPERMAN'S LIFE AND WHAT WAS LEFT OF THE HEROES BANDED TOGETHER TO FIGHT THE SYNDICATE. THIS SUPER-VILLAIN TEAM THAT HAD DECODER RINGS OR SOMETHING.
YEAH. OKAY.
THEN ALL THE BAD GUYS THAT HELPED OUT GOT A PRESIDENTIAL PARDON? THAT'S GOING TO BE HARD TO SPIN INTO A POSITIVE NO MATTER WHAT HAPPENED.
STEVE TREVOR IS A SUPER-SECRET DUPLICITOUS AGENT OF A.R.G.U.S.--
--SO IF THERE'S ONE THING I'VE LEARNED IN MY EIGHTEEN YEARS, IT'S NOT TO TRUST ANY "AGENT" OF ANYTHING.
PARALLEL HEROES FROM ANOTHER EARTH SIMILAR TO OURS TRYING TO TAKE OVER?
KIND OF SCARY TO THINK OF A SECOND SUPERMAN FLYING AROUND, LET ALONE A BAD ONE.
TREVOR'S PROBABLY JUST TRYING TO SCARE ME. WHICH MIGHT HAVE WORKED LAST WEEK. BUT NOW? AFTER ALL I'VE BEEN THROUGH?
GOING HEAD TO HEAD--LITERALLY-- WITH DESPERO AND COMING OUT THE OTHER SIDE.
I'M A DIFFERENT PERSON NOW.
EVEN MY FRIENDS...

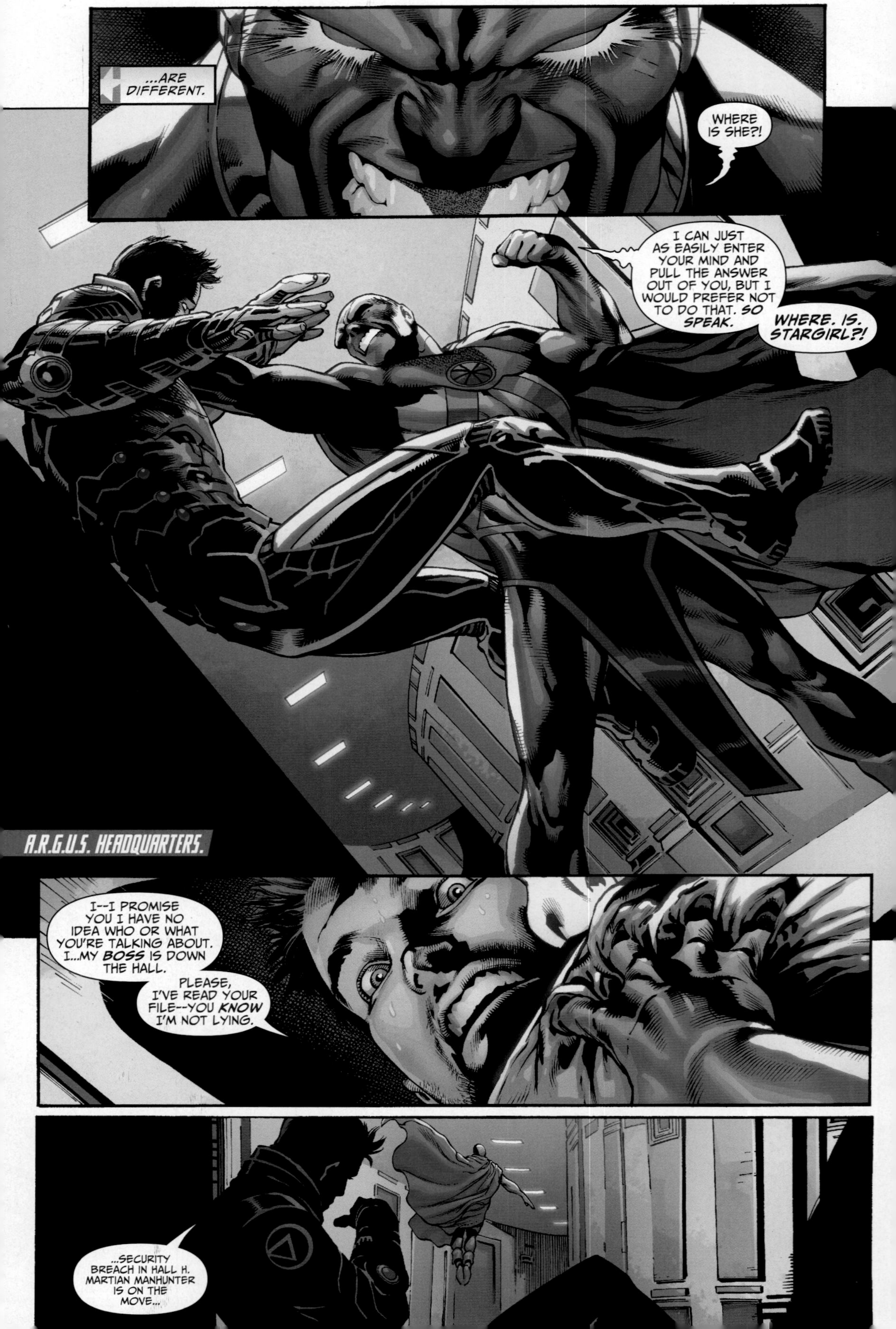
...ARE DIFFERENT.
WHERE IS SHE?!
I CAN JUST AS EASILY ENTER YOUR MIND AND PULL THE ANSWER OUT OF YOU, BUT I WOULD PREFER NOT TO DO THAT. SO SPEAK.
WHERE. IS. STARGIRL?!
A.R.G.U.S. HEADQUARTERS.
I--I PROMISE YOU I HAVE NO IDEA WHO OR WHAT YOU'RE TALKING ABOUT. I...MY BOSS IS DOWN THE HALL.
PLEASE, I'VE READ YOUR FILE--YOU KNOW I'M NOT LYING.
...SECURITY BREACH IN HALL H. MARTIAN MANHUNTER IS ON THE MOVE...

WHAT HAPPENED TO THE REST OF THE TEAM?

I CAN'T TELL YOU MOST OF IT BECAUSE...OF COURSE IT'S CLASSIFIED.

LET'S JUST SAY THAT THE JLA IS TAKING ALL THE HEAT FOR EVERYTHING THAT WENT DOWN--THE VILLAINS TAKING OVER AND THE GRID GOING DOWN.

THERE'S NO SPINNING THIS INTO A POSITIVE. THE JLA IS A SHIP THAT'S ALREADY SUNK. AND YOU NEED TO MAKE SURE YOU DON'T GET SUCKED DOWN WITH IT. BUT WHAT I *CAN* SAY IS THIS...

I'M YOUNG. I GET IT.

NO ONE WANTS TO TELL ME WHAT'S GOING ON, BUT EVERYONE WANTS TO TELL ME WHAT TO DO.

SITTING IN THIS FREAKY INTERROGATION ROOM WITH STEVE TREVOR WOULD HAVE MADE ME SICK TO MY STOMACH LAST WEEK. BUT NOW...I FIND THAT I'M *HUMORING* HIM.

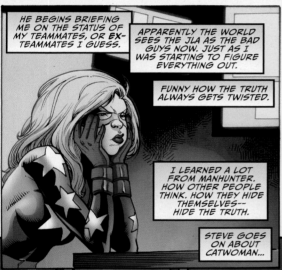

HE BEGINS BRIEFING ME ON THE STATUS OF MY TEAMMATES, OR EX-TEAMMATES I GUESS.

APPARENTLY THE WORLD SEES THE JLA AS THE BAD GUYS NOW. JUST AS I WAS STARTING TO FIGURE EVERYTHING OUT.

FUNNY HOW THE TRUTH ALWAYS GETS TWISTED.

I LEARNED A LOT FROM MANHUNTER. HOW OTHER PEOPLE THINK. HOW THEY HIDE THEMSELVES-- HIDE THE TRUTH.

STEVE GOES ON ABOUT CATWOMAN...

TALKS ABOUT HOW SHE'S GONE BACK TO A LIFE OF CRIME.

GOTHAM CITY.

HE THROWS IN SOME DETAILS ABOUT AN OBSCURE JEWEL IN SOME FARAWAY MUSEUM THAT SHE APPARENTLY COULDN'T LIVE WITHOUT...

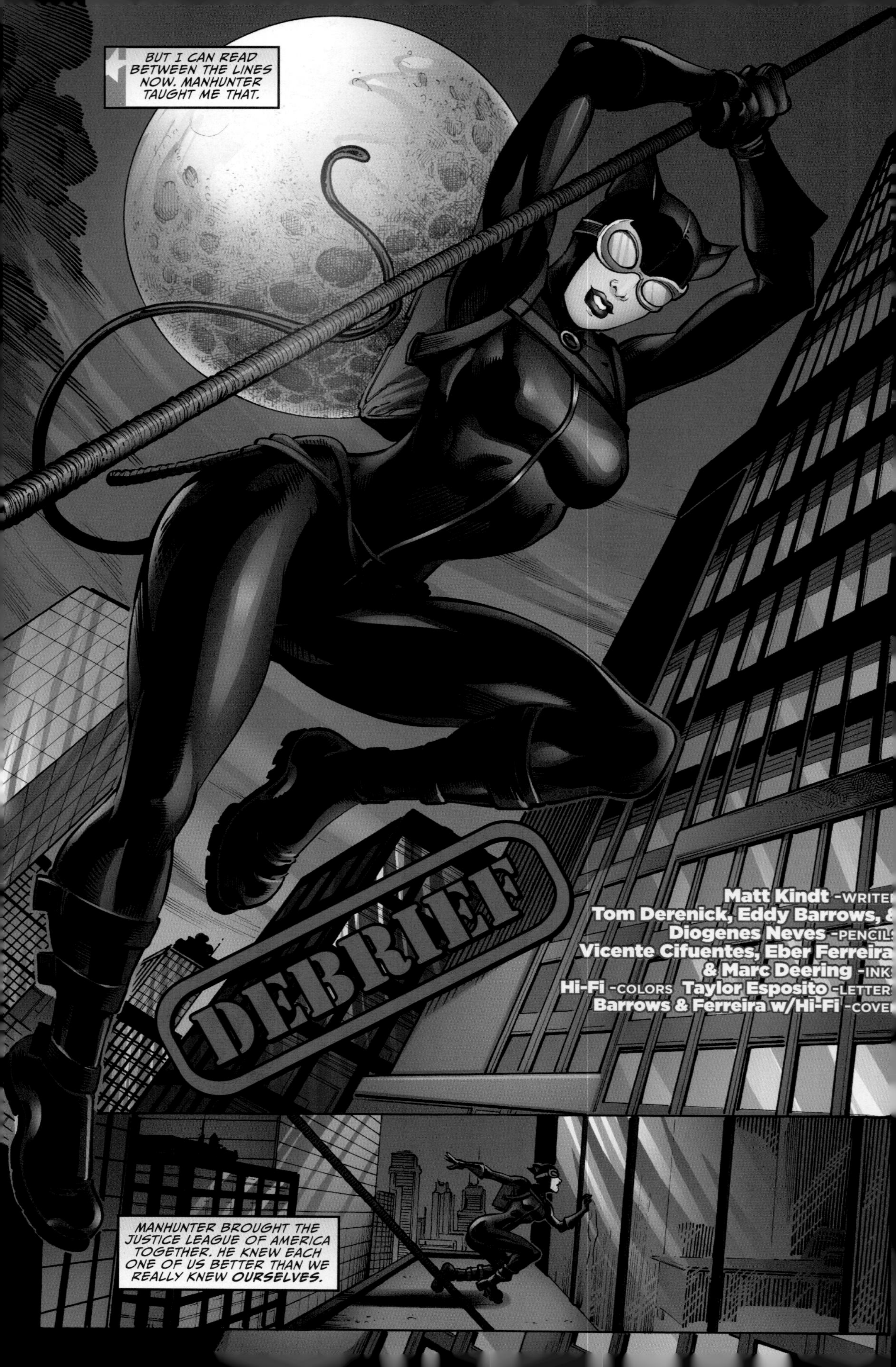

BUT I CAN READ BETWEEN THE LINES NOW. MANHUNTER TAUGHT ME THAT.
DEBRIEF
Matt Kindt -WRITE
Tom Derenick, Eddy Barrows, &
Diogenes Neves -PENCIL
Vicente Cifuentes, Eber Ferreira
& Marc Deering -INK
Hi-Fi -COLORS Taylor Esposito -LETTER
Barrows & Ferreira w/Hi-Fi -COVE
MANHUNTER BROUGHT THE JUSTICE LEAGUE OF AMERICA TOGETHER. HE KNEW EACH ONE OF US BETTER THAN WE REALLY KNEW OURSELVES.

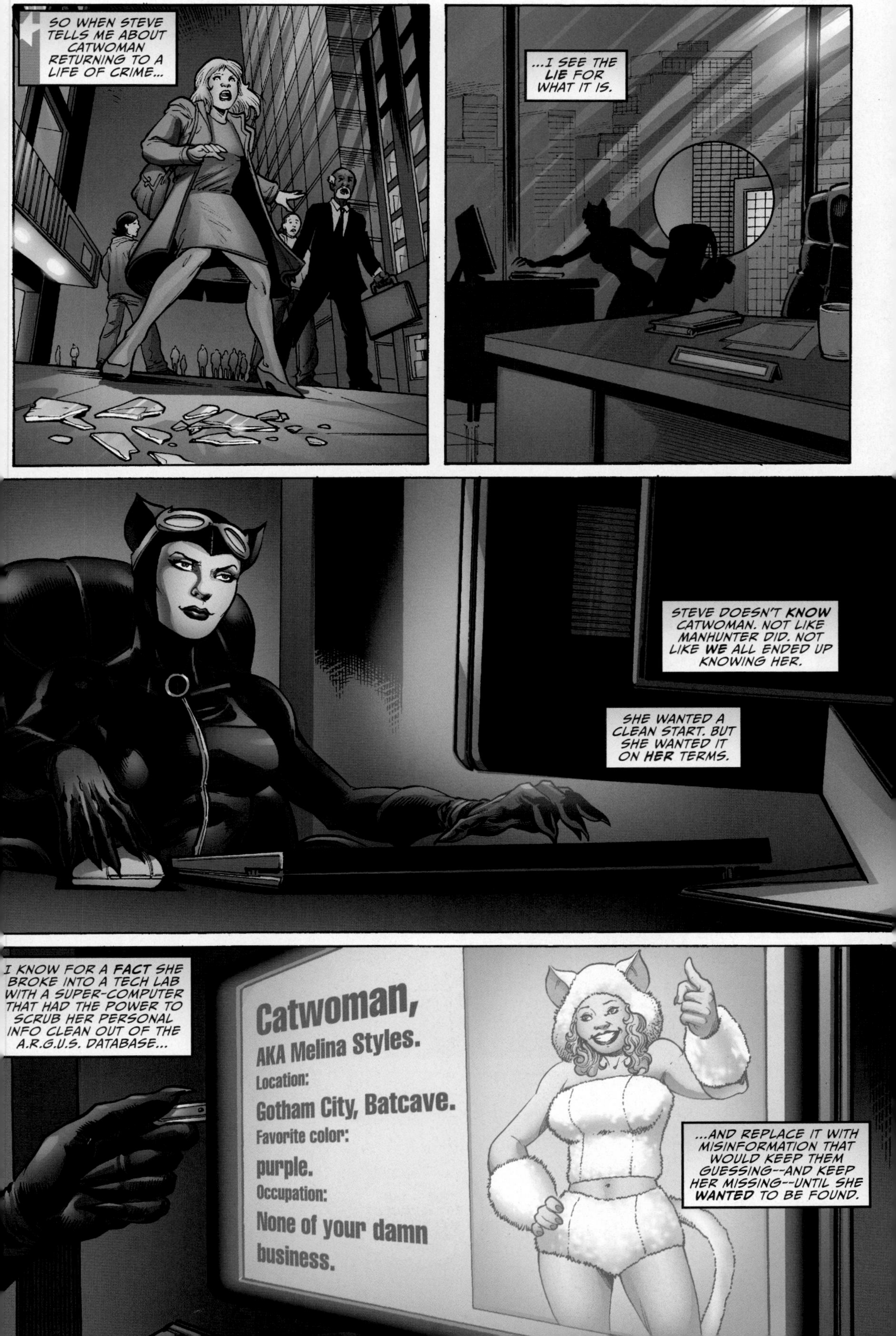
SO WHEN STEVE TELLS ME ABOUT CATWOMAN RETURNING TO A LIFE OF CRIME...
...I SEE THE LIE FOR WHAT IT IS.
STEVE DOESN'T KNOW CATWOMAN. NOT LIKE MANHUNTER DID. NOT LIKE WE ALL ENDED UP KNOWING HER.
SHE WANTED A CLEAN START. BUT SHE WANTED IT ON HER TERMS.
I KNOW FOR A FACT SHE BROKE INTO A TECH LAB WITH A SUPER-COMPUTER THAT HAD THE POWER TO SCRUB HER PERSONAL INFO CLEAN OUT OF THE A.R.G.U.S. DATABASE...
Catwoman,
AKA Melina Styles.
Location:
Gotham City, Batcave.
Favorite color:
purple.
Occupation:
None of your damn business.
...AND REPLACE IT WITH MISINFORMATION THAT WOULD KEEP THEM GUESSING--AND KEEP HER MISSING--UNTIL SHE WANTED TO BE FOUND.

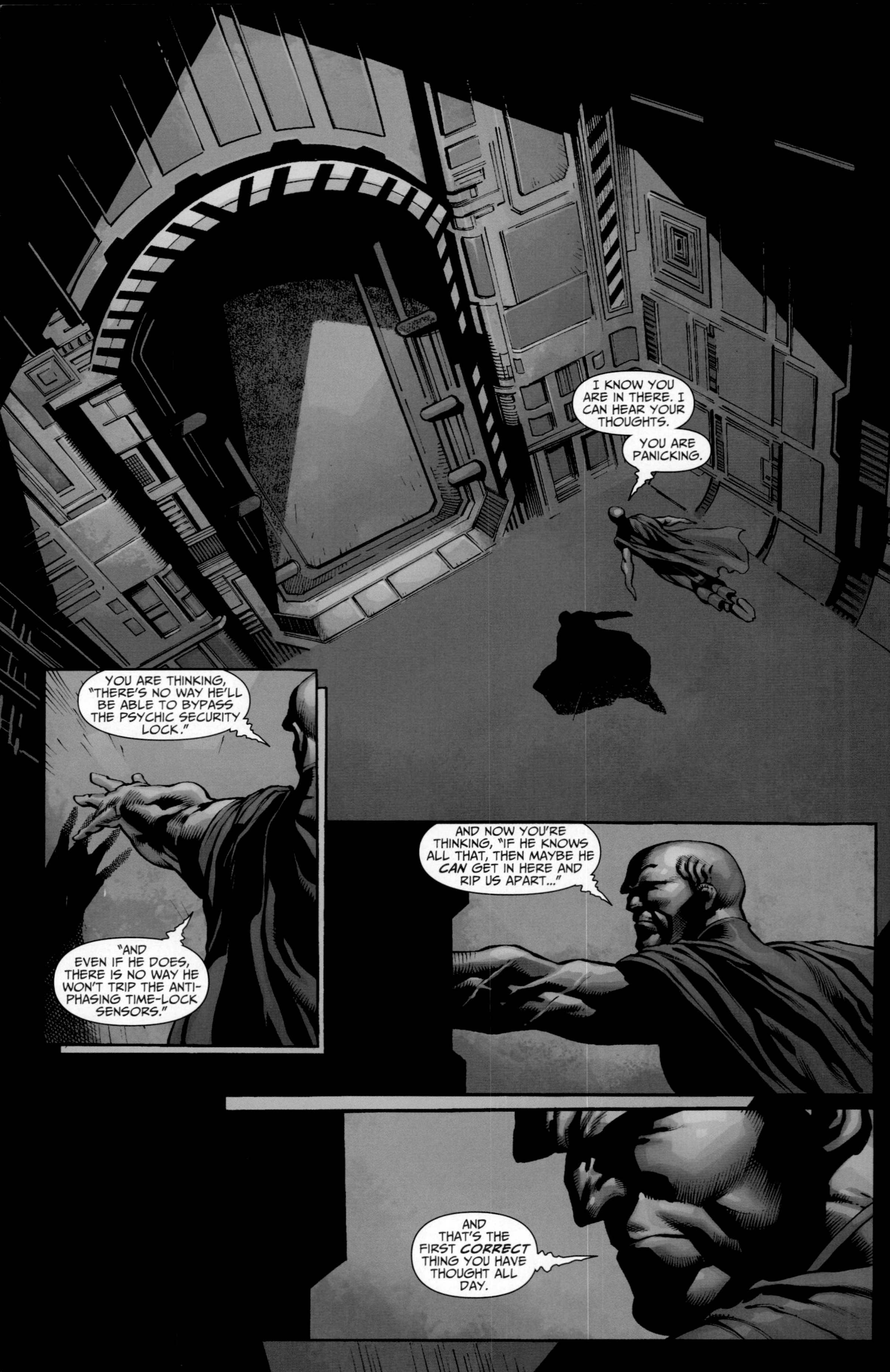
I KNOW YOU ARE IN THERE. I CAN HEAR YOUR THOUGHTS.
YOU ARE PANICKING.
YOU ARE THINKING, "THERE'S NO WAY HE'LL BE ABLE TO BYPASS THE PSYCHIC SECURITY LOCK."
"AND EVEN IF HE DOES, THERE IS NO WAY HE WON'T TRIP THE ANTI-PHASING TIME-LOCK SENSORS."
AND NOW YOU'RE THINKING, "IF HE KNOWS ALL THAT, THEN MAYBE HE CAN GET IN HERE AND RIP US APART..."
AND THAT'S THE FIRST CORRECT THING YOU HAVE THOUGHT ALL DAY.

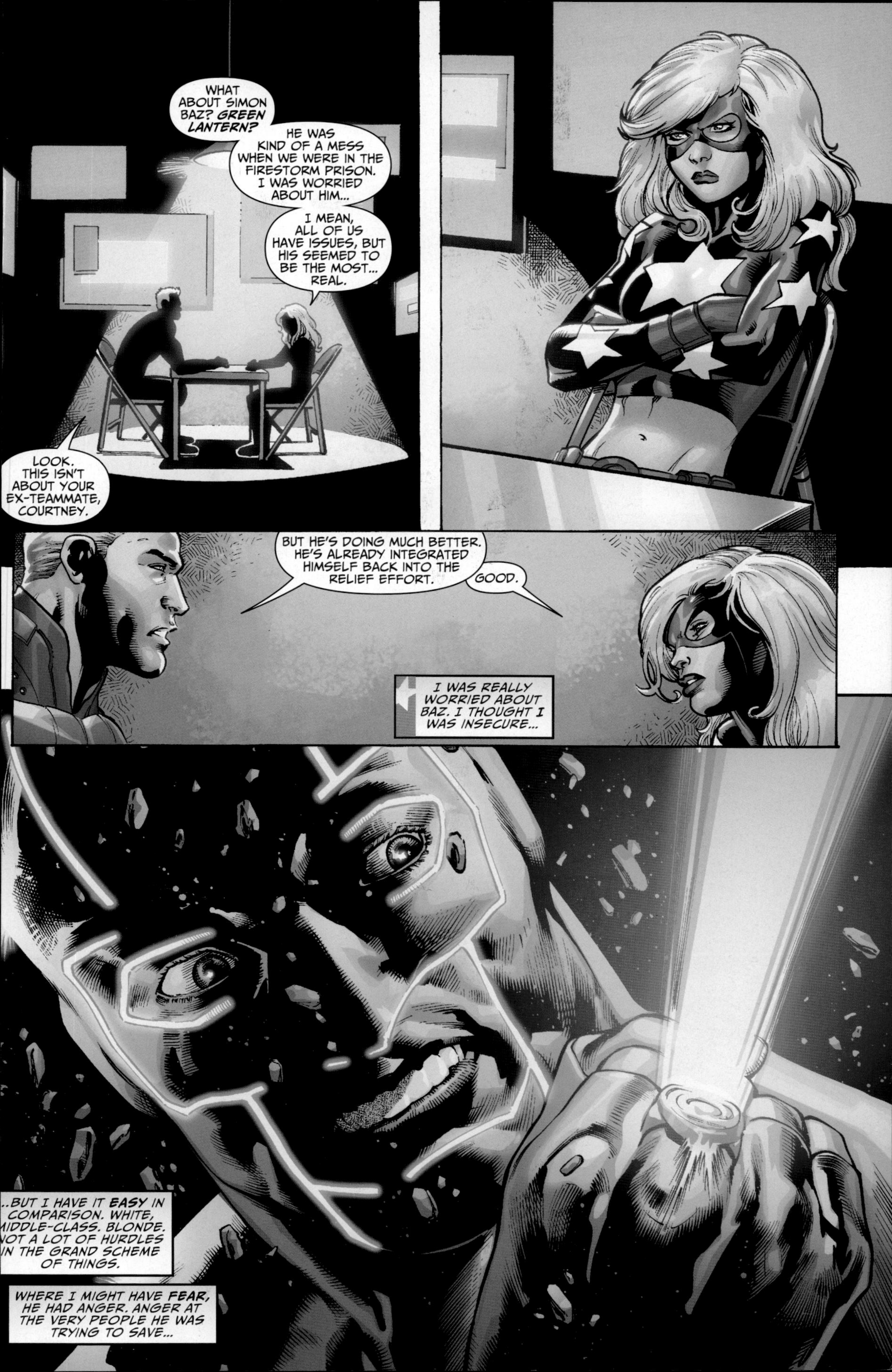

WHAT ABOUT SIMON BAZ? GREEN LANTERN?
HE WAS KIND OF A MESS WHEN WE WERE IN THE FIRESTORM PRISON. I WAS WORRIED ABOUT HIM...
I MEAN, ALL OF US HAVE ISSUES, BUT HIS SEEMED TO BE THE MOST... REAL.
LOOK. THIS ISN'T ABOUT YOUR EX-TEAMMATE, COURTNEY.
BUT HE'S DOING MUCH BETTER. HE'S ALREADY INTEGRATED HIMSELF BACK INTO THE RELIEF EFFORT.
GOOD.
I WAS REALLY WORRIED ABOUT BAZ. I THOUGHT I WAS INSECURE...
...BUT I HAVE IT EASY IN COMPARISON. WHITE, MIDDLE-CLASS. BLONDE. NOT A LOT OF HURDLES IN THE GRAND SCHEME OF THINGS.
WHERE I MIGHT HAVE FEAR, HE HAD ANGER. ANGER AT THE VERY PEOPLE HE WAS TRYING TO SAVE...

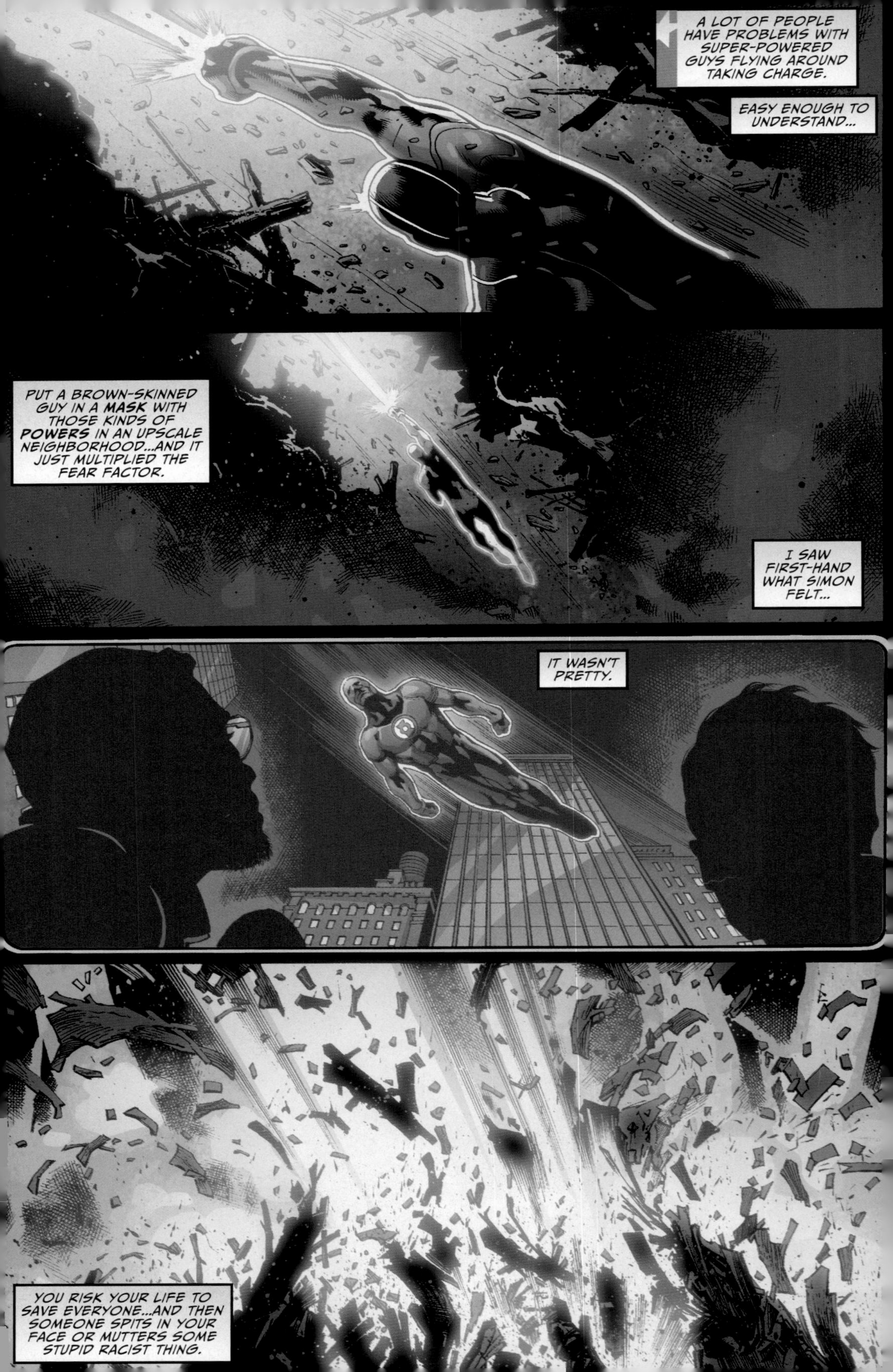
A LOT OF PEOPLE HAVE PROBLEMS WITH SUPER-POWERED GUYS FLYING AROUND TAKING CHARGE.
EASY ENOUGH TO UNDERSTAND...
PUT A BROWN-SKINNED GUY IN A MASK WITH THOSE KINDS OF POWERS IN AN UPSCALE NEIGHBORHOOD...AND IT JUST MULTIPLIED THE FEAR FACTOR.
I SAW FIRST-HAND WHAT SIMON FELT...
IT WASN'T PRETTY.
YOU RISK YOUR LIFE TO SAVE EVERYONE...AND THEN SOMEONE SPITS IN YOUR FACE OR MUTTERS SOME STUPID RACIST THING.

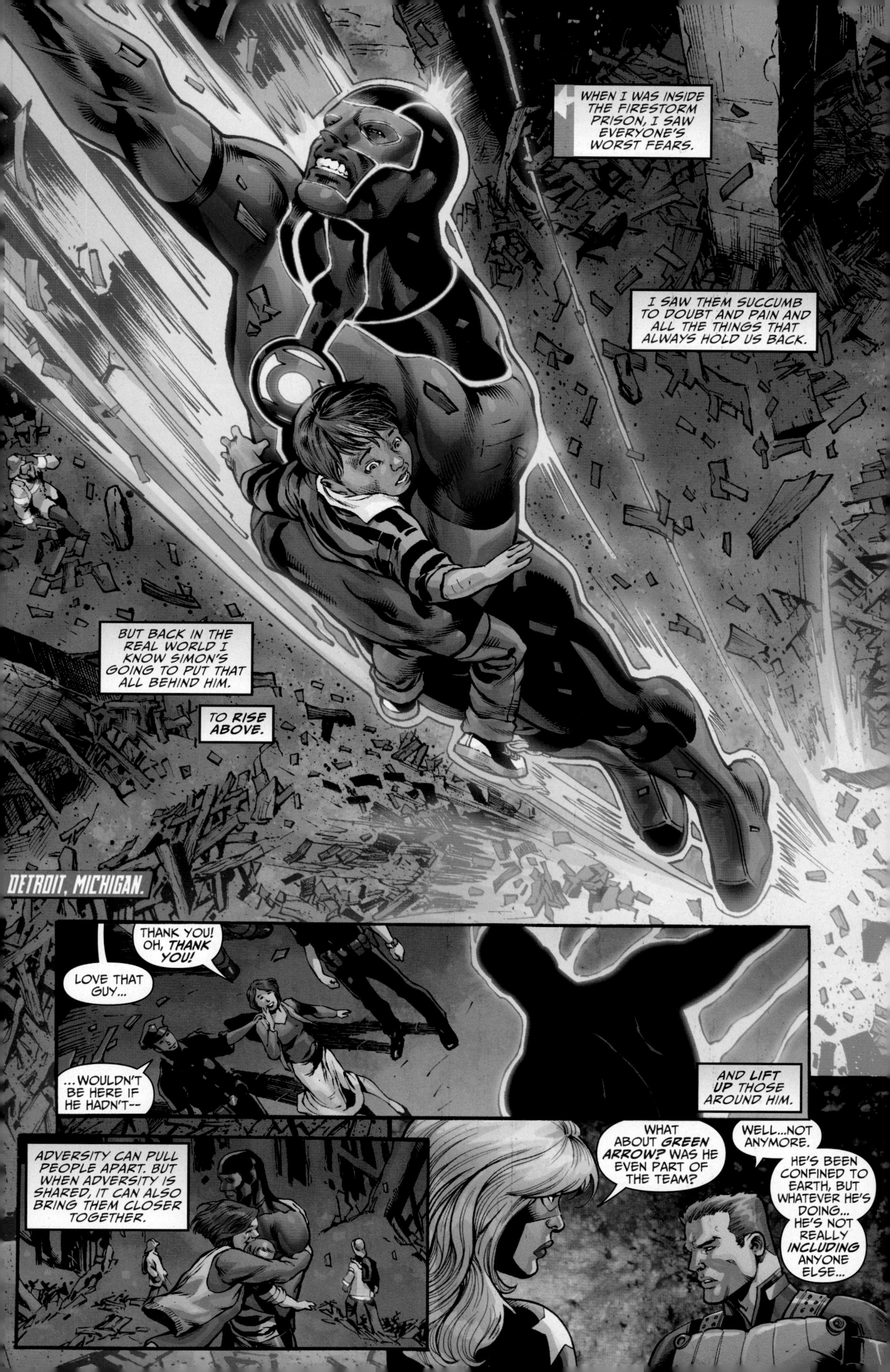
WHEN I WAS INSIDE THE FIRESTORM PRISON, I SAW EVERYONE'S WORST FEARS.
I SAW THEM SUCCUMB TO DOUBT AND PAIN AND ALL THE THINGS THAT ALWAYS HOLD US BACK.
BUT BACK IN THE REAL WORLD I KNOW SIMON'S GOING TO PUT THAT ALL BEHIND HIM.
TO RISE ABOVE.
DETROIT, MICHIGAN.
THANK YOU! OH, THANK YOU!
LOVE THAT GUY...
...WOULDN'T BE HERE IF HE HADN'T--
AND LIFT UP THOSE AROUND HIM.
ADVERSITY CAN PULL PEOPLE APART. BUT WHEN ADVERSITY IS SHARED, IT CAN ALSO BRING THEM CLOSER TOGETHER.
WHAT ABOUT GREEN ARROW? WAS HE EVEN PART OF THE TEAM?
WELL...NOT ANYMORE.
HE'S BEEN CONFINED TO EARTH, BUT WHATEVER HE'S DOING... HE'S NOT REALLY INCLUDING ANYONE ELSE...

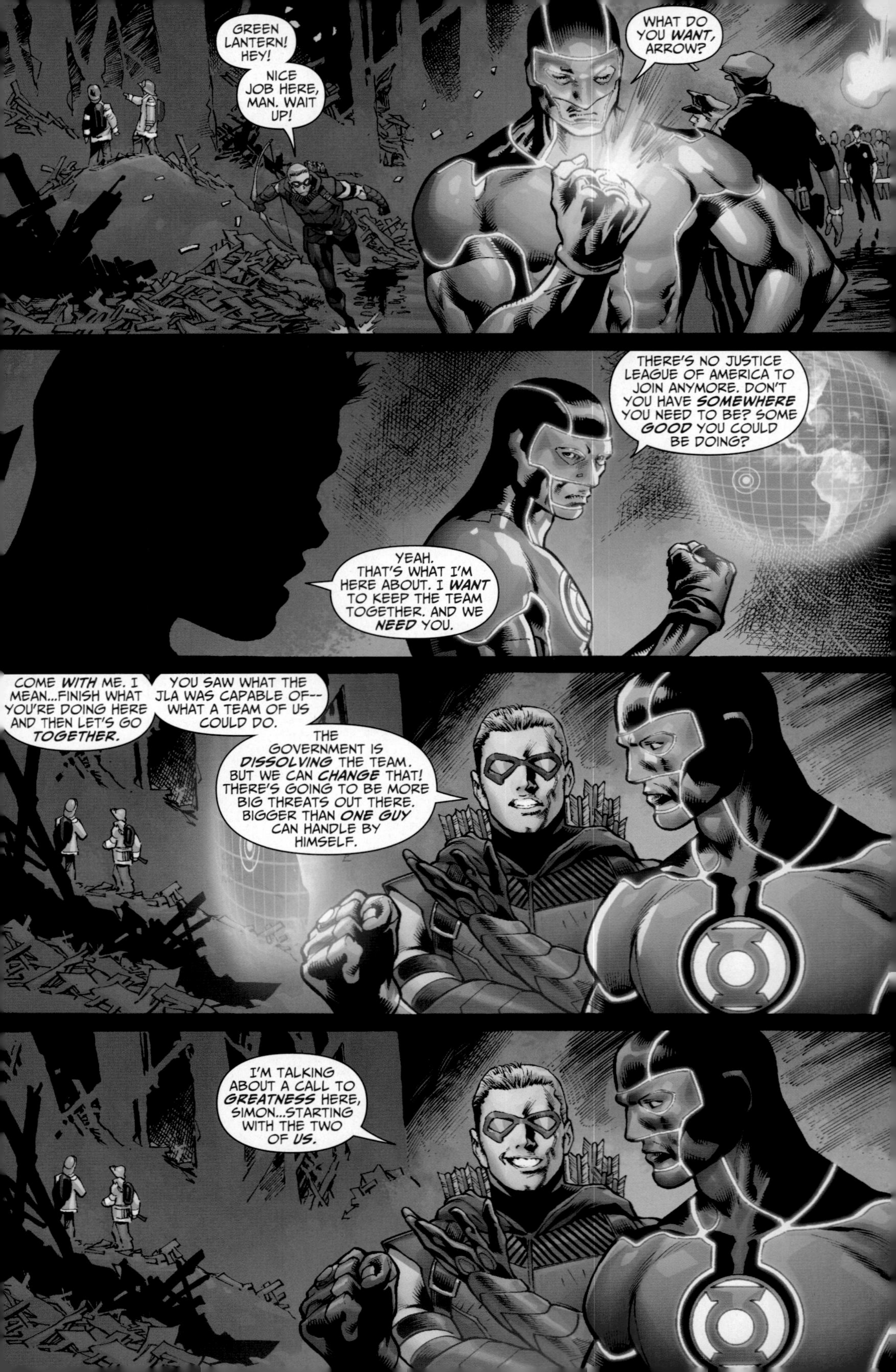
GREEN LANTERN! HEY!
NICE JOB HERE, MAN. WAIT UP!
WHAT DO YOU WANT, ARROW?
THERE'S NO JUSTICE LEAGUE OF AMERICA TO JOIN ANYMORE. DON'T YOU HAVE SOMEWHERE YOU NEED TO BE? SOME GOOD YOU COULD BE DOING?
YEAH. THAT'S WHAT I'M HERE ABOUT. I WANT TO KEEP THE TEAM TOGETHER. AND WE NEED YOU.
COME WITH ME. I MEAN...FINISH WHAT YOU'RE DOING HERE AND THEN LET'S GO TOGETHER.
YOU SAW WHAT THE JLA WAS CAPABLE OF-- WHAT A TEAM OF US COULD DO.
THE GOVERNMENT IS DISSOLVING THE TEAM. BUT WE CAN CHANGE THAT! THERE'S GOING TO BE MORE BIG THREATS OUT THERE. BIGGER THAN ONE GUY CAN HANDLE BY HIMSELF.
I'M TALKING ABOUT A CALL TO GREATNESS HERE, SIMON...STARTING WITH THE TWO OF US.

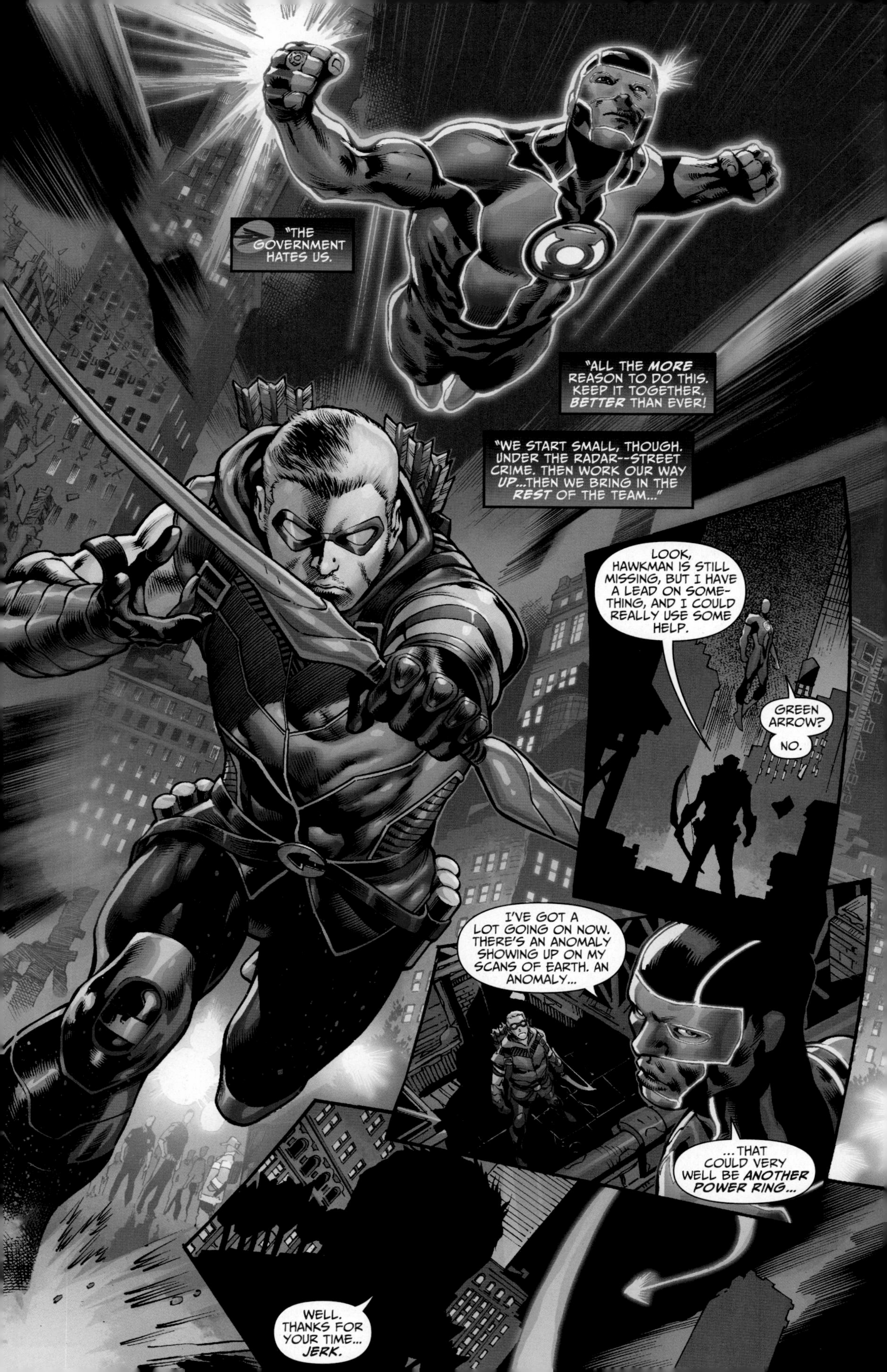
"THE GOVERNMENT HATES US.
"ALL THE MORE REASON TO DO THIS. KEEP IT TOGETHER. BETTER THAN EVER!
"WE START SMALL, THOUGH. UNDER THE RADAR--STREET CRIME. THEN WORK OUR WAY UP...THEN WE BRING IN THE REST OF THE TEAM..."
LOOK, HAWKMAN IS STILL MISSING, BUT I HAVE A LEAD ON SOME-THING, AND I COULD REALLY USE SOME HELP.
GREEN ARROW?
NO.
I'VE GOT A LOT GOING ON NOW. THERE'S AN ANOMALY SHOWING UP ON MY SCANS OF EARTH. AN ANOMALY...
...THAT COULD VERY WELL BE ANOTHER POWER RING...
WELL. THANKS FOR YOUR TIME... JERK.

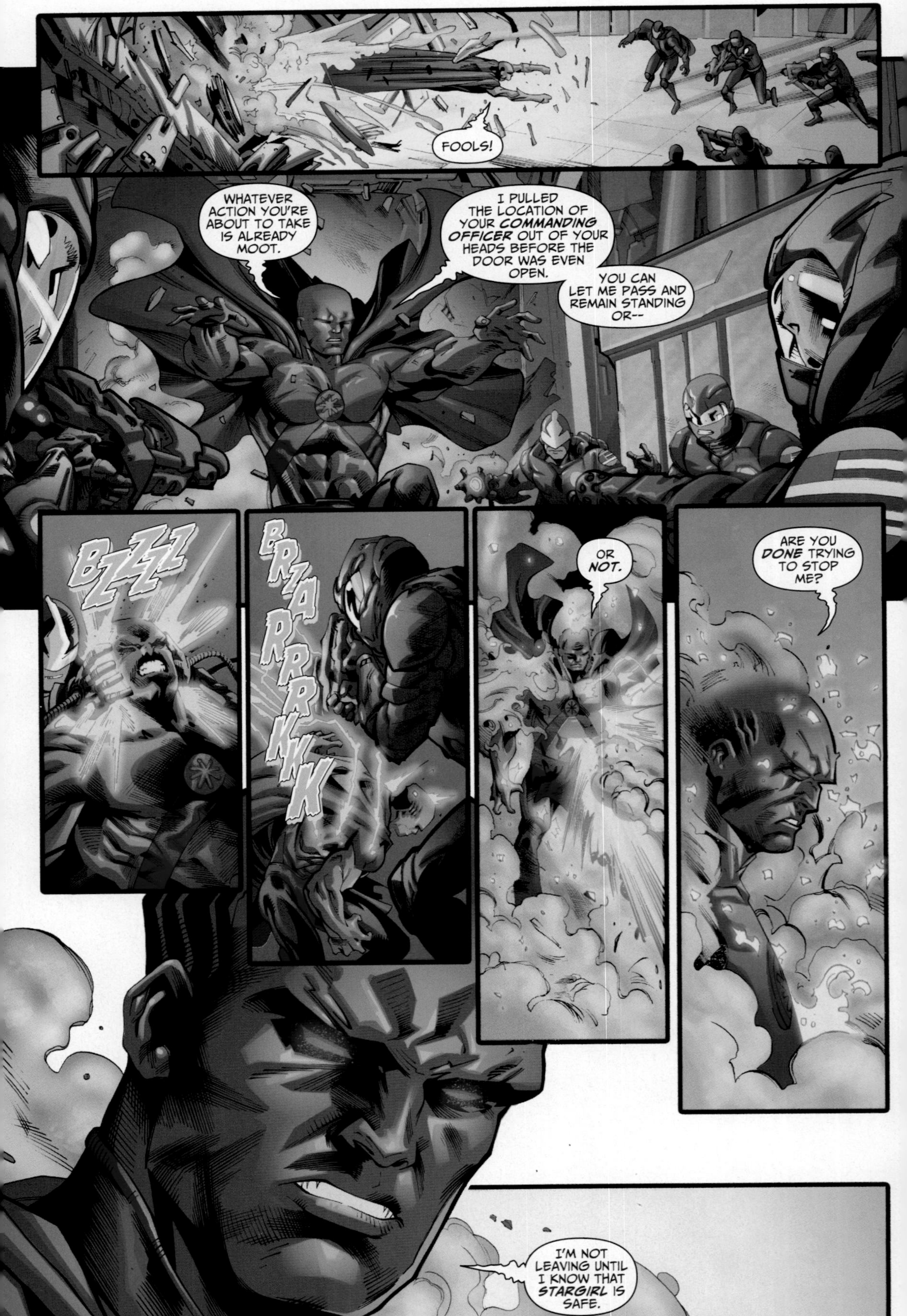
FOOLS!
WHATEVER ACTION YOU'RE ABOUT TO TAKE IS ALREADY MOOT.
I PULLED THE LOCATION OF YOUR COMMANDING OFFICER OUT OF YOUR HEADS BEFORE THE DOOR WAS EVEN OPEN.
YOU CAN LET ME PASS AND REMAIN STANDING OR--
BZZZZ
BRZAARRRKKK
OR NOT.
ARE YOU DONE TRYING TO STOP ME?
I'M NOT LEAVING UNTIL I KNOW THAT STARGIRL IS SAFE.

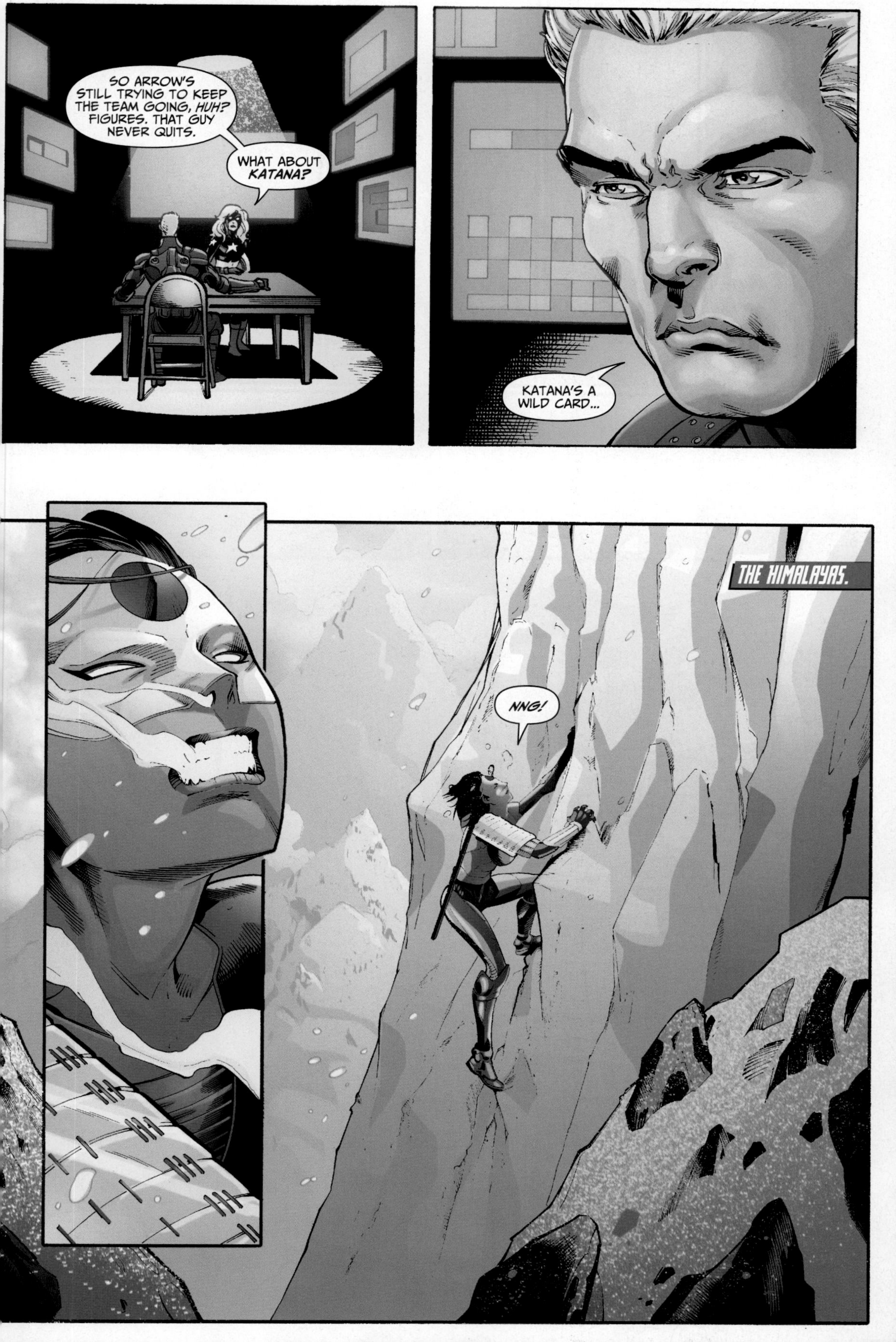
SO ARROW'S STILL TRYING TO KEEP THE TEAM GOING, *HUH?* FIGURES. THAT GUY NEVER QUITS.
WHAT ABOUT *KATANA?*
KATANA'S A WILD CARD...
THE HIMALAYAS.
NNG!

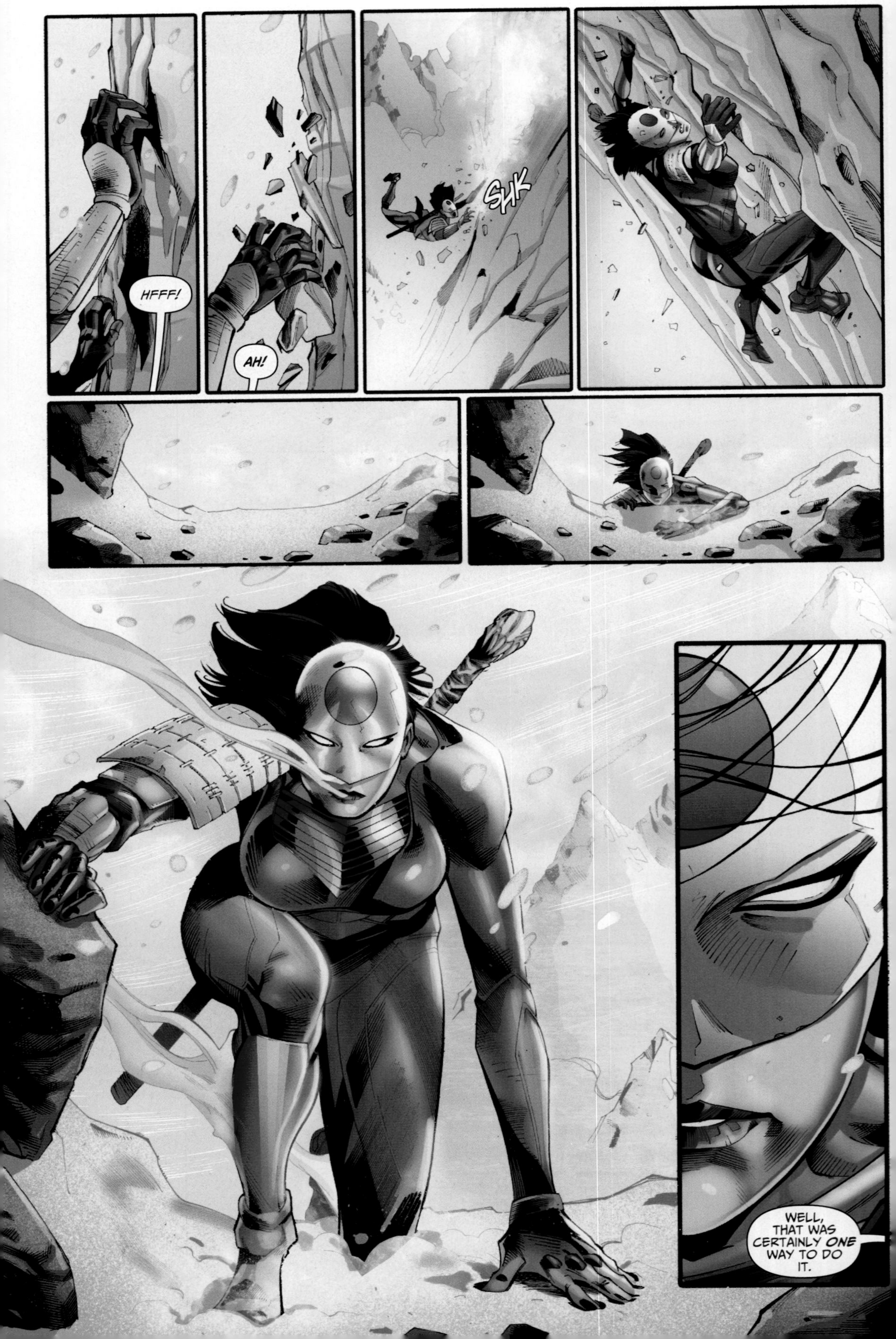
HFFF!
AH!
SHK
WELL, THAT WAS CERTAINLY ONE WAY TO DO IT.

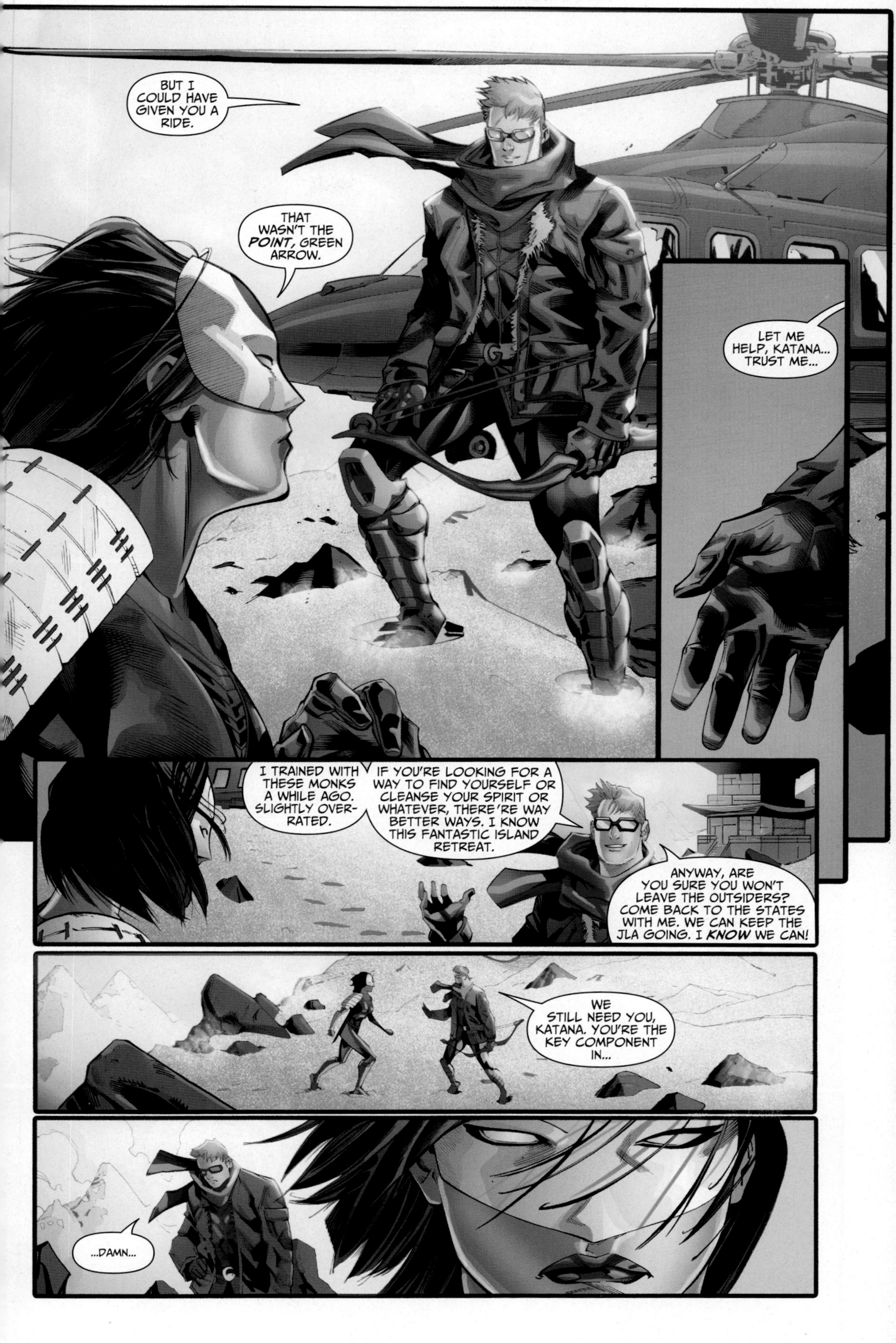
BUT I COULD HAVE GIVEN YOU A RIDE.
THAT WASN'T THE *POINT*, GREEN ARROW.
LET ME HELP, KATANA... TRUST ME...
I TRAINED WITH THESE MONKS A WHILE AGO. SLIGHTLY OVER-RATED.
IF YOU'RE LOOKING FOR A WAY TO FIND YOURSELF OR CLEANSE YOUR SPIRIT OR WHATEVER, THERE'RE WAY BETTER WAYS. I KNOW THIS FANTASTIC ISLAND RETREAT.
ANYWAY, ARE YOU SURE YOU WON'T LEAVE THE OUTSIDERS? COME BACK TO THE STATES WITH ME. WE CAN KEEP THE JLA GOING. I *KNOW* WE CAN!
WE STILL NEED YOU, KATANA. YOU'RE THE KEY COMPONENT IN...
...DAMN...

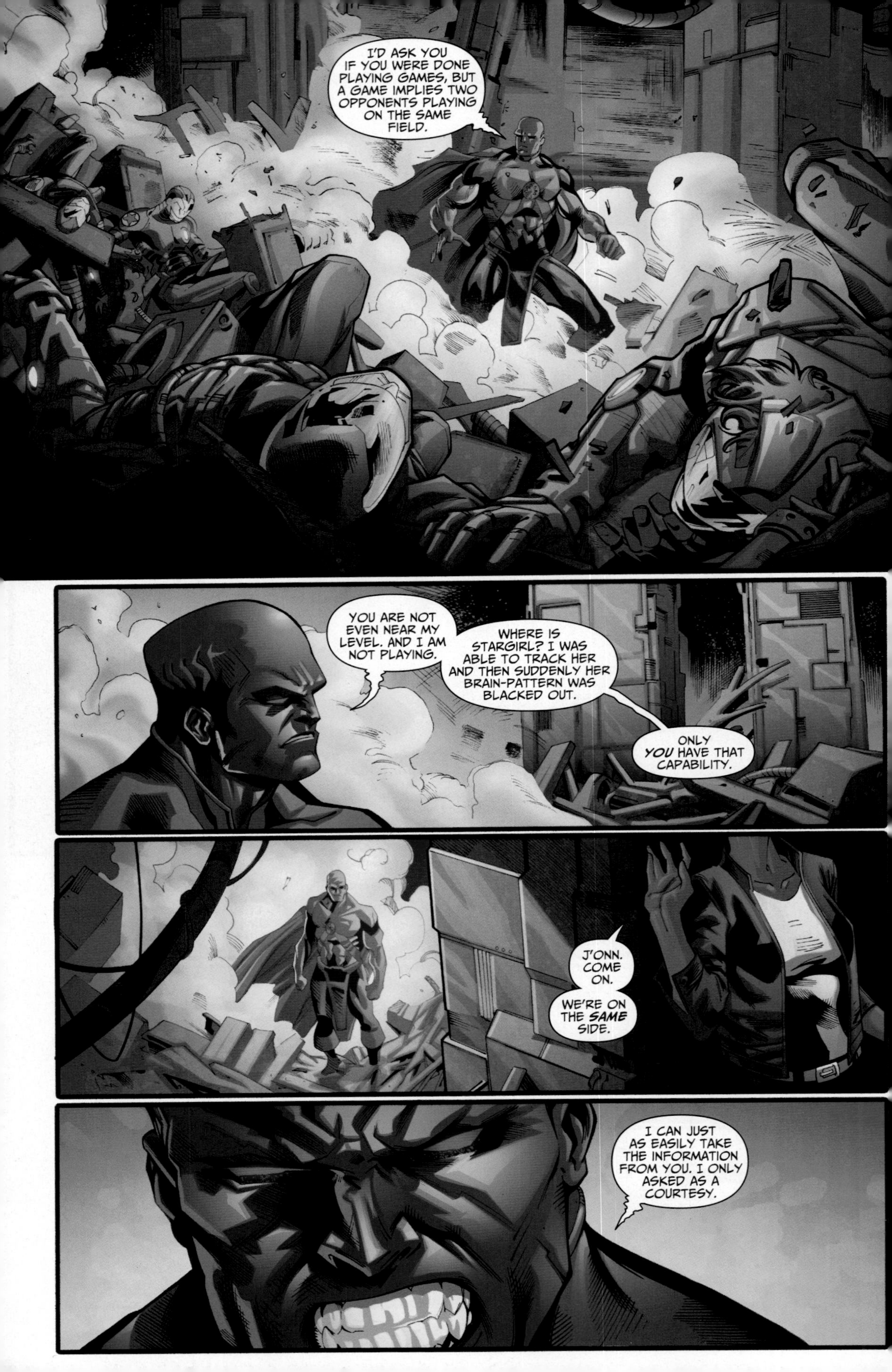
I'D ASK YOU IF YOU WERE DONE PLAYING GAMES, BUT A GAME IMPLIES TWO OPPONENTS PLAYING ON THE SAME FIELD.
YOU ARE NOT EVEN NEAR MY LEVEL. AND I AM NOT PLAYING.
WHERE IS STARGIRL? I WAS ABLE TO TRACK HER AND THEN SUDDENLY HER BRAIN-PATTERN WAS BLACKED OUT.
ONLY *YOU* HAVE THAT CAPABILITY.
J'ONN. COME ON.
WE'RE ON THE *SAME* SIDE.
I CAN JUST AS EASILY TAKE THE INFORMATION FROM YOU. I ONLY ASKED AS A COURTESY.

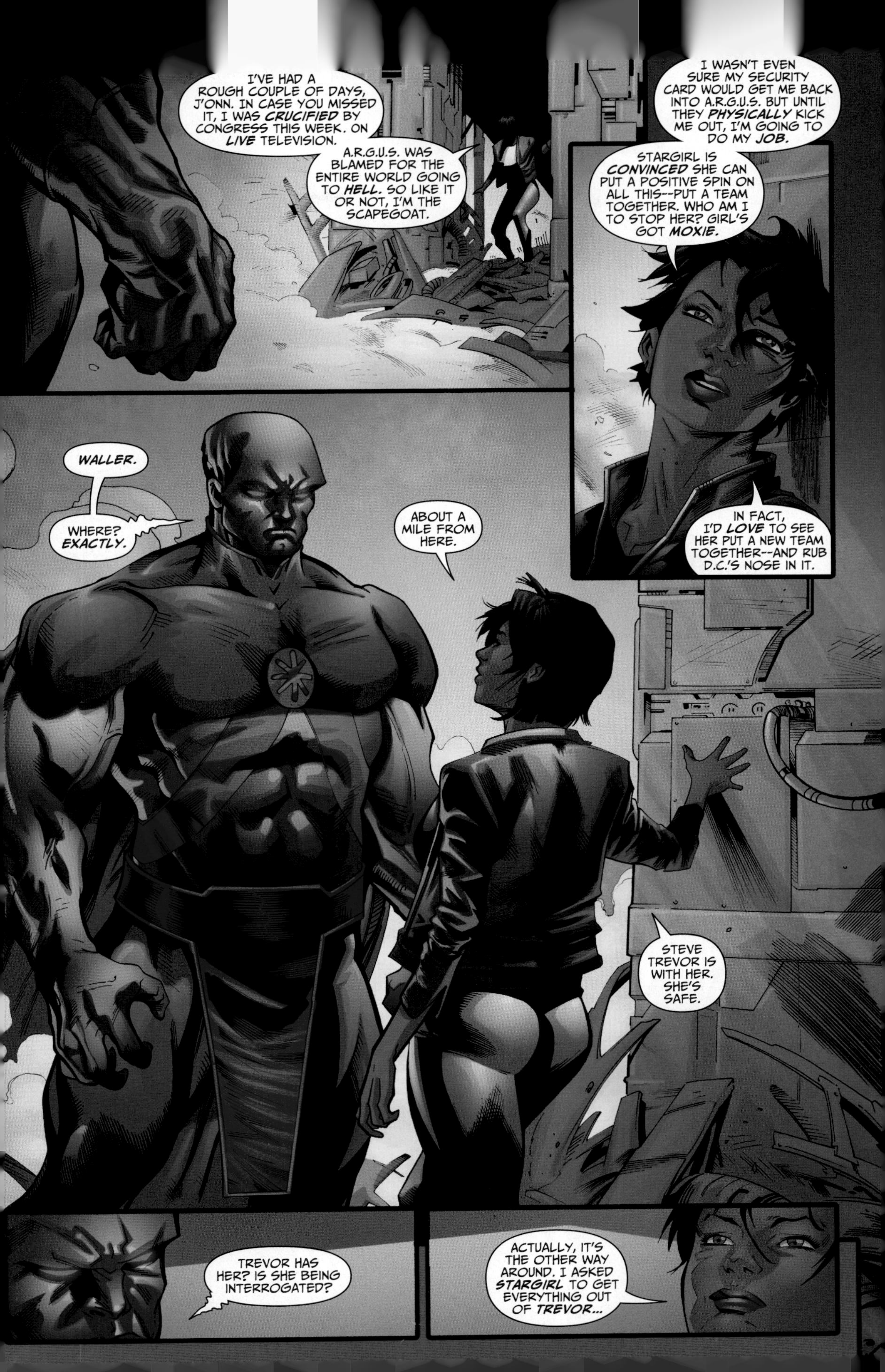
I'VE HAD A ROUGH COUPLE OF DAYS, J'ONN. IN CASE YOU MISSED IT, I WAS CRUCIFIED BY CONGRESS THIS WEEK. ON LIVE TELEVISION.
A.R.G.U.S. WAS BLAMED FOR THE ENTIRE WORLD GOING TO HELL. SO LIKE IT OR NOT, I'M THE SCAPEGOAT.
I WASN'T EVEN SURE MY SECURITY CARD WOULD GET ME BACK INTO A.R.G.U.S. BUT UNTIL THEY PHYSICALLY KICK ME OUT, I'M GOING TO DO MY JOB.
STARGIRL IS CONVINCED SHE CAN PUT A POSITIVE SPIN ON ALL THIS--PUT A TEAM TOGETHER. WHO AM I TO STOP HER? GIRL'S GOT MOXIE.
IN FACT, I'D LOVE TO SEE HER PUT A NEW TEAM TOGETHER--AND RUB D.C.'S NOSE IN IT.
WALLER.
WHERE? EXACTLY.
ABOUT A MILE FROM HERE.
STEVE TREVOR IS WITH HER. SHE'S SAFE.
TREVOR HAS HER? IS SHE BEING INTERROGATED?
ACTUALLY, IT'S THE OTHER WAY AROUND. I ASKED STARGIRL TO GET EVERYTHING OUT OF TREVOR...

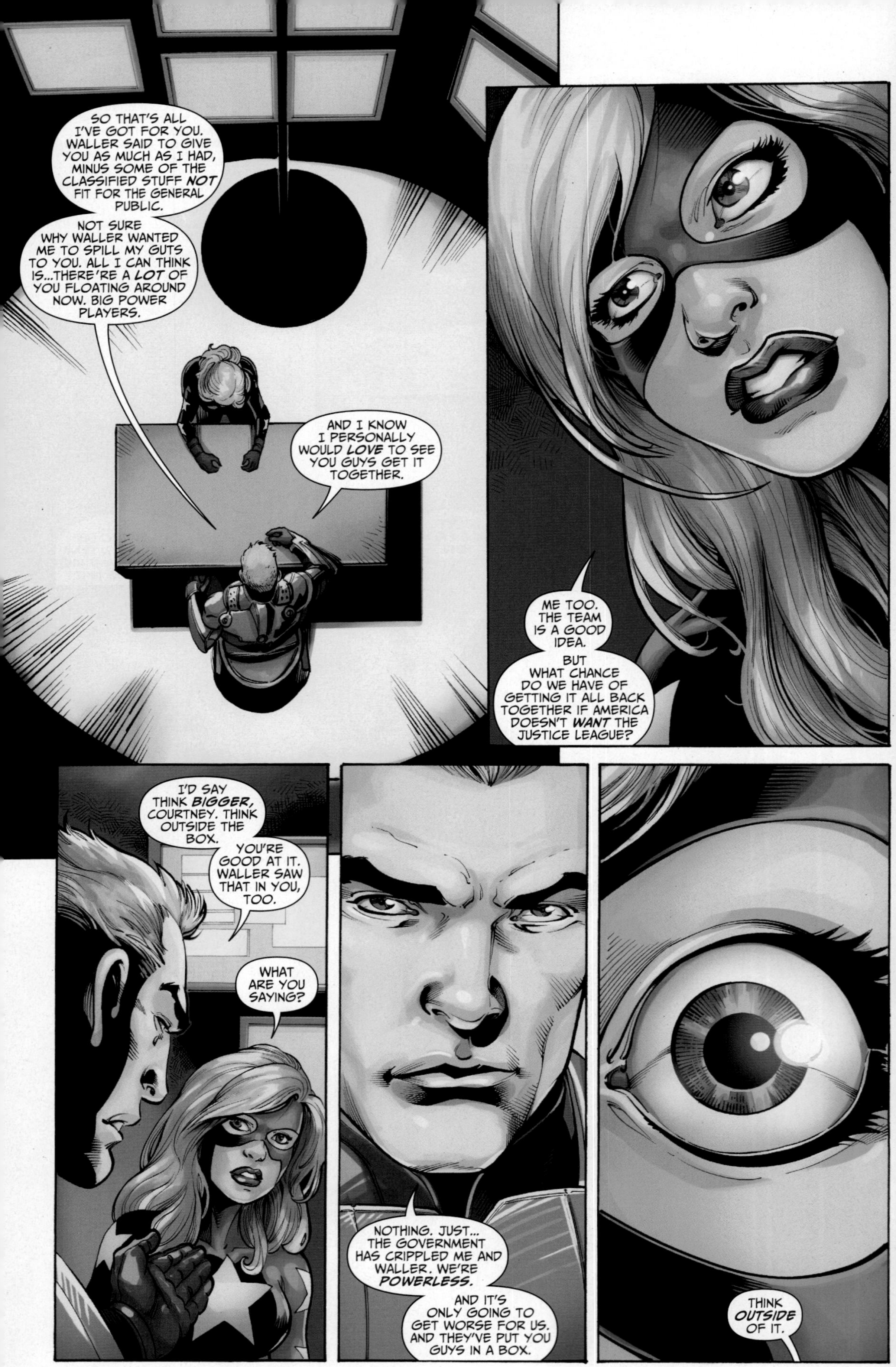
SO THAT'S ALL I'VE GOT FOR YOU. WALLER SAID TO GIVE YOU AS MUCH AS I HAD, MINUS SOME OF THE CLASSIFIED STUFF NOT FIT FOR THE GENERAL PUBLIC.
NOT SURE WHY WALLER WANTED ME TO SPILL MY GUTS TO YOU. ALL I CAN THINK IS...THERE'RE A LOT OF YOU FLOATING AROUND NOW. BIG POWER PLAYERS.
AND I KNOW I PERSONALLY WOULD LOVE TO SEE YOU GUYS GET IT TOGETHER.
ME TOO. THE TEAM IS A GOOD IDEA.
BUT WHAT CHANCE DO WE HAVE OF GETTING IT ALL BACK TOGETHER IF AMERICA DOESN'T WANT THE JUSTICE LEAGUE?
I'D SAY THINK BIGGER, COURTNEY. THINK OUTSIDE THE BOX.
YOU'RE GOOD AT IT. WALLER SAW THAT IN YOU, TOO.
WHAT ARE YOU SAYING?
NOTHING. JUST... THE GOVERNMENT HAS CRIPPLED ME AND WALLER. WE'RE POWERLESS.
AND IT'S ONLY GOING TO GET WORSE FOR US. AND THEY'VE PUT YOU GUYS IN A BOX.
THINK OUTSIDE OF IT.

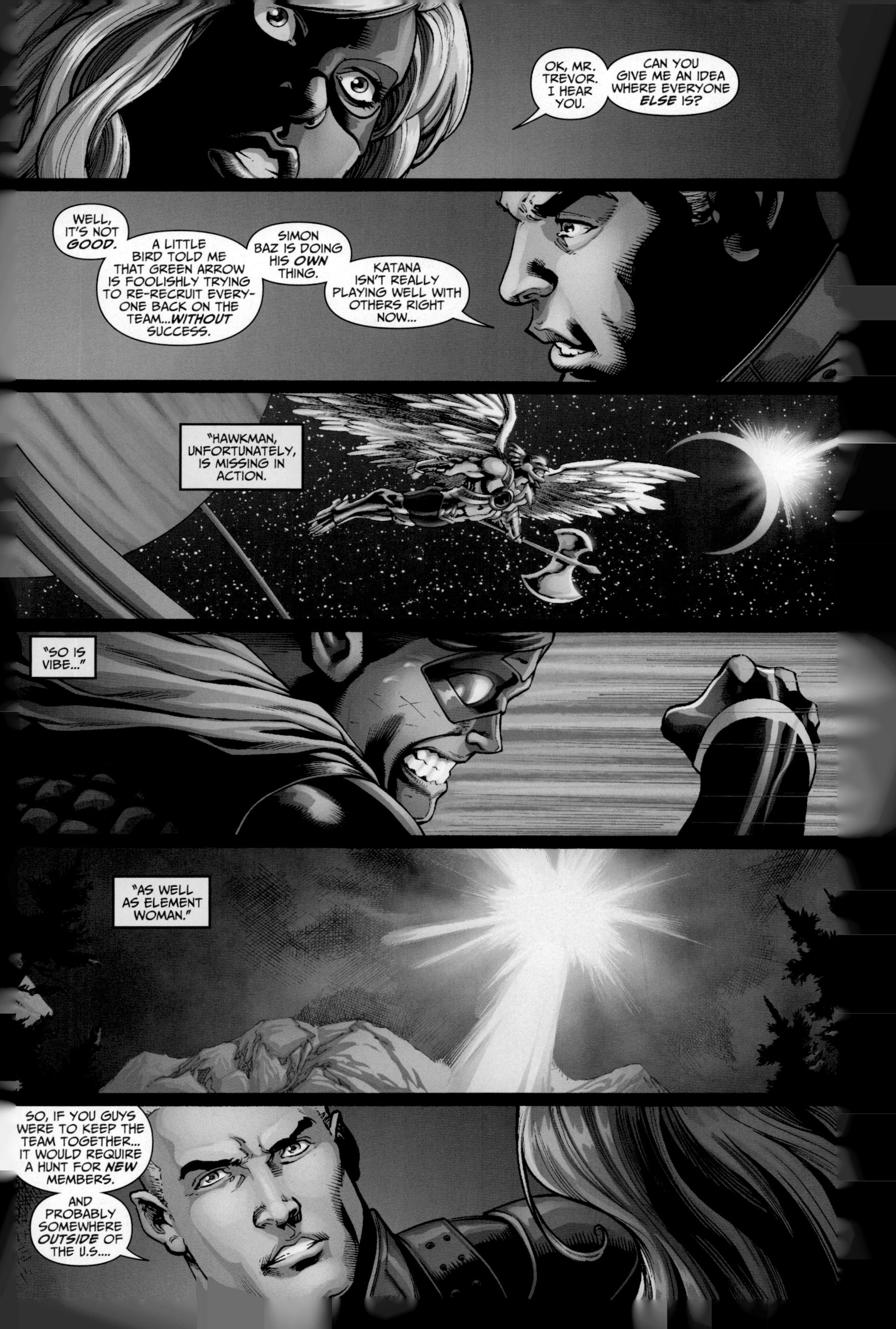
OK, MR. TREVOR. I HEAR YOU.
CAN YOU GIVE ME AN IDEA WHERE EVERYONE *ELSE* IS?
WELL, IT'S NOT *GOOD.*
A LITTLE BIRD TOLD ME THAT GREEN ARROW IS FOOLISHLY TRYING TO RE-RECRUIT EVERY-ONE BACK ON THE TEAM...*WITHOUT* SUCCESS.
SIMON BAZ IS DOING HIS *OWN* THING.
KATANA ISN'T REALLY PLAYING WELL WITH OTHERS RIGHT NOW...
"HAWKMAN, UNFORTUNATELY, IS MISSING IN ACTION.
"SO IS VIBE..."
"AS WELL AS ELEMENT WOMAN."
SO, IF YOU GUYS WERE TO KEEP THE TEAM TOGETHER... IT WOULD REQUIRE A HUNT FOR *NEW* MEMBERS.
AND PROBABLY SOMEWHERE *OUTSIDE* OF THE U.S....

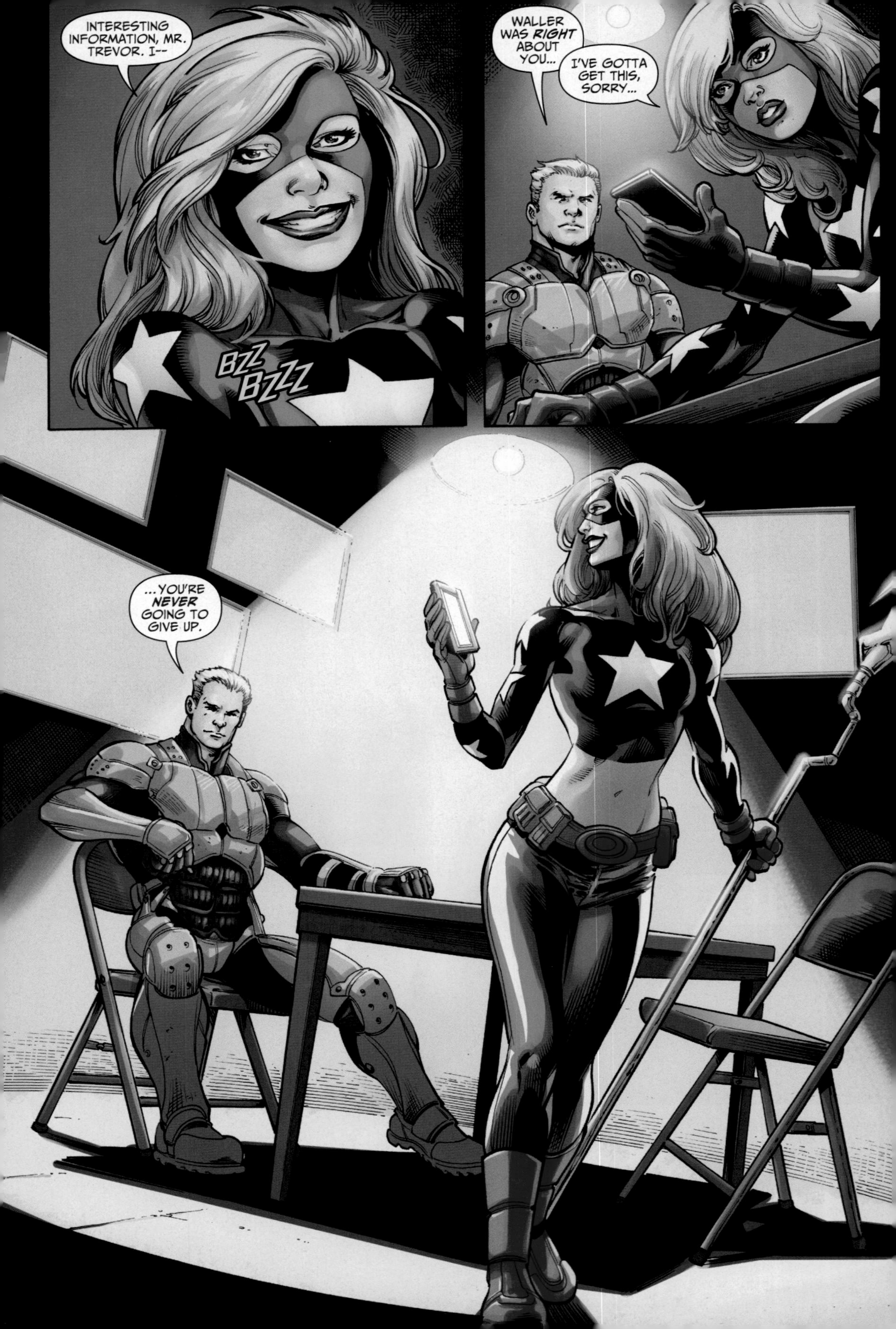
INTERESTING INFORMATION, MR. TREVOR. I--
BZZ BZZZ
WALLER WAS RIGHT ABOUT YOU...
I'VE GOTTA GET THIS, SORRY...
...YOU'RE NEVER GOING TO GIVE UP.

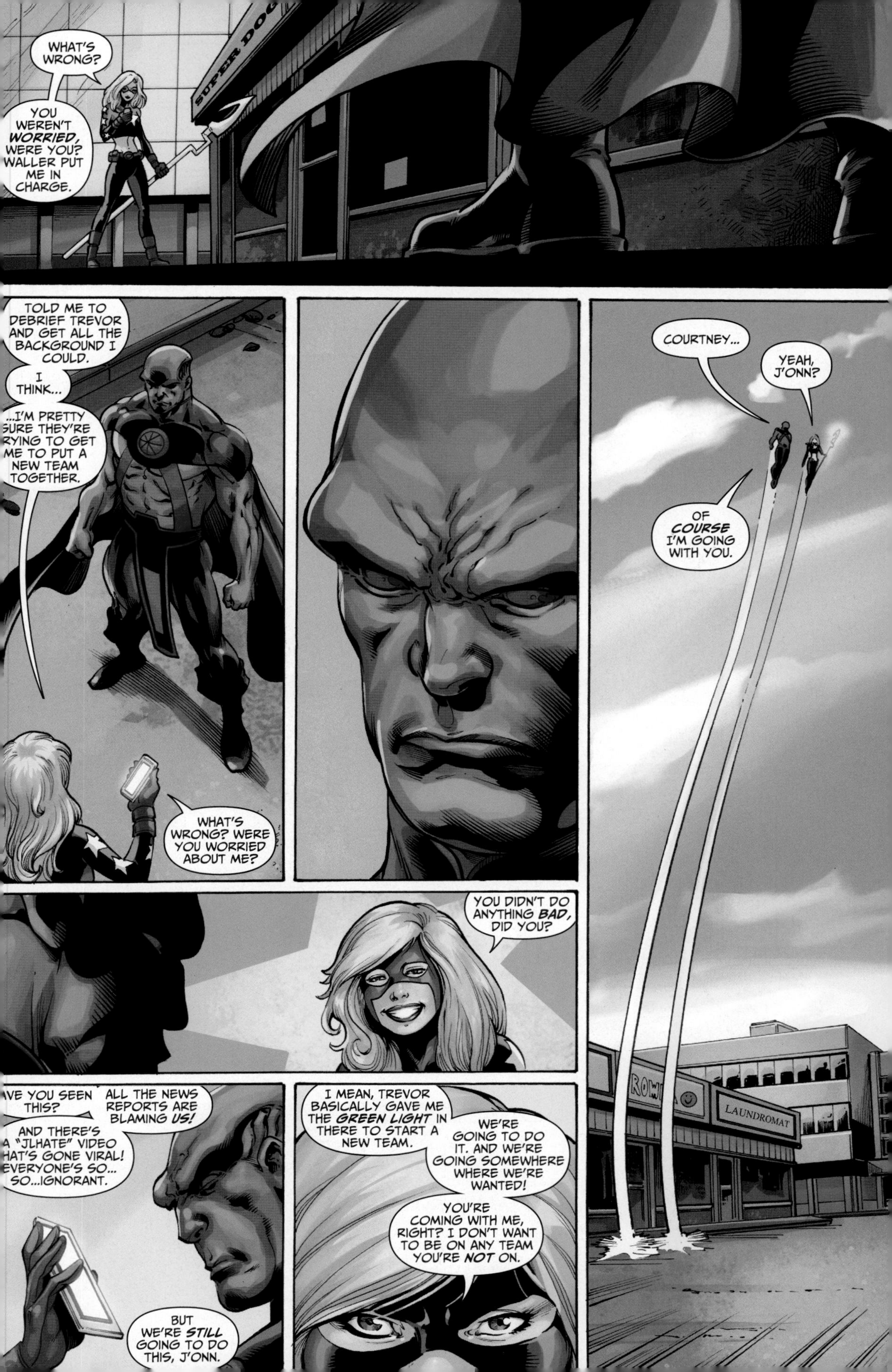
WHAT'S WRONG?
YOU WEREN'T WORRIED, WERE YOU? WALLER PUT ME IN CHARGE.
SUPER DOG
TOLD ME TO DEBRIEF TREVOR AND GET ALL THE BACKGROUND I COULD.
I THINK...
...I'M PRETTY SURE THEY'RE TRYING TO GET ME TO PUT A NEW TEAM TOGETHER.
WHAT'S WRONG? WERE YOU WORRIED ABOUT ME?
COURTNEY...
YEAH, J'ONN?
OF COURSE I'M GOING WITH YOU.
LAUNDROMAT
YOU DIDN'T DO ANYTHING BAD, DID YOU?
AVE YOU SEEN THIS?
ALL THE NEWS REPORTS ARE BLAMING US!
AND THERE'S A "JLHATE" VIDEO THAT'S GONE VIRAL! EVERYONE'S SO... SO...IGNORANT.
BUT WE'RE STILL GOING TO DO THIS, J'ONN.
I MEAN, TREVOR BASICALLY GAVE ME THE GREEN LIGHT IN THERE TO START A NEW TEAM.
WE'RE GOING TO DO IT. AND WE'RE GOING SOMEWHERE WHERE WE'RE WANTED!
YOU'RE COMING WITH ME, RIGHT? I DON'T WANT TO BE ON ANY TEAM YOU'RE NOT ON.

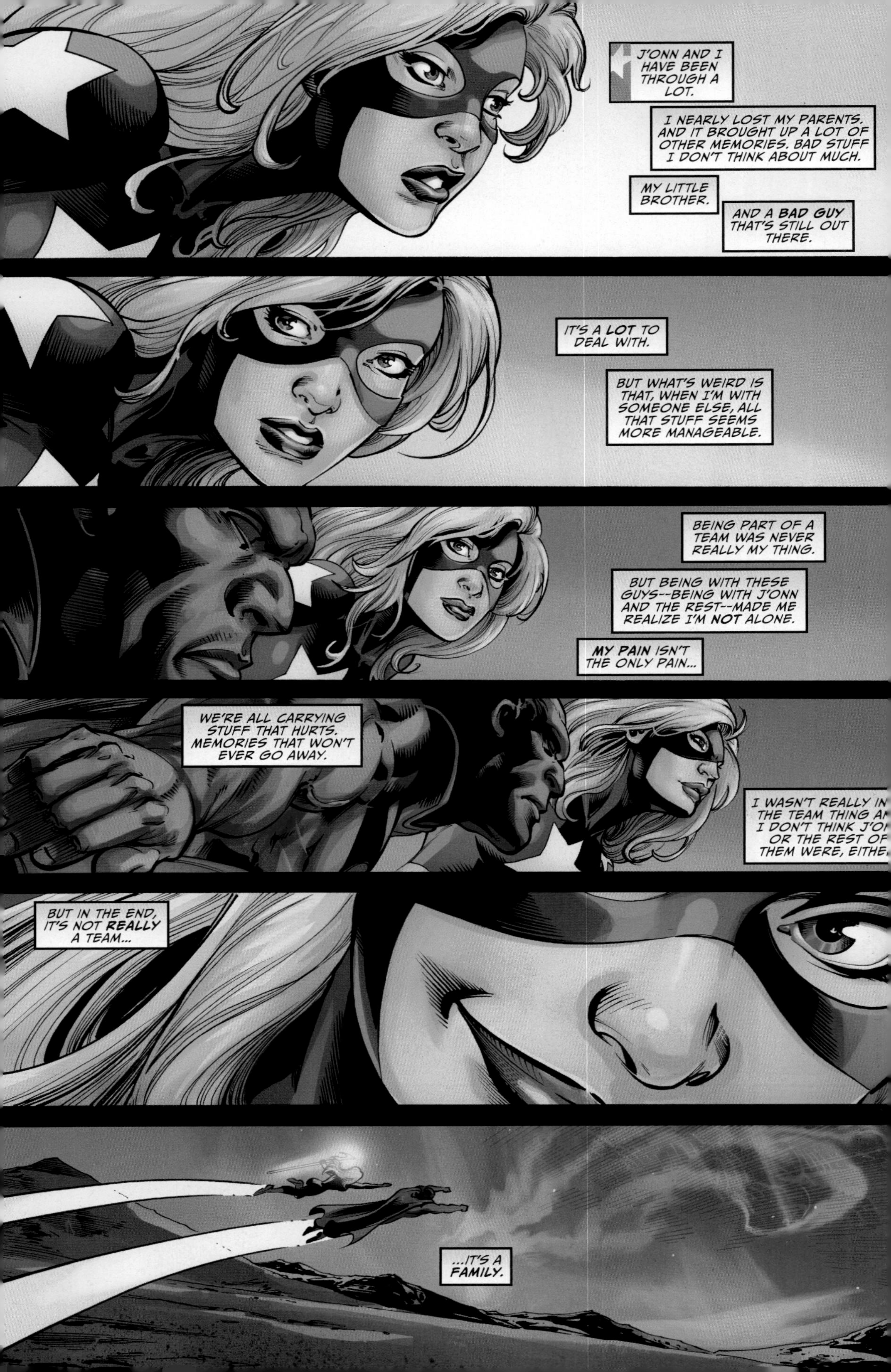
J'ONN AND I HAVE BEEN THROUGH A LOT.
I NEARLY LOST MY PARENTS. AND IT BROUGHT UP A LOT OF OTHER MEMORIES. BAD STUFF I DON'T THINK ABOUT MUCH.
MY LITTLE BROTHER.
AND A BAD GUY THAT'S STILL OUT THERE.
IT'S A LOT TO DEAL WITH.
BUT WHAT'S WEIRD IS THAT, WHEN I'M WITH SOMEONE ELSE, ALL THAT STUFF SEEMS MORE MANAGEABLE.
BEING PART OF A TEAM WAS NEVER REALLY MY THING.
BUT BEING WITH THESE GUYS--BEING WITH J'ONN AND THE REST--MADE ME REALIZE I'M NOT ALONE.
MY PAIN ISN'T THE ONLY PAIN...
WE'RE ALL CARRYING STUFF THAT HURTS. MEMORIES THAT WON'T EVER GO AWAY.
I WASN'T REALLY IN THE TEAM THING AN I DON'T THINK J'ON OR THE REST OF THEM WERE, EITHE
BUT IN THE END, IT'S NOT REALLY A TEAM...
...IT'S A FAMILY.

VARIANT COVER GALLERY

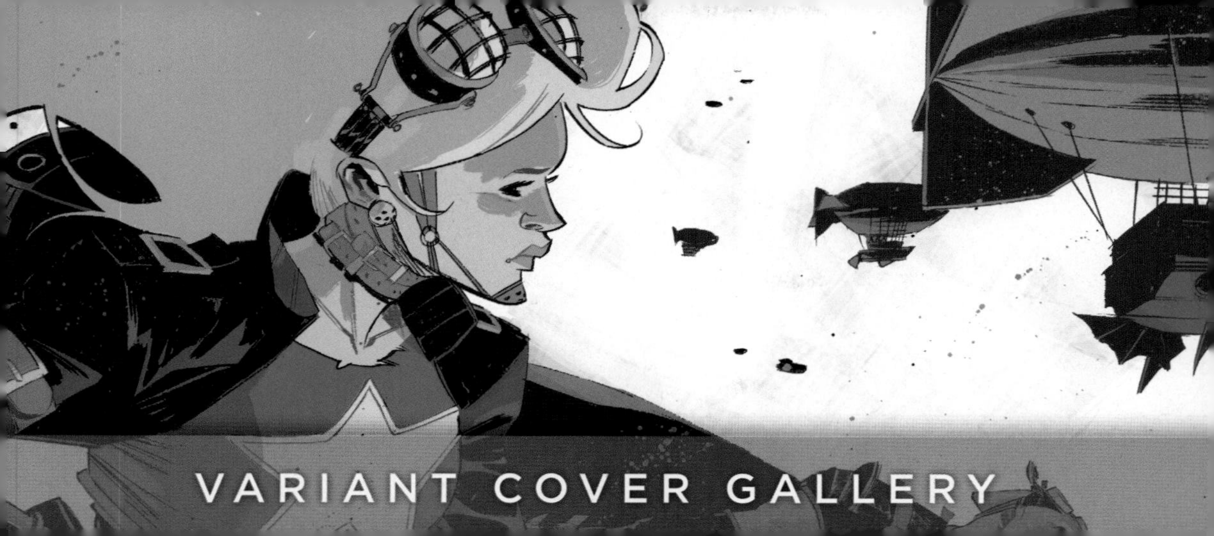

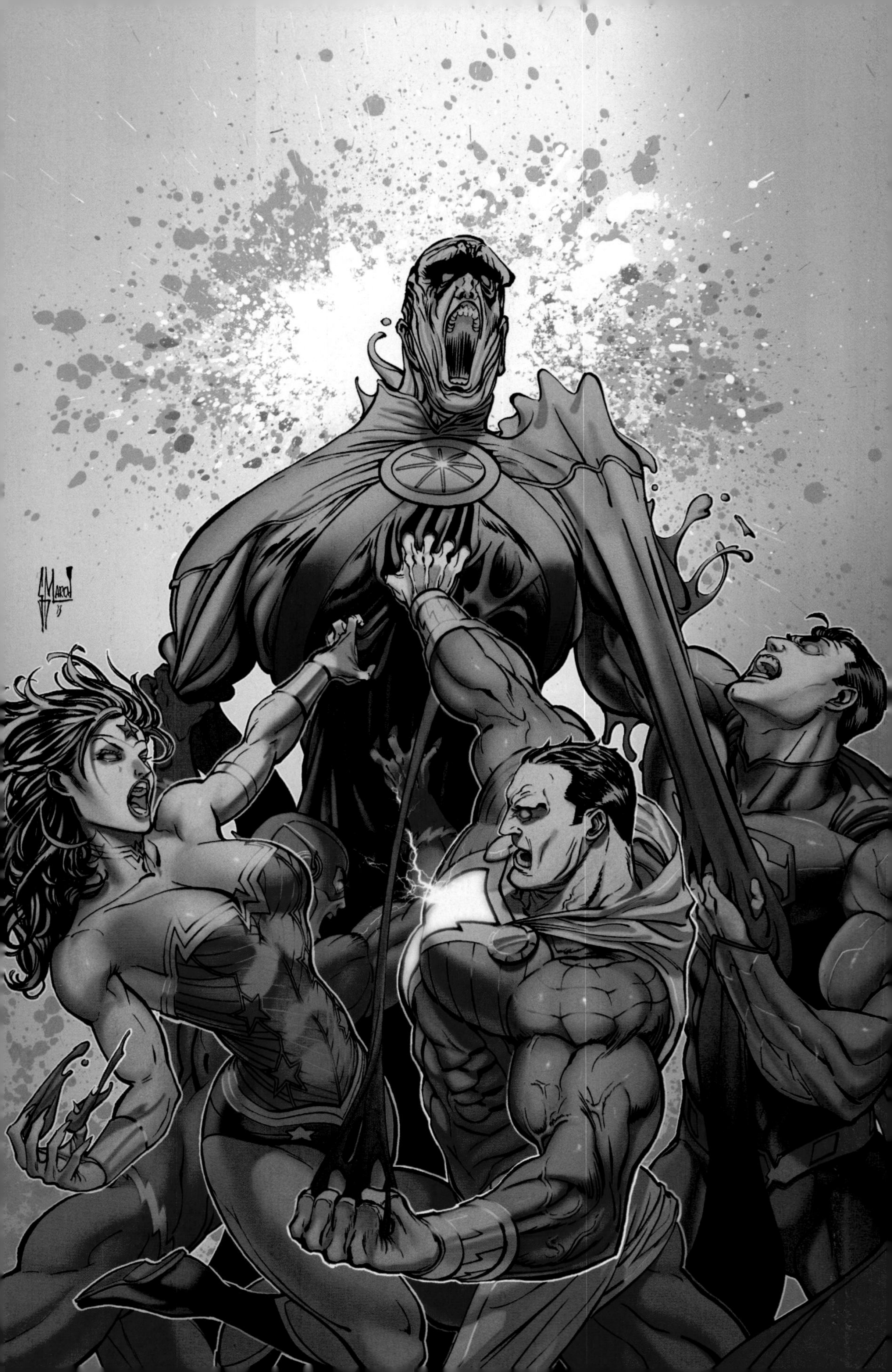

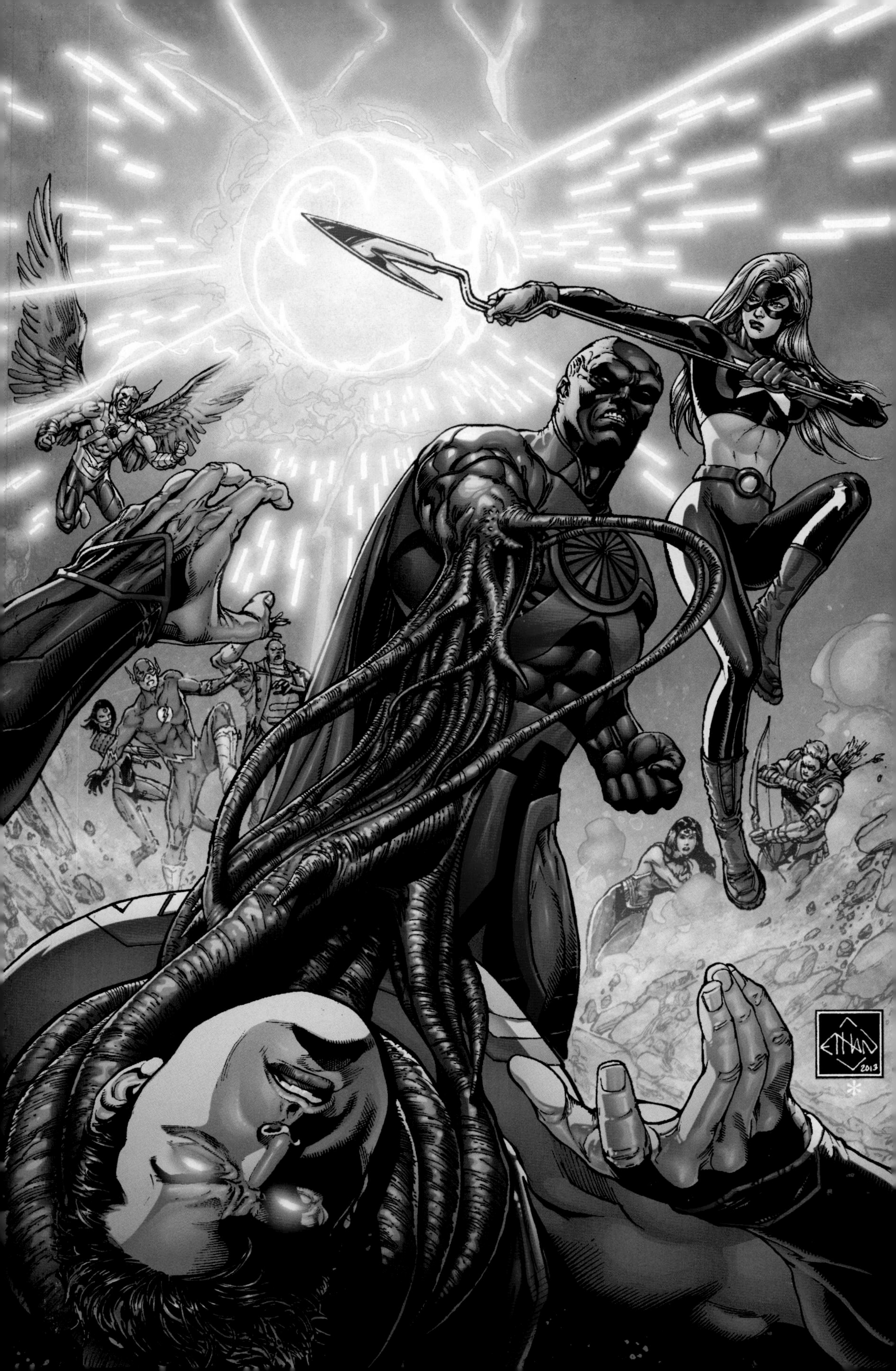
ETHAN
2013

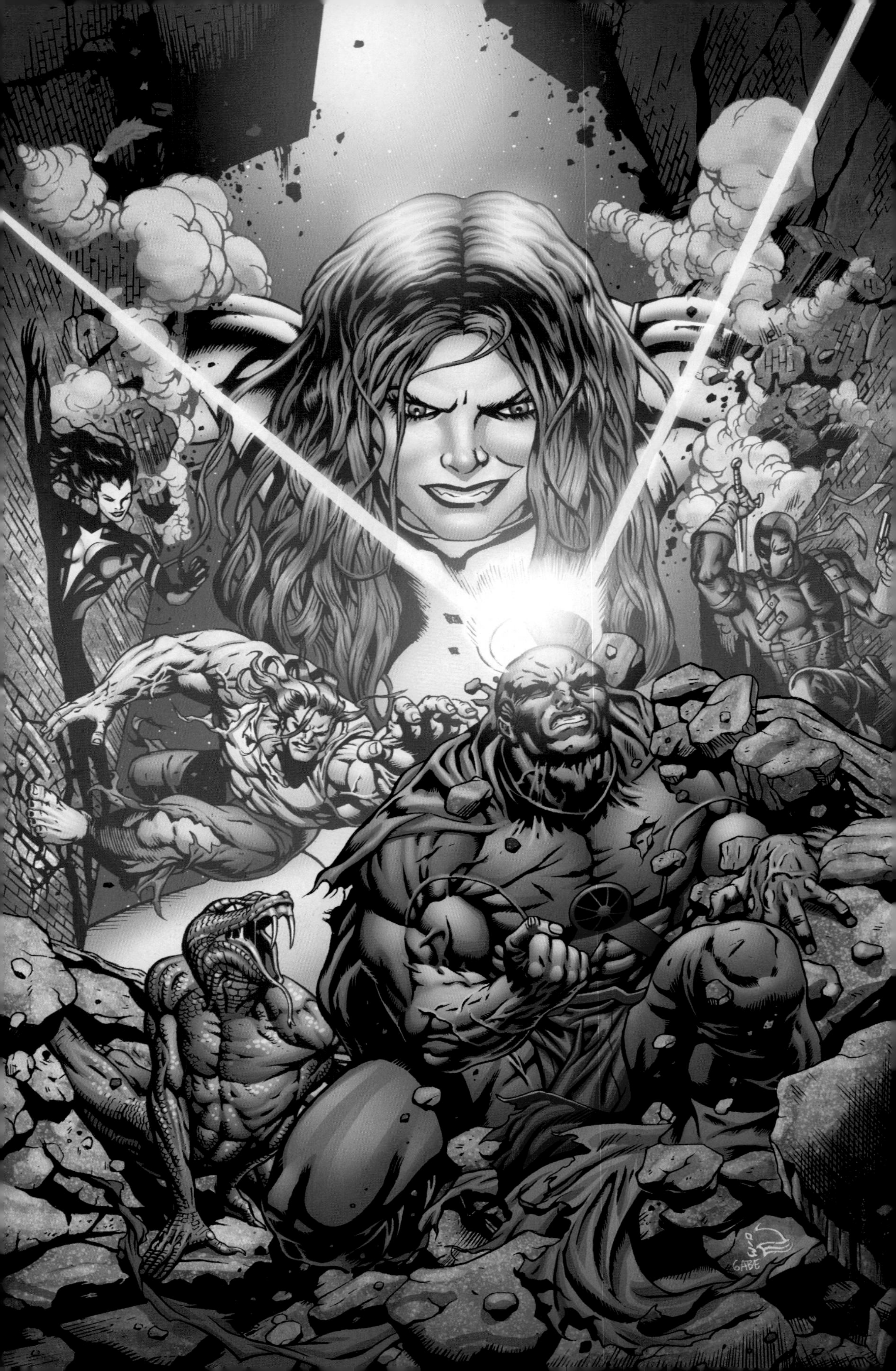
GABE

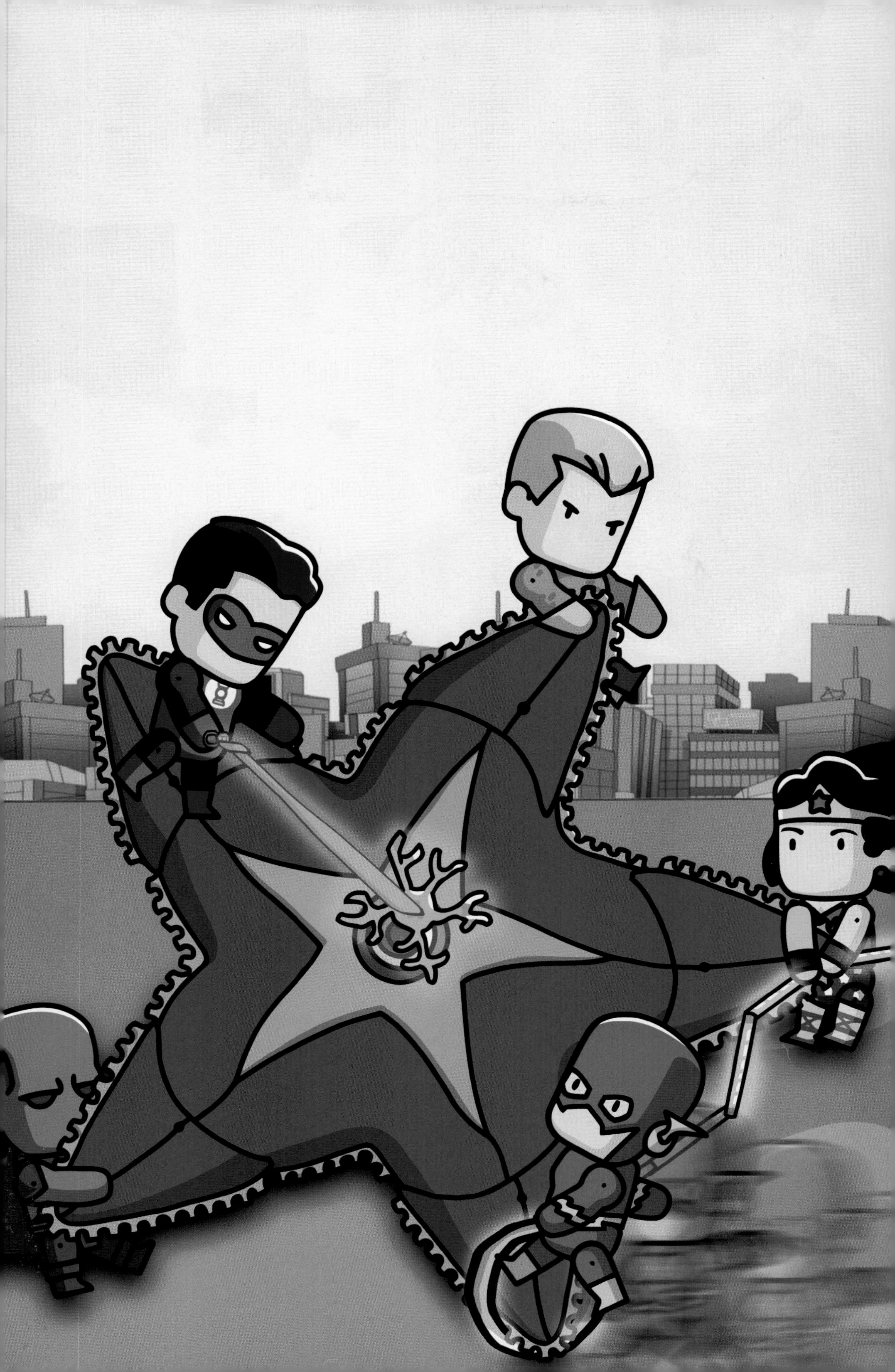

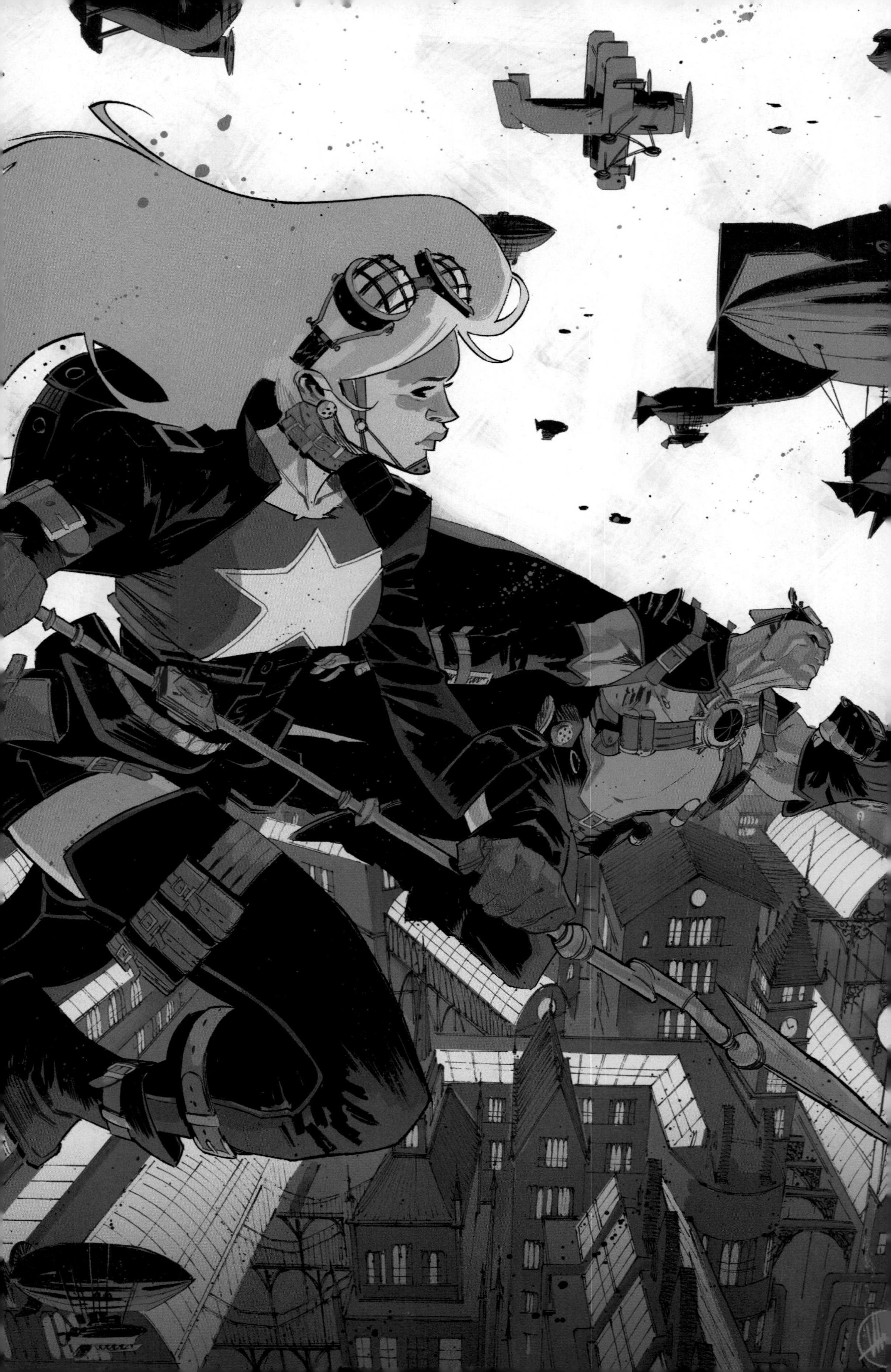

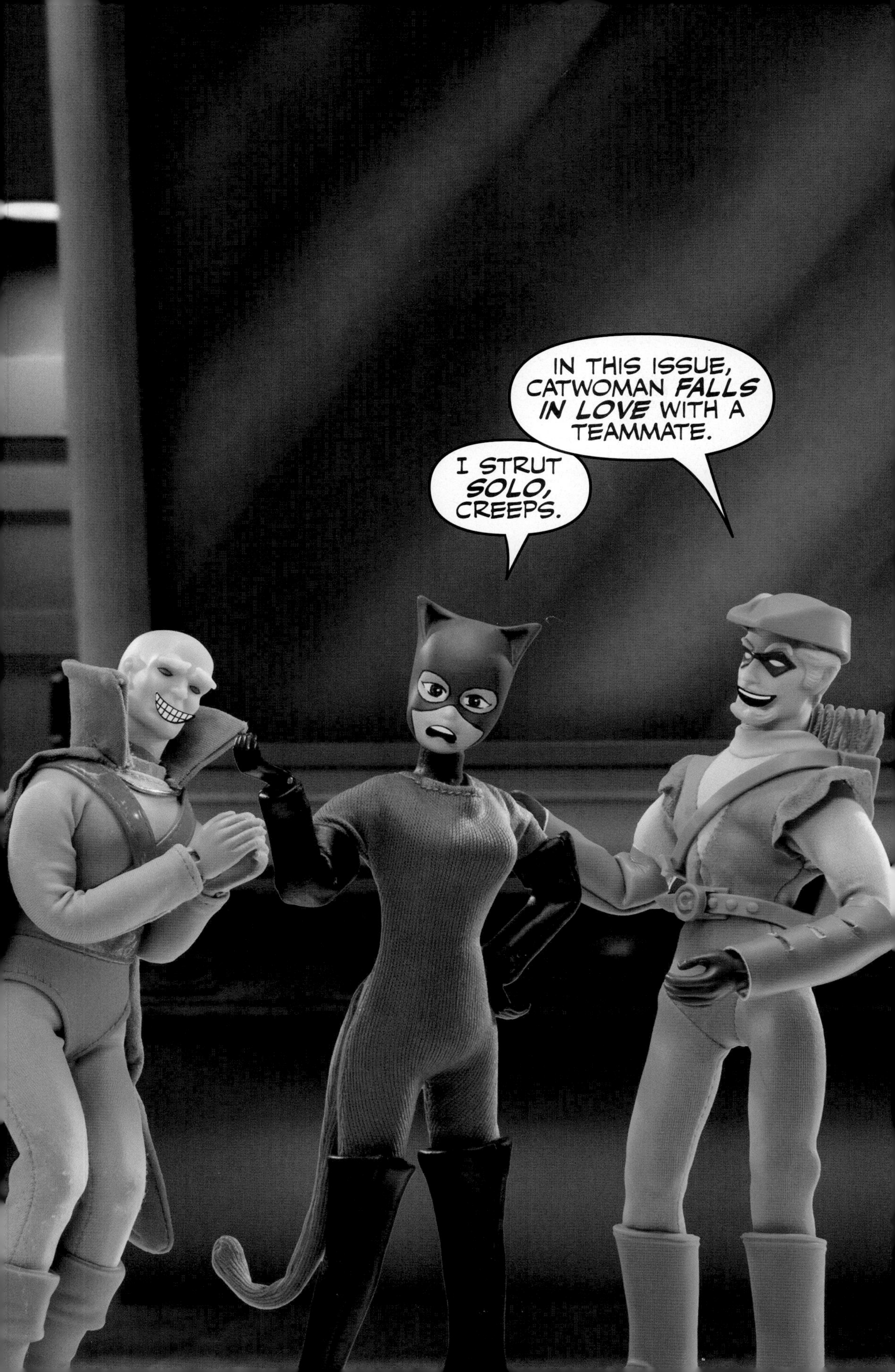
IN THIS ISSUE, CATWOMAN FALLS IN LOVE WITH A TEAMMATE.
I STRUT SOLO, CREEPS.

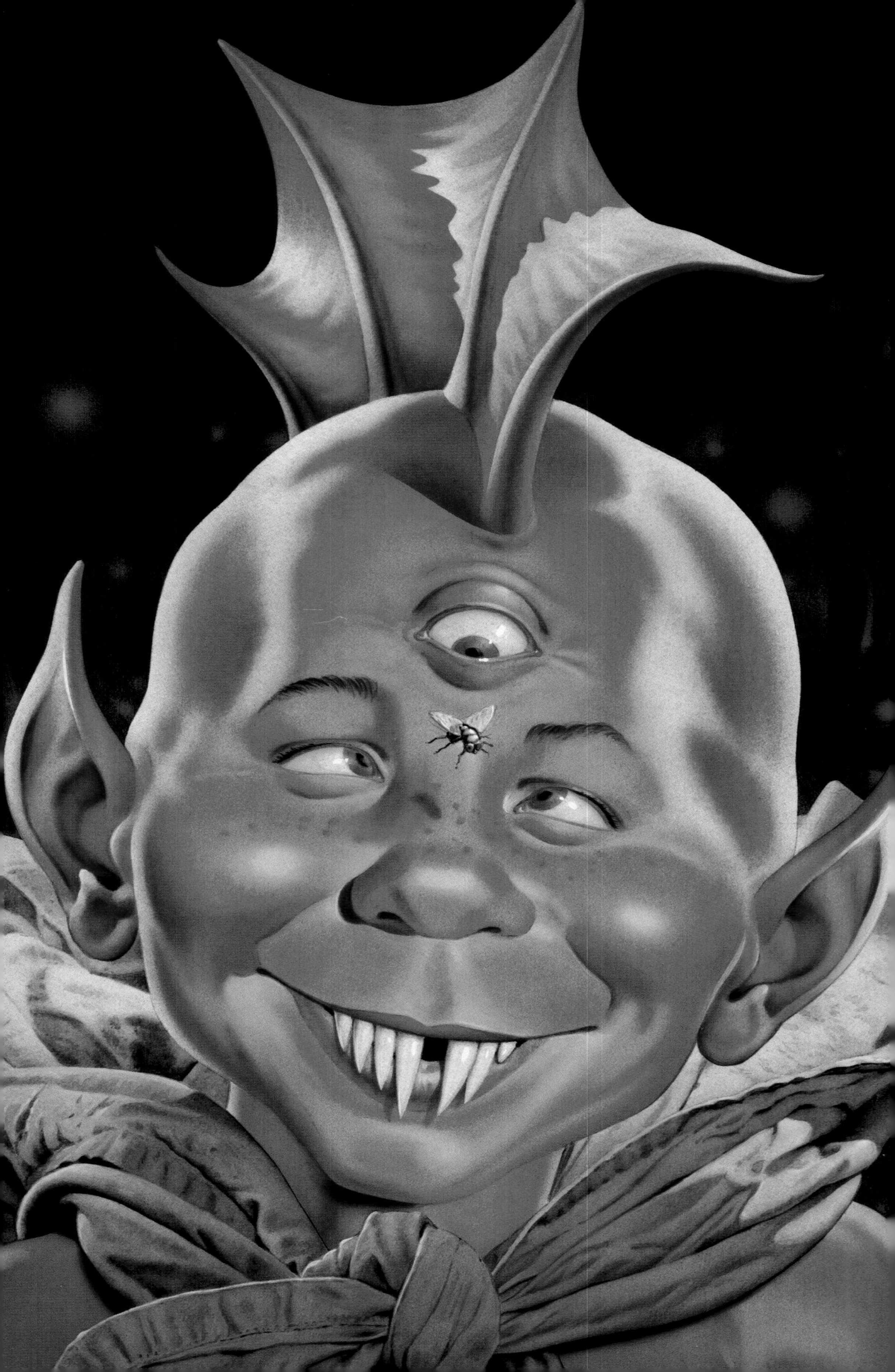

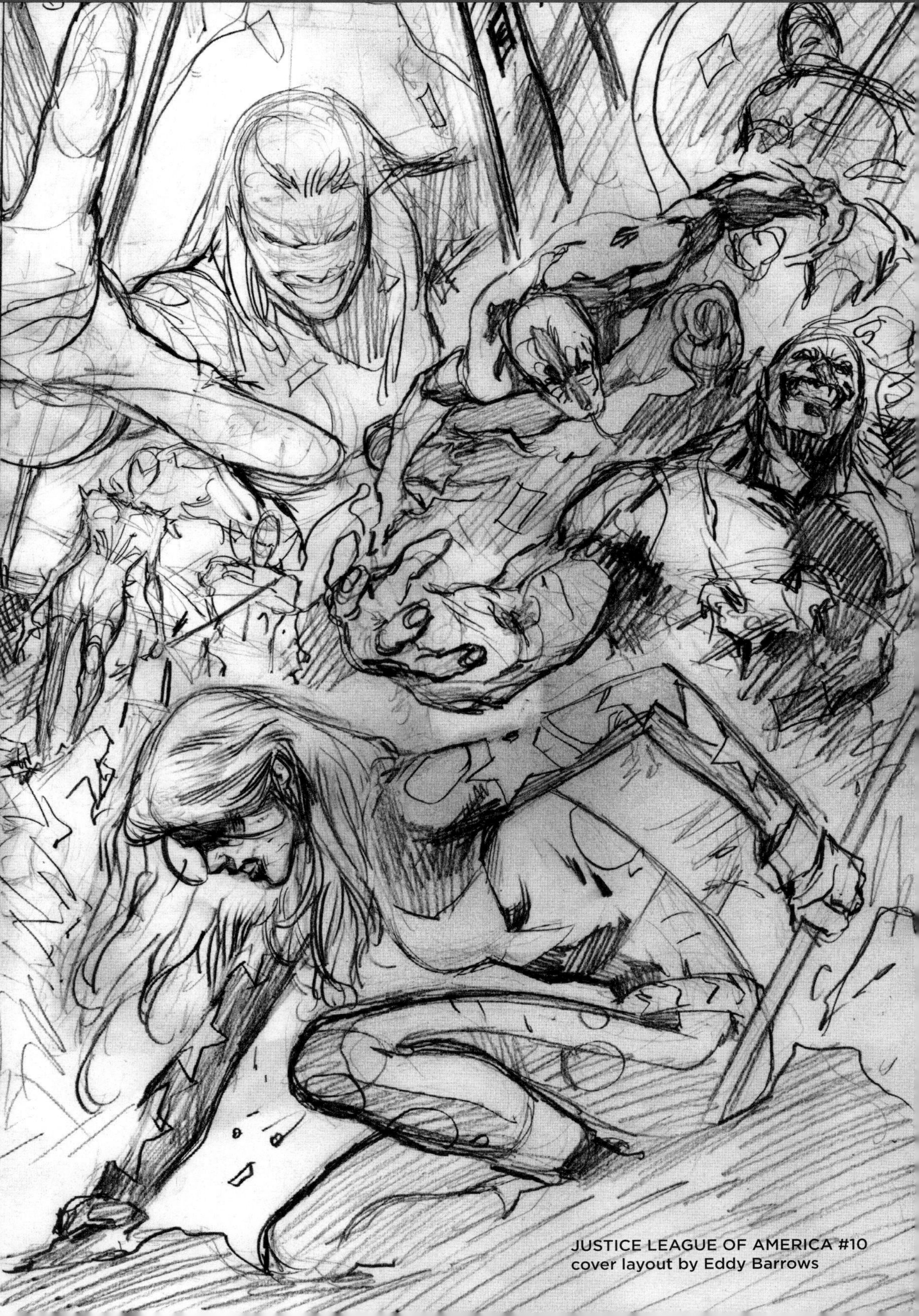

JUSTICE LEAGUE OF AMERICA #10
cover layout by Eddy Barrows

JUSTICE LEAGUE OF AMERICA #8
cover layout by Ken Lashley

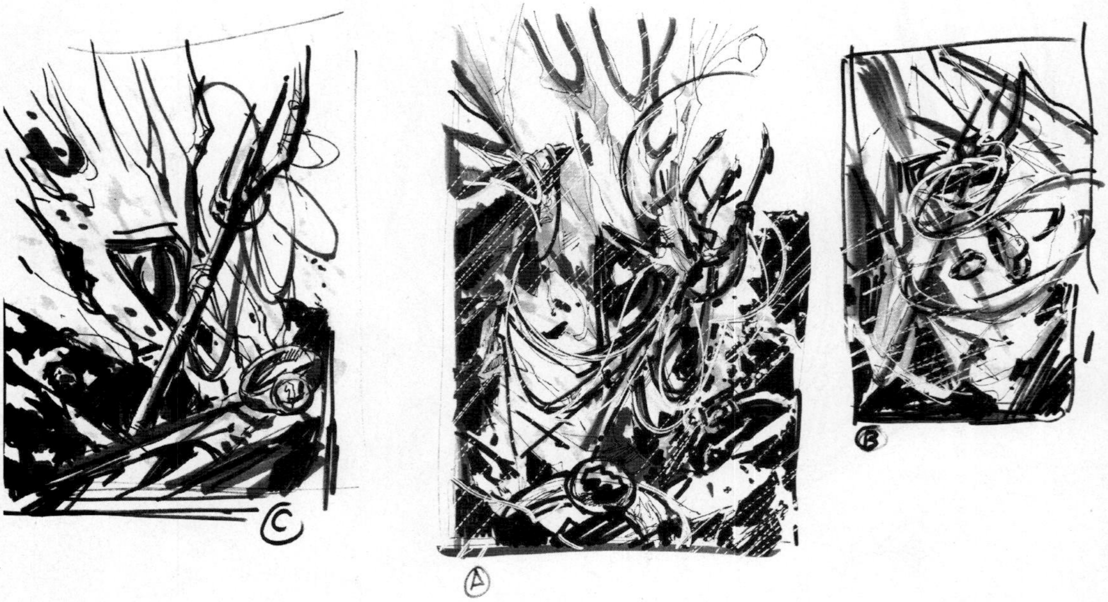
C
A
B

JUSTICE LEAGUE OF AMERICA #9
cover layout by Doug Mahnke

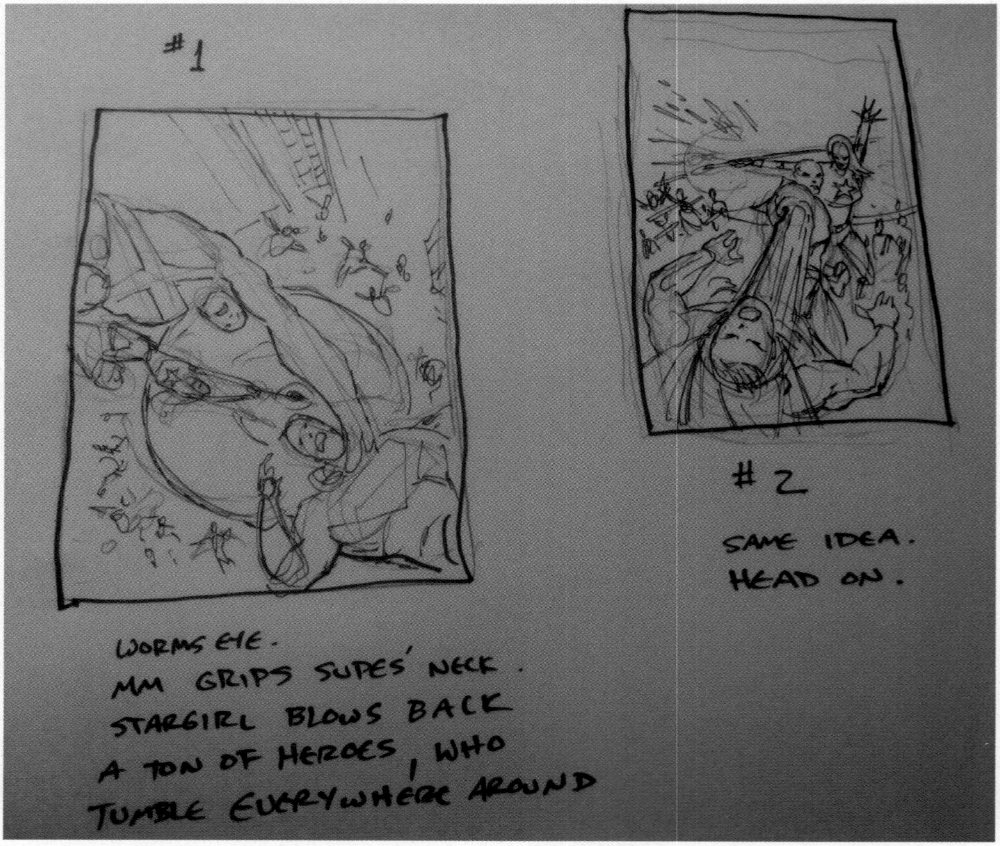
#1
#2
SAME IDEA.
HEAD ON.
WORMS EYE.
MM GRIPS SUPES' NECK.
STARGIRL BLOWS BACK
A TON OF HEROES, WHO
TUMBLE EVERYWHERE AROUND

JUSTICE LEAGUE OF AMERICA #11 and #12
cover layouts and pencils by Eddy Barrows

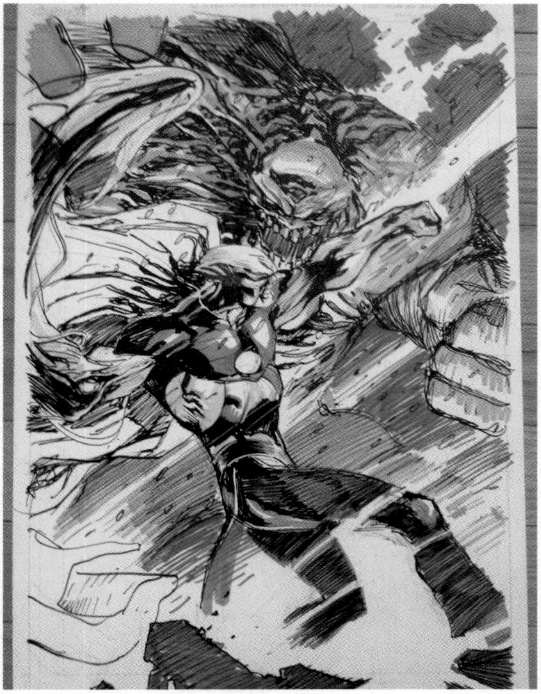

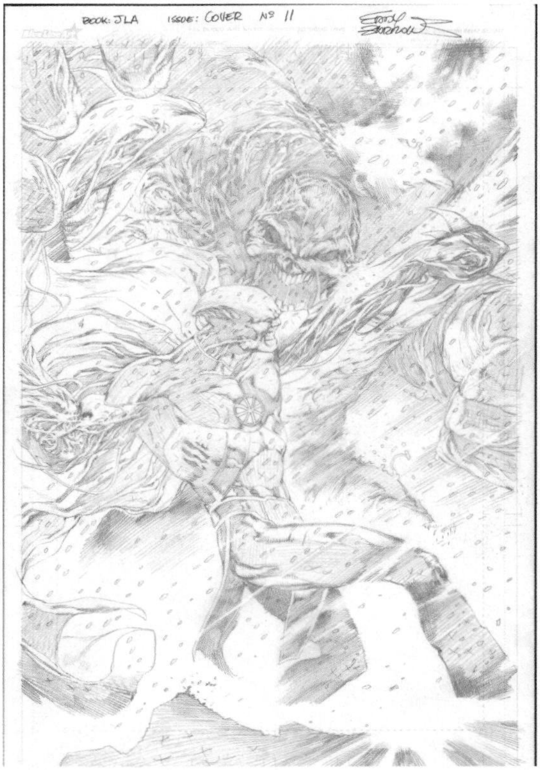
BOOK: JLA ISSUE: COVER Nº 11

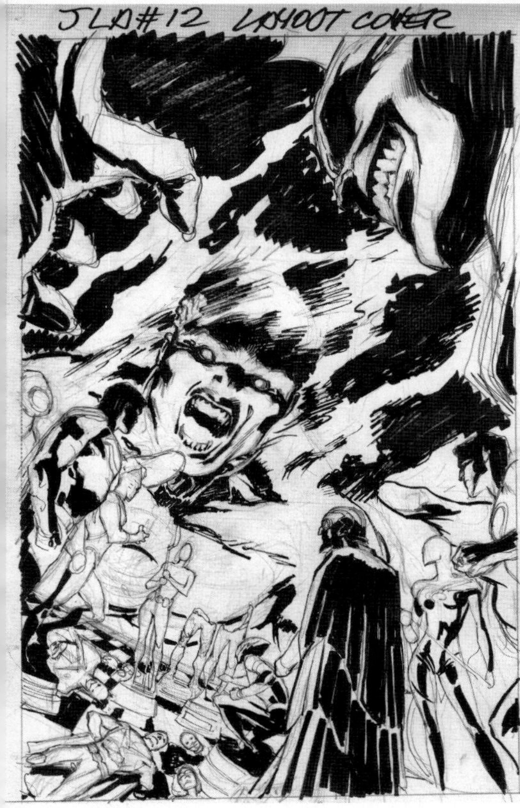
JLA#12 LAYOUT COVER

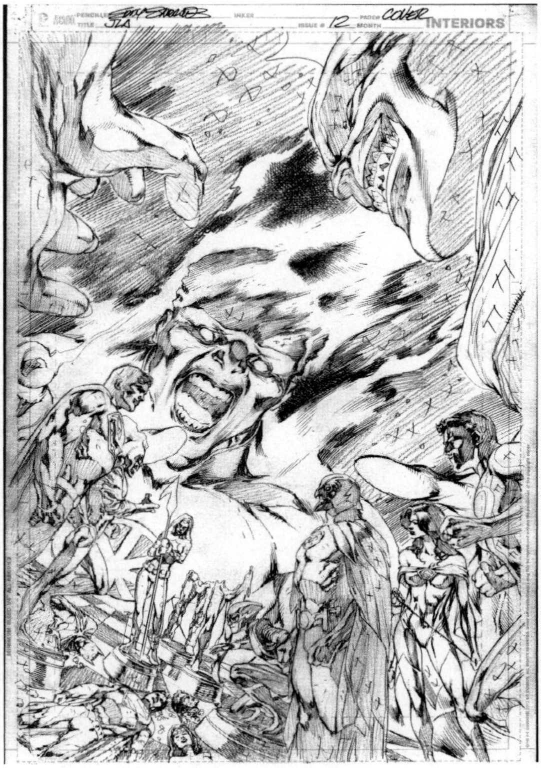
TITLE JLA
ISSUE # 12
COVER
INTERIORS

JUSTICE LEAGUE OF AMERICA #13 and #14
cover layouts and #14 pencils by Eddy Barrows

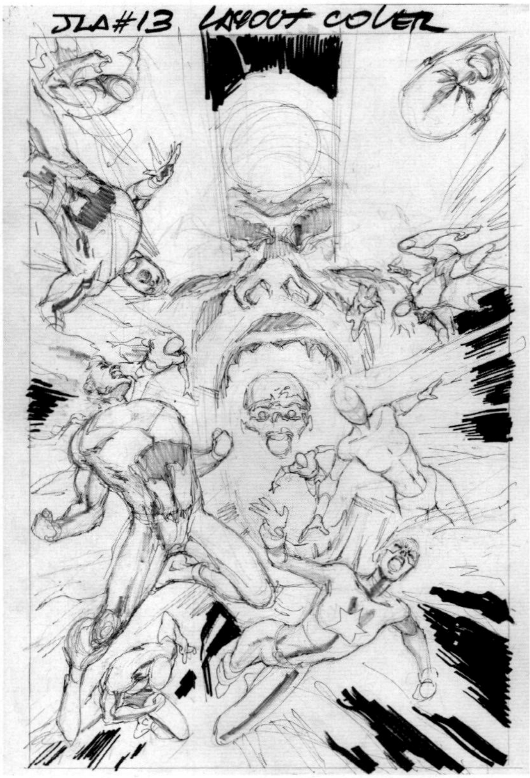
JLA#13 LAYOUT COVER

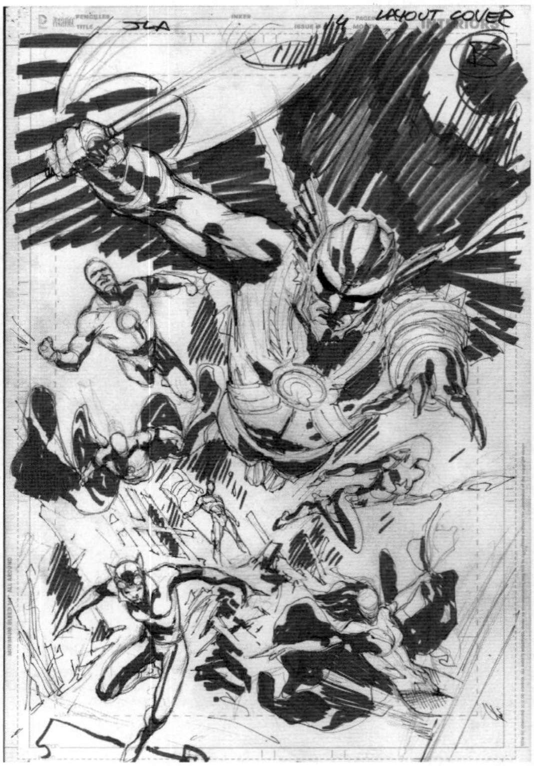
JLA
14
LAYOUT COVER

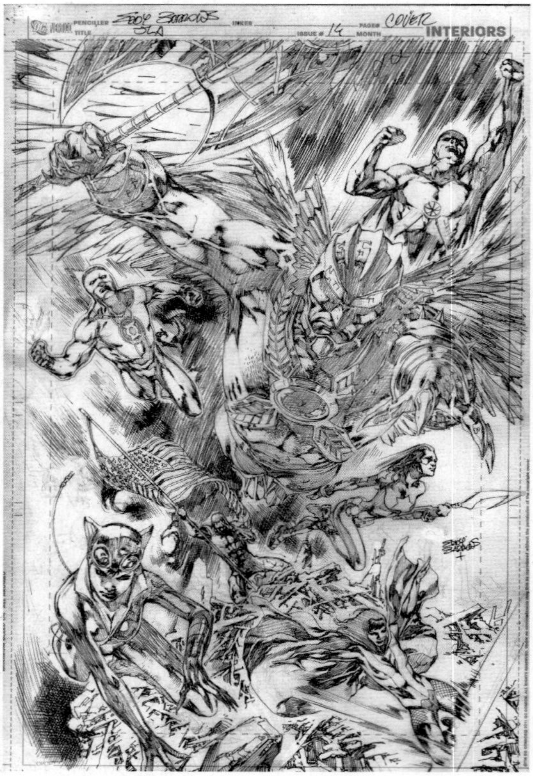
EDDY BARROWS
JLA
14
COVER
INTERIORS

Alternate cover idea for JUSTICE LEAGUE OF AMERICA #14
by Eddy Barrows

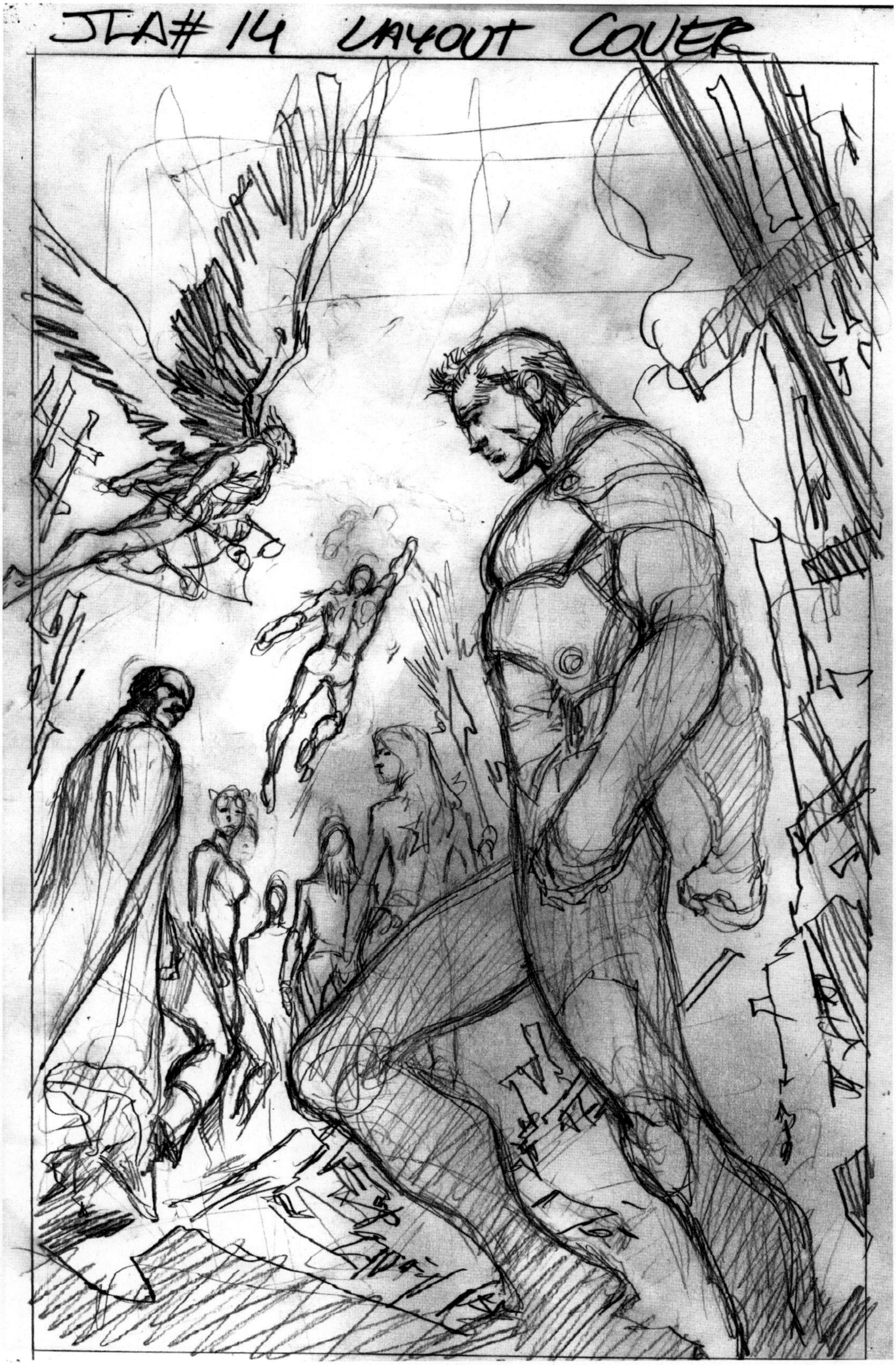
JLA# 14 LAYOUT COVER

JUSTICE LEAGUE OF AMERICA #8 variant cover layouts by Guillem March

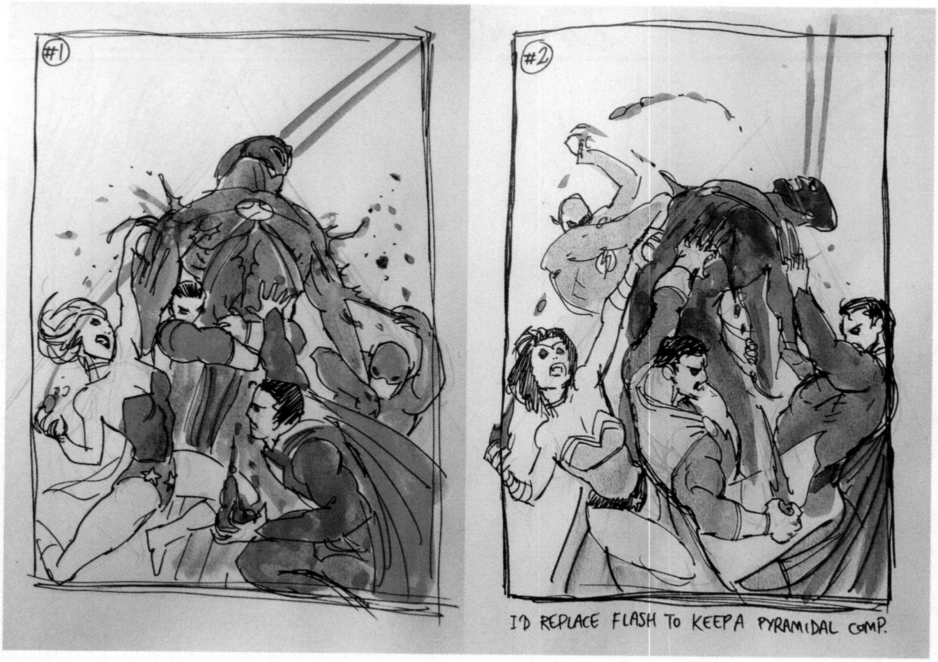
#1
#2
I'D REPLACE FLASH TO KEEP A PYRAMIDAL COMP.

JUSTICE LEAGUE OF AMERICA #10 variant cover layout and pencils by Dale Eaglesham

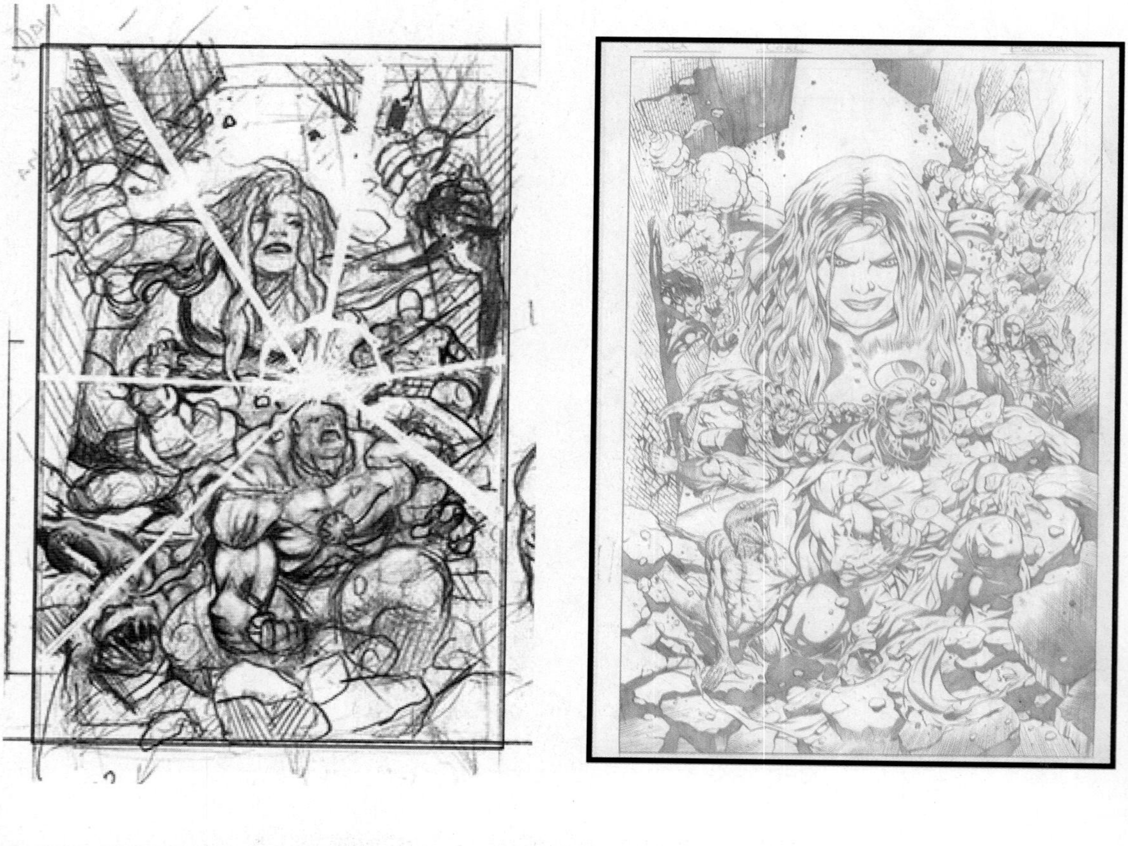

START AT THE BEGINNING!

JUSTICE LEAGUE VOLUME 1: ORIGIN

AQUAMAN VOLUME 1: THE TRENCH

THE SAVAGE HAWKMAN VOLUME 1: DARKNESS RISING

GREEN ARROW VOLUME 1: THE MIDAS TOUCH

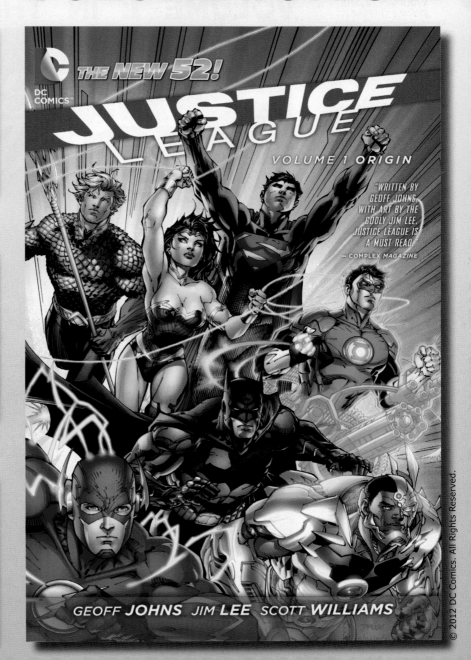

GEOFF JOHNS JIM LEE SCOTT WILLIAMS

"Maniacally brilliant."
—THE NEW YORK TIMES

"A stirringly mythic, emotionally resonant, and gloriously alternative take on the Man of Steel."
—ENTERTAINMENT WEEKLY

"Taking the Man of Steel back to his roots and into the future at the same time, ALL-STAR SUPERMAN is exciting, bold and supercool...all the makings of a classic."
—VARIETY

GRANT MORRISON
with FRANK QUITELY

FINAL CRISIS

with J.G. JONES, CARLOS PACHECO & DOUG MAHNKE

BATMAN: ARKHAM ASYLUM

with DAVE McKEAN

SEVEN SOLDIERS OF VICTORY VOLS. 1 & 2

with J.H. WILLIAMS III & VARIOUS ARTISTS

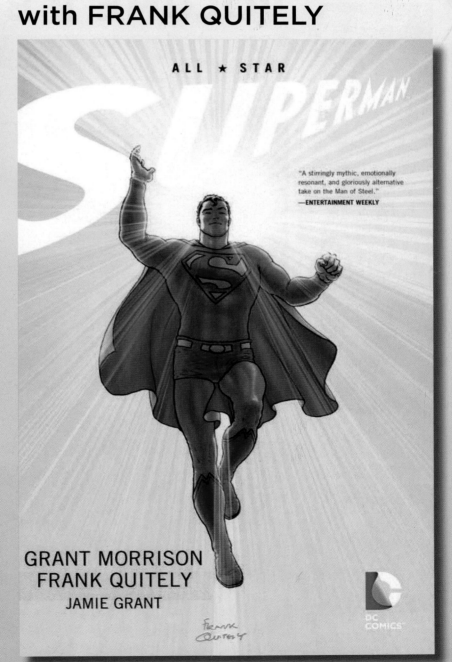

ALL ★ STAR SUPERMAN

"A stirringly mythic, emotionally resonant, and gloriously alternative take on the Man of Steel."
—ENTERTAINMENT WEEKLY

GRANT MORRISON
FRANK QUITELY

Jamie Grant

DC COMICS

"Clear storytelling at its best. It's an intriguing concept and easy to grasp."—THE NEW YORK TIMES

"Azzarello is rebuilding the mythology of Wonder Woman."—CRAVE ONLINE

START AT THE BEGINNING!

WONDER WOMAN VOLUME 1: BLOOD

WONDER WOMAN
VOL. 2: GUTS

by BRIAN
AZZARELLO and
CLIFF CHIANG

WONDER WOMAN
VOL. 3: IRON

by BRIAN
AZZARELLO and
CLIFF CHIANG

SUPERGIRL VOL. 1:
LAST DAUGHTER OF
KRYPTON

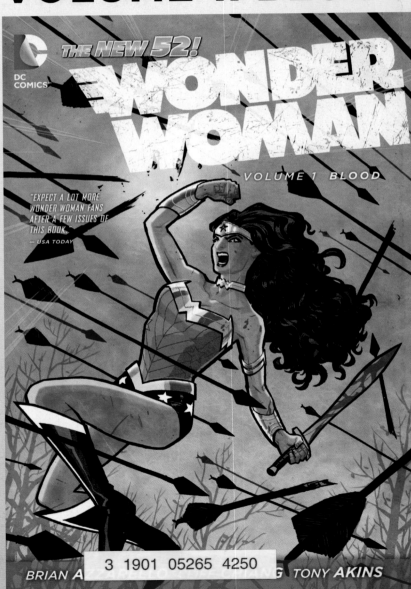